eensy weensy MONSTER

Volume 1

By Masami Tsuda

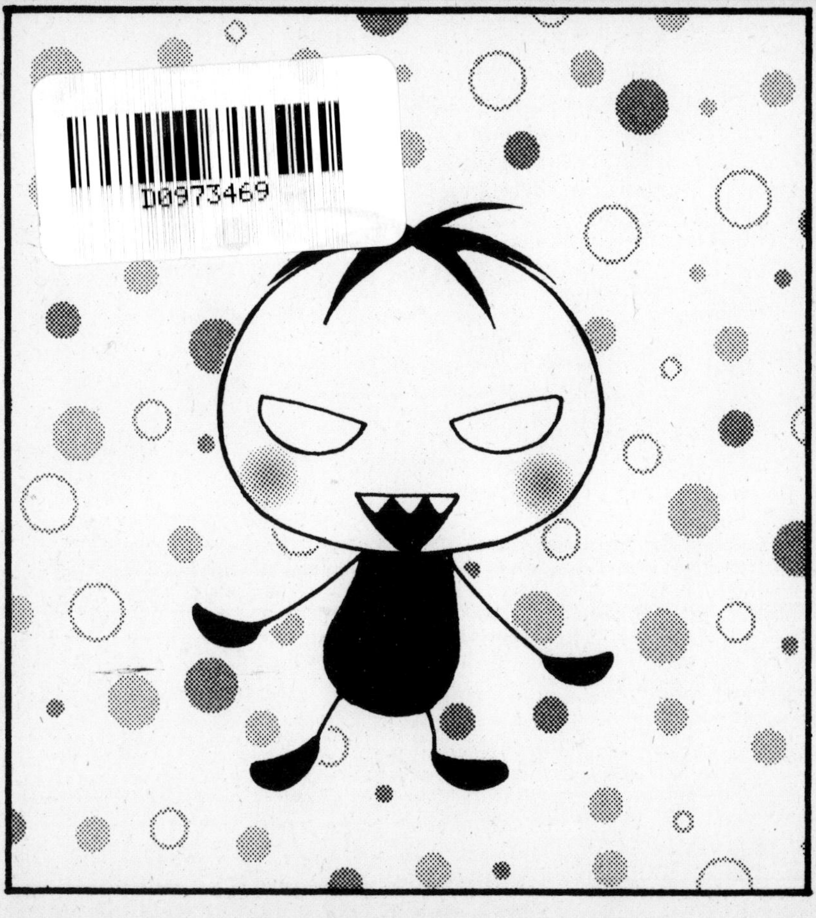

Eensy Weensy Monster Volume 1
Created By Masami Tsuda

Translation - Noi Sasaki
English Adaptation - Clint Bickham
Retouch and Lettering - Star Print Brokers
Production Artist - Rui Kyo
Graphic Designer - Rachel Macek

Editor - Lillian Diaz-Przybyl
Print Production Manager - Lucas Rivera
Managing Editor - Vy Nguyen
Senior Designer - Louis Csontos
Art Director - Al-Insan Lashley
Director of Sales and Manufacturing - Allyson De Simone
Associate Publisher - Marco F. Pavia
President and C.O.O. - John Parker
C.E.O. and Chief Creative Officer - Stu Levy

A **TOKYOPOP** Manga

TOKYOPOP and are trademarks or registered trademarks of TOKYOPOP Inc.

TOKYOPOP Inc.
5900 Wilshire Blvd. Suite 2000
Los Angeles, CA 90036

E-mail: info@TOKYOPOP.com
Come visit us online at www.TOKYOPOP.com

ISBN: 978-1-4278-1651-1

First TOKYOPOP printing: December 2010
10 9 8 7 6 5 4 3 2 1
Printed in the USA

eensy weensy MONSTER

Volume 1
By Masami Tsuda

HAMBURG // LONDON // LOS ANGELES // TOKYO

■ Contents ■

Eensy-weensy MONSTER

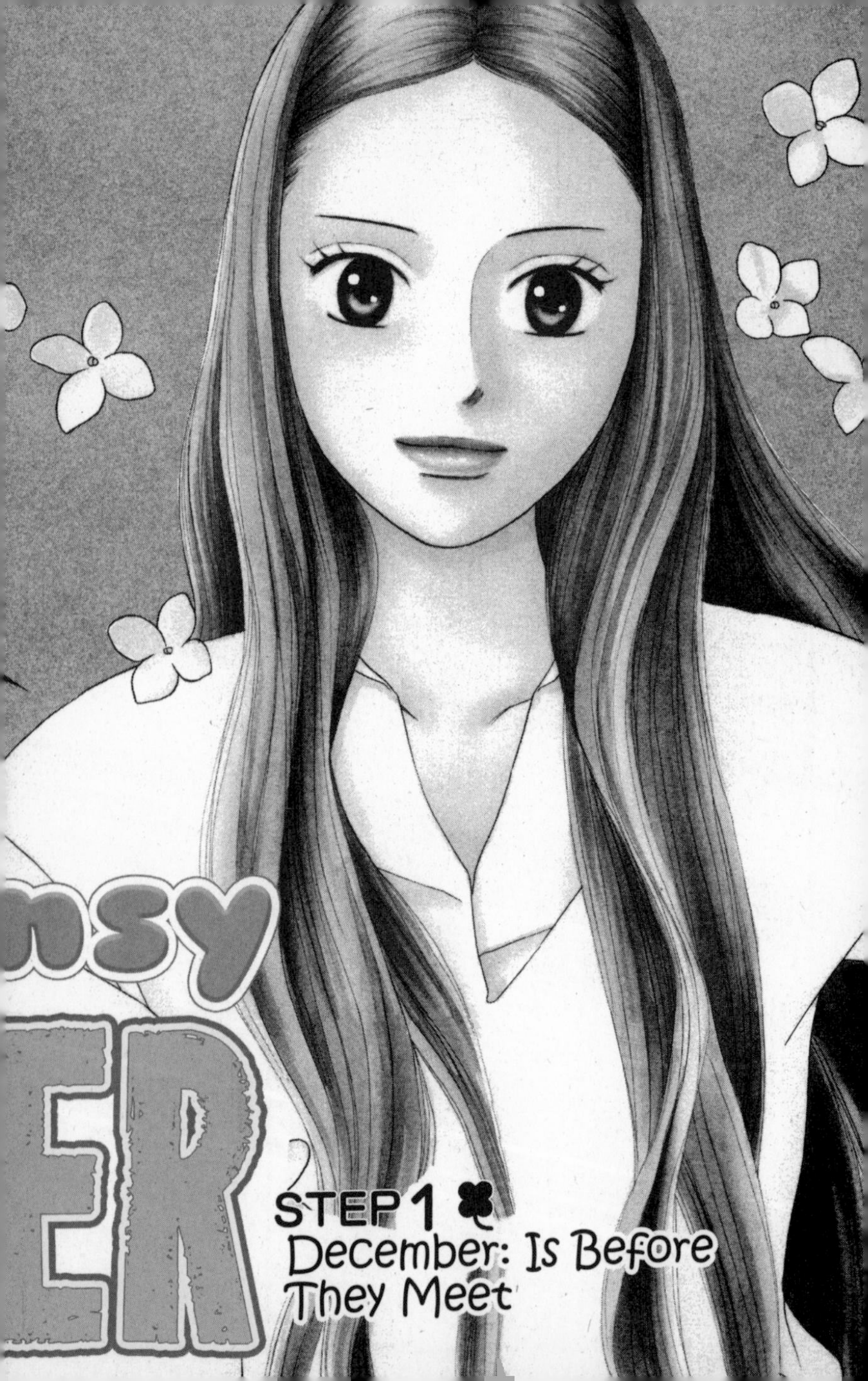
nsy
ER
STEP 1
December: Is Before They Meet

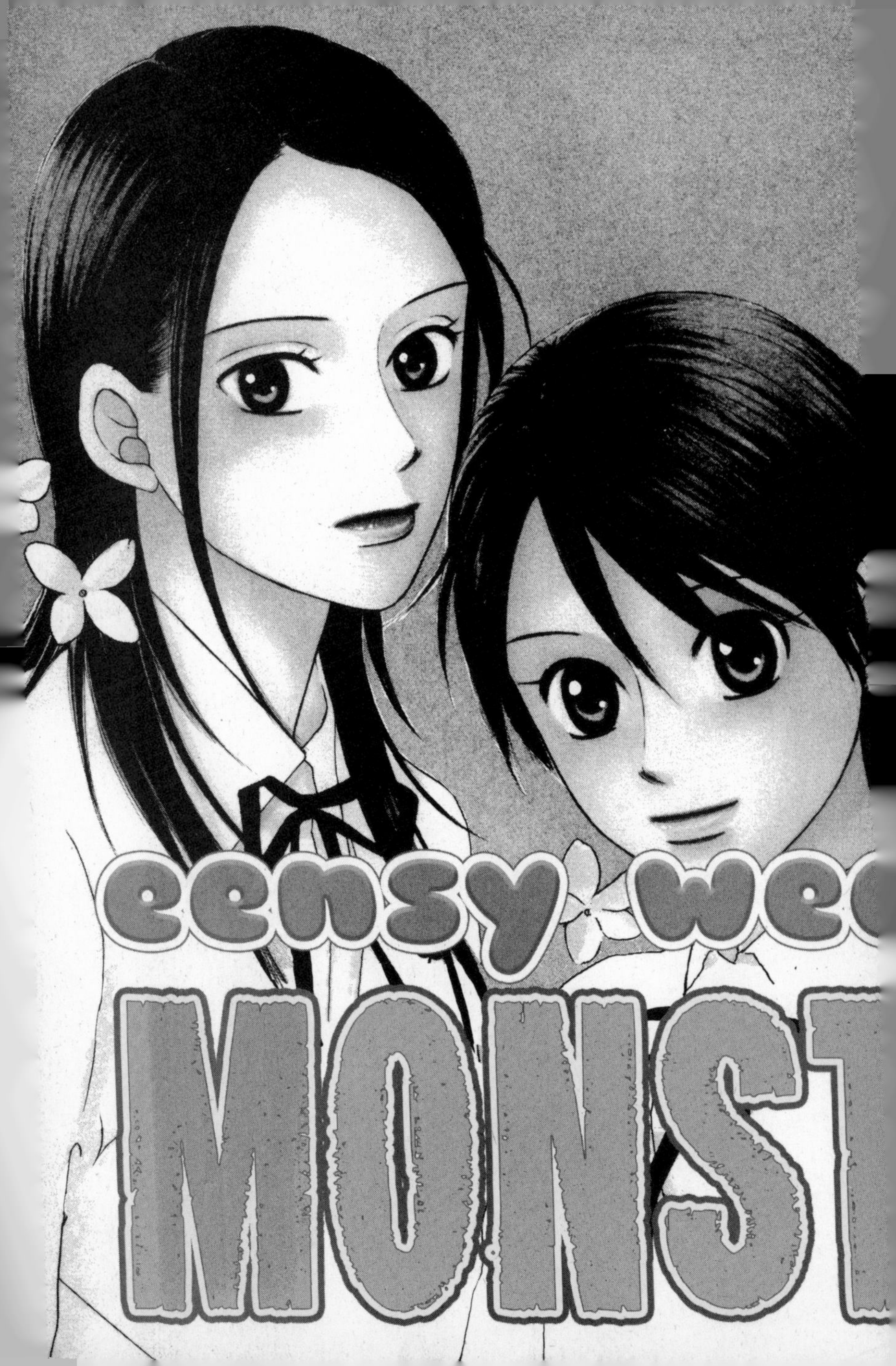
eensy we
MONST

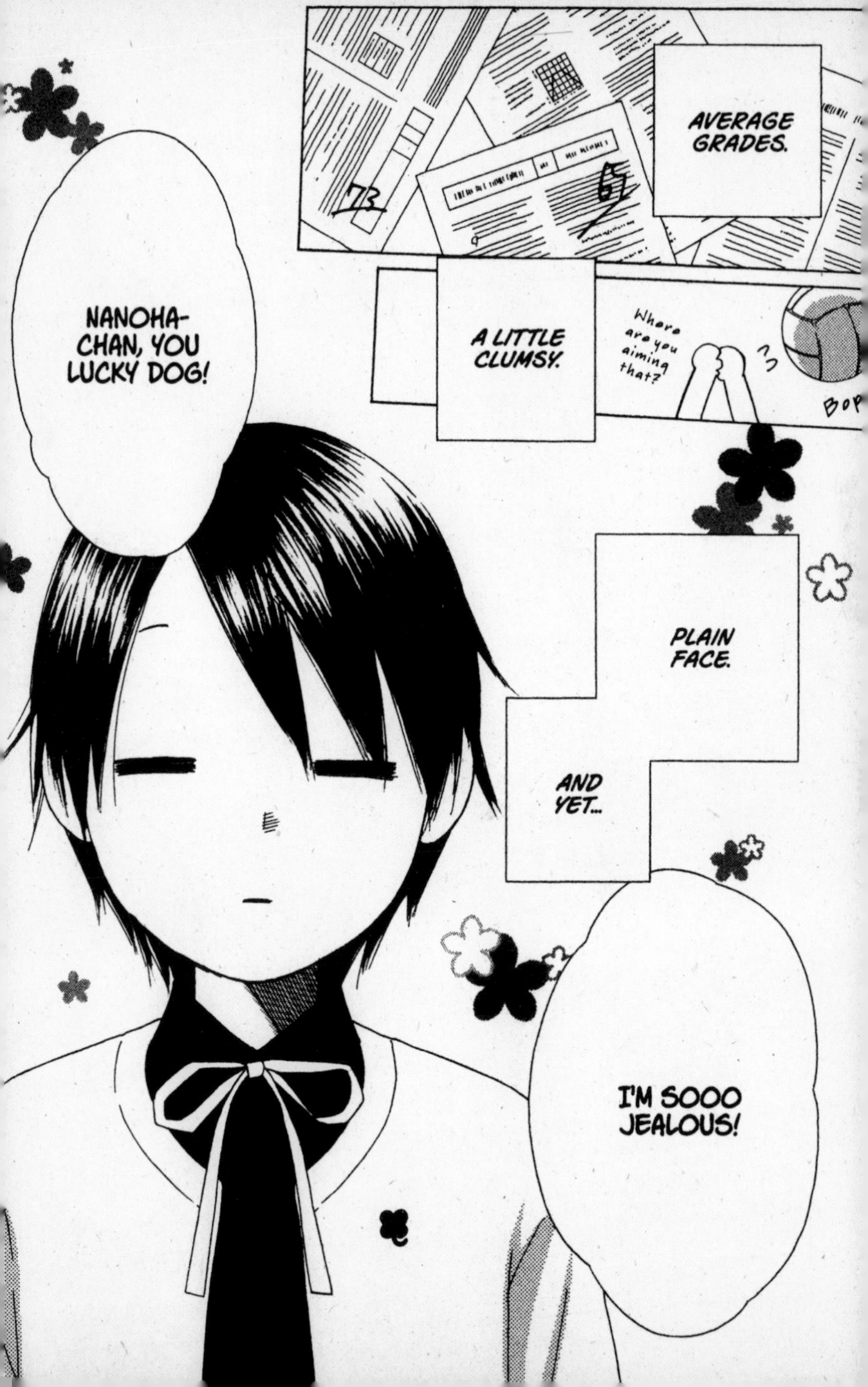
AVERAGE GRADES.
73
67
Where are you aiming that?
Bop
A LITTLE CLUMSY.
PLAIN FACE.
AND YET...
NANOHA-CHAN, YOU LUCKY DOG!
I'M SOOO JEALOUS!

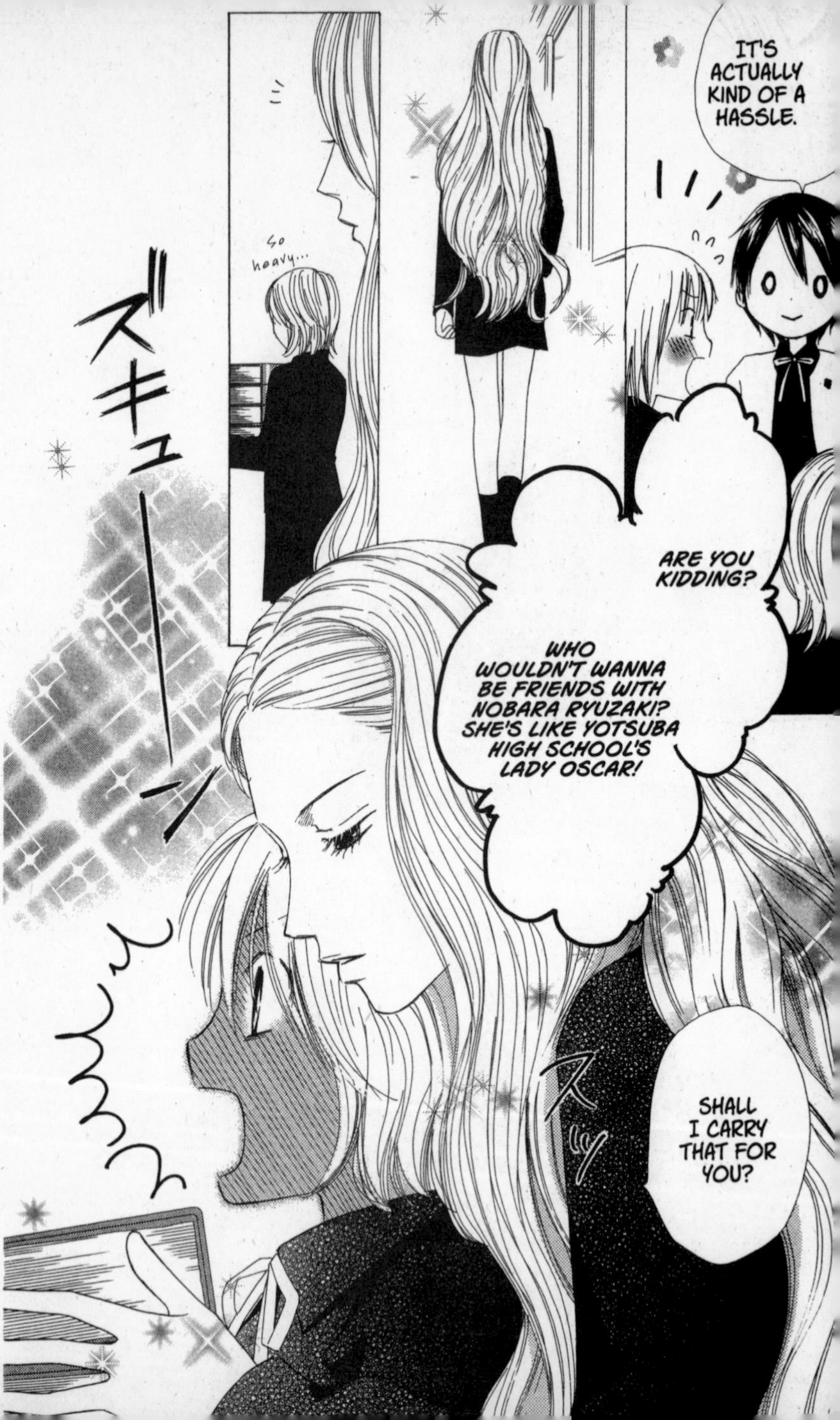
IT'S ACTUALLY KIND OF A HASSLE.
So heavy...
ARE YOU KIDDING?
WHO WOULDN'T WANNA BE FRIENDS WITH NOBARA RYUZAKI? SHE'S LIKE YOTSUBA HIGH SCHOOL'S LADY OSCAR!
SHALL I CARRY THAT FOR YOU?

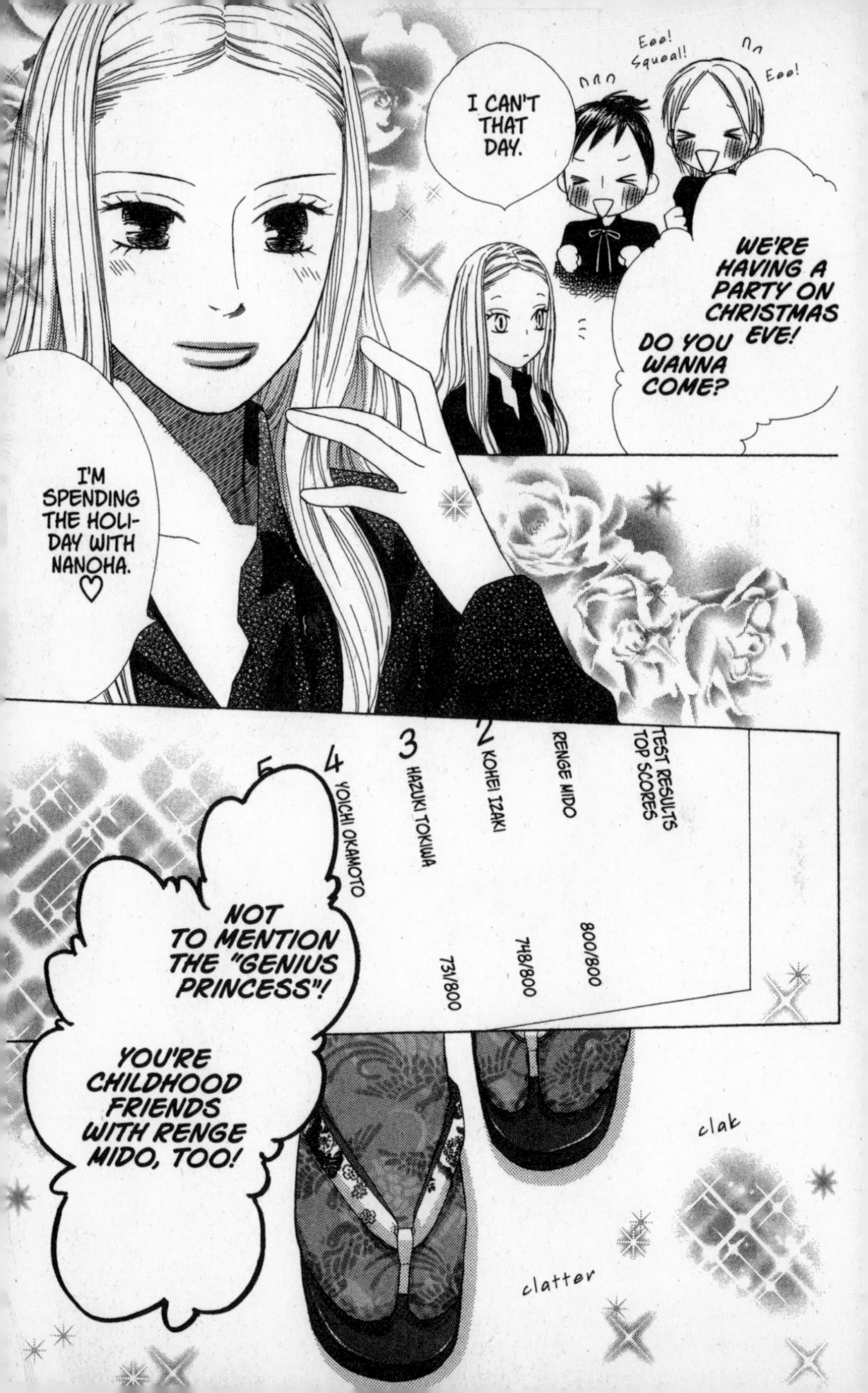
Eee! Squeal!
Eee!
WE'RE HAVING A PARTY ON CHRISTMAS EVE!
DO YOU WANNA COME?
I CAN'T THAT DAY.
I'M SPENDING THE HOLI-DAY WITH NANOHA. ♡
TEST RESULTS TOP SCORES
RENGE MIDO 800/800
2 KOHEI IZAKI 748/800
3 HAZUKI TOKIWA 731/800
4 YOICHI OKAMOTO
5
NOT TO MENTION THE "GENIUS PRINCESS"!
YOU'RE CHILDHOOD FRIENDS WITH RENGE MIDO, TOO!
clak
clatter

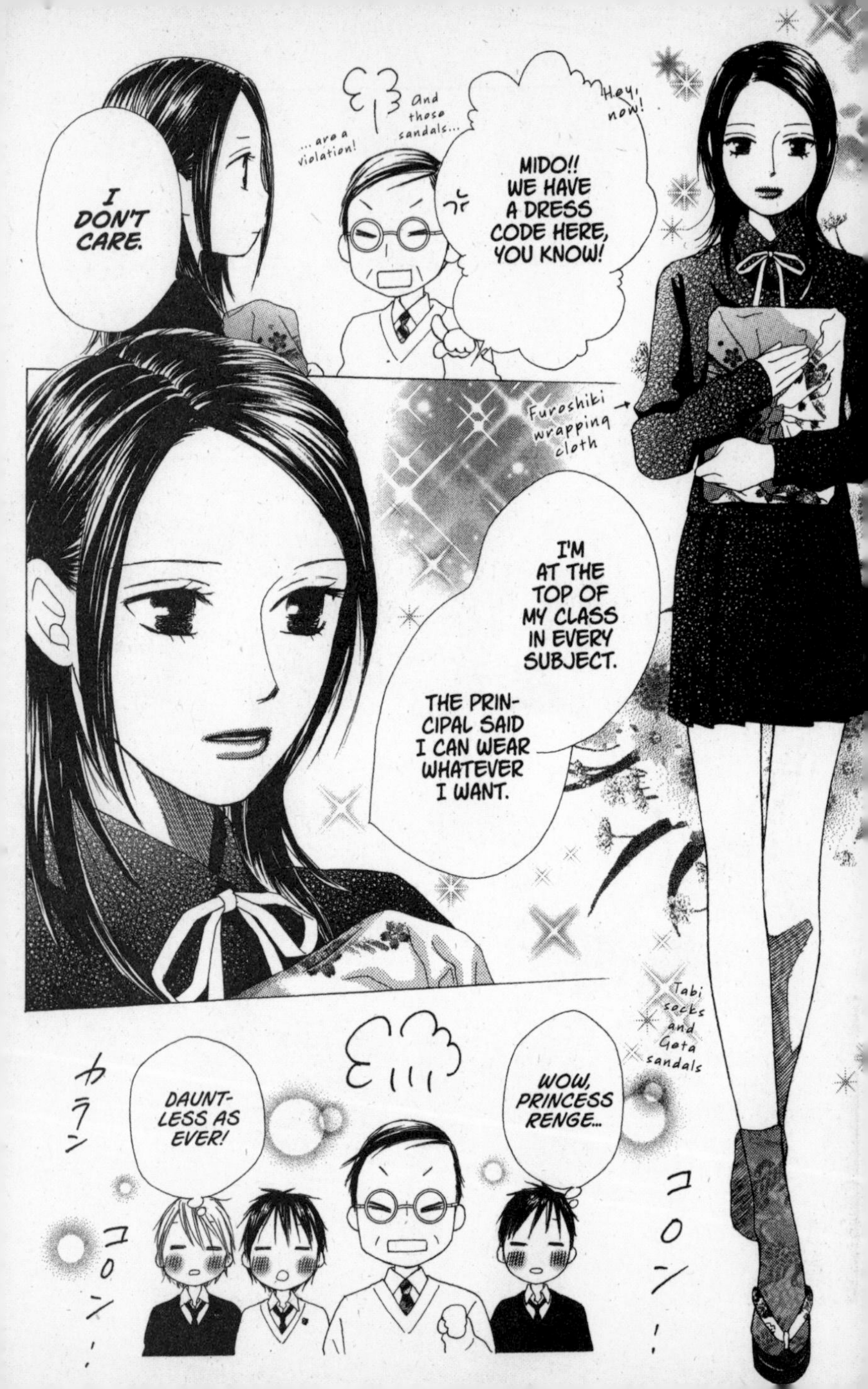
Furoshiki wrapping cloth
Tabi socks and Geta sandals
コロン!
Hey, now!
MIDO!! WE HAVE A DRESS CODE HERE, YOU KNOW!
and those sandals...
...are a violation!
I DON'T CARE.
I'M AT THE TOP OF MY CLASS IN EVERY SUBJECT.
THE PRINCIPAL SAID I CAN WEAR WHATEVER I WANT.
WOW, PRINCESS RENGE...
DAUNTLESS AS EVER!
カラン
コロン!

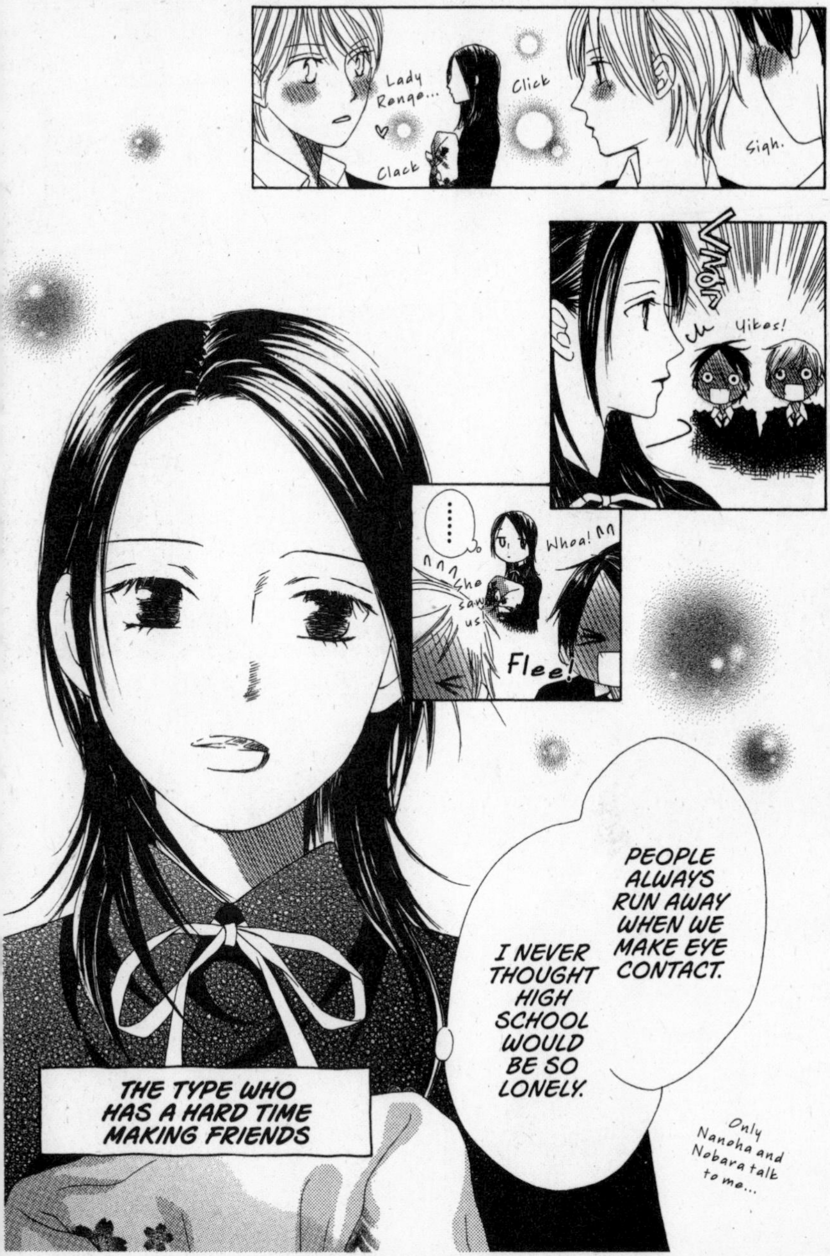
Sigh.
Click
Lady Renge...
Clack
Yikes!
......
Whoa!
She saw us!
Flee!
PEOPLE ALWAYS RUN AWAY WHEN WE MAKE EYE CONTACT.
I NEVER THOUGHT HIGH SCHOOL WOULD BE SO LONELY.
THE TYPE WHO HAS A HARD TIME MAKING FRIENDS
Only Nanoha and Nobara talk to me...

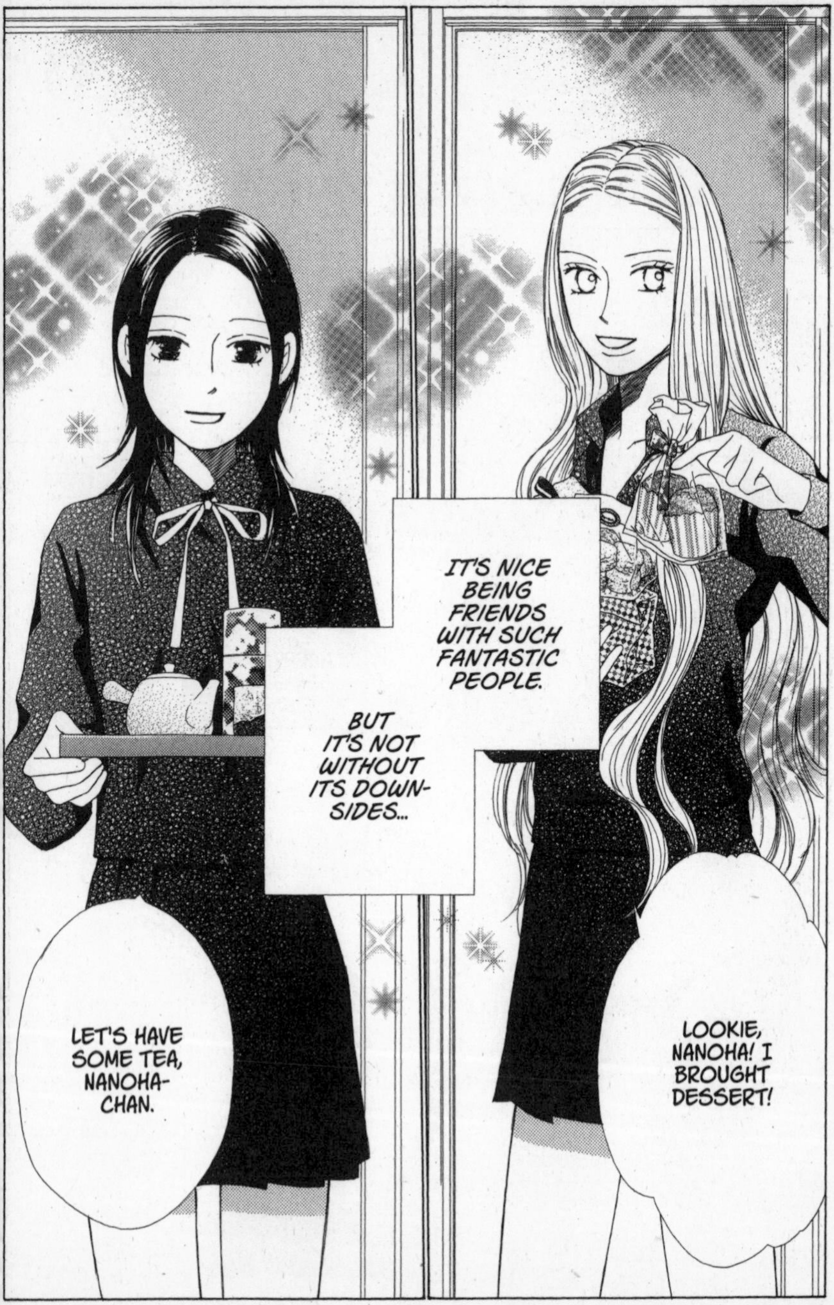
IT'S NICE BEING FRIENDS WITH SUCH FANTASTIC PEOPLE.
LOOKIE, NANOHA! I BROUGHT DESSERT!
BUT IT'S NOT WITHOUT ITS DOWN-SIDES...
LET'S HAVE SOME TEA, NANOHA-CHAN.

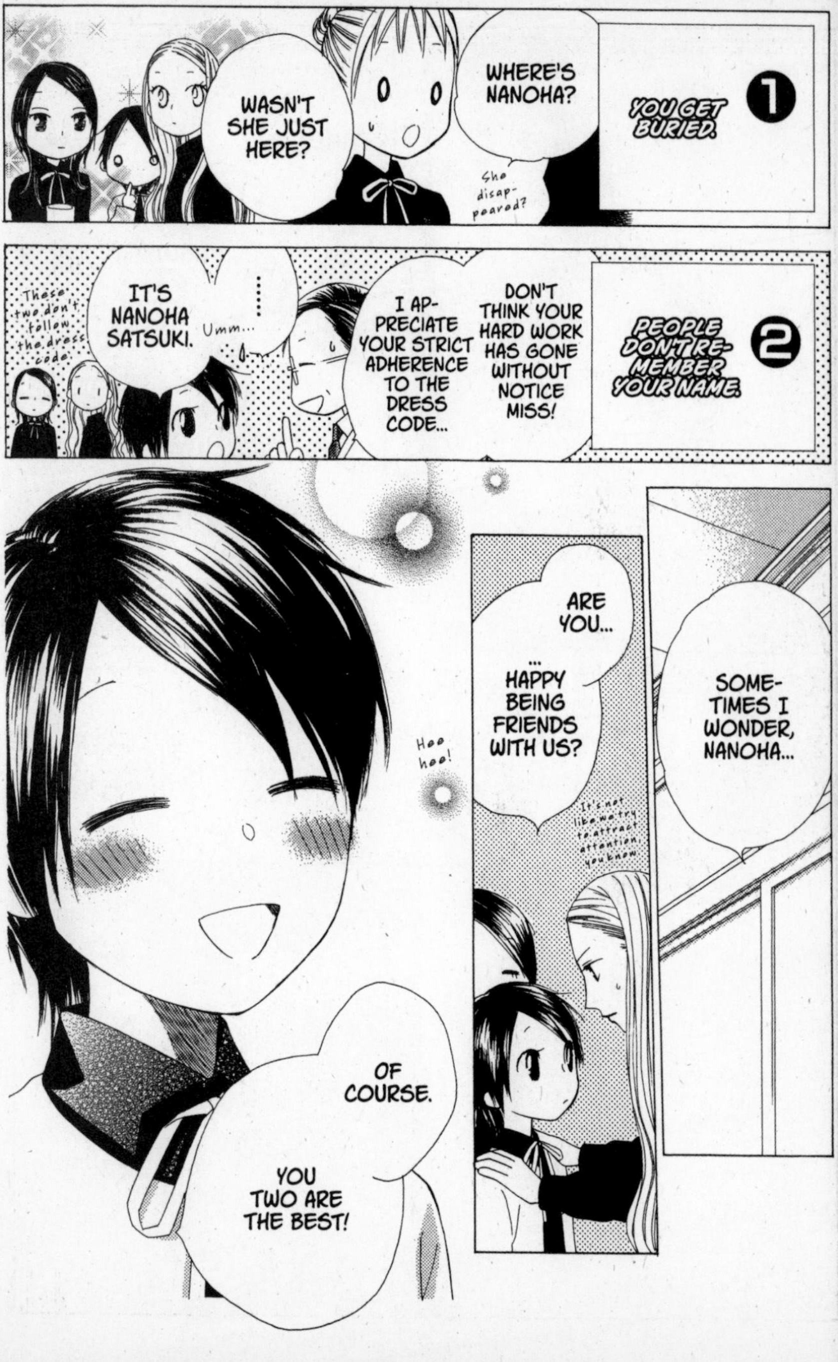
1
YOU GET BURIED.
WHERE'S NANOHA?
She disappeared?
WASN'T SHE JUST HERE?
2
PEOPLE DON'T RE-MEMBER YOUR NAME.
DON'T THINK YOUR HARD WORK HAS GONE WITHOUT NOTICE MISS!
I AP-PRECIATE YOUR STRICT ADHERENCE TO THE DRESS CODE...
......
Umm...
IT'S NANOHA SATSUKI.
These two don't follow the dress code.
SOME-TIMES I WONDER, NANOHA...
ARE YOU...
... HAPPY BEING FRIENDS WITH US?
It's not like we try to attract attention, you know.
Hee hee!
OF COURSE.
YOU TWO ARE THE BEST!

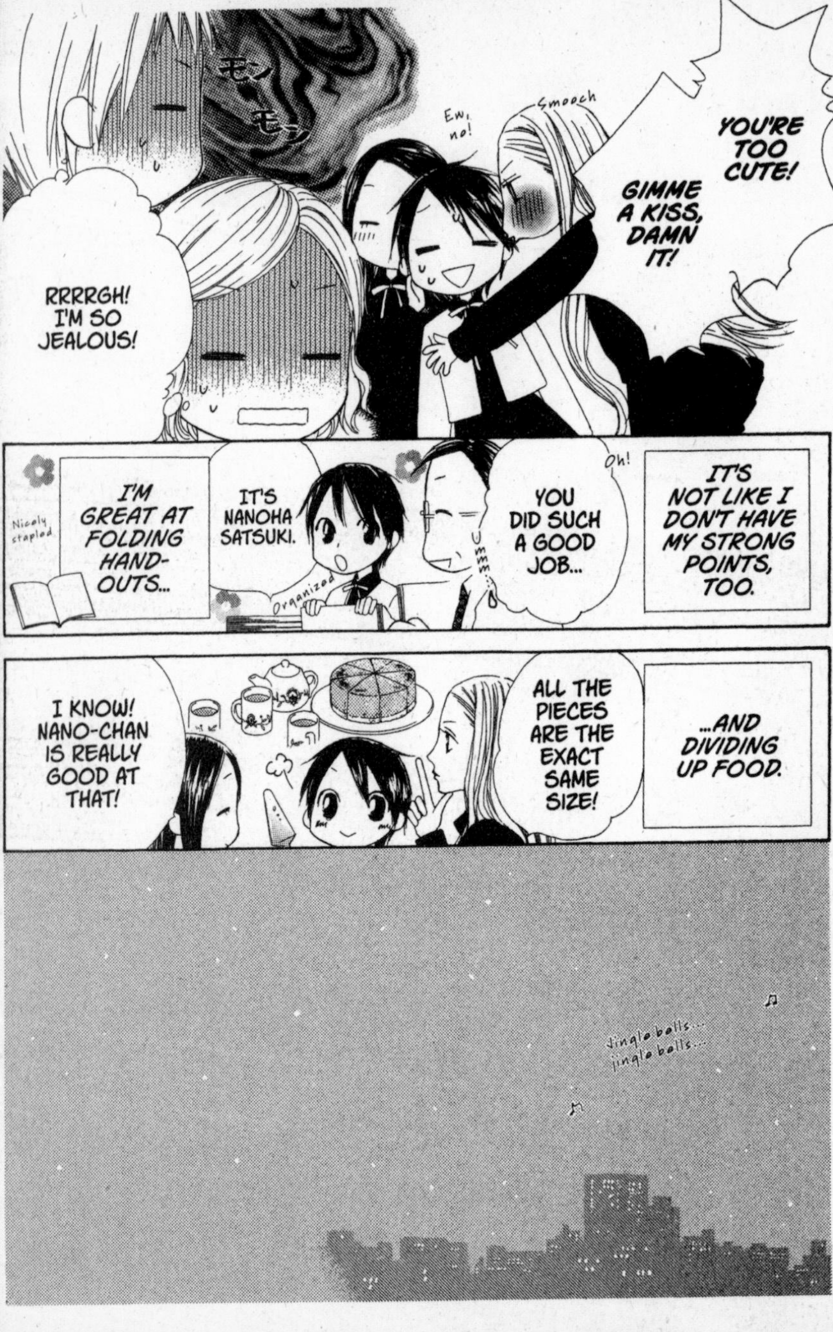
YOU'RE TOO CUTE!
GIMME A KISS, DAMN IT!
Smooch
Ew, no!
モン モン
RRRRGH! I'M SO JEALOUS!
IT'S NOT LIKE I DON'T HAVE MY STRONG POINTS, TOO.
Oh!
YOU DID SUCH A GOOD JOB...
IT'S NANOHA SATSUKI.
Organized
I'M GREAT AT FOLDING HAND-OUTS...
Nicely stapled
...AND DIVIDING UP FOOD.
ALL THE PIECES ARE THE EXACT SAME SIZE!
I KNOW! NANO-CHAN IS REALLY GOOD AT THAT!
jingle bells...
jingle bells...

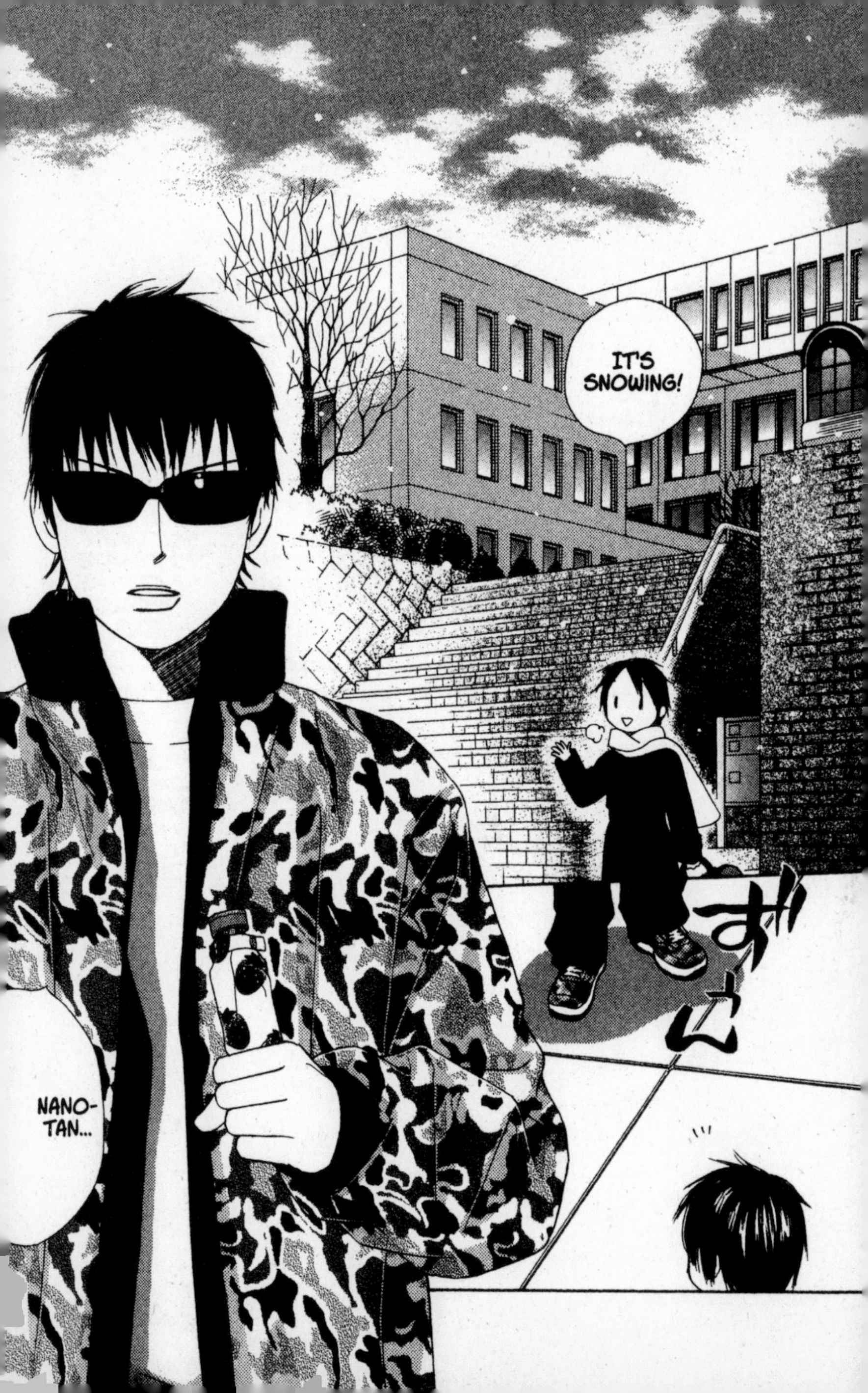
IT'S SNOWING!
ずーん
NANO-TAN...

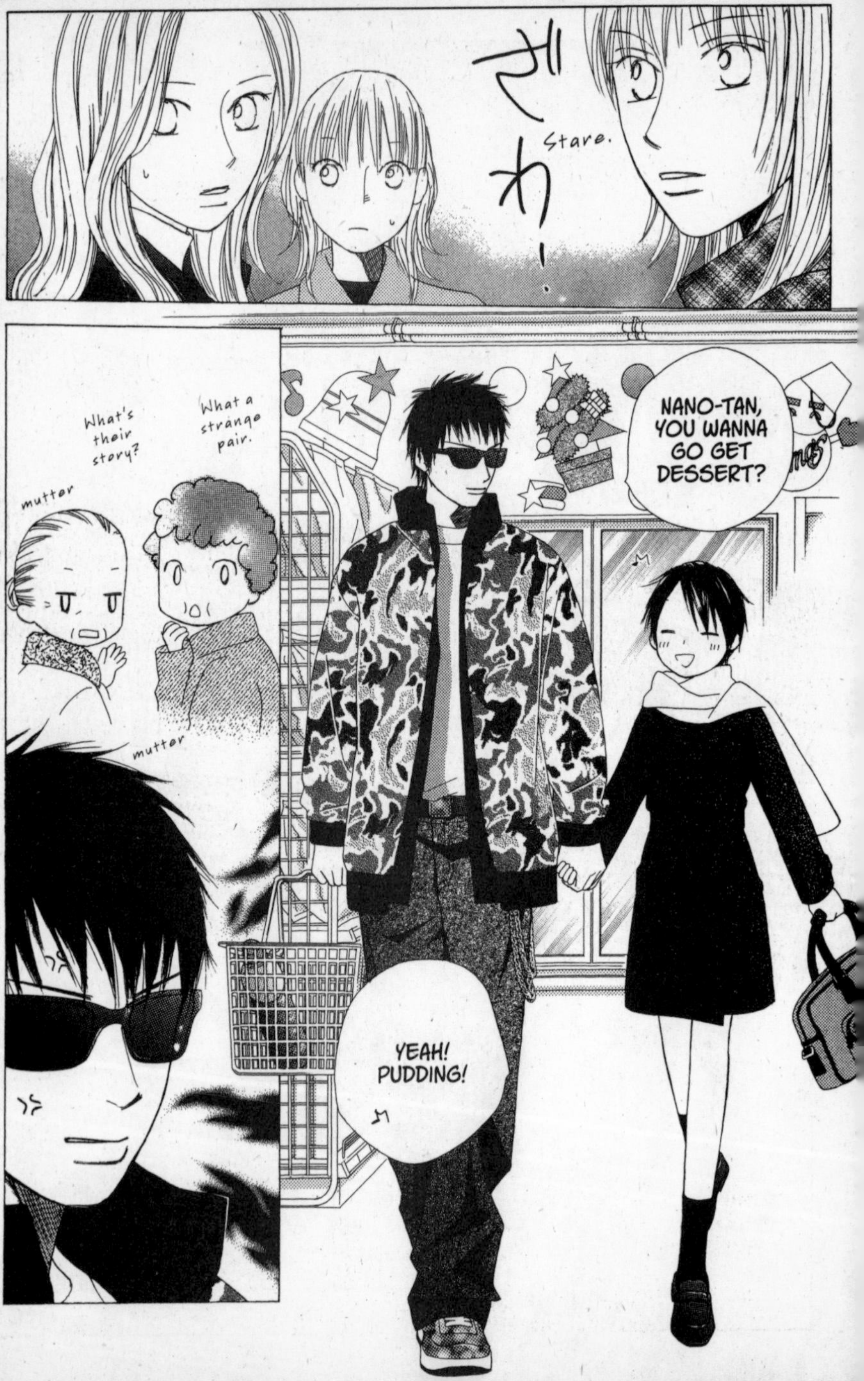
ざわ
Stare.
NANO-TAN, YOU WANNA GO GET DESSERT?
YEAH! PUDDING!
What a strange pair.
What's their story?
mutter
mutter

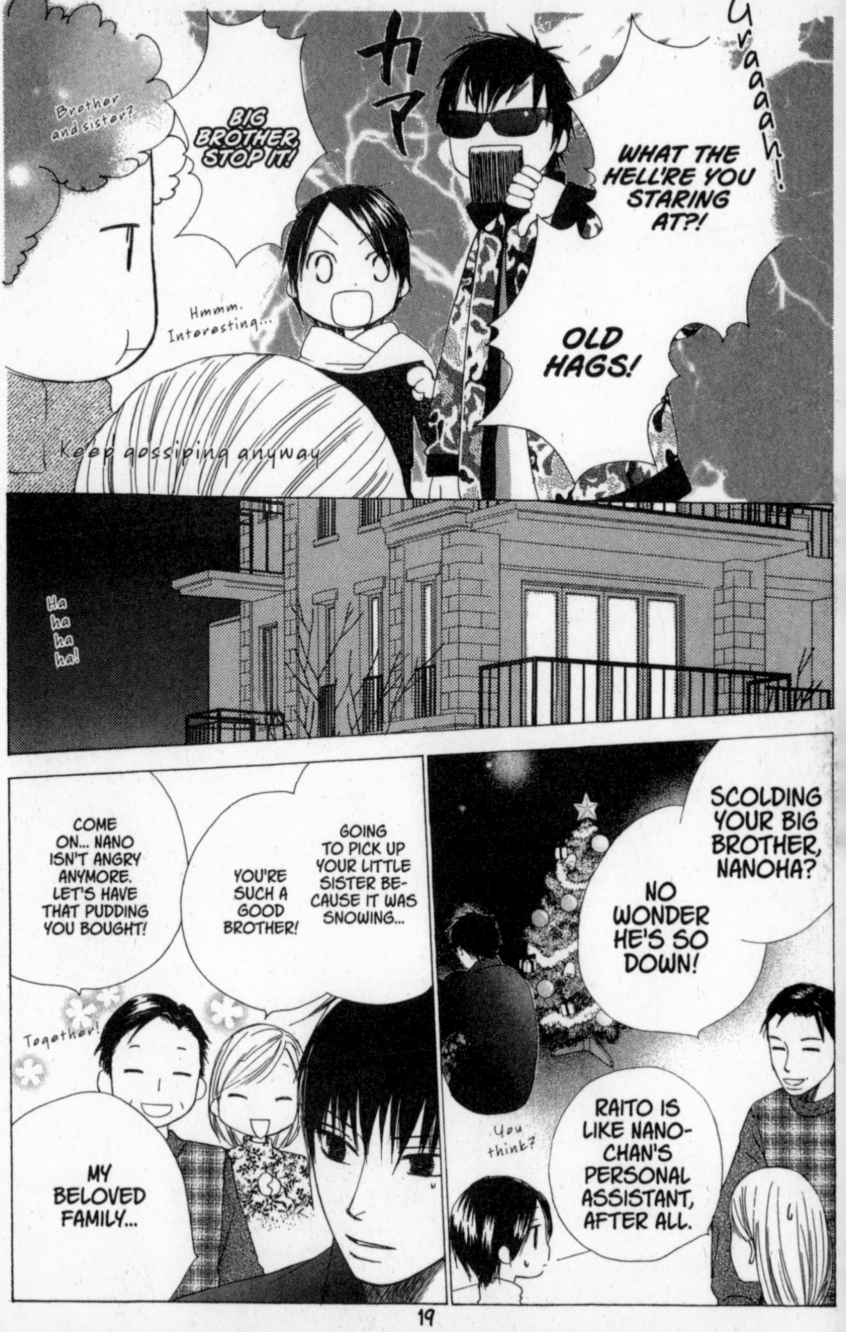
Graaaah!
WHAT THE HELL'RE YOU STARING AT?!
カァ
OLD HAGS!
BIG BROTHER, STOP IT!
Brother and sister?
Hmmm. Interesting...
Keep gossiping anyway
Ha ha ha ha!
SCOLDING YOUR BIG BROTHER, NANOHA?
NO WONDER HE'S SO DOWN!
RAITO IS LIKE NANO-CHAN'S PERSONAL ASSISTANT, AFTER ALL.
You think?
GOING TO PICK UP YOUR LITTLE SISTER BE-CAUSE IT WAS SNOWING...
YOU'RE SUCH A GOOD BROTHER!
COME ON... NANO ISN'T ANGRY ANYMORE. LET'S HAVE THAT PUDDING YOU BOUGHT!
Together!
MY BELOVED FAMILY...

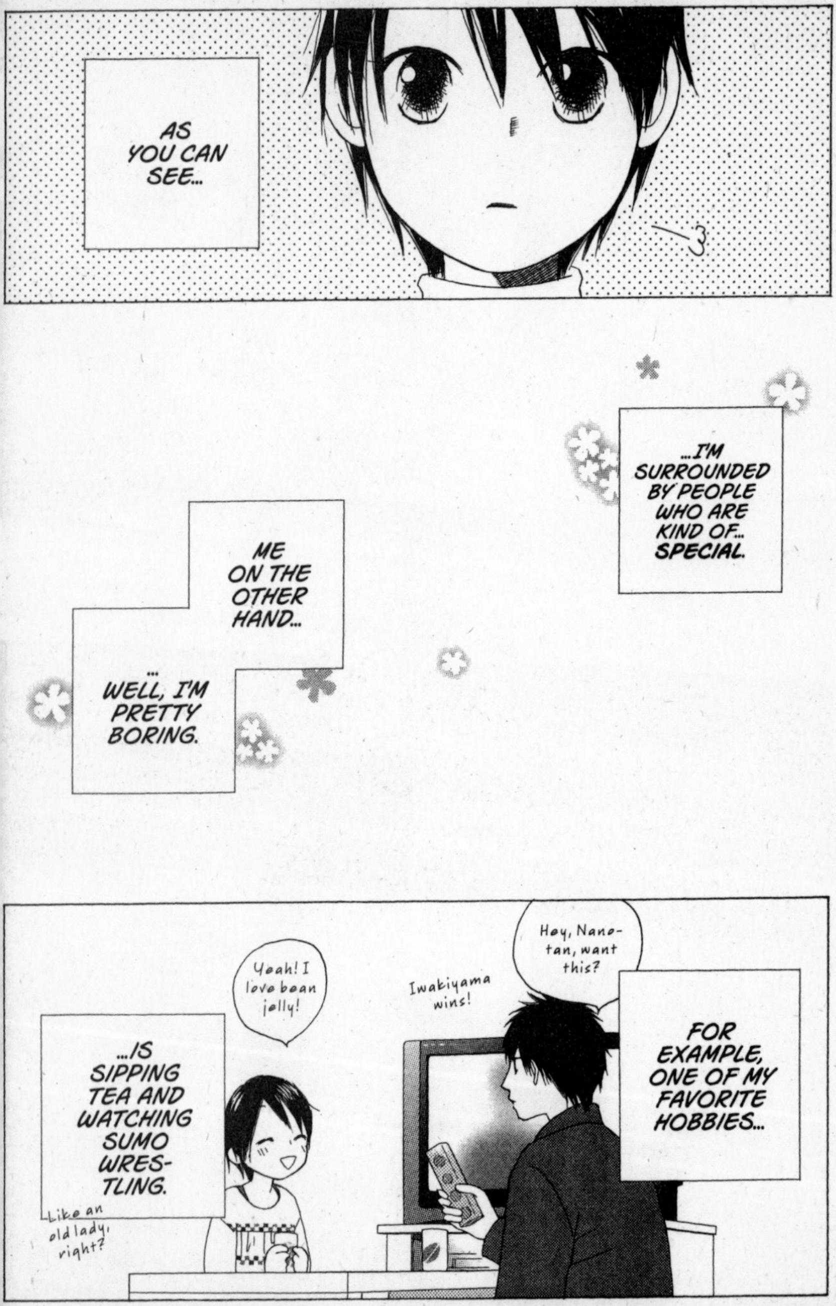
AS YOU CAN SEE...
...I'M SURROUNDED BY PEOPLE WHO ARE KIND OF... SPECIAL.
ME ON THE OTHER HAND...
... WELL, I'M PRETTY BORING.
FOR EXAMPLE, ONE OF MY FAVORITE HOBBIES...
Hey, Nano-tan, want this?
Iwakiyama wins!
Yeah! I love bean jelly!
...IS SIPPING TEA AND WATCHING SUMO WRES-TLING.
Like an old lady, right?

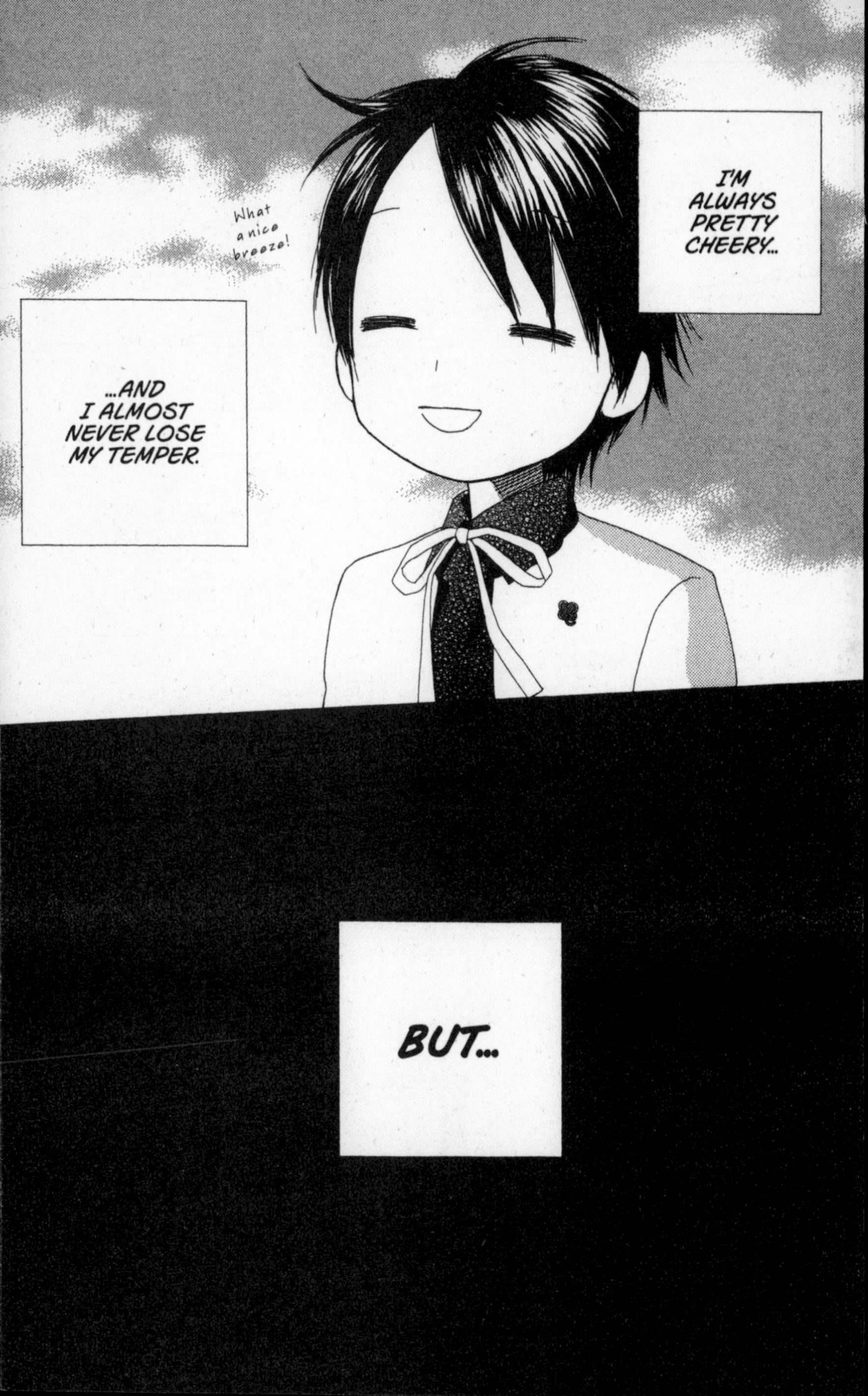
I'M ALWAYS PRETTY CHEERY...
What a nice breeze!
...AND I ALMOST NEVER LOSE MY TEMPER.
BUT...

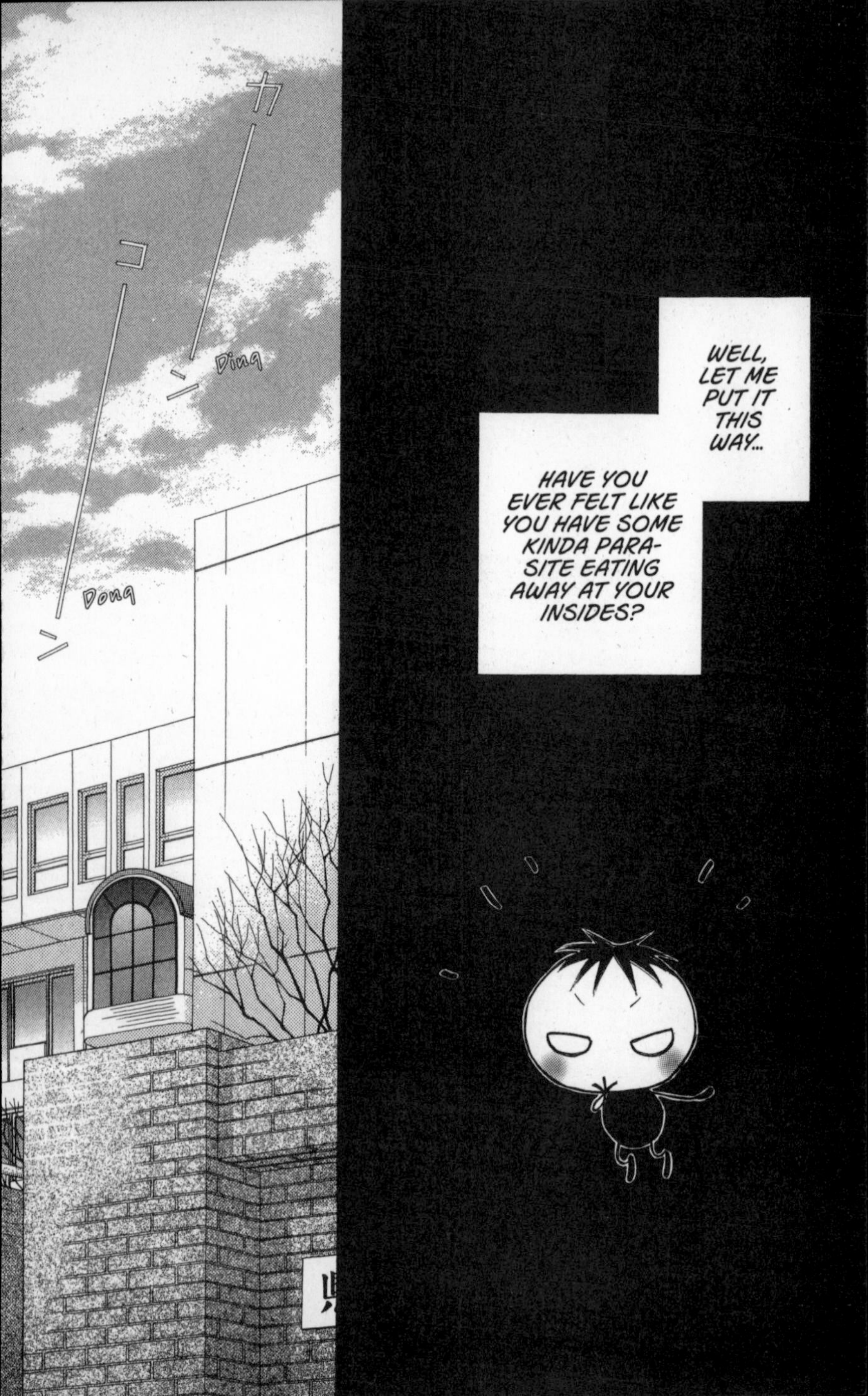
WELL, LET ME PUT IT THIS WAY...
HAVE YOU EVER FELT LIKE YOU HAVE SOME KINDA PARA-SITE EATING AWAY AT YOUR INSIDES?
カーン
Ding
コーン
Dong

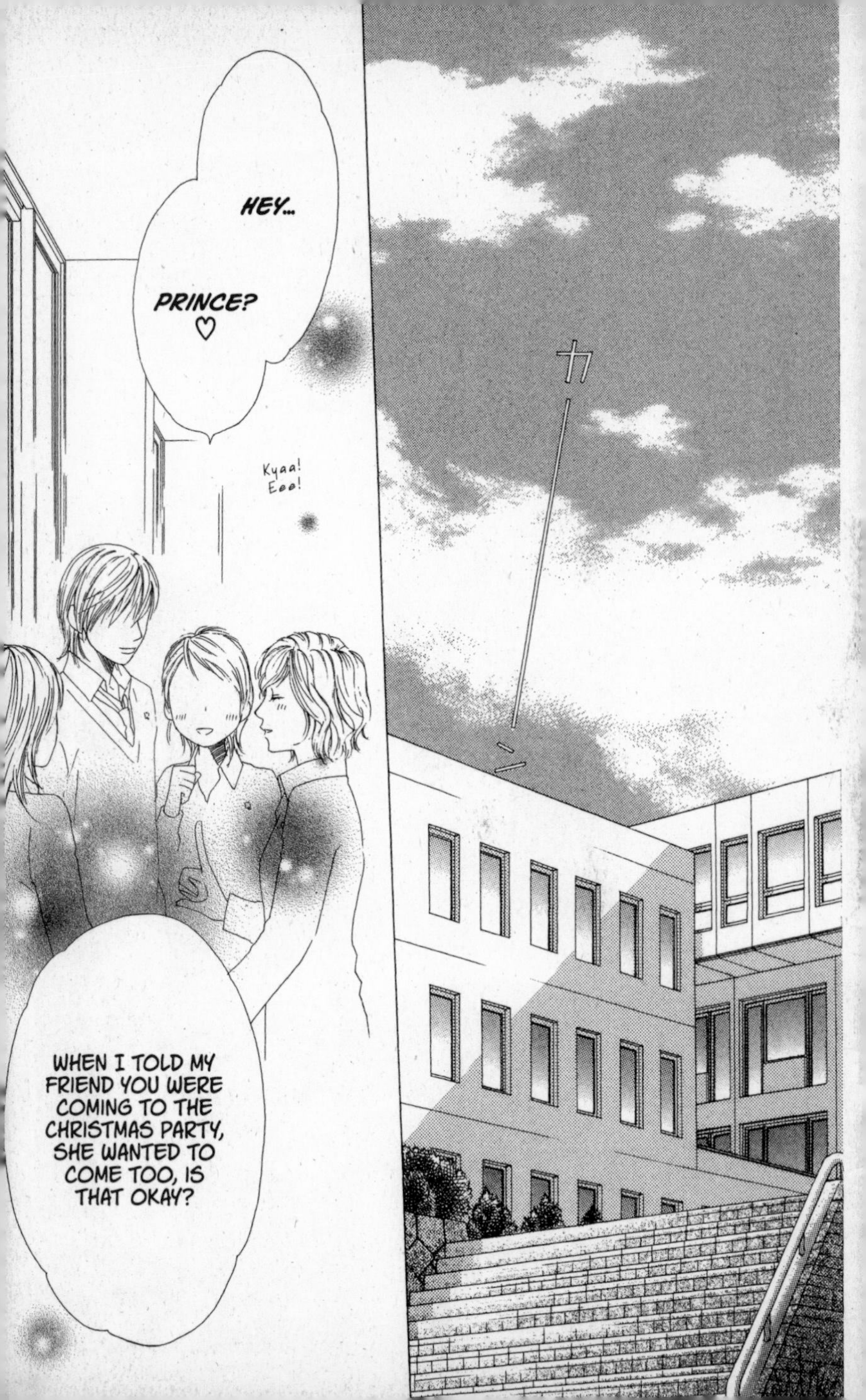
カ
HEY... PRINCE? ♡
Kyaa! Eee!
WHEN I TOLD MY FRIEND YOU WERE COMING TO THE CHRISTMAS PARTY, SHE WANTED TO COME TOO, IS THAT OKAY?

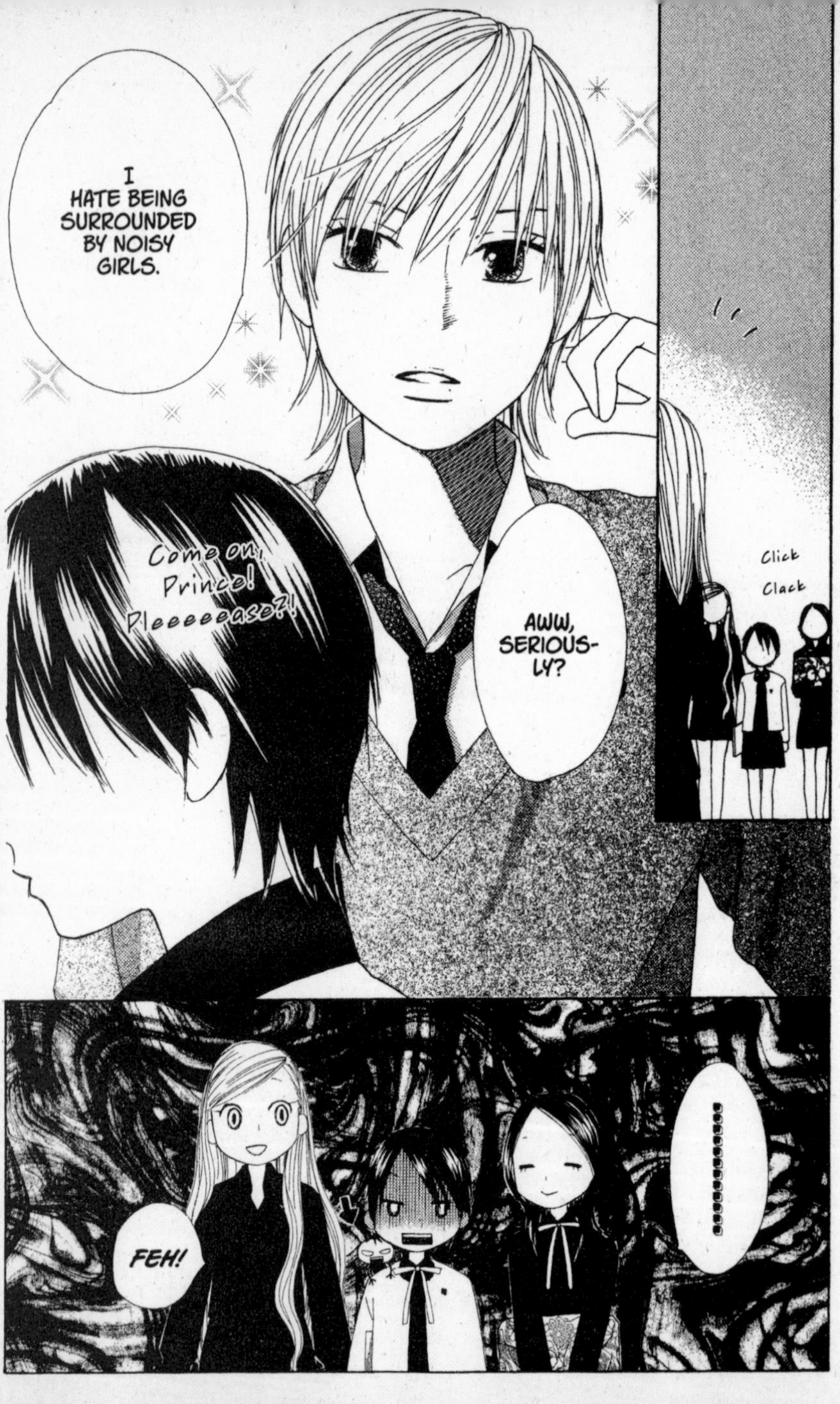
Click
Clack
I HATE BEING SURROUNDED BY NOISY GIRLS.
AWW, SERIOUS-LY?
Come on, Prince! Pleeeeease?!
....
FEH!

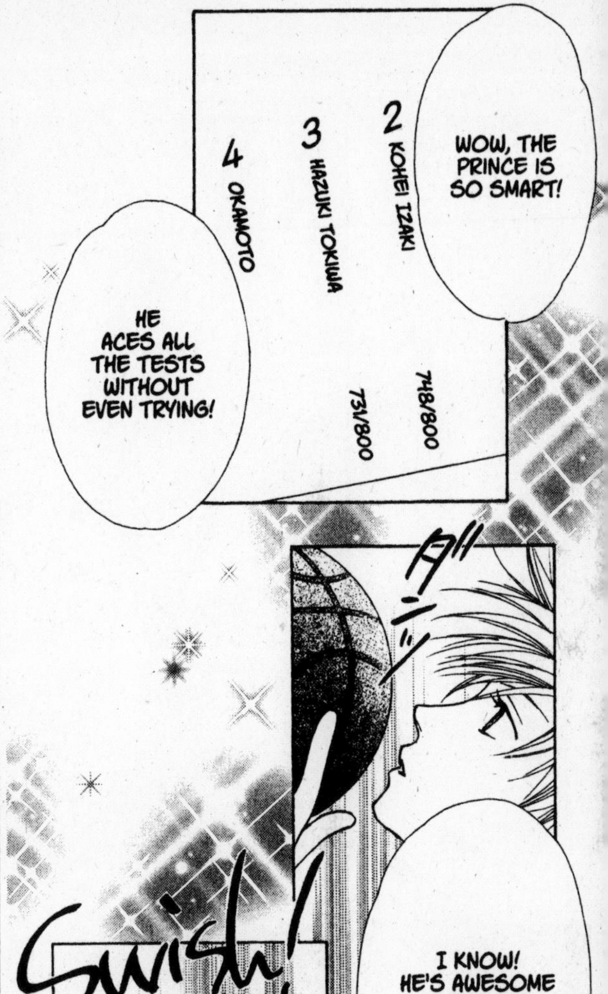
WOW, THE PRINCE IS SO SMART!
2 KOHEI IZAKI 748/800
3 HAZUKI TOKIWA 731/800
4 OKAMOTO
HE ACES ALL THE TESTS WITHOUT EVEN TRYING!
I KNOW! HE'S AWESOME AT SPORTS, TOO!
Swish!

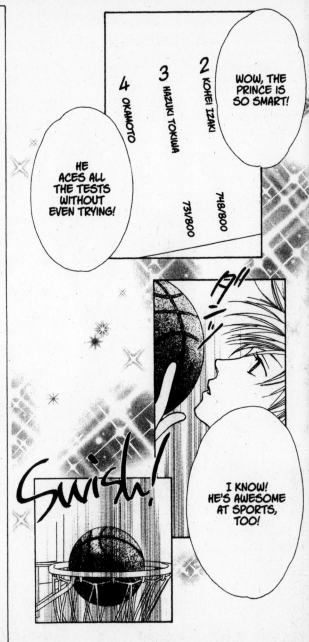

1

Hello! This is my 26th manga, Eensy-Weensy Monster volume one!

I started this series because I wanted to draw something happy and cute.

This little guy isn't very happy, though.

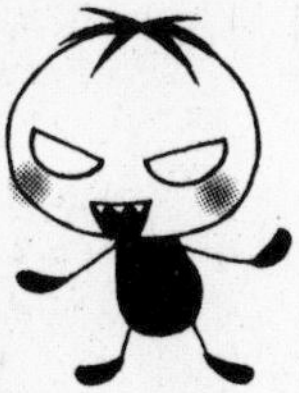

I hope you have as much fun reading this as I had drawing it!

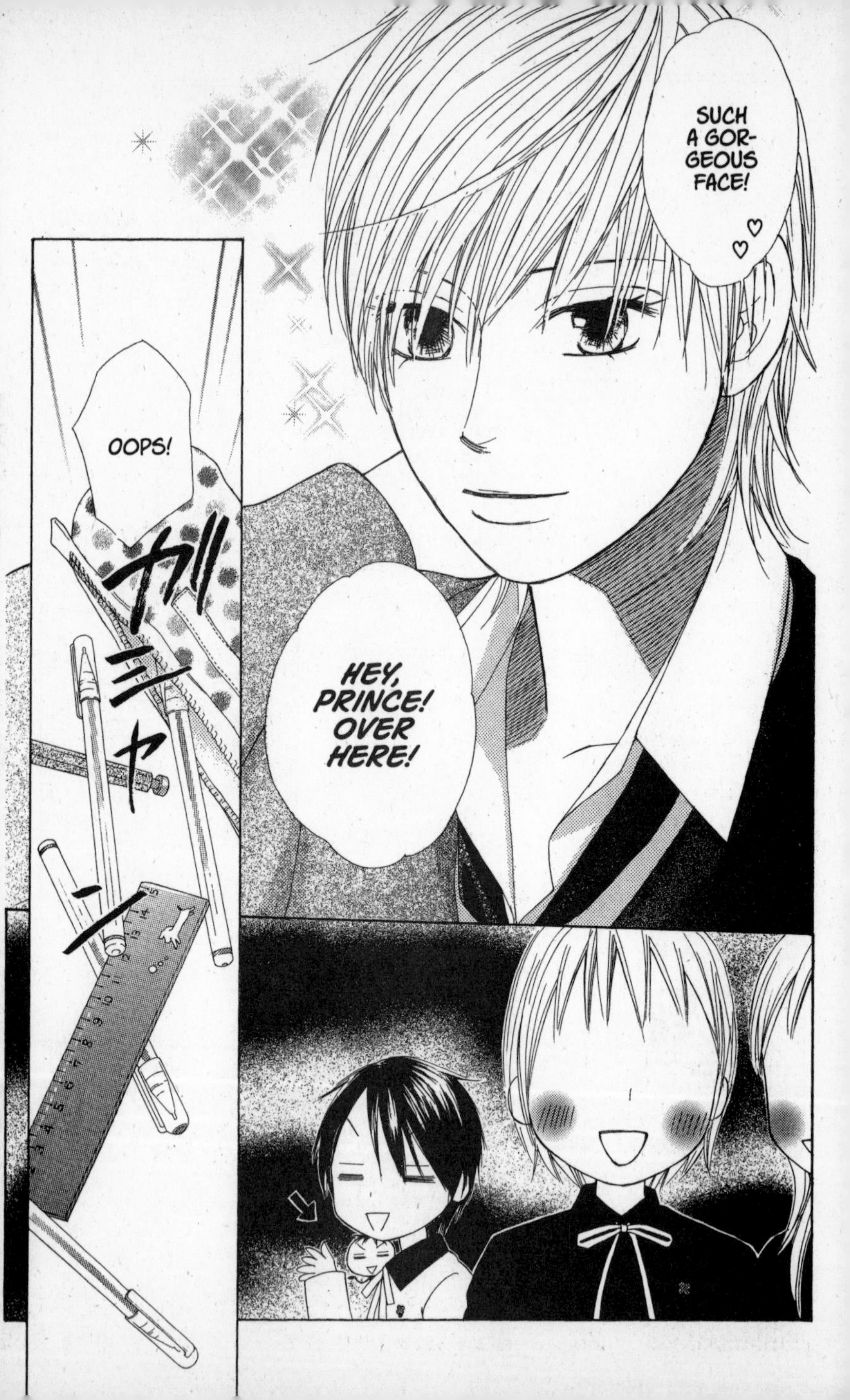
SUCH A GOR-GEOUS FACE!
HEY, PRINCE! OVER HERE!
OOPS!
ガシャーン

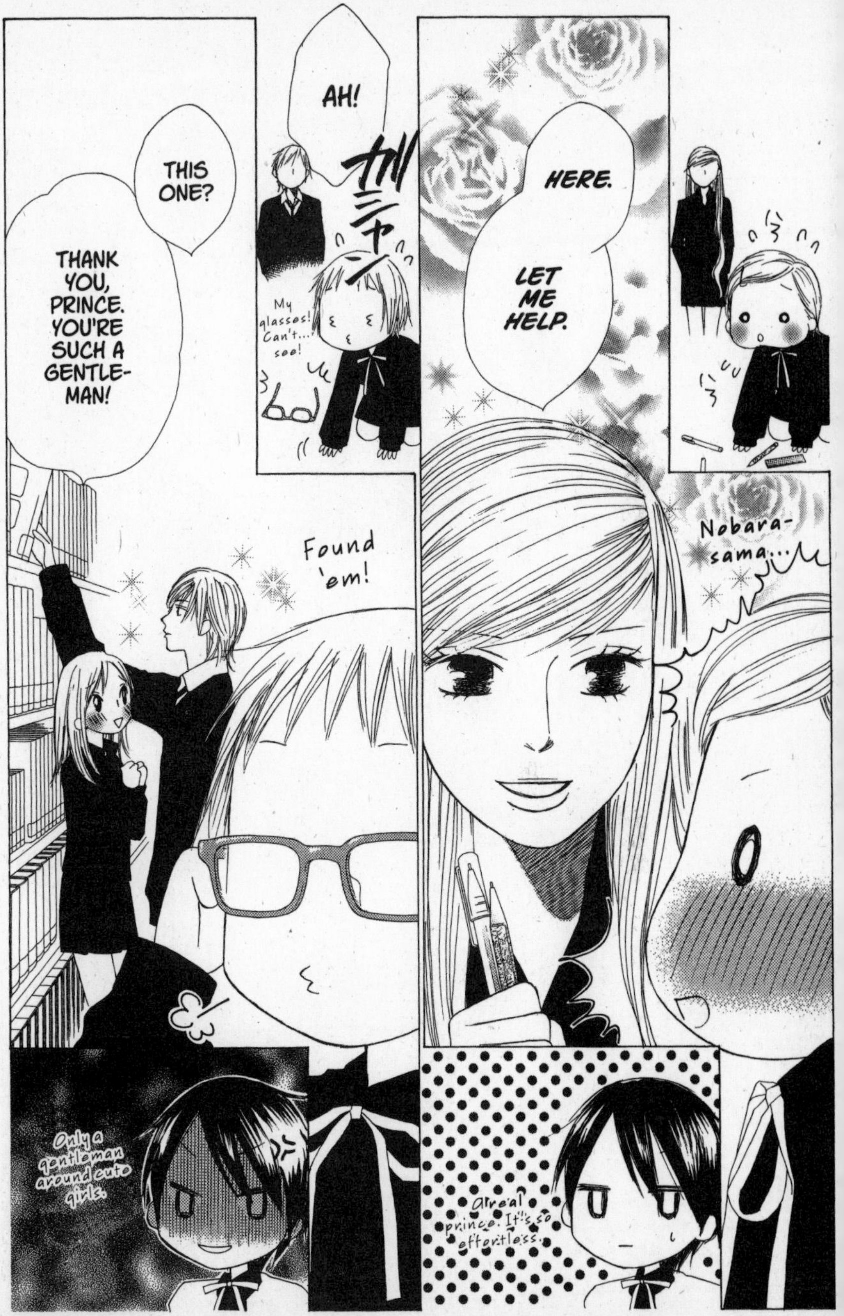
HERE.
LET ME HELP.
Nobara-sama...
AH!
My glasses! Can't... see!
THIS ONE?
THANK YOU, PRINCE. YOU'RE SUCH A GENTLE-MAN!
Found 'em!
A real prince. It's so effortless.
Only a gentleman around cute girls.

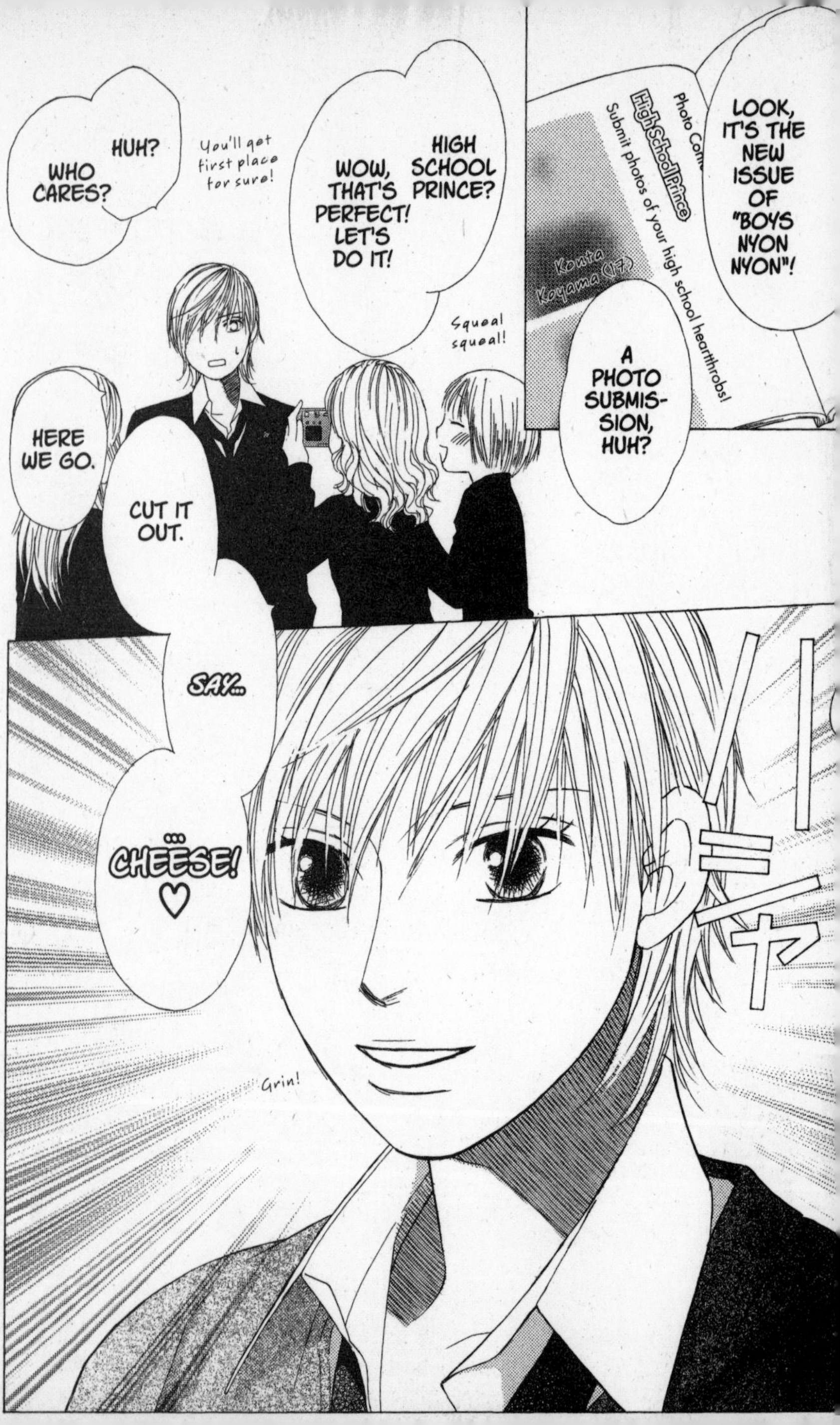
LOOK, IT'S THE NEW ISSUE OF "BOYS NYON NYON"!
High School Prince
Submit photos of your high school heartthrobs!
Kouta Koyama (17)
A PHOTO SUBMISSION, HUH?
HIGH SCHOOL PRINCE?
WOW, THAT'S PERFECT! LET'S DO IT!
You'll get first place for sure!
HUH? WHO CARES?
Squeal squeal!
HERE WE GO.
CUT IT OUT.
SAY...
...CHEESE! ♡
Grin!

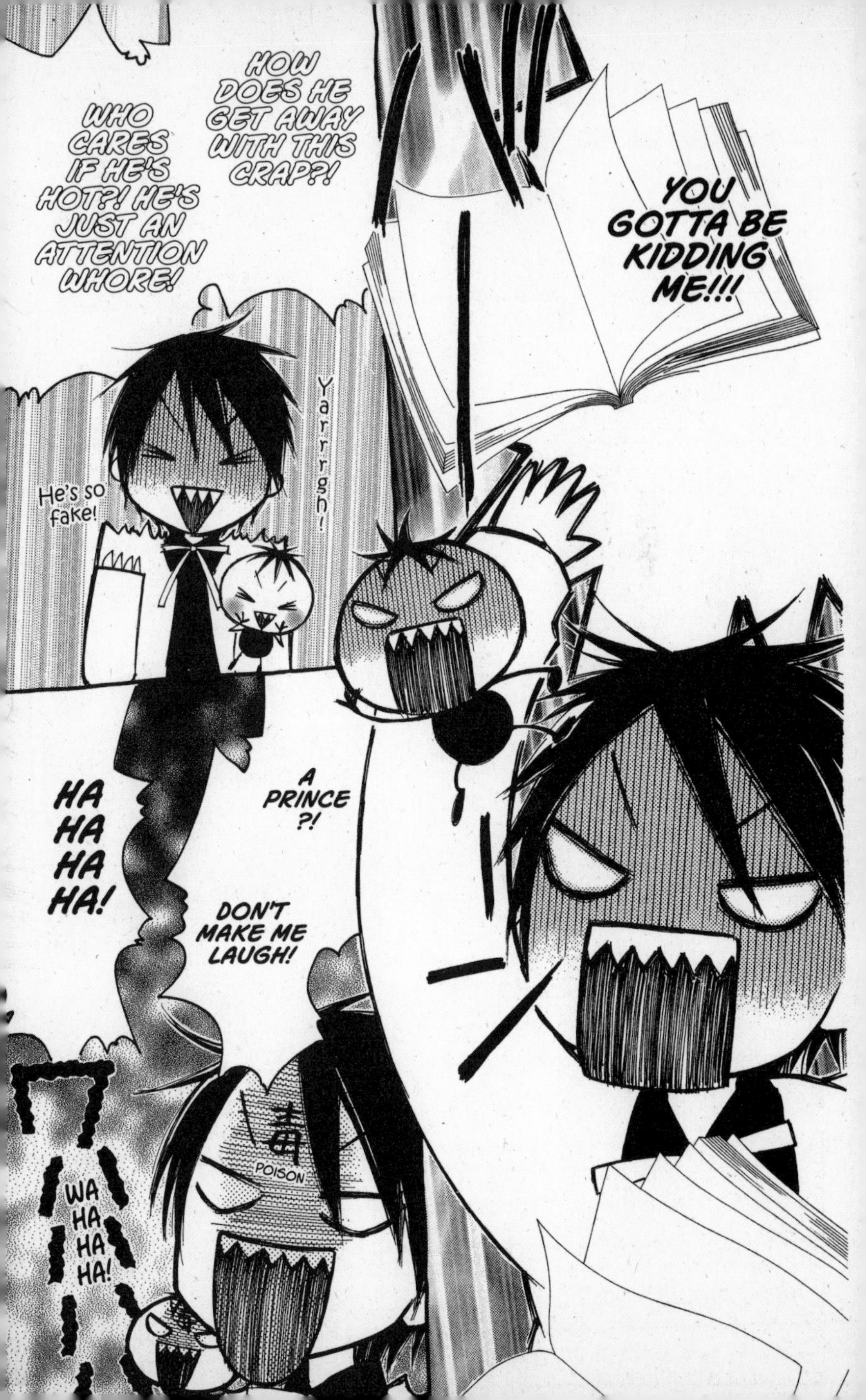
YOU GOTTA BE KIDDING ME!!!
HOW DOES HE GET AWAY WITH THIS CRAP?!
WHO CARES IF HE'S HOT?! HE'S JUST AN ATTENTION WHORE!
Yarrrgh!
He's so fake!
A PRINCE?!
DON'T MAKE ME LAUGH!
HA HA HA HA!
POISON
WA HA HA HA!

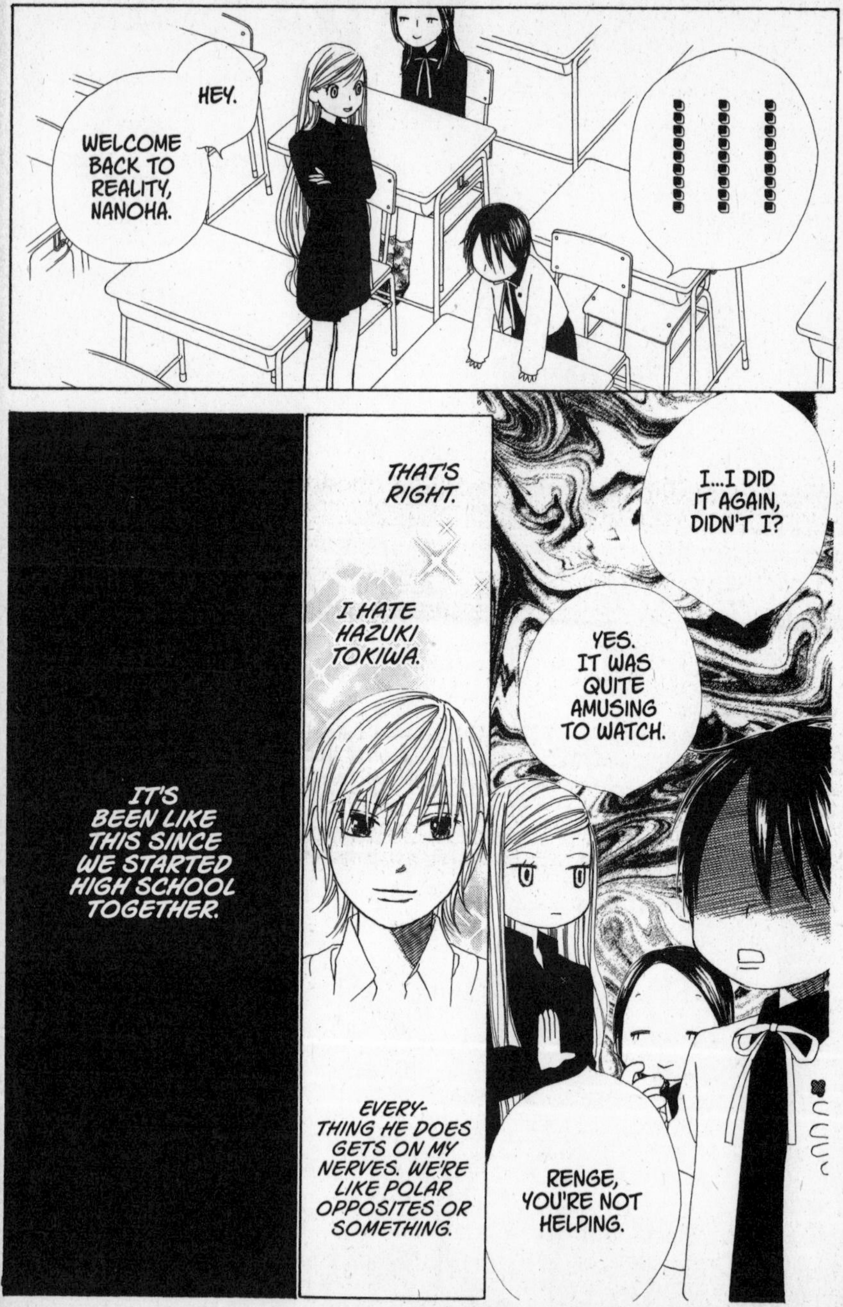
HEY.
WELCOME BACK TO REALITY, NANOHA.
I...I DID IT AGAIN, DIDN'T I?
YES. IT WAS QUITE AMUSING TO WATCH.
RENGE, YOU'RE NOT HELPING.
THAT'S RIGHT.
I HATE HAZUKI TOKIWA.
EVERY-THING HE DOES GETS ON MY NERVES. WE'RE LIKE POLAR OPPOSITES OR SOMETHING.
IT'S BEEN LIKE THIS SINCE WE STARTED HIGH SCHOOL TOGETHER.

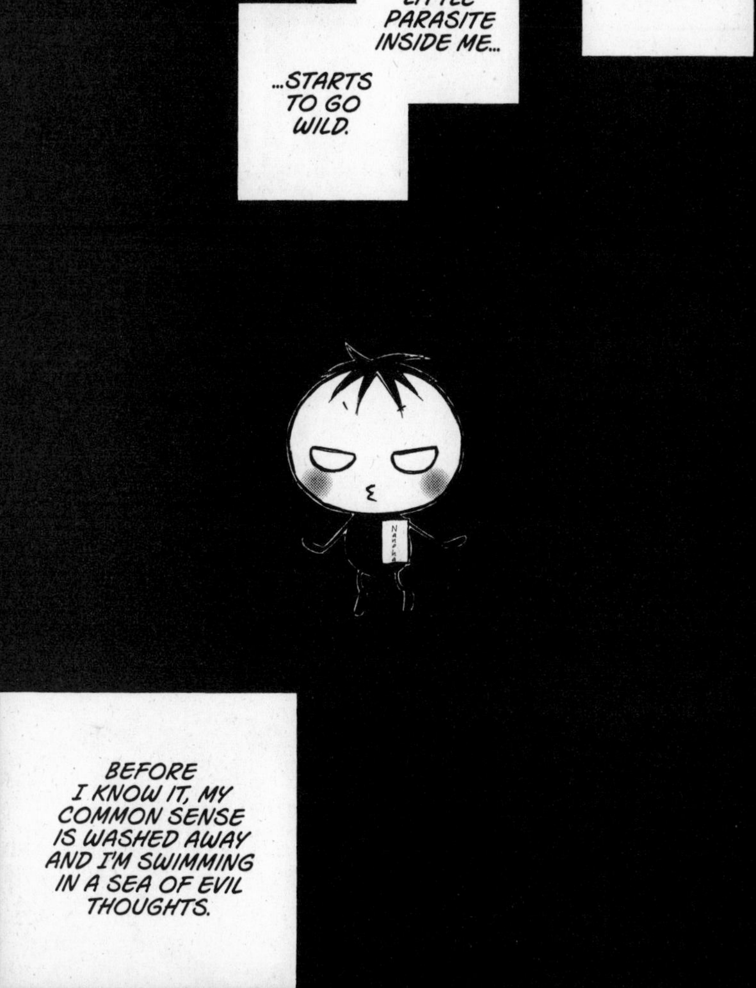
PARASITE INSIDE ME...
...STARTS TO GO WILD.
BEFORE I KNOW IT, MY COMMON SENSE IS WASHED AWAY AND I'M SWIMMING IN A SEA OF EVIL THOUGHTS.

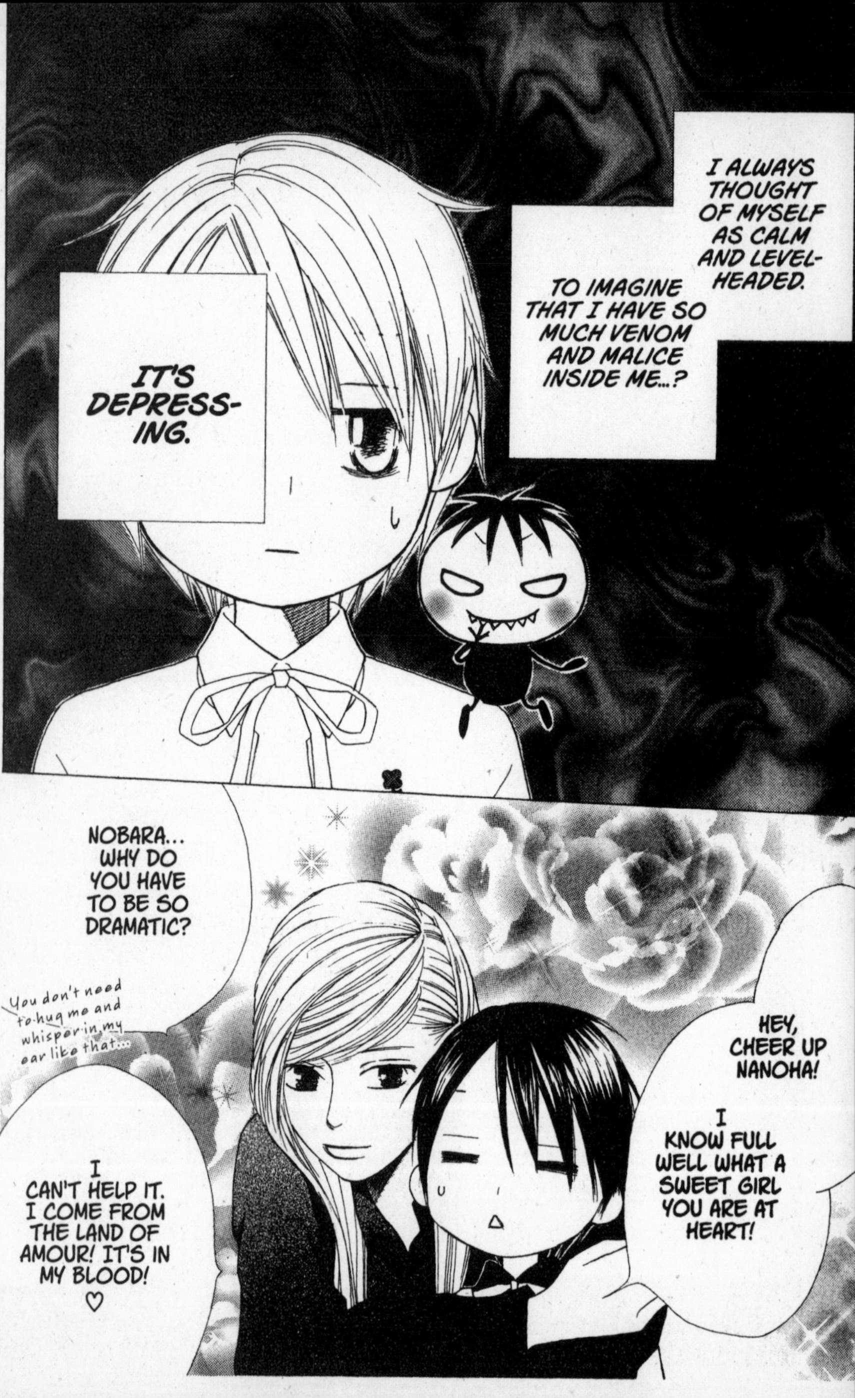
I ALWAYS THOUGHT OF MYSELF AS CALM AND LEVEL-HEADED.
TO IMAGINE THAT I HAVE SO MUCH VENOM AND MALICE INSIDE ME...?
IT'S DEPRESS-ING.
HEY, CHEER UP NANOHA!
I KNOW FULL WELL WHAT A SWEET GIRL YOU ARE AT HEART!
NOBARA... WHY DO YOU HAVE TO BE SO DRAMATIC?
You don't need to hug me and whisper in my ear like that...
I CAN'T HELP IT. I COME FROM THE LAND OF AMOUR! IT'S IN MY BLOOD! ♡

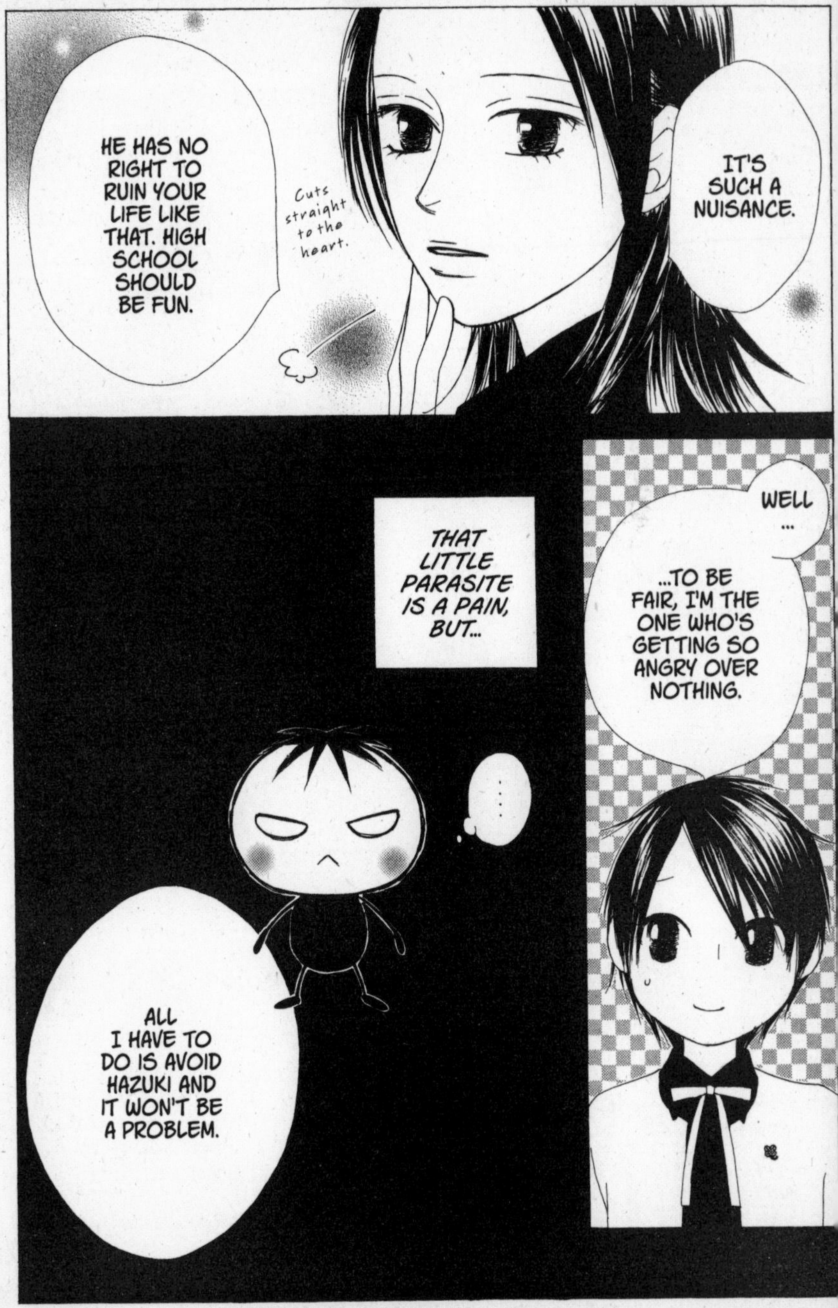
IT'S SUCH A NUISANCE.
Cuts straight to the heart.
HE HAS NO RIGHT TO RUIN YOUR LIFE LIKE THAT. HIGH SCHOOL SHOULD BE FUN.
WELL ...
...TO BE FAIR, I'M THE ONE WHO'S GETTING SO ANGRY OVER NOTHING.
THAT LITTLE PARASITE IS A PAIN, BUT...
ALL I HAVE TO DO IS AVOID HAZUKI AND IT WON'T BE A PROBLEM.

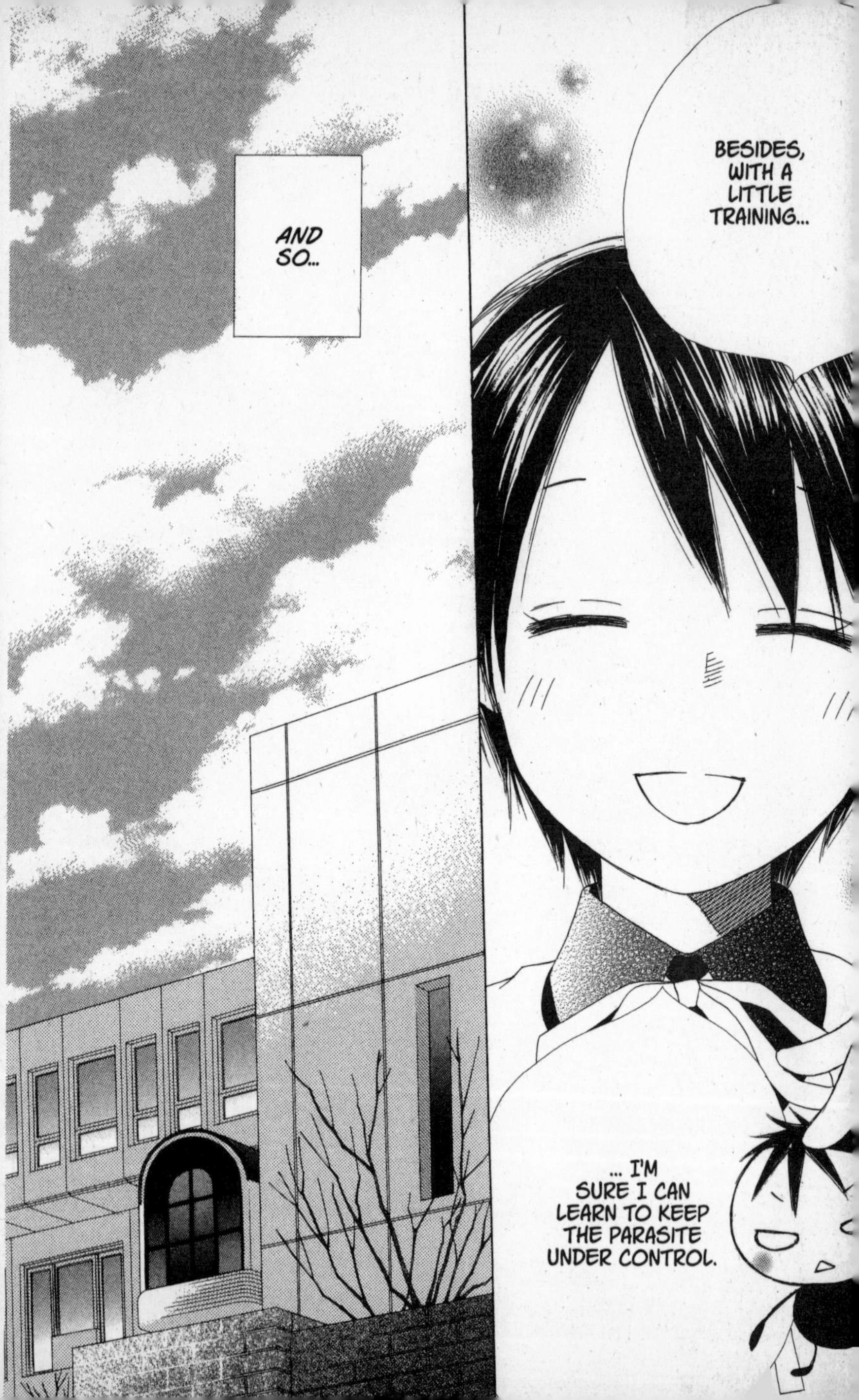
BESIDES, WITH A LITTLE TRAINING...
... I'M SURE I CAN LEARN TO KEEP THE PARASITE UNDER CONTROL.
AND SO...

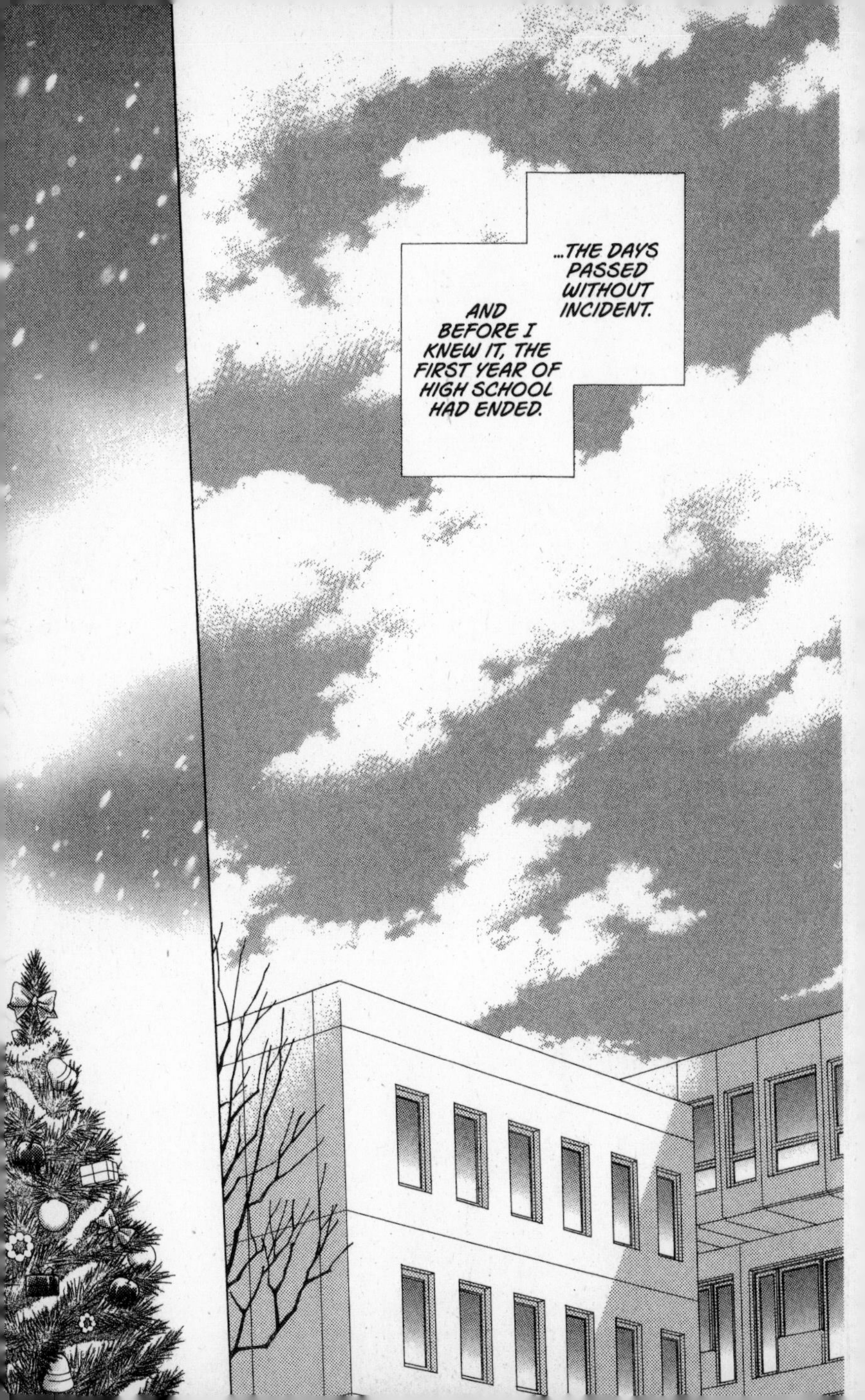
...THE DAYS PASSED WITHOUT INCIDENT.
AND BEFORE I KNEW IT, THE FIRST YEAR OF HIGH SCHOOL HAD ENDED.

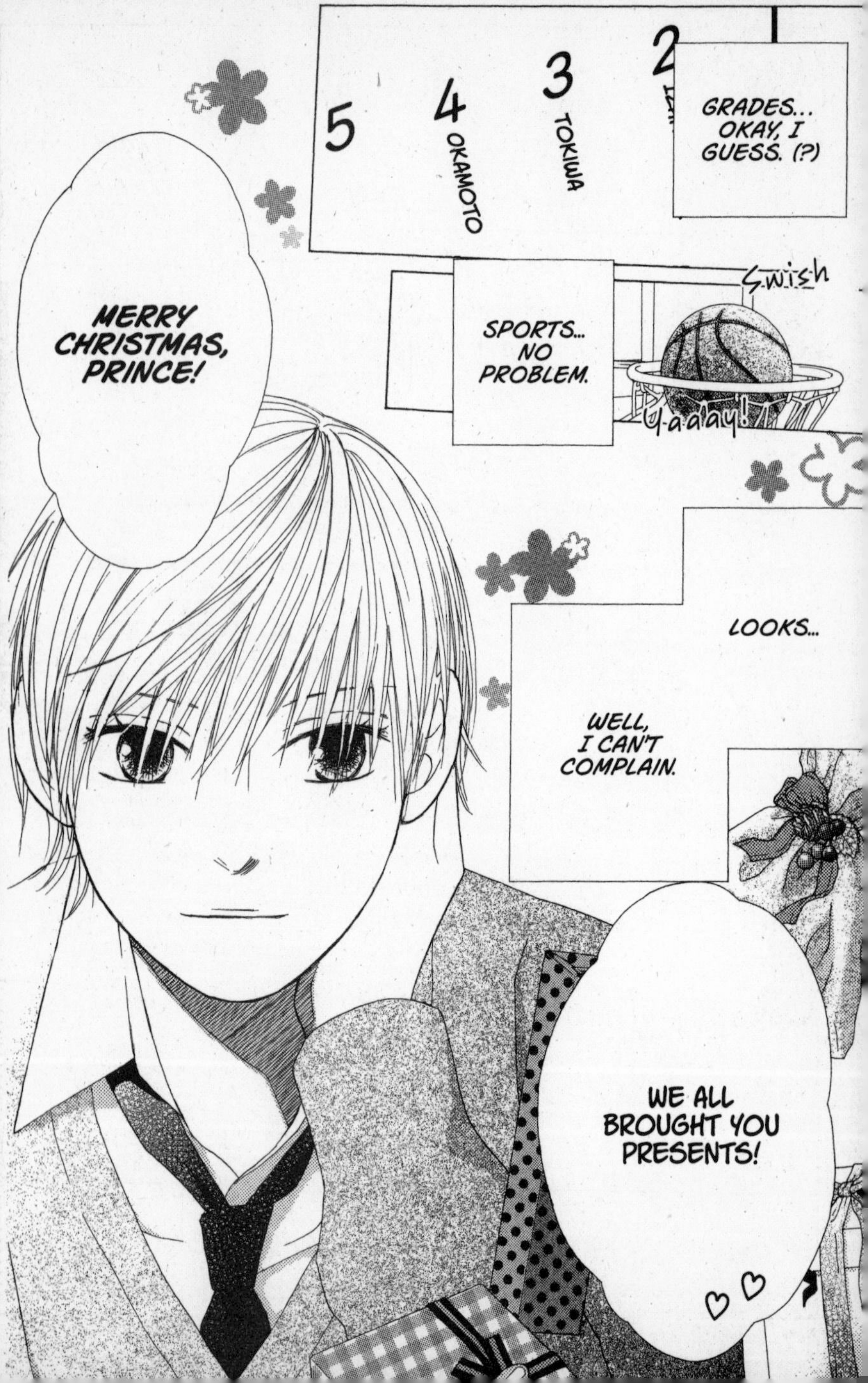
GRADES... OKAY, I GUESS. (?)
2
3
TOKIWA
4
OKAMOTO
5
SWISH
Y-A-A-A-Y!
SPORTS... NO PROBLEM.
LOOKS...
WELL, I CAN'T COMPLAIN.
MERRY CHRISTMAS, PRINCE!
WE ALL BROUGHT YOU PRESENTS!

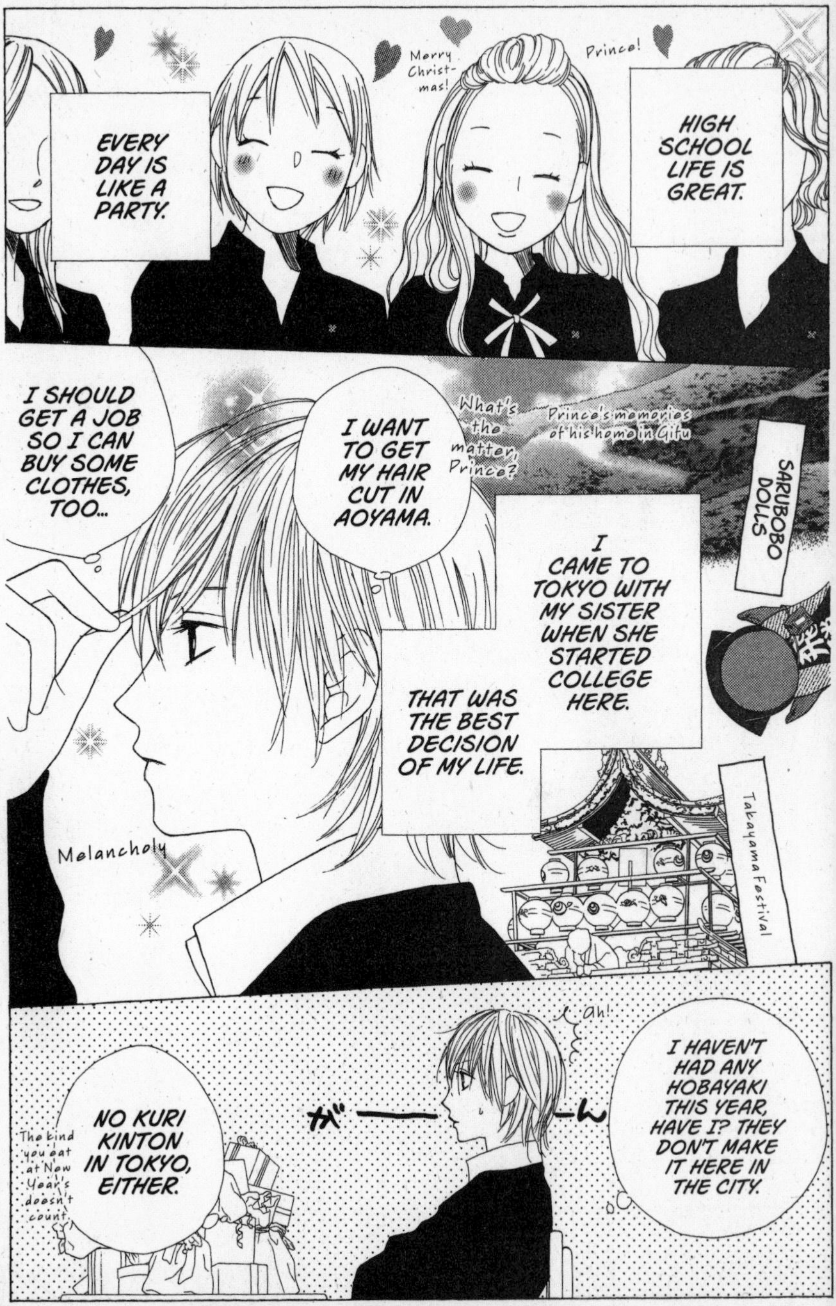
Prince!
HIGH SCHOOL LIFE IS GREAT.
Merry Christmas!
EVERY DAY IS LIKE A PARTY.
SARUBOBO DOLLS
Prince's memories of his home in Gifu
I CAME TO TOKYO WITH MY SISTER WHEN SHE STARTED COLLEGE HERE.
What's the matter, Prince?
I WANT TO GET MY HAIR CUT IN AOYAMA.
I SHOULD GET A JOB SO I CAN BUY SOME CLOTHES, TOO...
THAT WAS THE BEST DECISION OF MY LIFE.
Takayama Festival
Melancholy
I HAVEN'T HAD ANY HOBAYAKI THIS YEAR, HAVE I? THEY DON'T MAKE IT HERE IN THE CITY.
ah!
ガーーーーん
NO KURI KINTON IN TOKYO, EITHER.
The kind you eat at New Year's doesn't count.

Note: Hobayaki is a regional dish from Gifu. Kuri kinton is a chestnut desert.

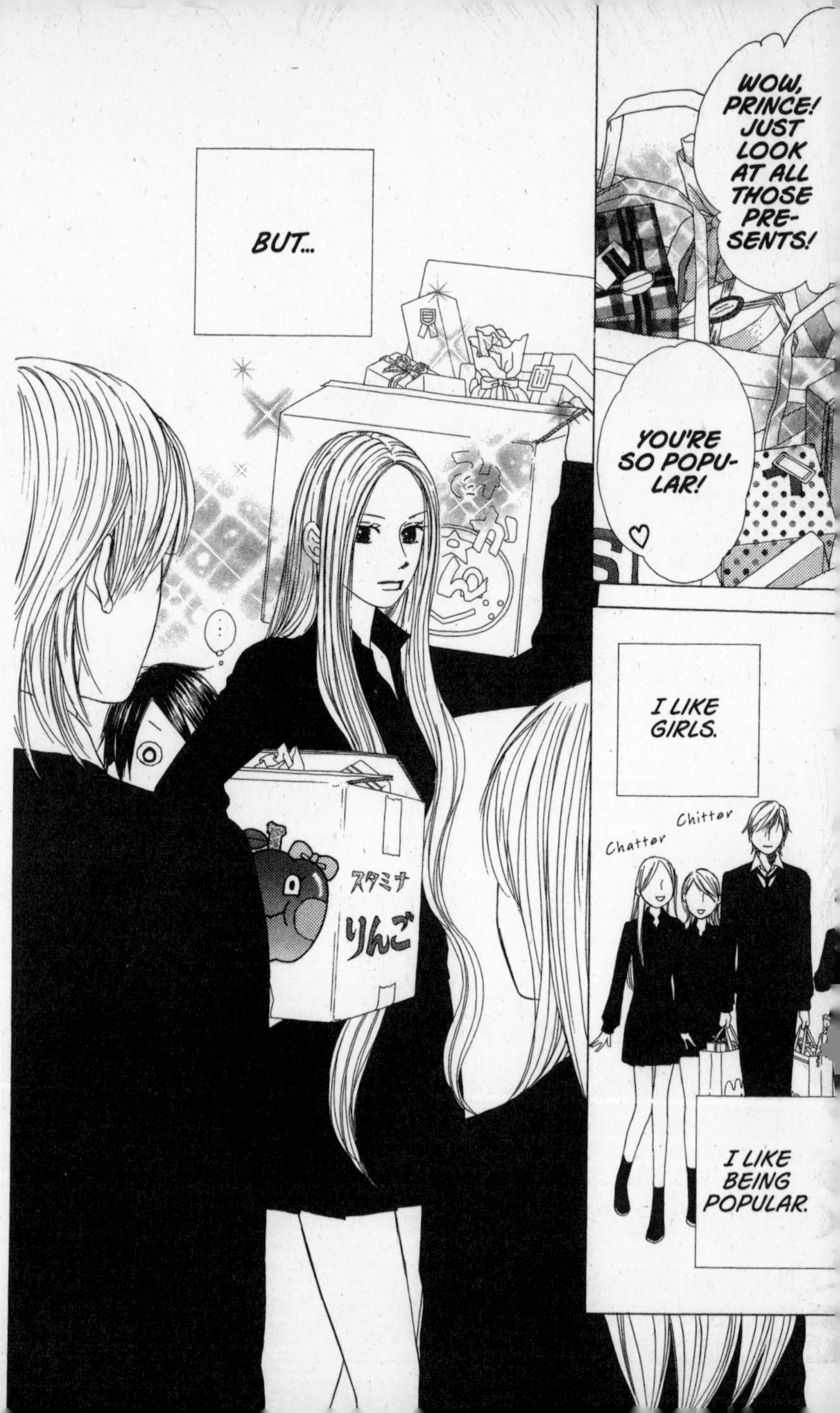
WOW, PRINCE! JUST LOOK AT ALL THOSE PRE-SENTS!
YOU'RE SO POPU-LAR!
I LIKE GIRLS.
Chitter
Chatter
I LIKE BEING POPULAR.
BUT...
スタミナ
りんご

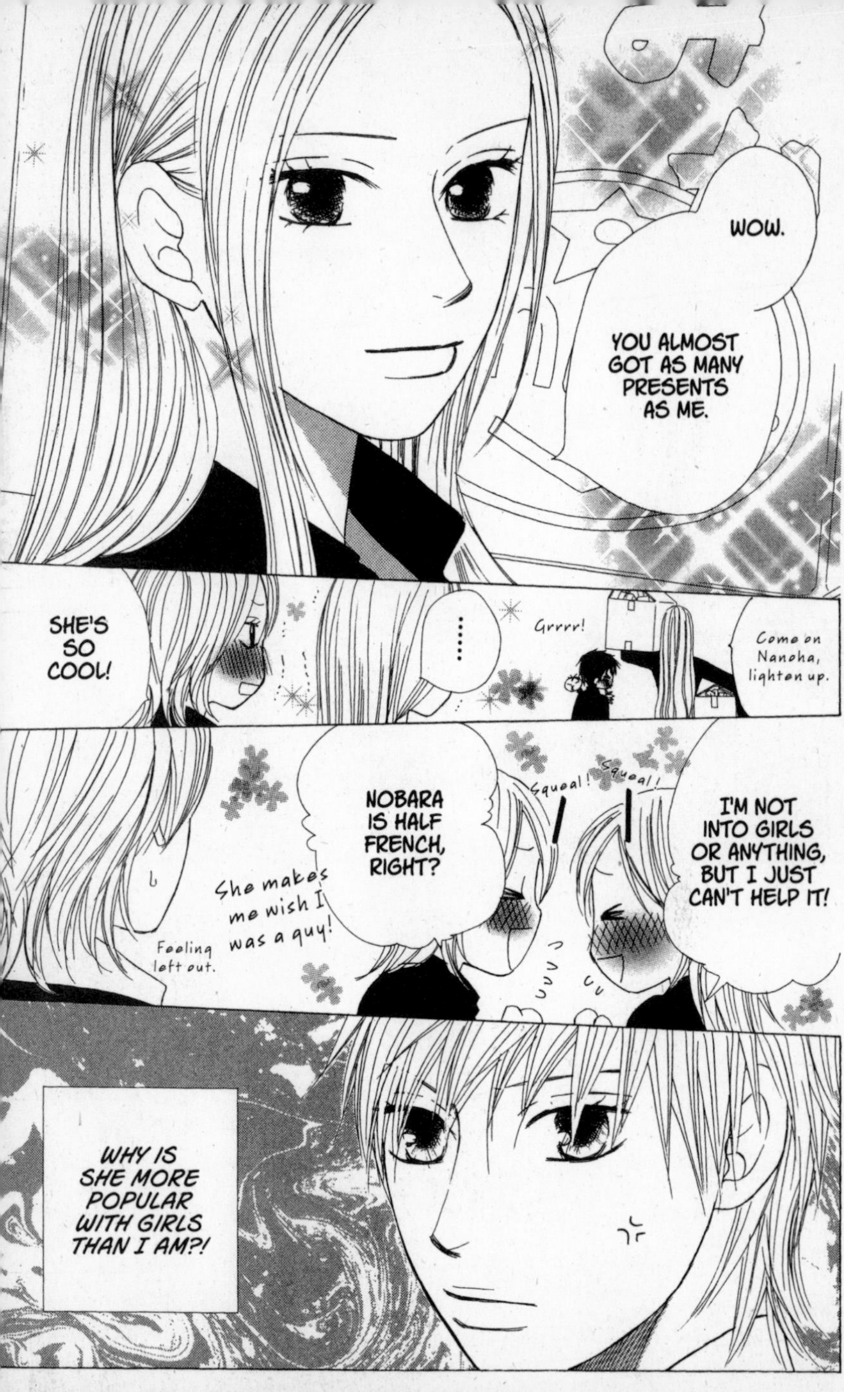
WOW.
YOU ALMOST GOT AS MANY PRESENTS AS ME.
Come on Nanoha, lighten up.
Grrrr!
......
SHE'S SO COOL!
I'M NOT INTO GIRLS OR ANYTHING, BUT I JUST CAN'T HELP IT!
Squeal!
Squeal!
NOBARA IS HALF FRENCH, RIGHT?
She makes me wish I was a guy!
Feeling left out.
WHY IS SHE MORE POPULAR WITH GIRLS THAN I AM?!

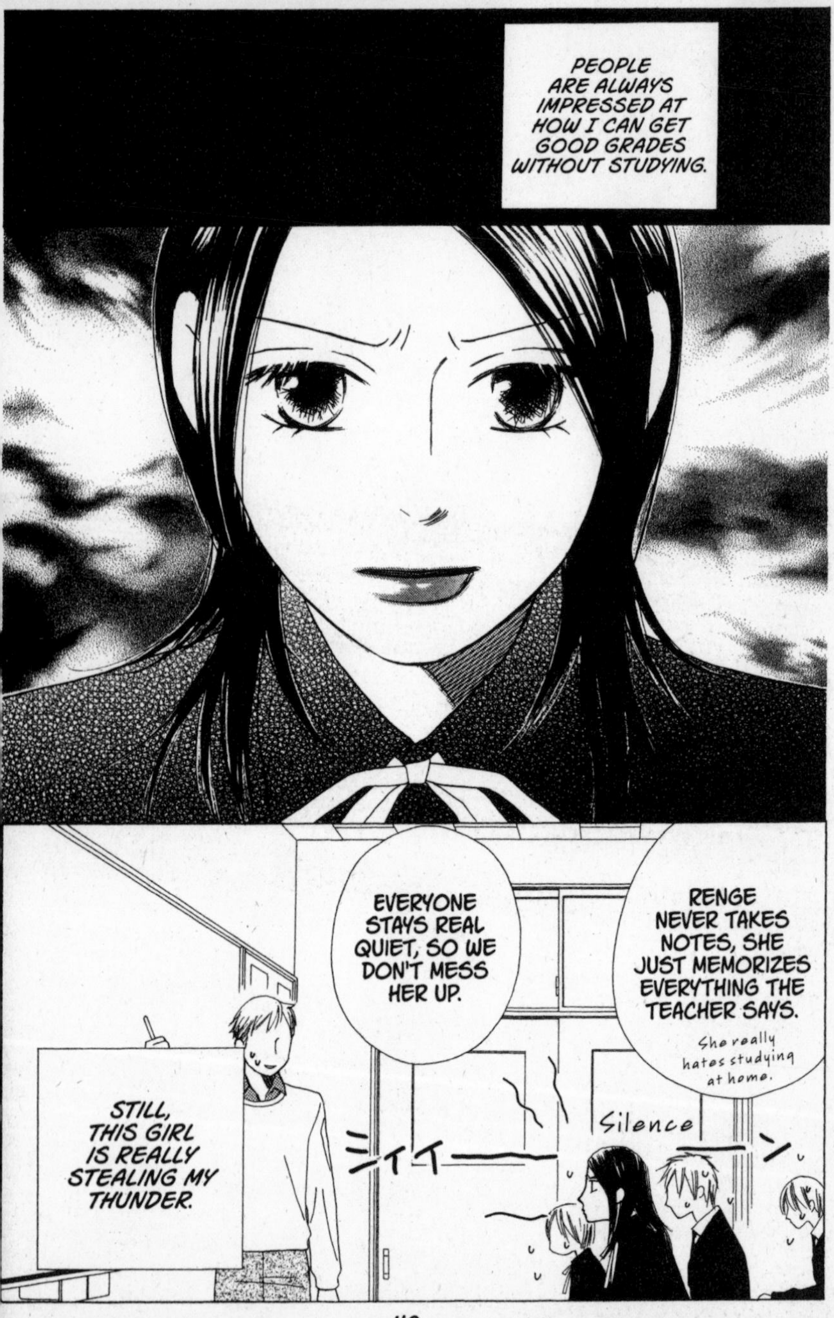
PEOPLE ARE ALWAYS IMPRESSED AT HOW I CAN GET GOOD GRADES WITHOUT STUDYING.
RENGE NEVER TAKES NOTES, SHE JUST MEMORIZES EVERYTHING THE TEACHER SAYS.
She really hates studying at home.
EVERYONE STAYS REAL QUIET, SO WE DON'T MESS HER UP.
シイイ———ン
Silence
STILL, THIS GIRL IS REALLY STEALING MY THUNDER.

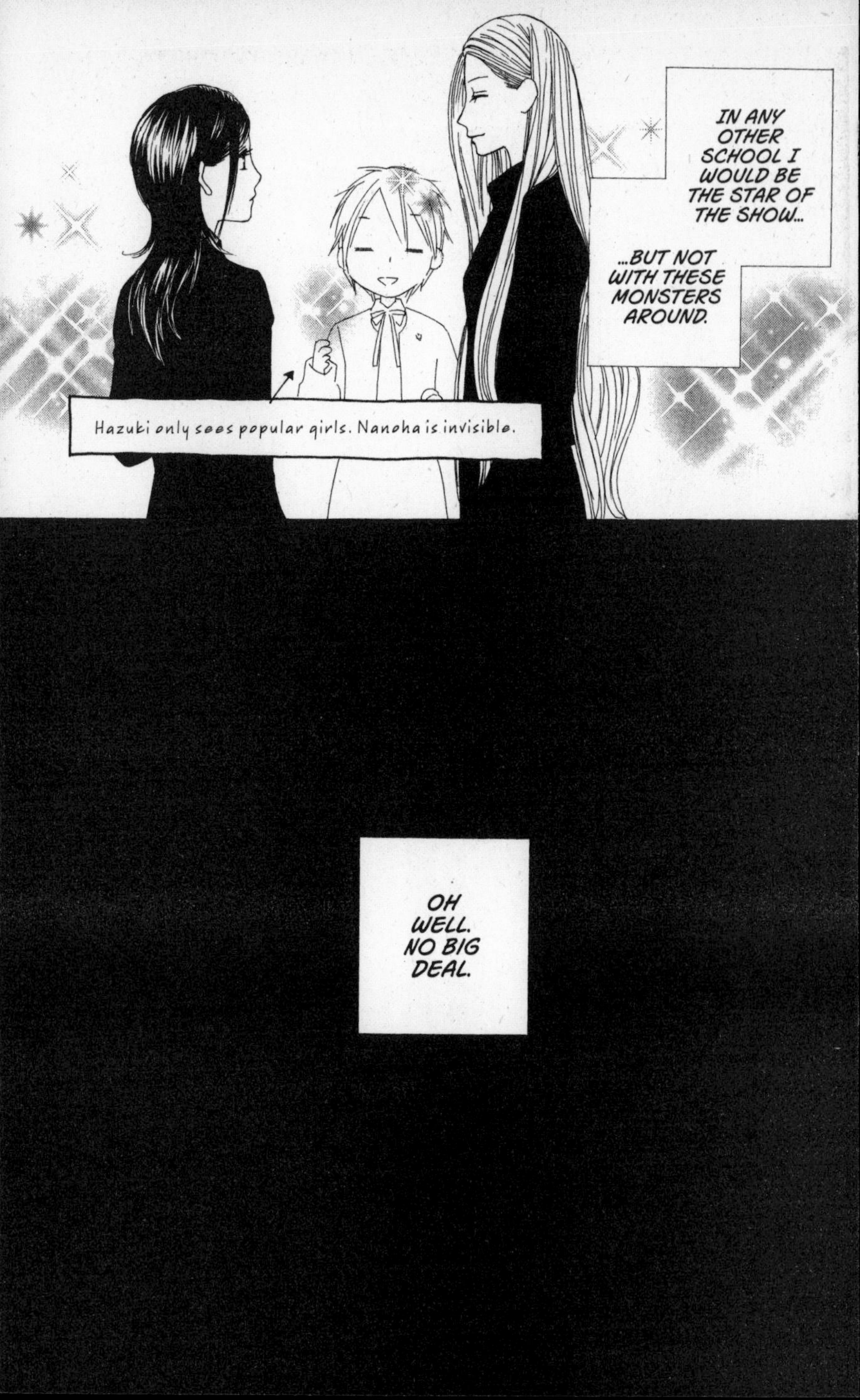
IN ANY OTHER SCHOOL I WOULD BE THE STAR OF THE SHOW...
...BUT NOT WITH THESE MONSTERS AROUND.
Hazuki only sees popular girls. Nanoha is invisible.
OH WELL. NO BIG DEAL.

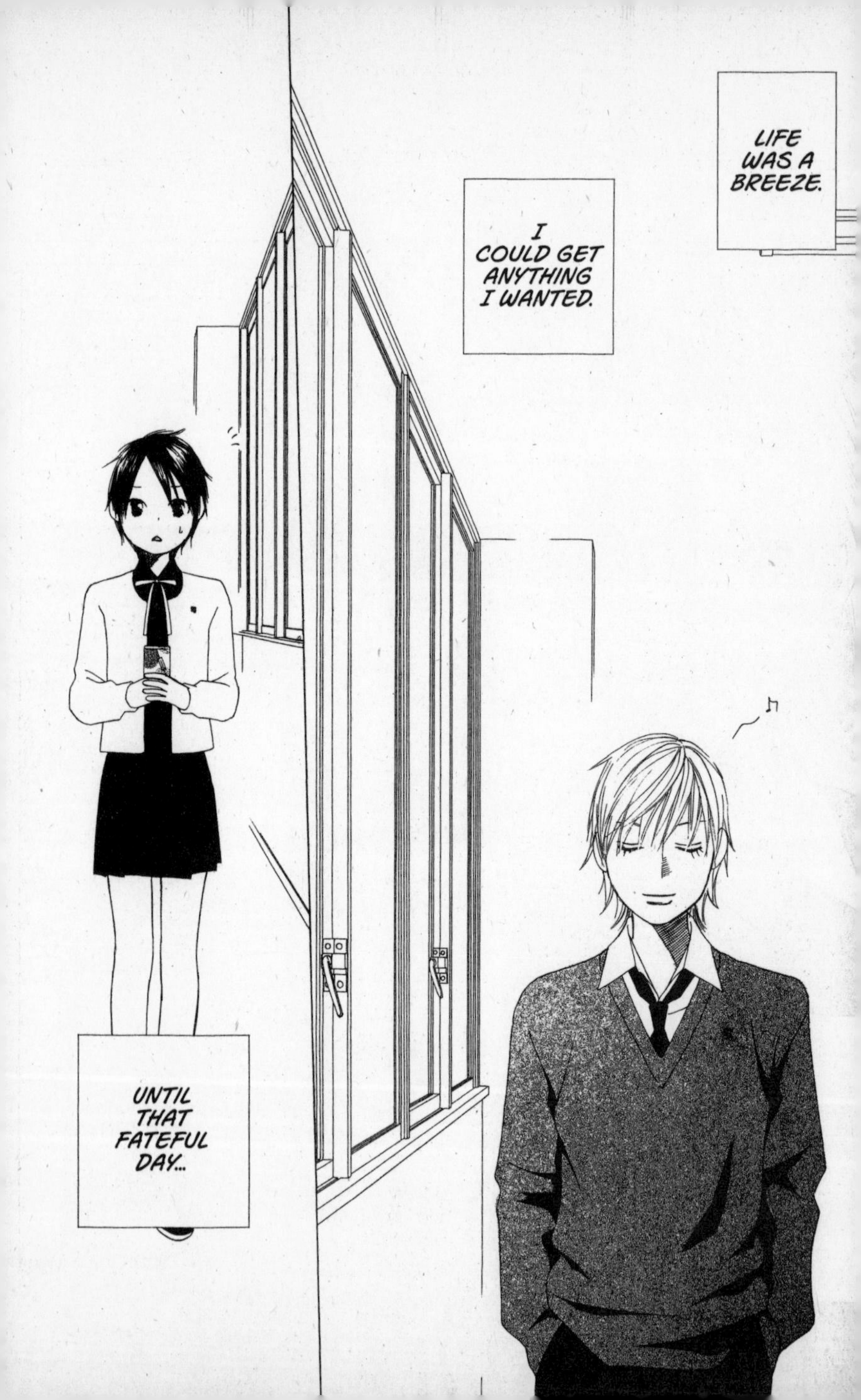
LIFE WAS A BREEZE.
I COULD GET ANYTHING I WANTED.
UNTIL THAT FATEFUL DAY...

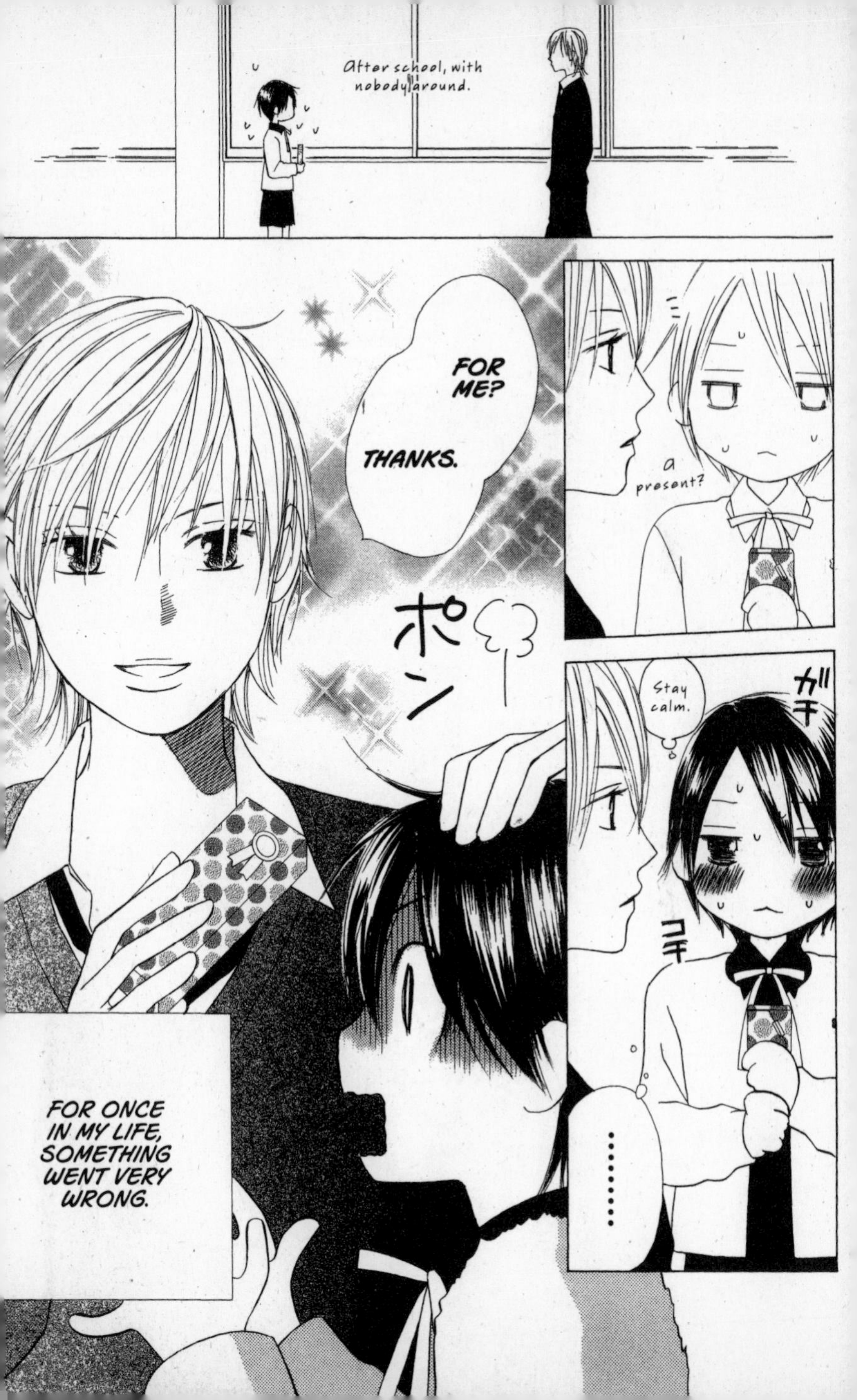

After school, with nobody around.
a present?
Stay calm.
ガチ
コチ
......
FOR ME?
THANKS.
ポン
FOR ONCE IN MY LIFE, SOMETHING WENT VERY WRONG.

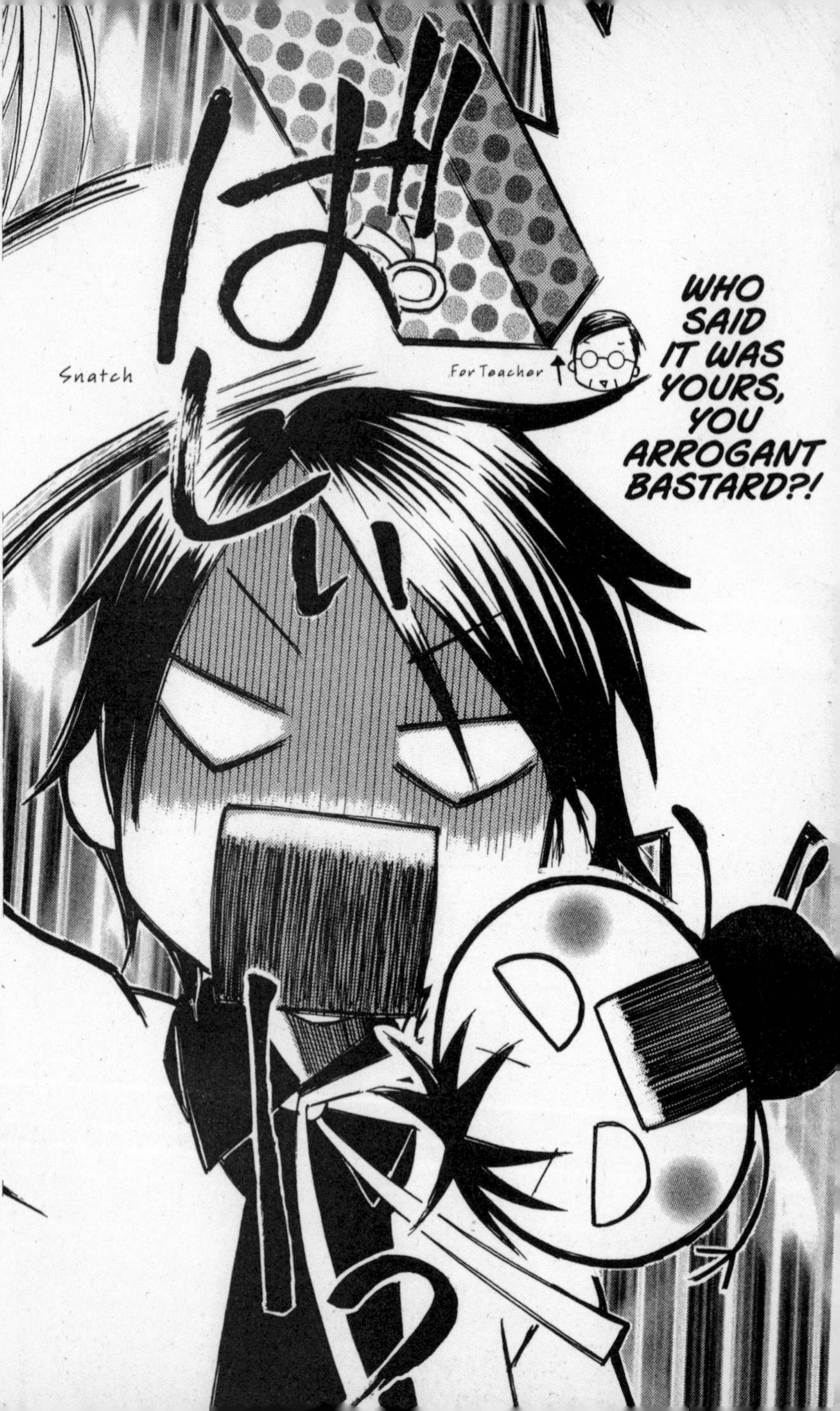
WHO SAID IT WAS YOURS, YOU ARROGANT BASTARD?!
For Teacher
Snatch

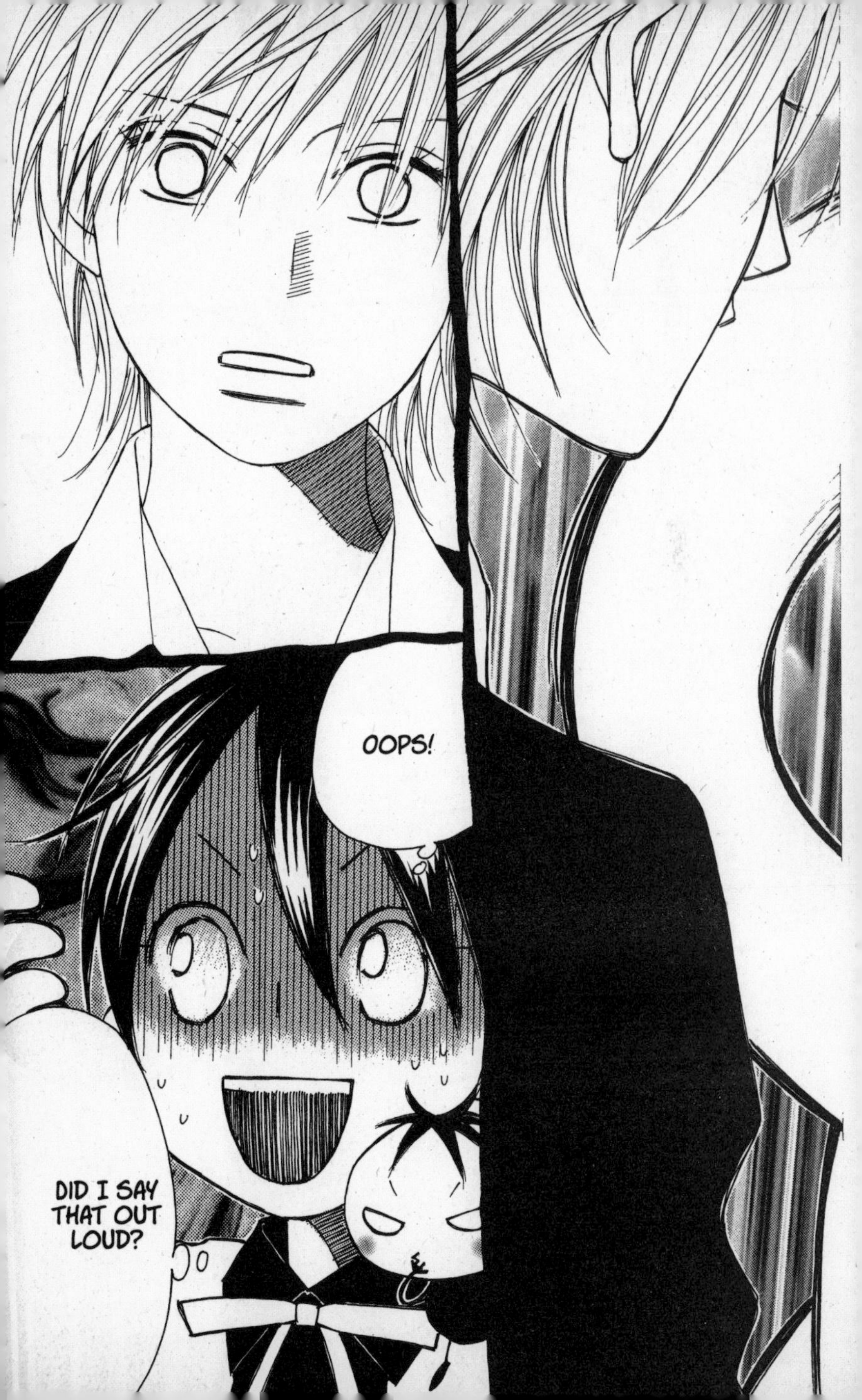
OOPS!
DID I SAY THAT OUT LOUD?

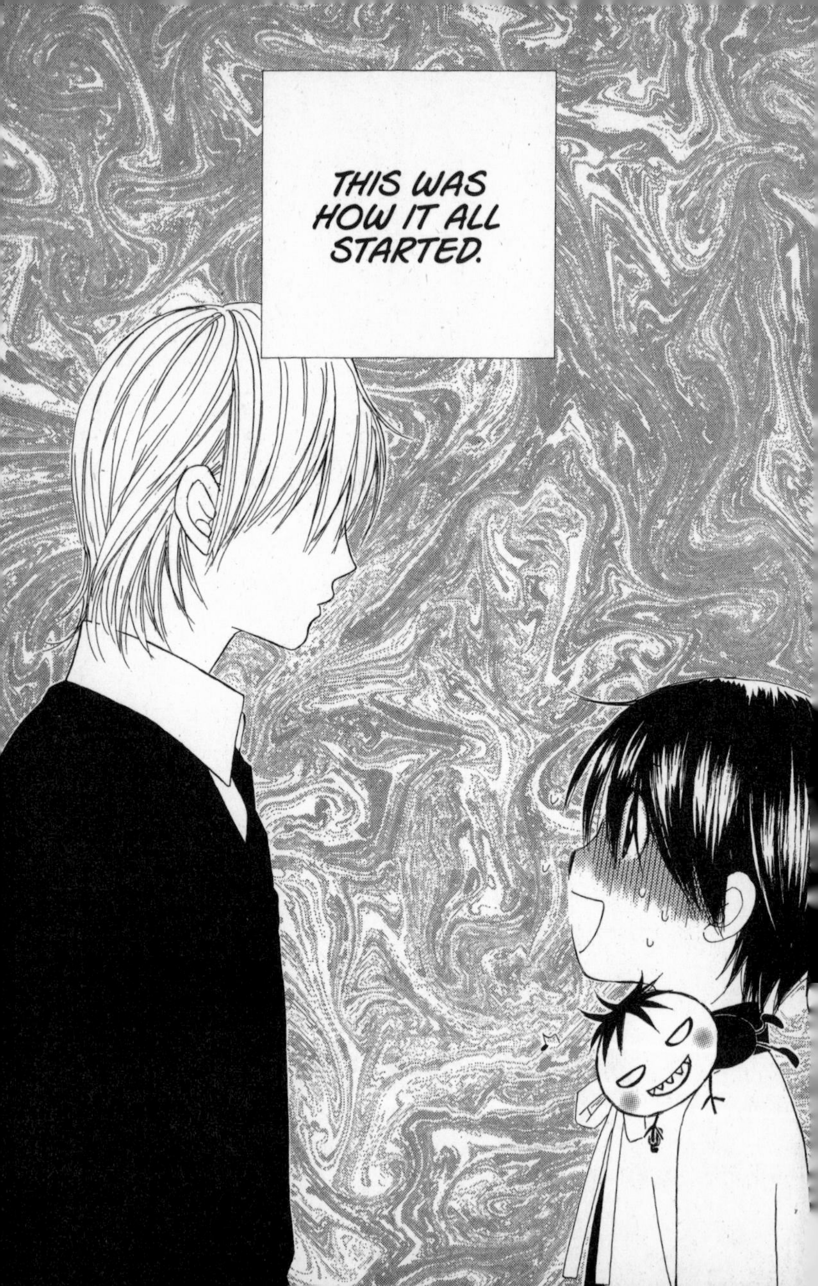
THIS WAS HOW IT ALL STARTED.

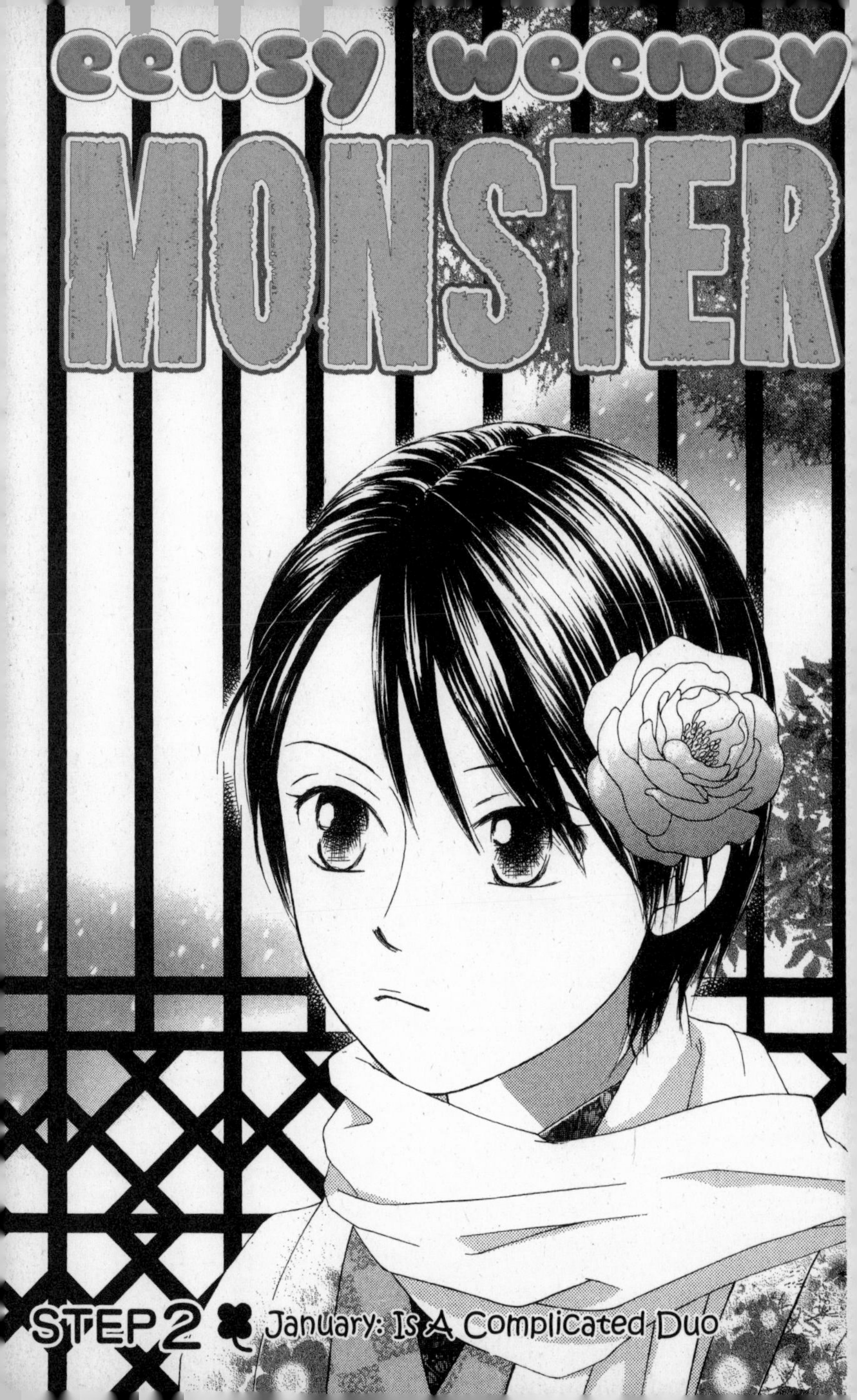
eensy weensy
MONSTER
STEP 2 January: Is A Complicated Duo

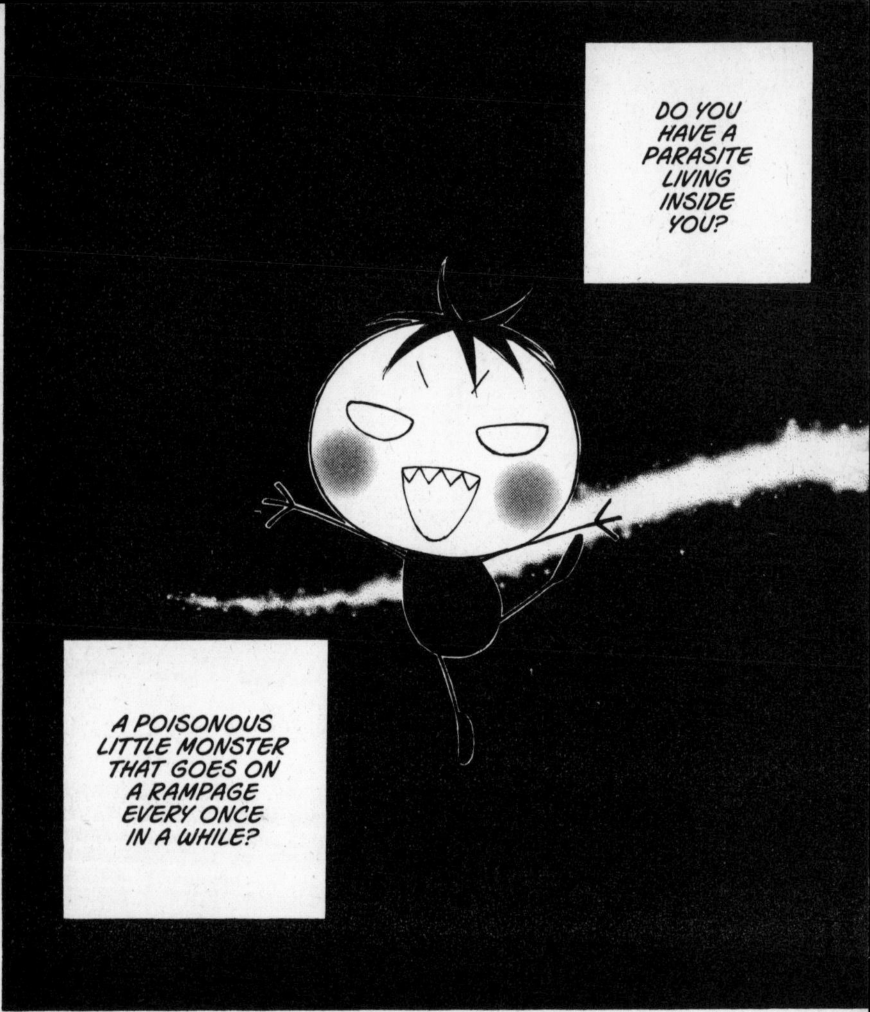
DO YOU HAVE A PARASITE LIVING INSIDE YOU?
A POISONOUS LITTLE MONSTER THAT GOES ON A RAMPAGE EVERY ONCE IN A WHILE?

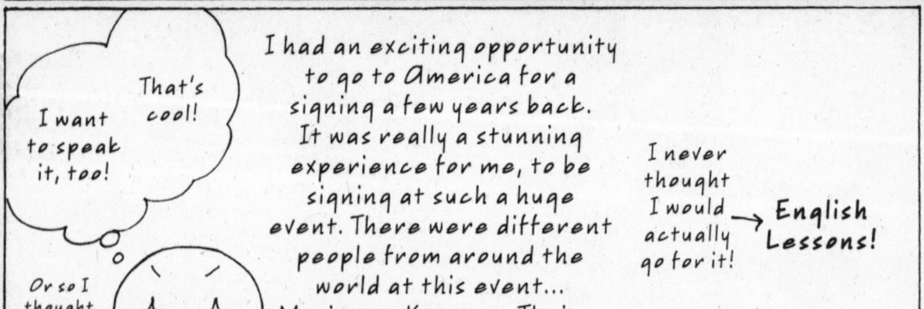
I had an exciting opportunity to go to America for a signing a few years back. It was really a stunning experience for me, to be signing at such a huge event. There were different people from around the world at this event... Mexicans, Koreans, Thais... all speaking English!
That's cool!
I want to speak it, too!
Or so I thought to myself.
I never thought I would actually go for it!
English Lessons!

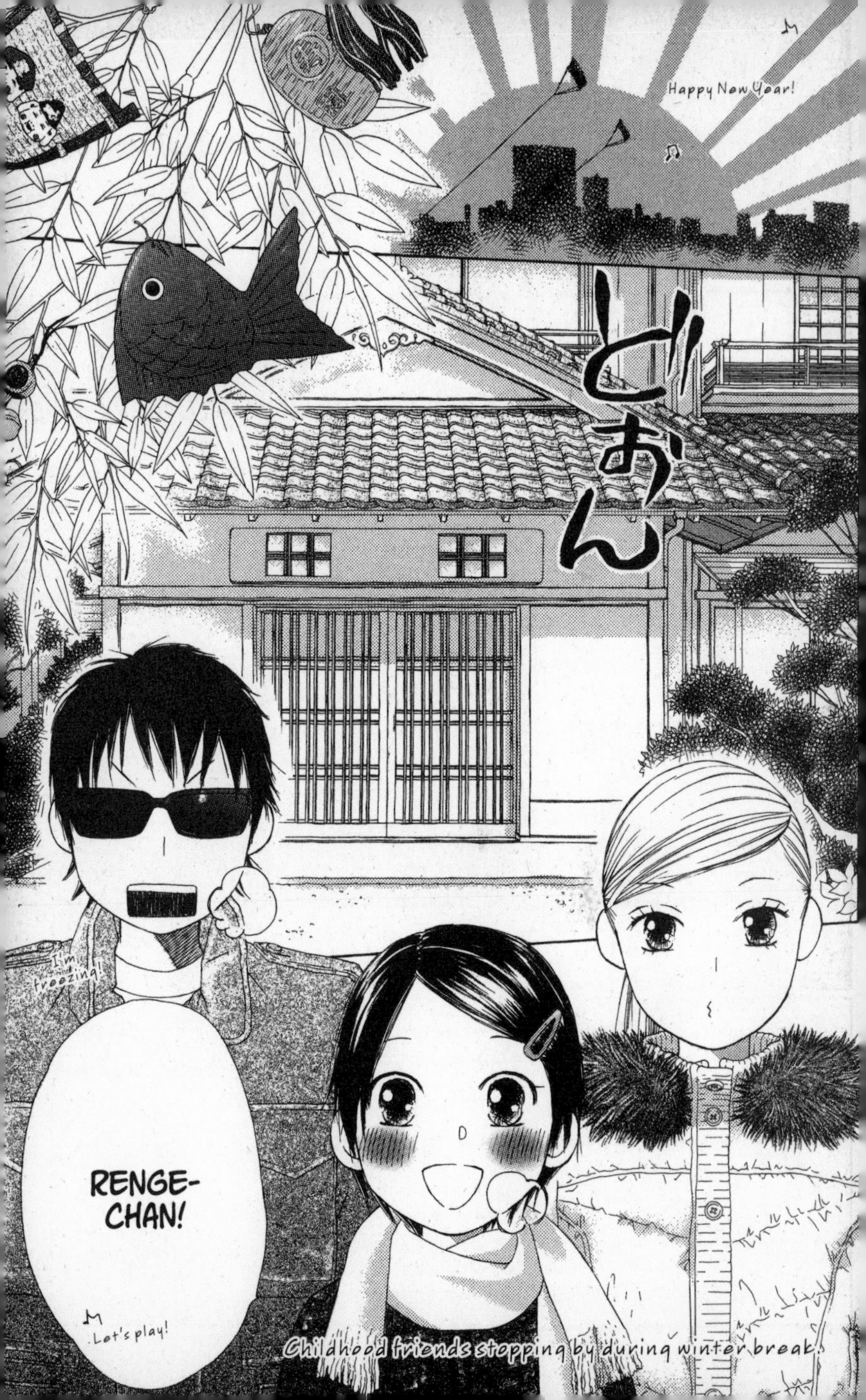
Happy New Year!
どおん
I'm freezing!
RENGE-CHAN!
Let's play!
Childhood friends stopping by during winter break.

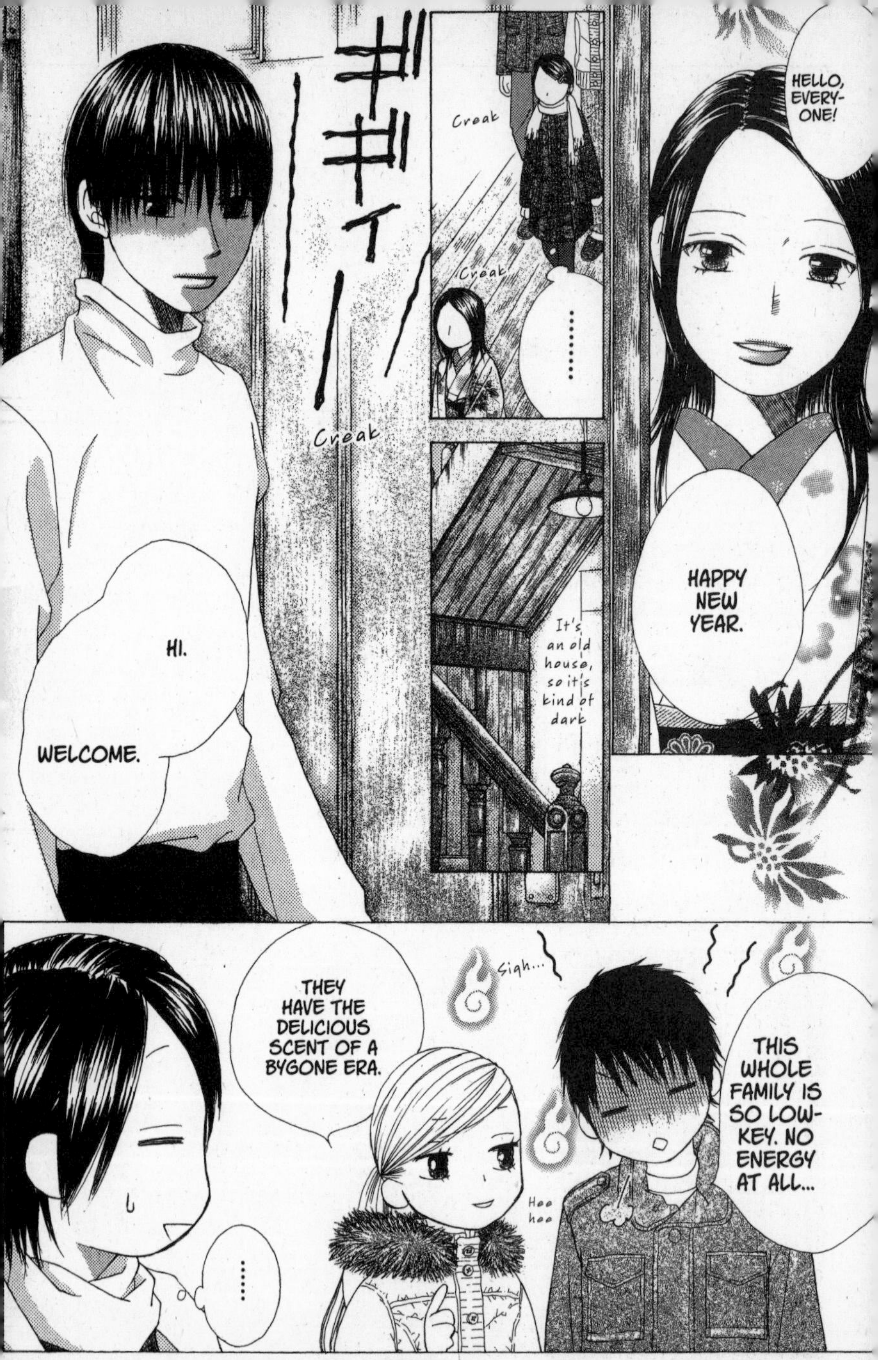
HELLO, EVERYONE!
HAPPY NEW YEAR.
Creak
Creak
......
It's an old house, so it's kind of dark
Creak
HI.
WELCOME.
Sigh...
THIS WHOLE FAMILY IS SO LOW-KEY. NO ENERGY AT ALL...
Hee hee
THEY HAVE THE DELICIOUS SCENT OF A BYGONE ERA.
......

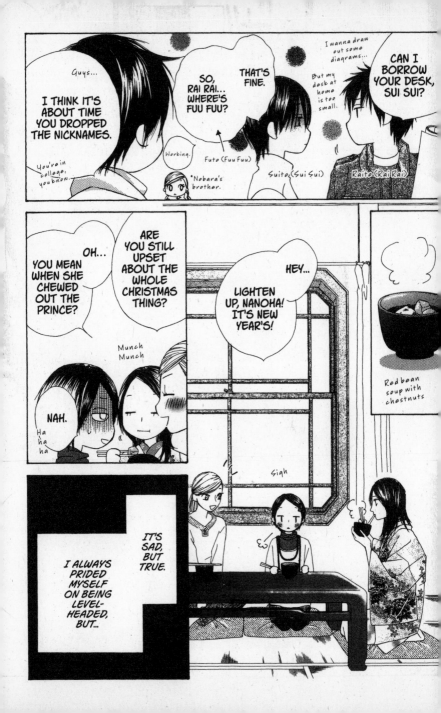

CAN I BORROW YOUR DESK, SUI SUI?
I wanna draw out some diagrams...
But my desk at home is too small.
Raito (Rai Rai)
THAT'S FINE.
Suito (Sui Sui)
SO, RAI RAI... WHERE'S FUU FUU?
Futo (Fuu Fuu)
Working.
*Nobara's brother.
Guys...
I THINK IT'S ABOUT TIME YOU DROPPED THE NICKNAMES.
You're in college, you know...
Red bean soup with chestnuts
ARE YOU STILL UPSET ABOUT THE WHOLE CHRISTMAS THING?
OH... YOU MEAN WHEN SHE CHEWED OUT THE PRINCE?
Munch Munch
NAH.
Ha ha ha
HEY... LIGHTEN UP, NANOHA! IT'S NEW YEAR'S!
Sigh
IT'S SAD, BUT TRUE.
I ALWAYS PRIDED MYSELF ON BEING LEVEL-HEADED, BUT...

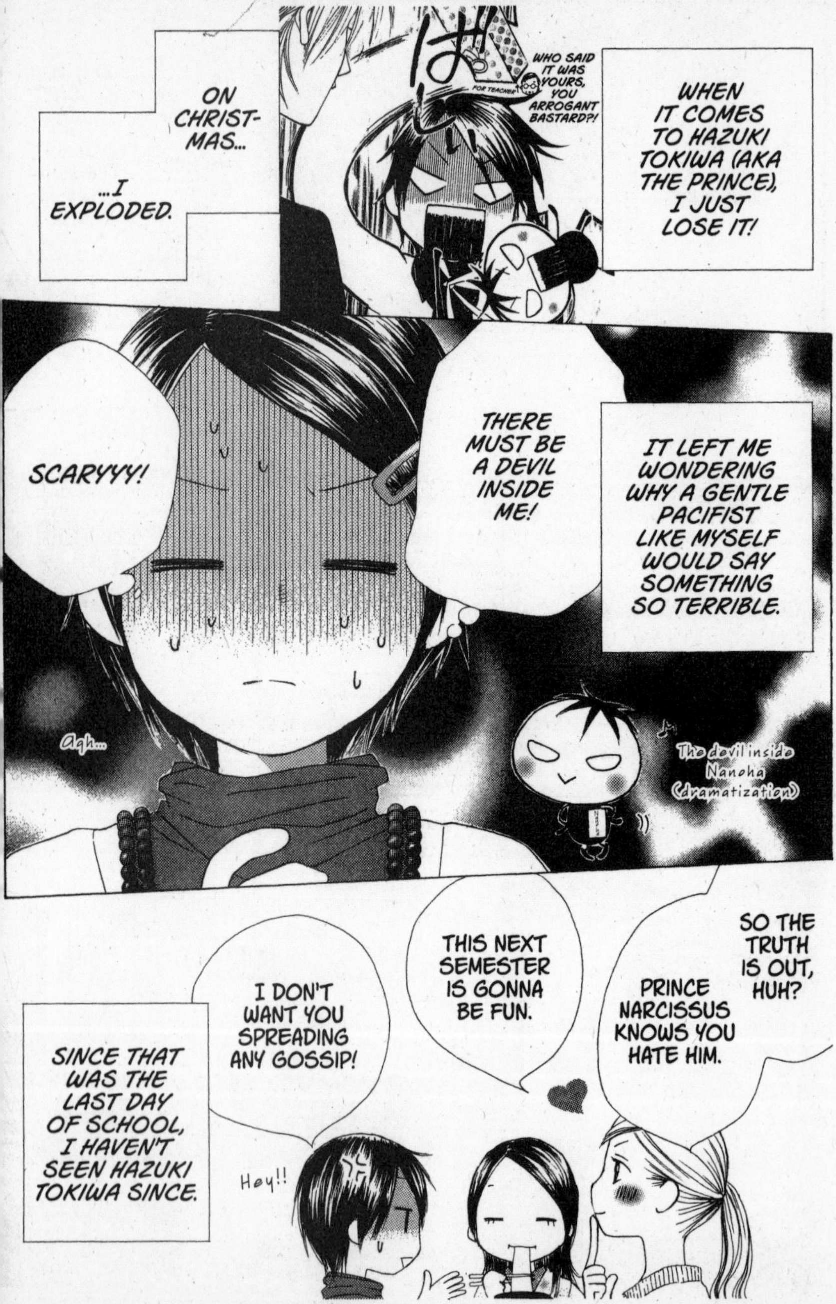

WHEN IT COMES TO HAZUKI TOKIWA (AKA THE PRINCE), I JUST LOSE IT!
WHO SAID IT WAS YOURS, YOU ARROGANT BASTARD?!
FOR TEACHER
ON CHRIST-MAS...
...I EXPLODED.
IT LEFT ME WONDERING WHY A GENTLE PACIFIST LIKE MYSELF WOULD SAY SOMETHING SO TERRIBLE.
THERE MUST BE A DEVIL INSIDE ME!
SCARYYY!
The devil inside Nanoha (dramatization)
Agh...
SO THE TRUTH IS OUT, HUH?
PRINCE NARCISSUS KNOWS YOU HATE HIM.
THIS NEXT SEMESTER IS GONNA BE FUN.
I DON'T WANT YOU SPREADING ANY GOSSIP!
Hey!!
SINCE THAT WAS THE LAST DAY OF SCHOOL, I HAVEN'T SEEN HAZUKI TOKIWA SINCE.

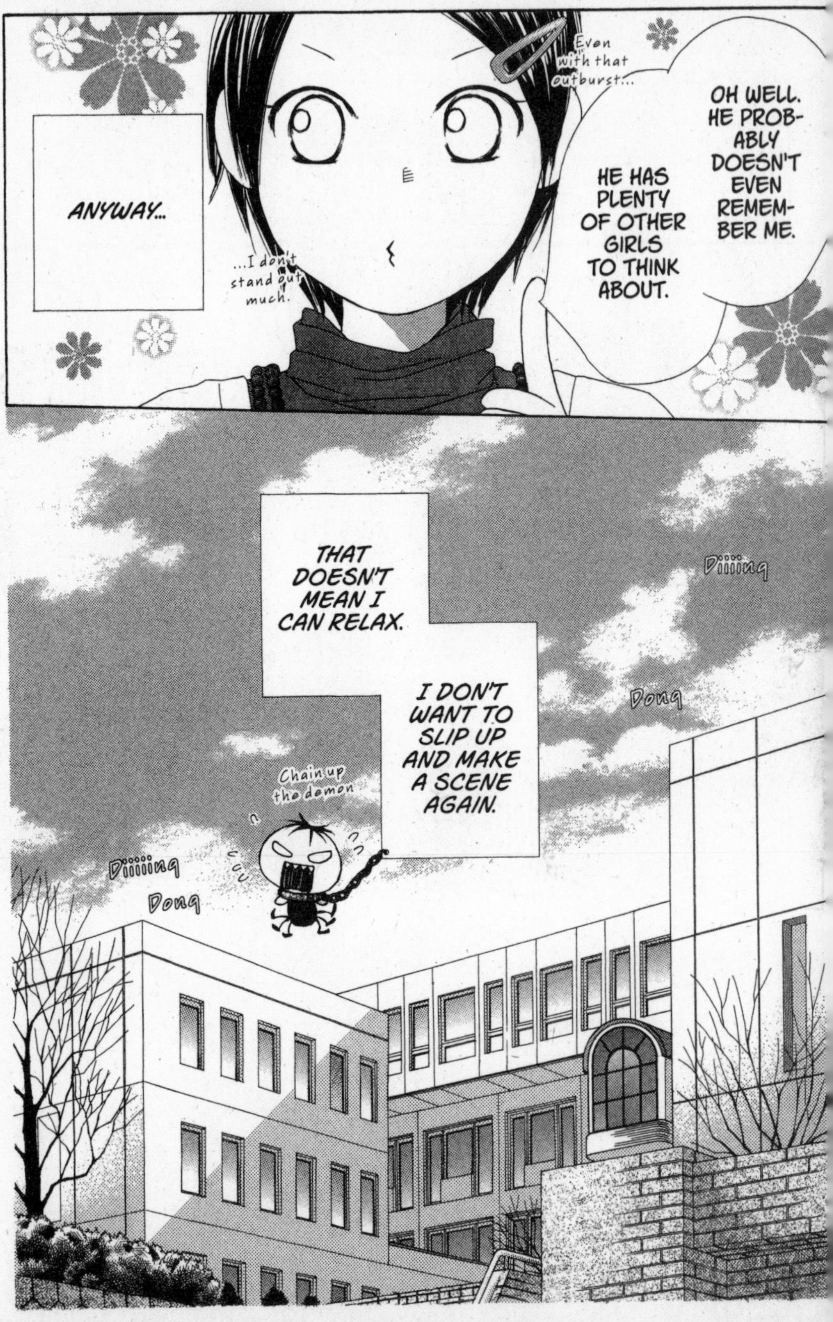
OH WELL. HE PROBABLY DOESN'T EVEN REMEMBER ME.
HE HAS PLENTY OF OTHER GIRLS TO THINK ABOUT.
Even with that outburst...
...I don't stand out much.
ANYWAY...
Diiiing
Dong
THAT DOESN'T MEAN I CAN RELAX.
I DON'T WANT TO SLIP UP AND MAKE A SCENE AGAIN.
Chain up the demon
Diiiing
Dong

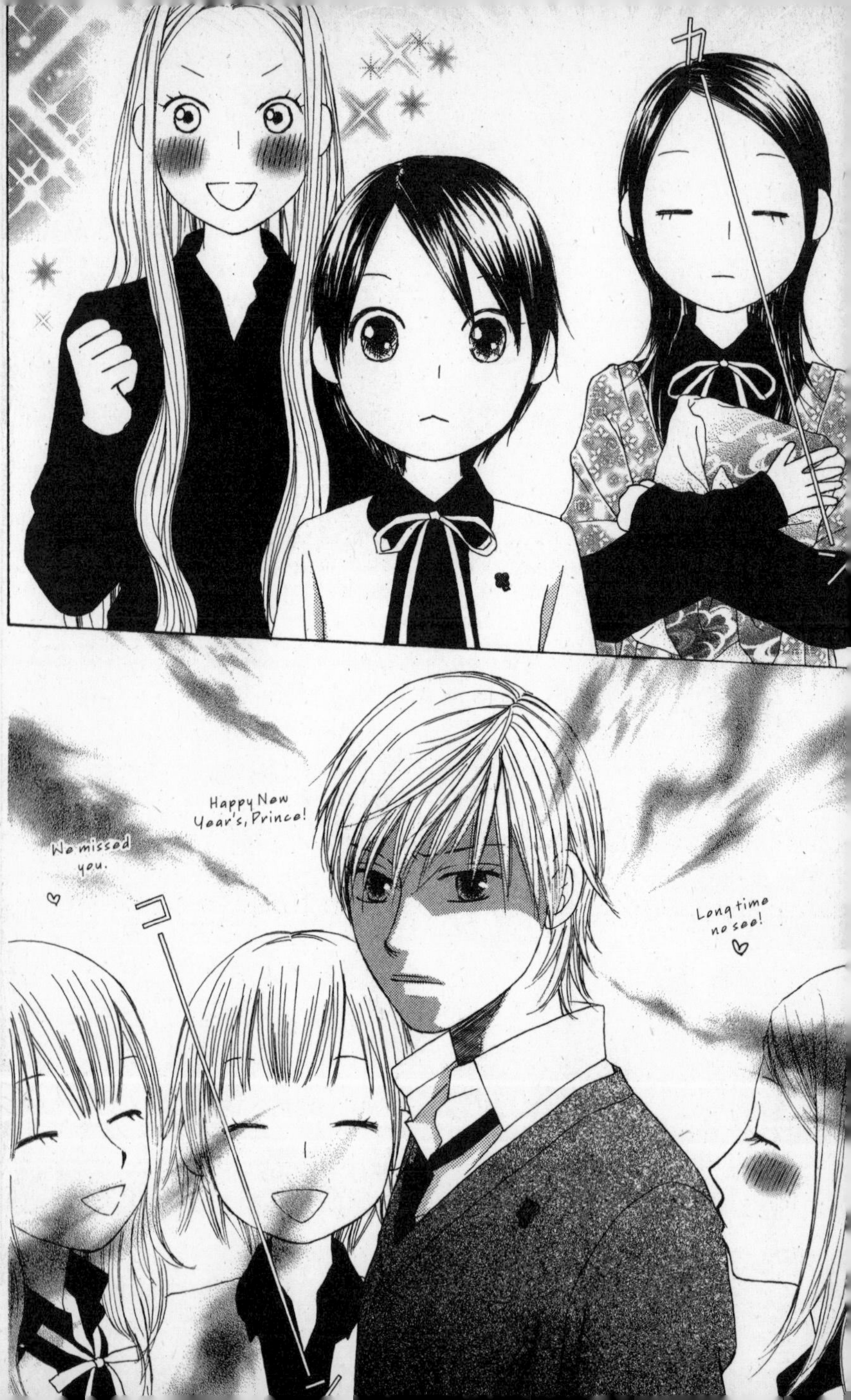
Long time no see!
Happy New Year's, Prince!
We missed you.

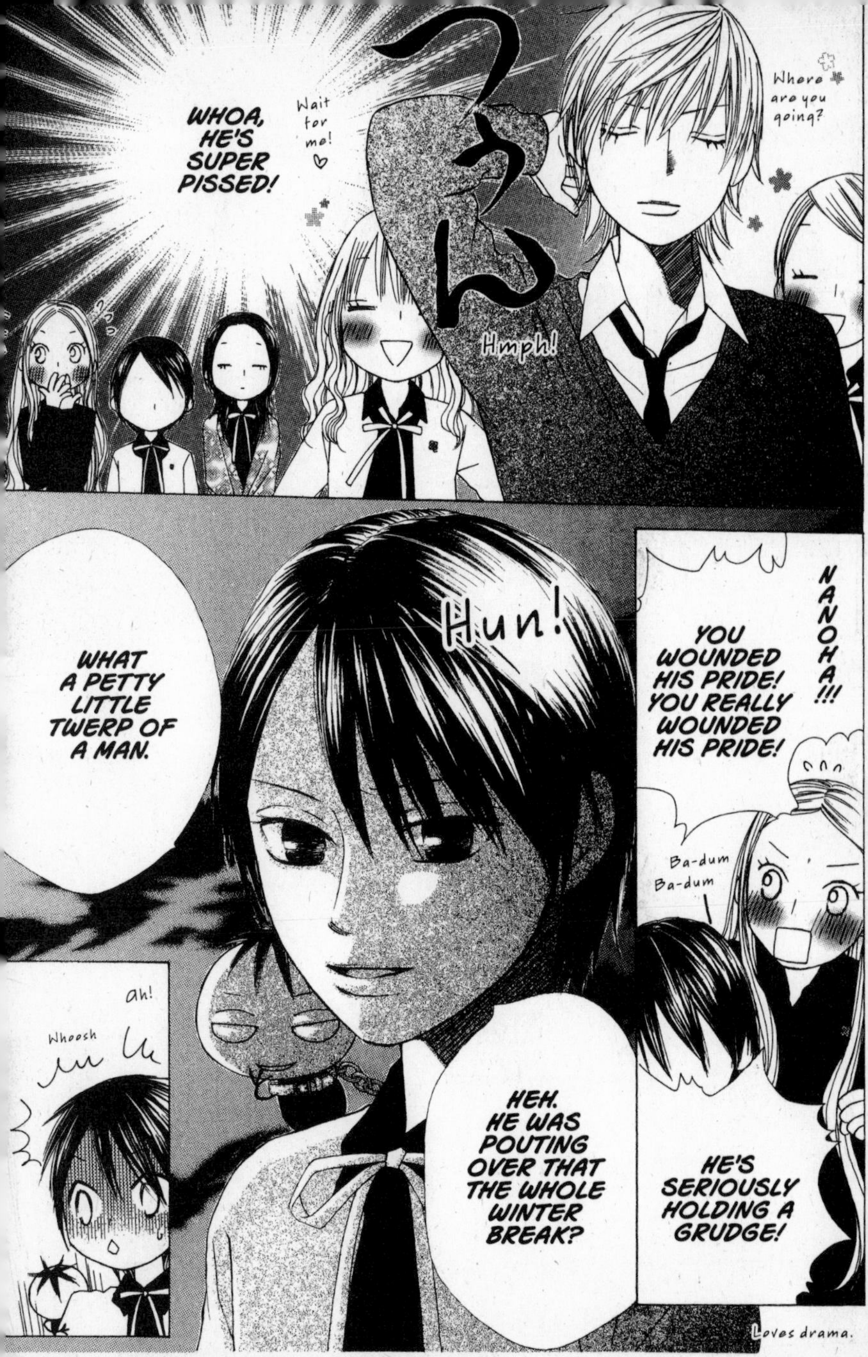
Where are you going?
Wait for me!
WHOA, HE'S SUPER PISSED!
Hmph!
NANOHA!!!
YOU WOUNDED HIS PRIDE! YOU REALLY WOUNDED HIS PRIDE!
Ba-dum Ba-dum
HE'S SERIOUSLY HOLDING A GRUDGE!
Hun!
WHAT A PETTY LITTLE TWERP OF A MAN.
HEH. HE WAS POUTING OVER THAT THE WHOLE WINTER BREAK?
ah!
Whoosh

Loves drama.

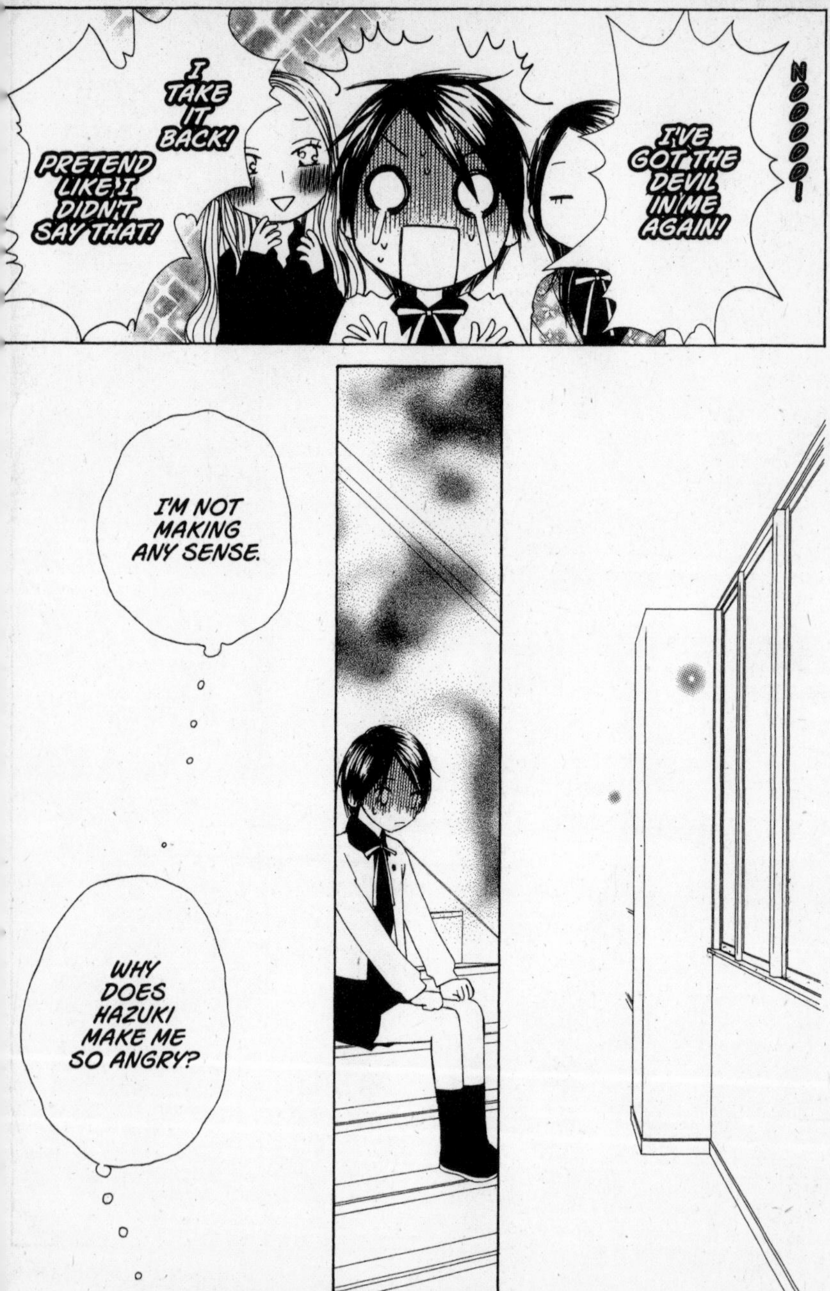
NOOOOOO!
I'VE GOT THE DEVIL IN ME AGAIN!
I TAKE IT BACK!
PRETEND LIKE I DIDN'T SAY THAT!
I'M NOT MAKING ANY SENSE.
WHY DOES HAZUKI MAKE ME SO ANGRY?

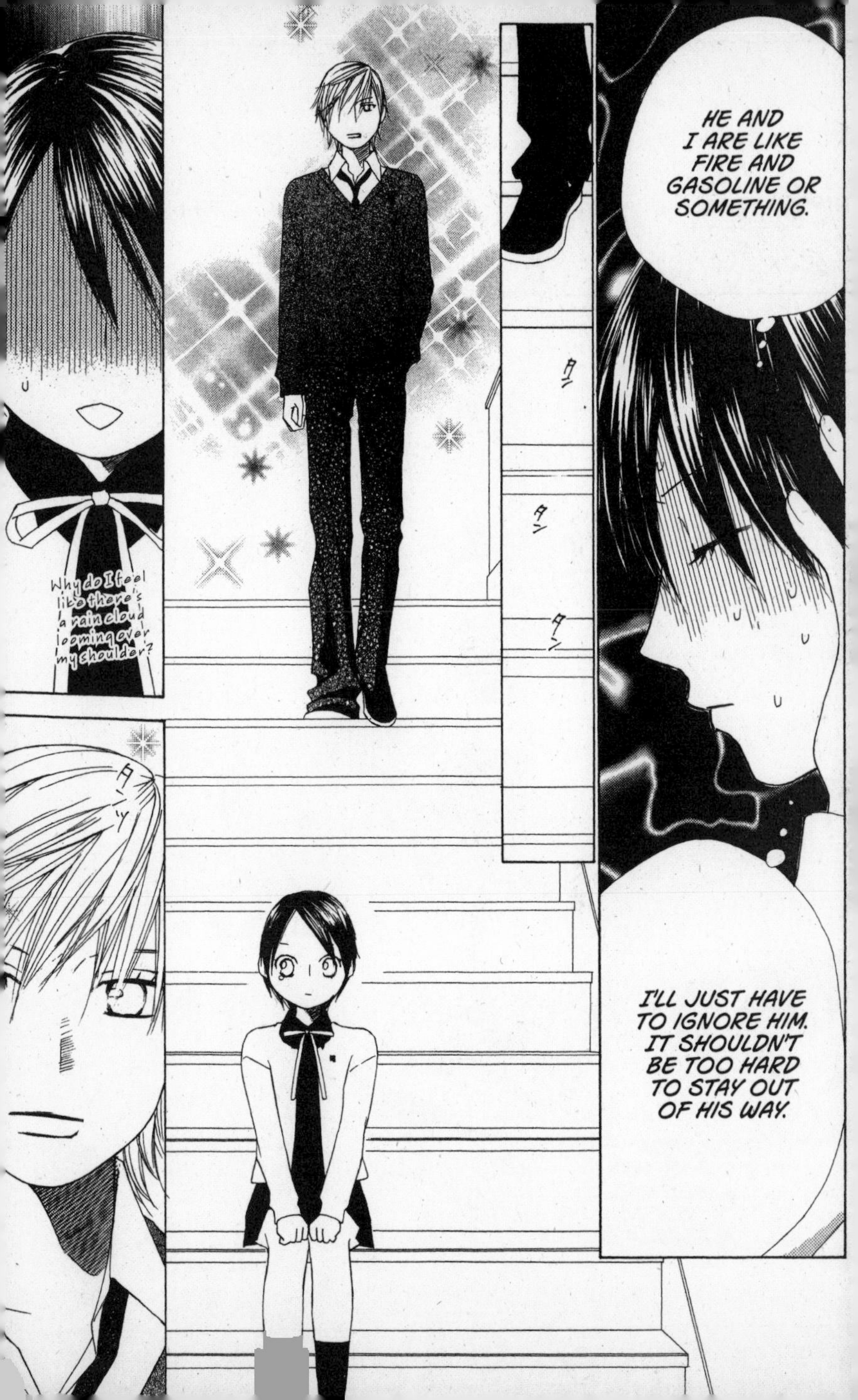
HE AND I ARE LIKE FIRE AND GASOLINE OR SOMETHING.
I'LL JUST HAVE TO IGNORE HIM. IT SHOULDN'T BE TOO HARD TO STAY OUT OF HIS WAY.
タン
タン
タン
Why do I feel like there's a rain cloud looming over my shoulder?

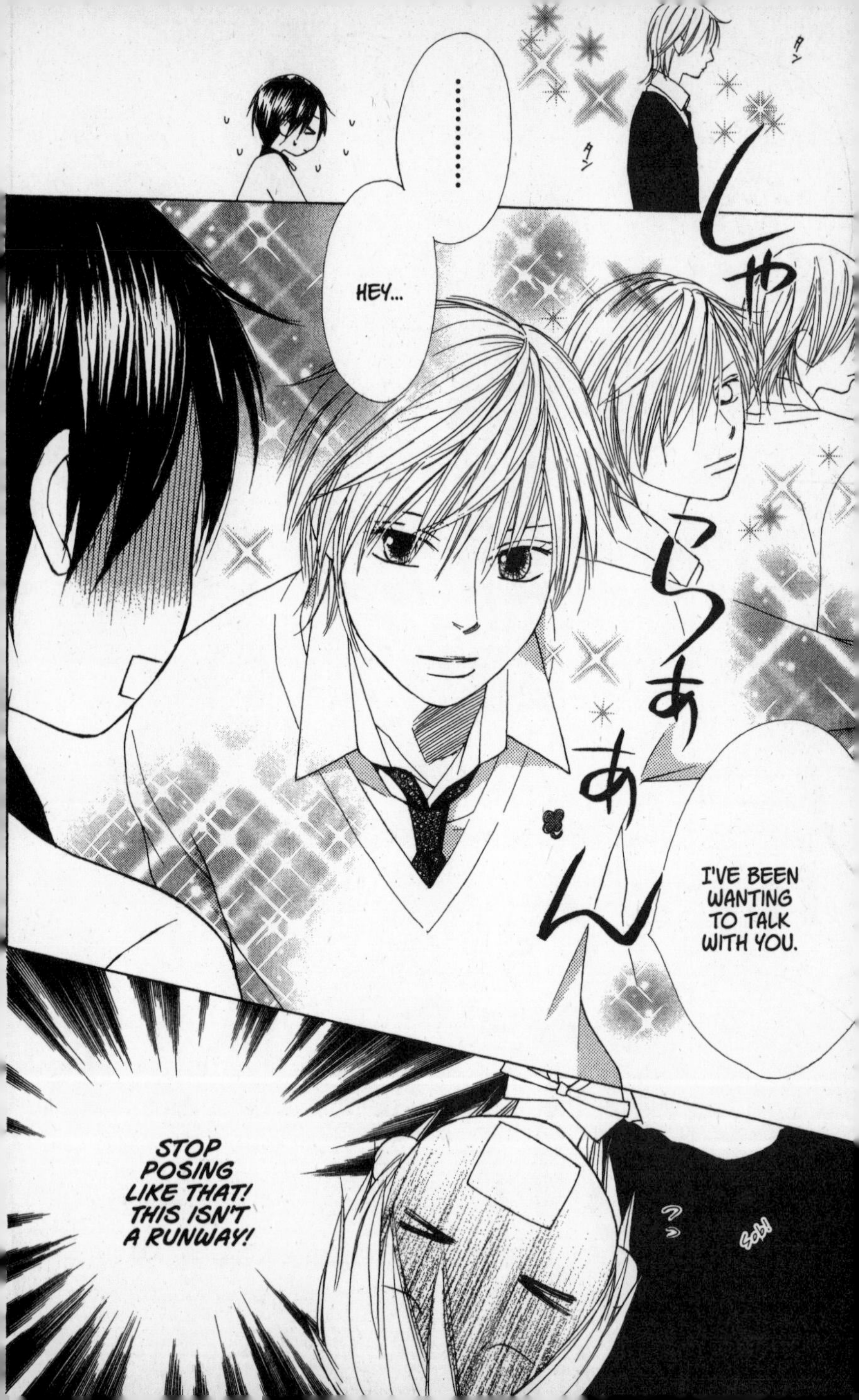
タン
タン
……
しゃらああん
HEY...
I'VE BEEN WANTING TO TALK WITH YOU.
STOP POSING LIKE THAT! THIS ISN'T A RUNWAY!
Sob!

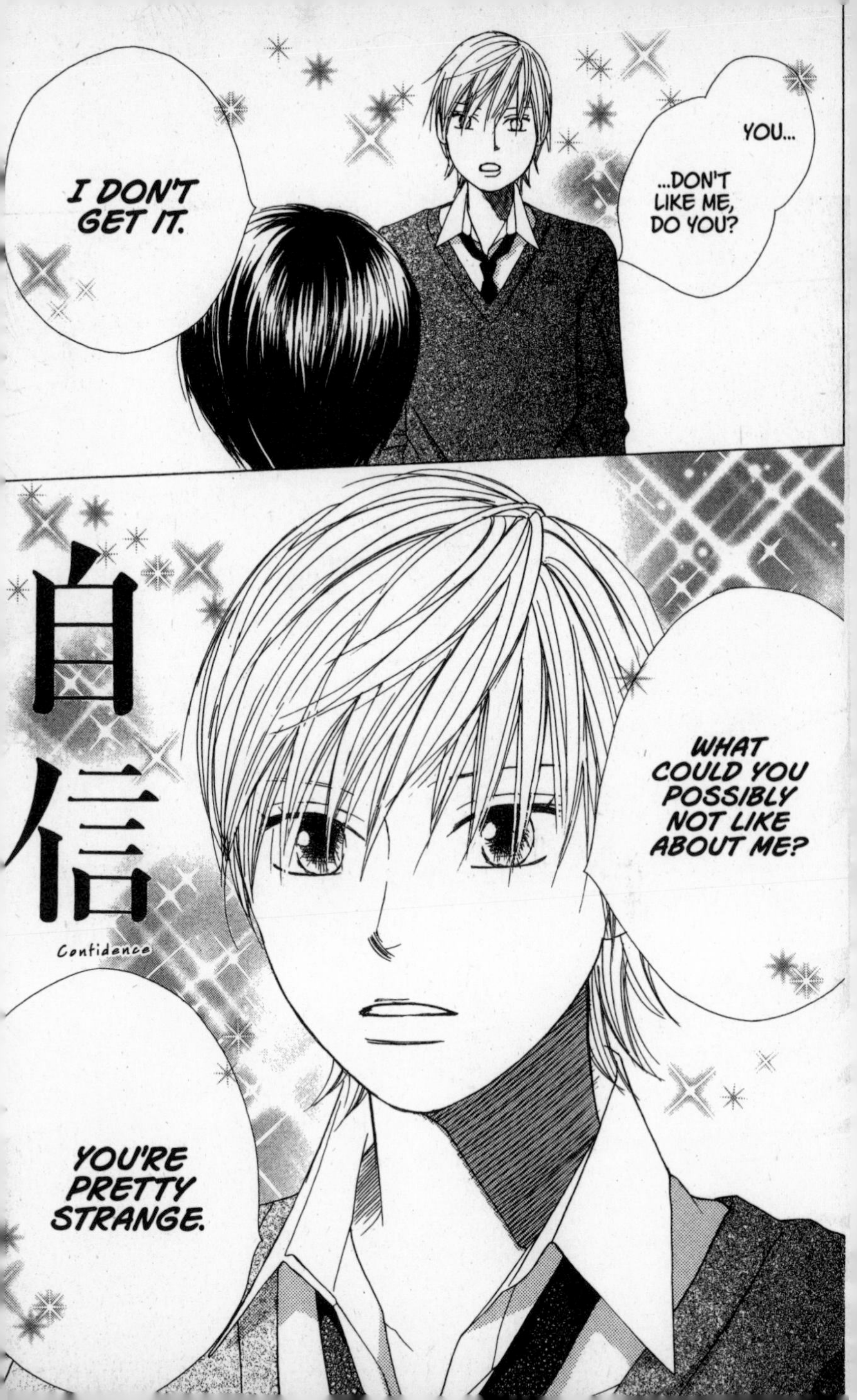
YOU... ...DON'T LIKE ME, DO YOU?
I DON'T GET IT.
WHAT COULD YOU POSSIBLY NOT LIKE ABOUT ME?
自信
Confidence
YOU'RE PRETTY STRANGE.

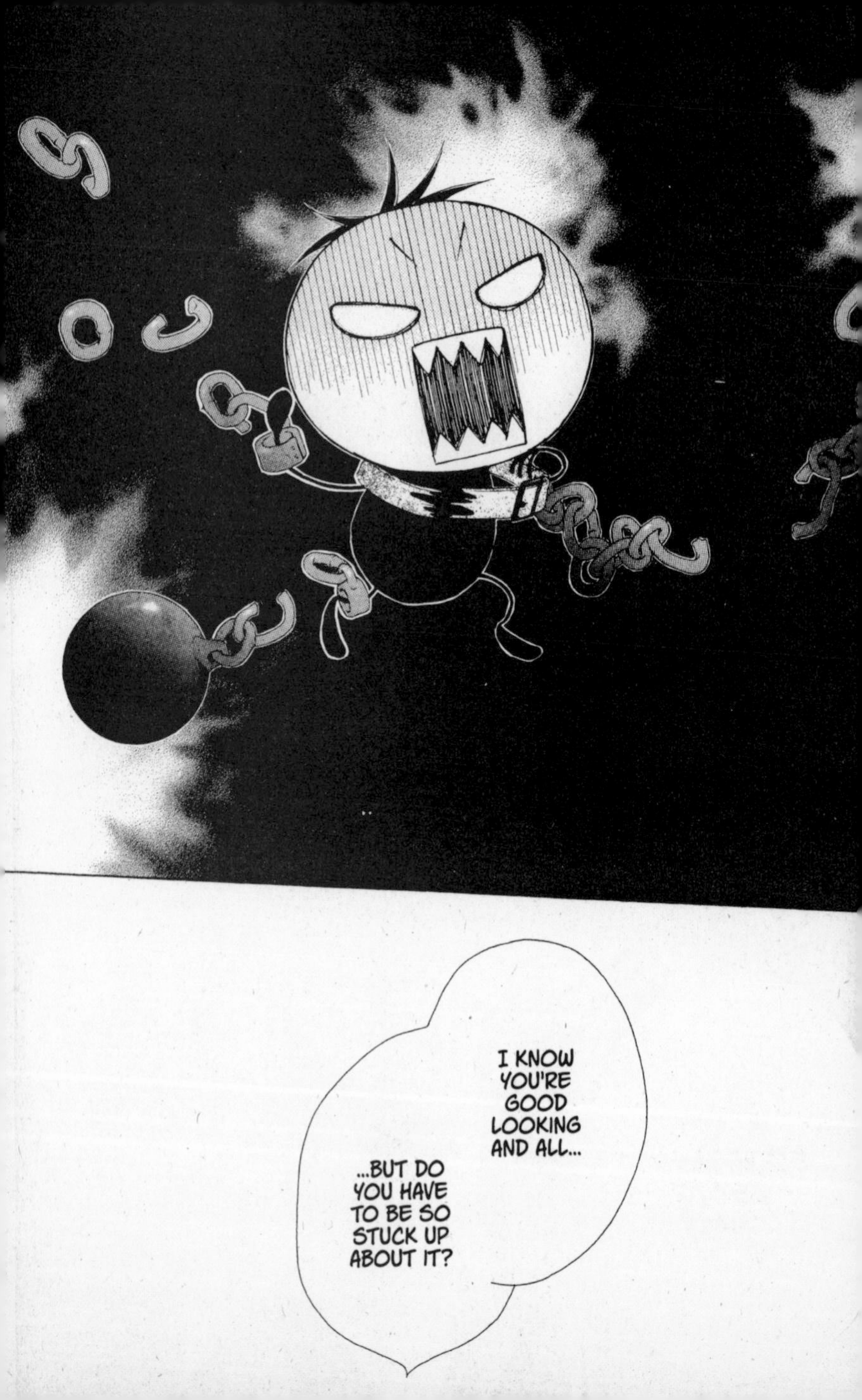
I KNOW YOU'RE GOOD LOOKING AND ALL...
...BUT DO YOU HAVE TO BE SO STUCK UP ABOUT IT?

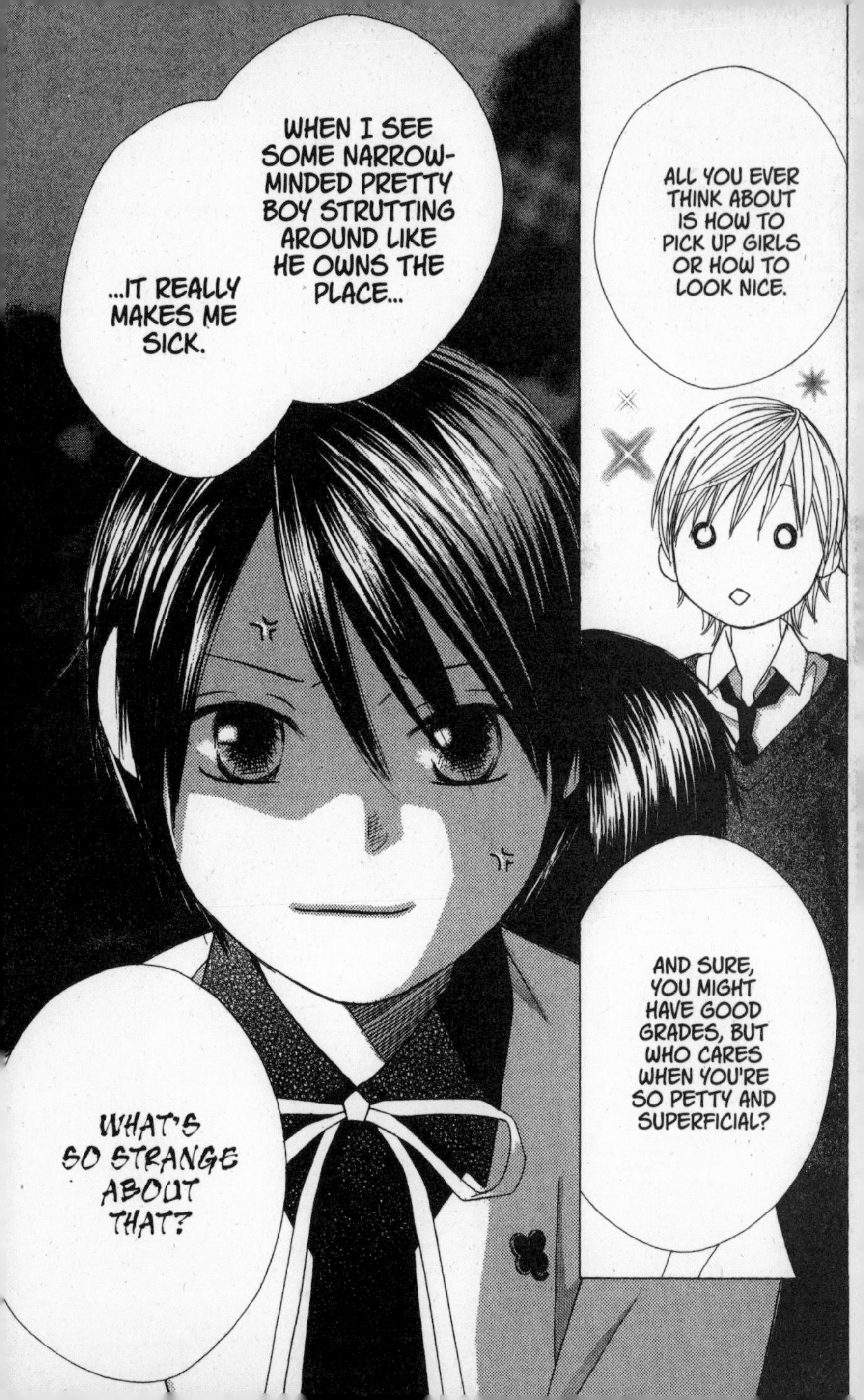
ALL YOU EVER THINK ABOUT IS HOW TO PICK UP GIRLS OR HOW TO LOOK NICE.
AND SURE, YOU MIGHT HAVE GOOD GRADES, BUT WHO CARES WHEN YOU'RE SO PETTY AND SUPERFICIAL?
WHEN I SEE SOME NARROW-MINDED PRETTY BOY STRUTTING AROUND LIKE HE OWNS THE PLACE...
...IT REALLY MAKES ME SICK.
WHAT'S SO STRANGE ABOUT THAT?

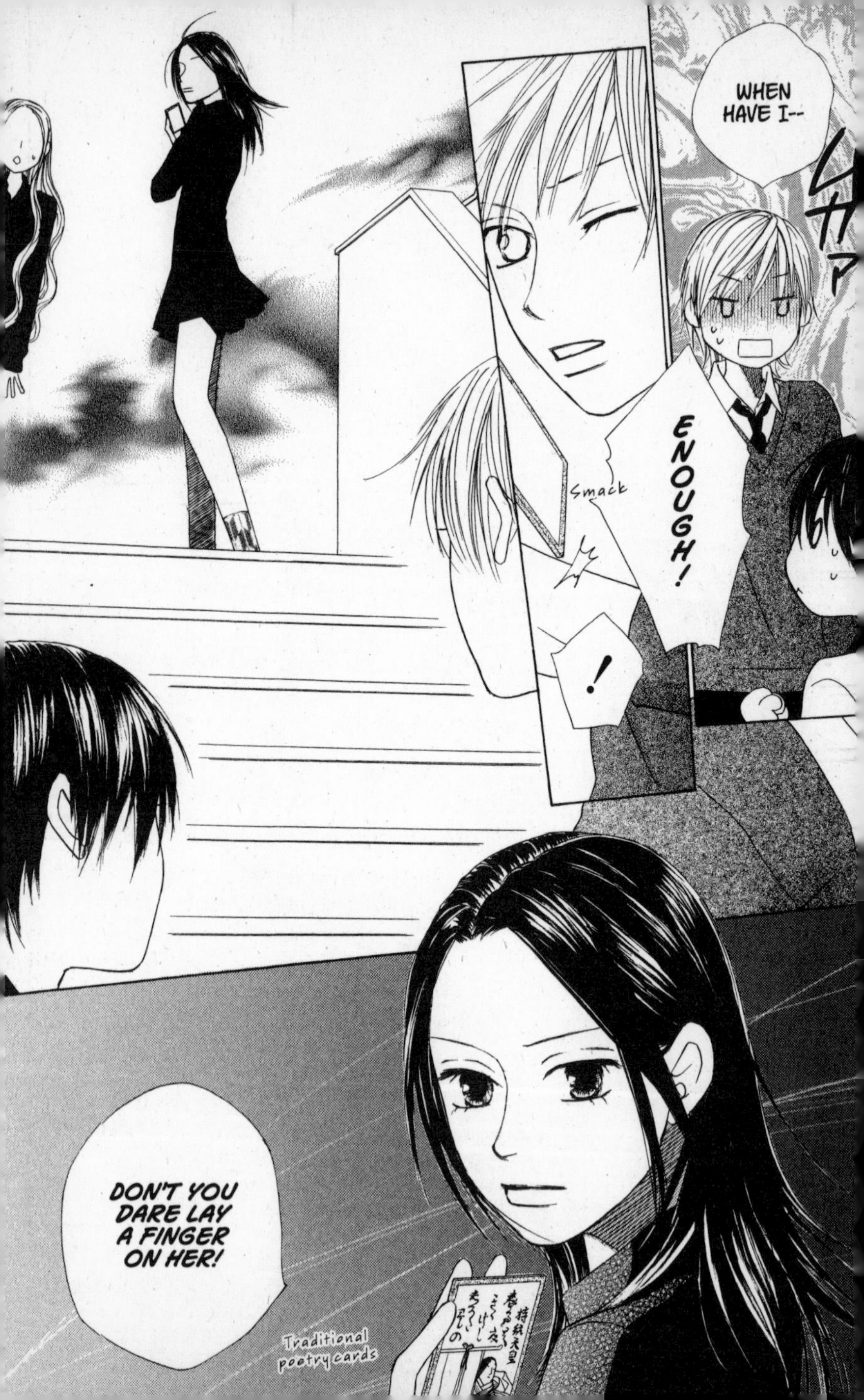
WHEN HAVE I--
ムカァ
ENOUGH!
Smack
!
DON'T YOU DARE LAY A FINGER ON HER!
Traditional poetry cards

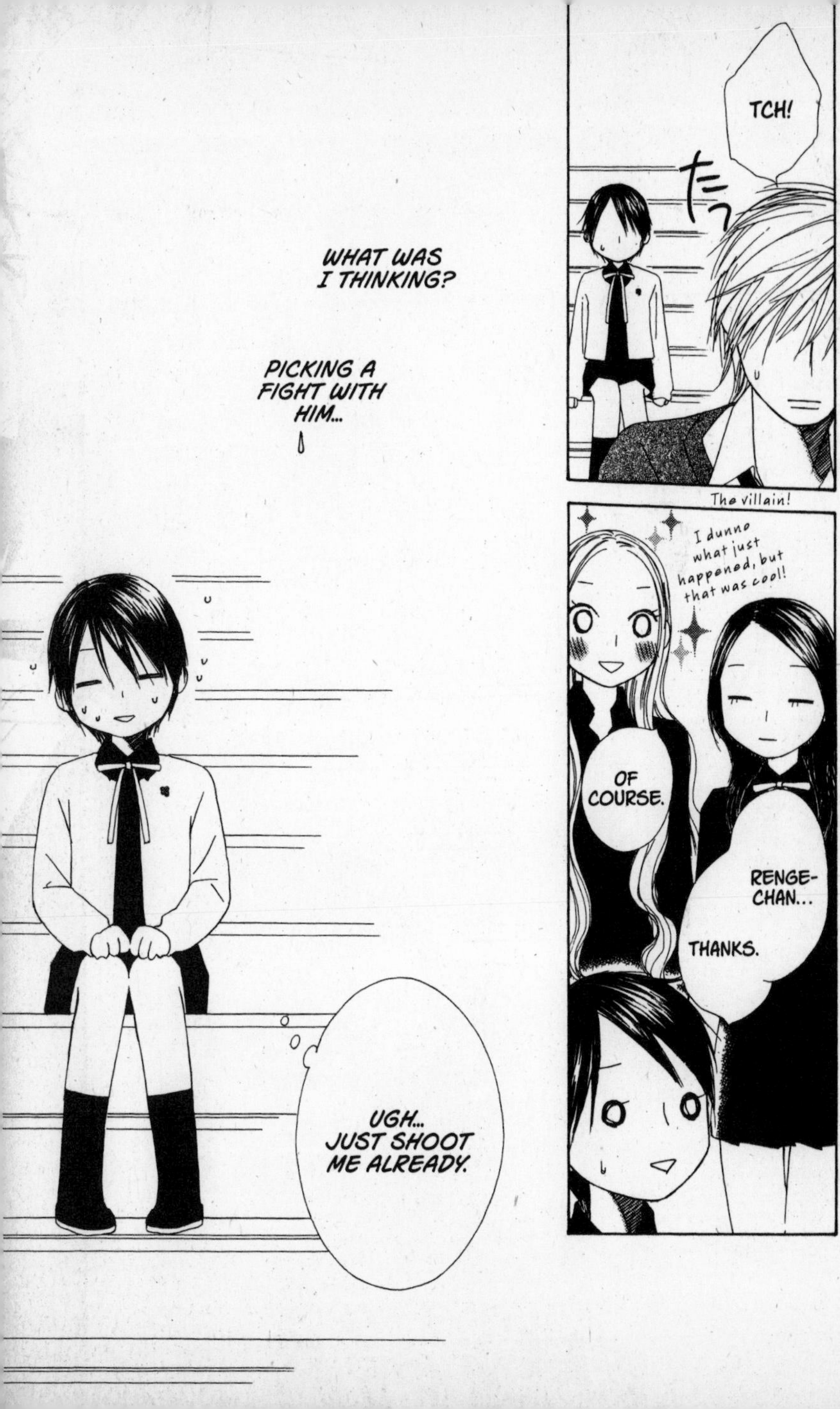
TCH!
たっ
The villain!
I dunno what just happened, but that was cool!
OF COURSE.
RENGE-CHAN...
THANKS.
WHAT WAS I THINKING?
PICKING A FIGHT WITH HIM...
UGH... JUST SHOOT ME ALREADY.

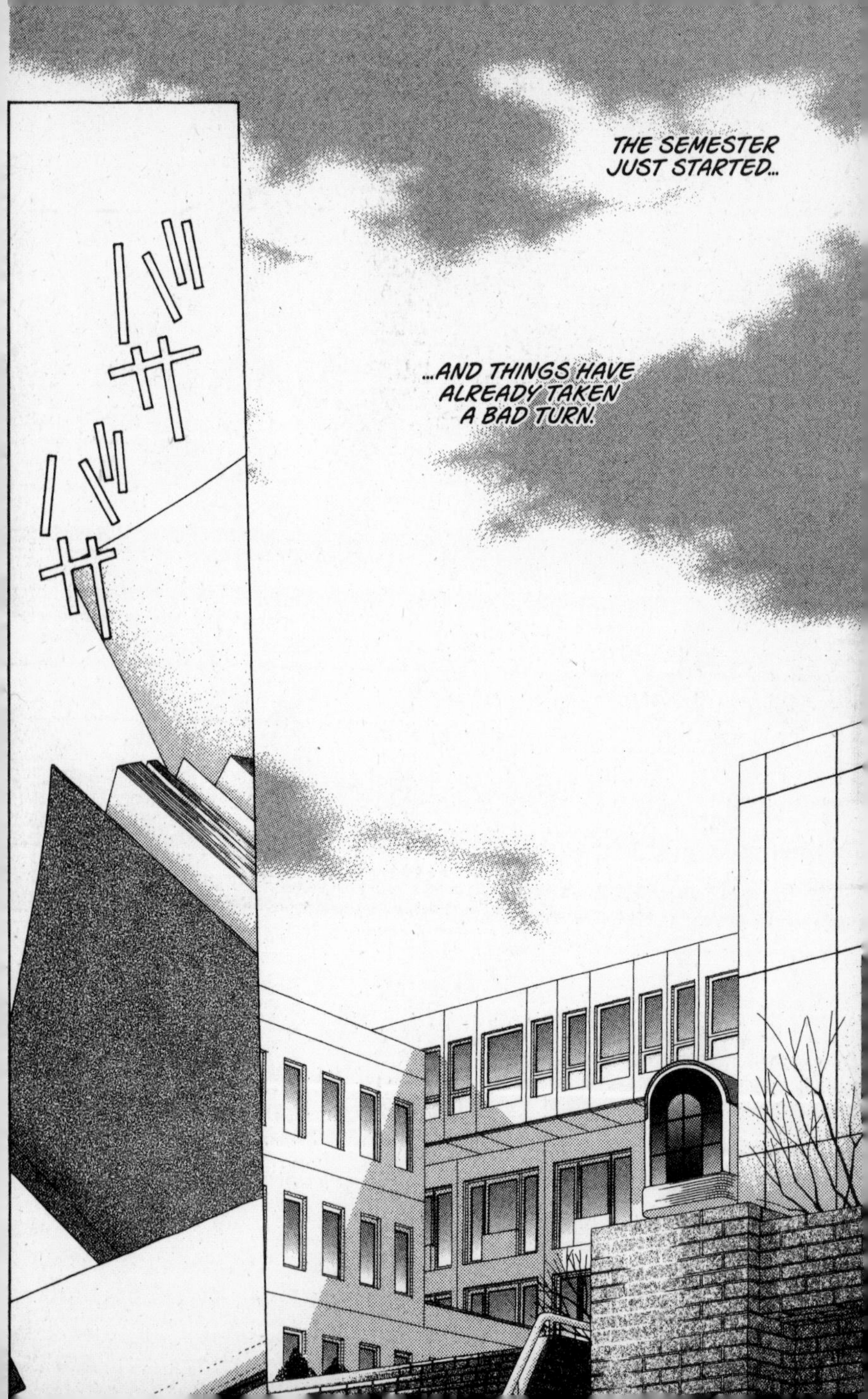
THE SEMESTER JUST STARTED...
...AND THINGS HAVE ALREADY TAKEN A BAD TURN.

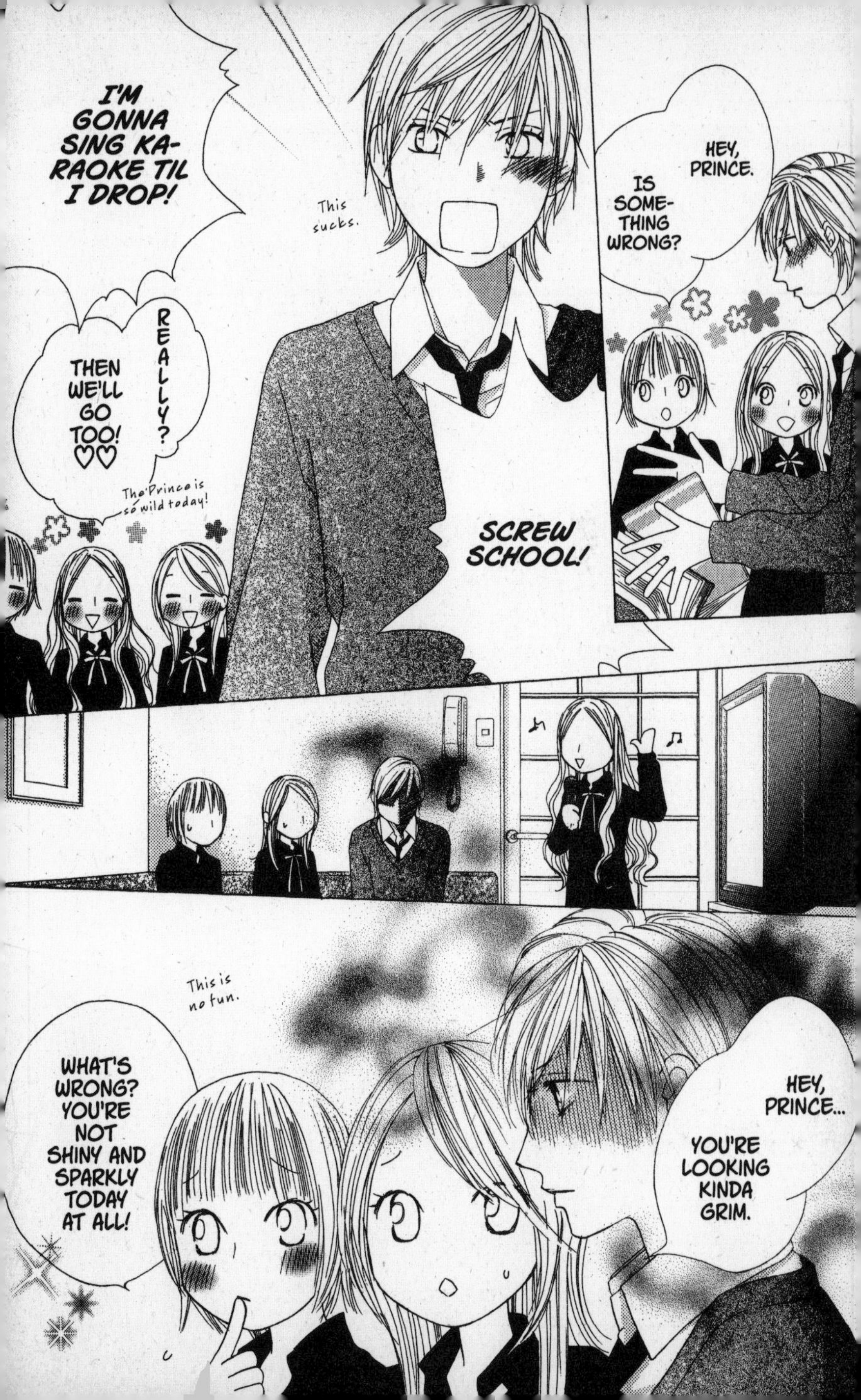
HEY, PRINCE.
IS SOMETHING WRONG?
This sucks.
SCREW SCHOOL!
I'M GONNA SING KARAOKE TIL I DROP!
REALLY?
THEN WE'LL GO TOO! ♡♡
The Prince is so wild today!
HEY, PRINCE...
YOU'RE LOOKING KINDA GRIM.
WHAT'S WRONG? YOU'RE NOT SHINY AND SPARKLY TODAY AT ALL!
This is no fun.

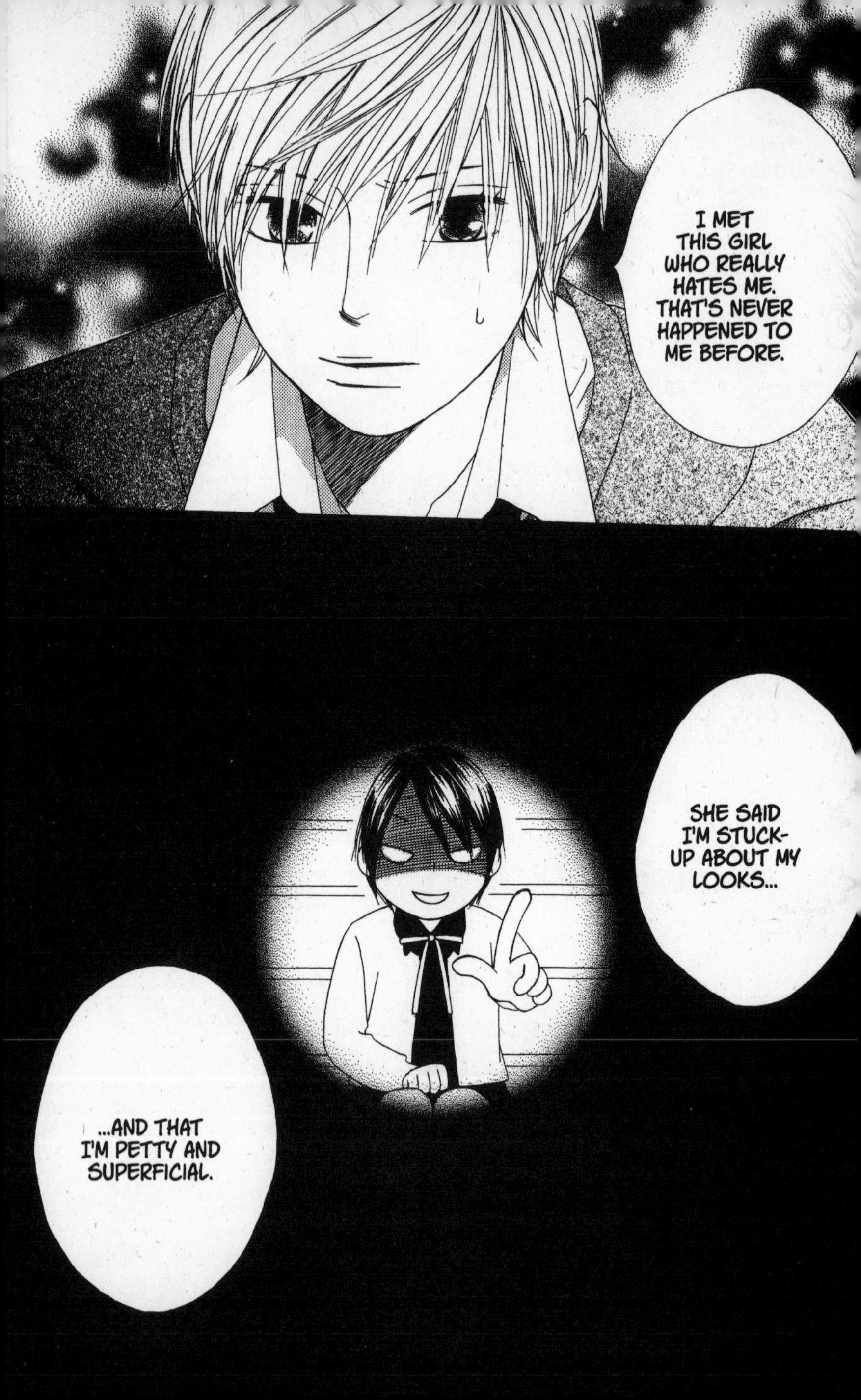
I MET THIS GIRL WHO REALLY HATES ME. THAT'S NEVER HAPPENED TO ME BEFORE.
SHE SAID I'M STUCK-UP ABOUT MY LOOKS...
...AND THAT I'M PETTY AND SUPERFICIAL.

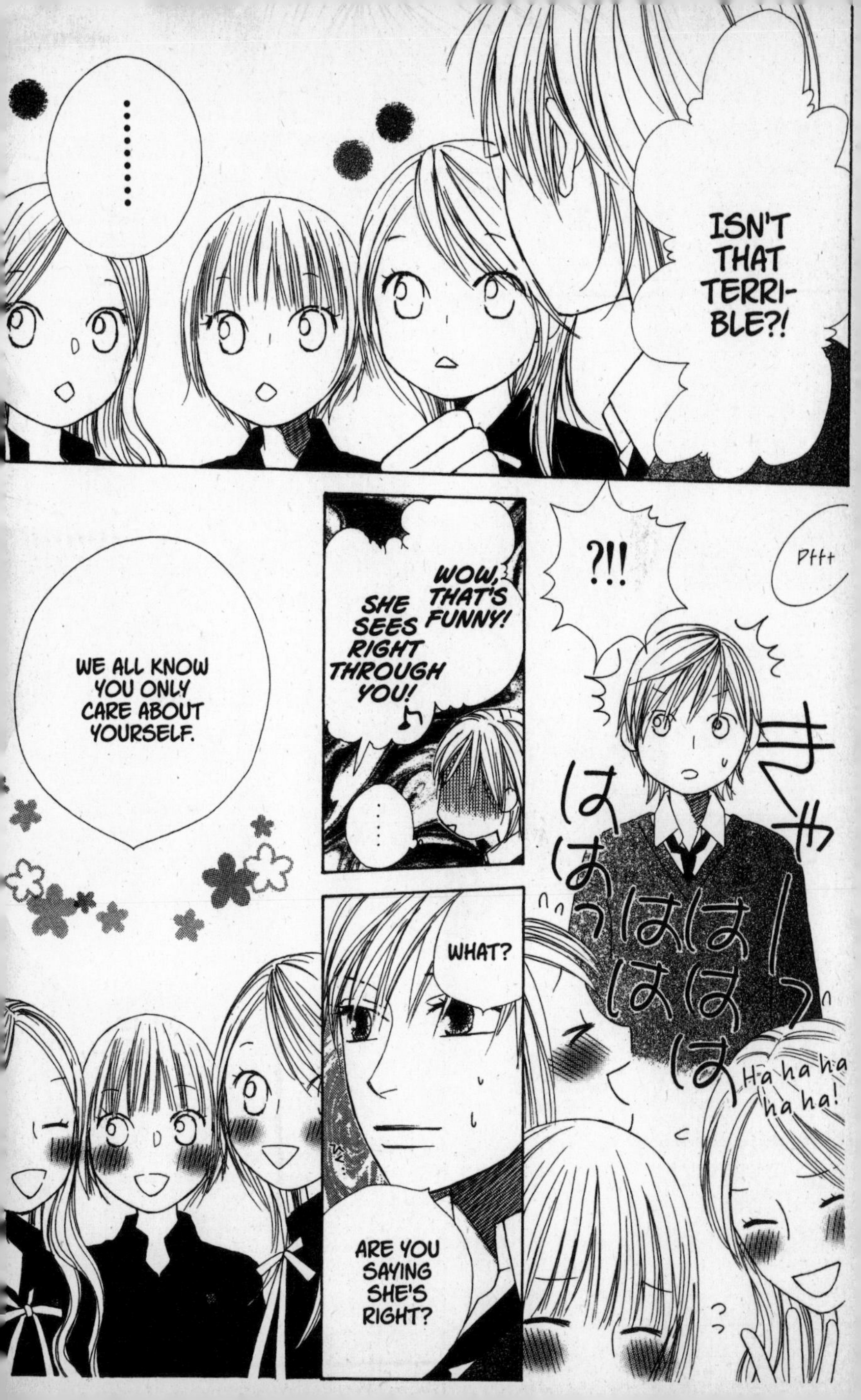
ISN'T THAT TERRI-BLE?!
......
?!!
Pfft
きゃーっ
はははははは
Ha ha ha ha ha!
WOW, THAT'S FUNNY! SHE SEES RIGHT THROUGH YOU!
......
WHAT?
ARE YOU SAYING SHE'S RIGHT?
WE ALL KNOW YOU ONLY CARE ABOUT YOURSELF.

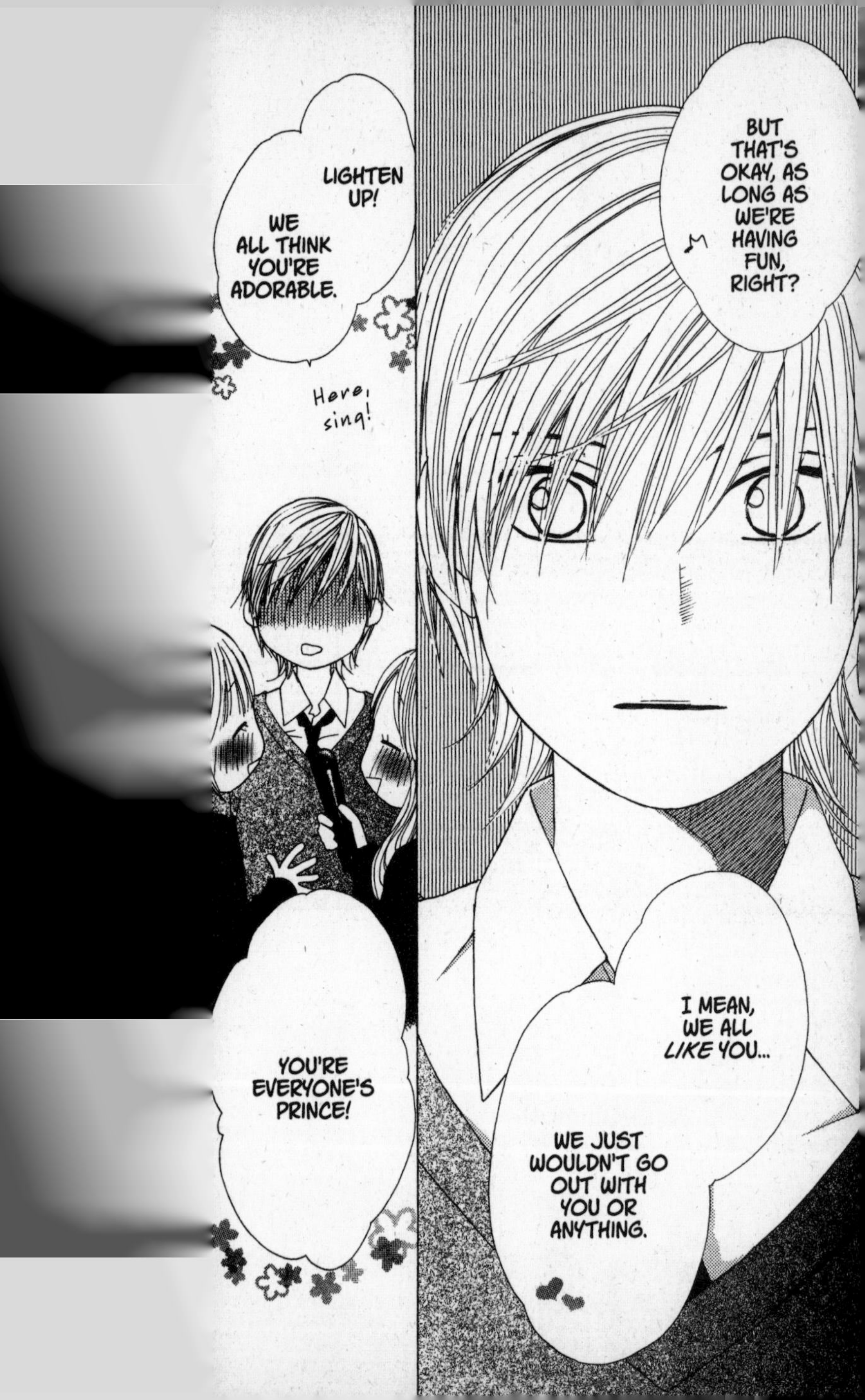
BUT THAT'S OKAY, AS LONG AS WE'RE HAVING FUN, RIGHT?
I MEAN, WE ALL *LIKE* YOU...
WE JUST WOULDN'T GO OUT WITH YOU OR ANYTHING.
LIGHTEN UP! WE ALL THINK YOU'RE ADORABLE.
Here, sing!
YOU'RE EVERYONE'S PRINCE!

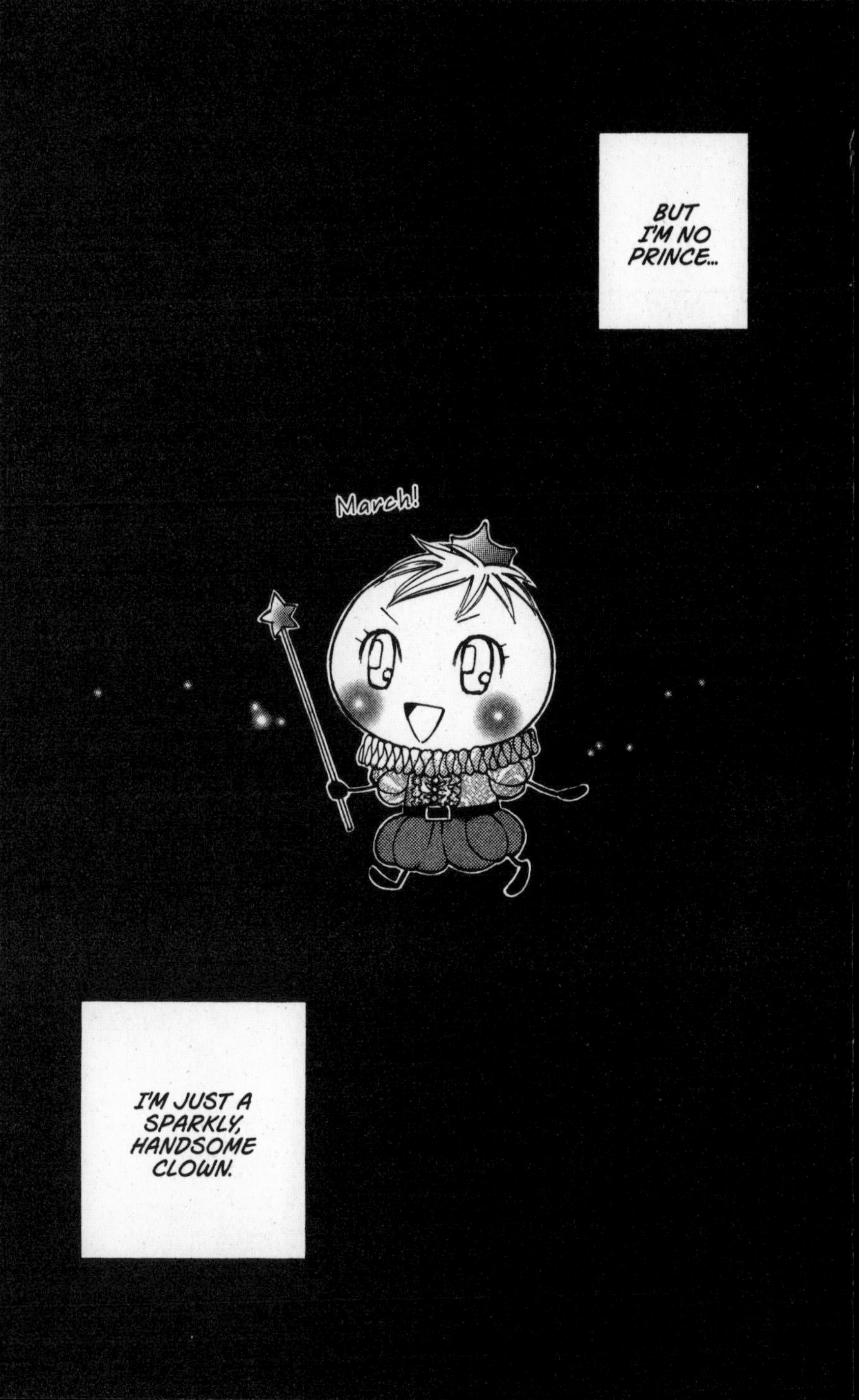
BUT I'M NO PRINCE...
March!
I'M JUST A SPARKLY, HANDSOME CLOWN.

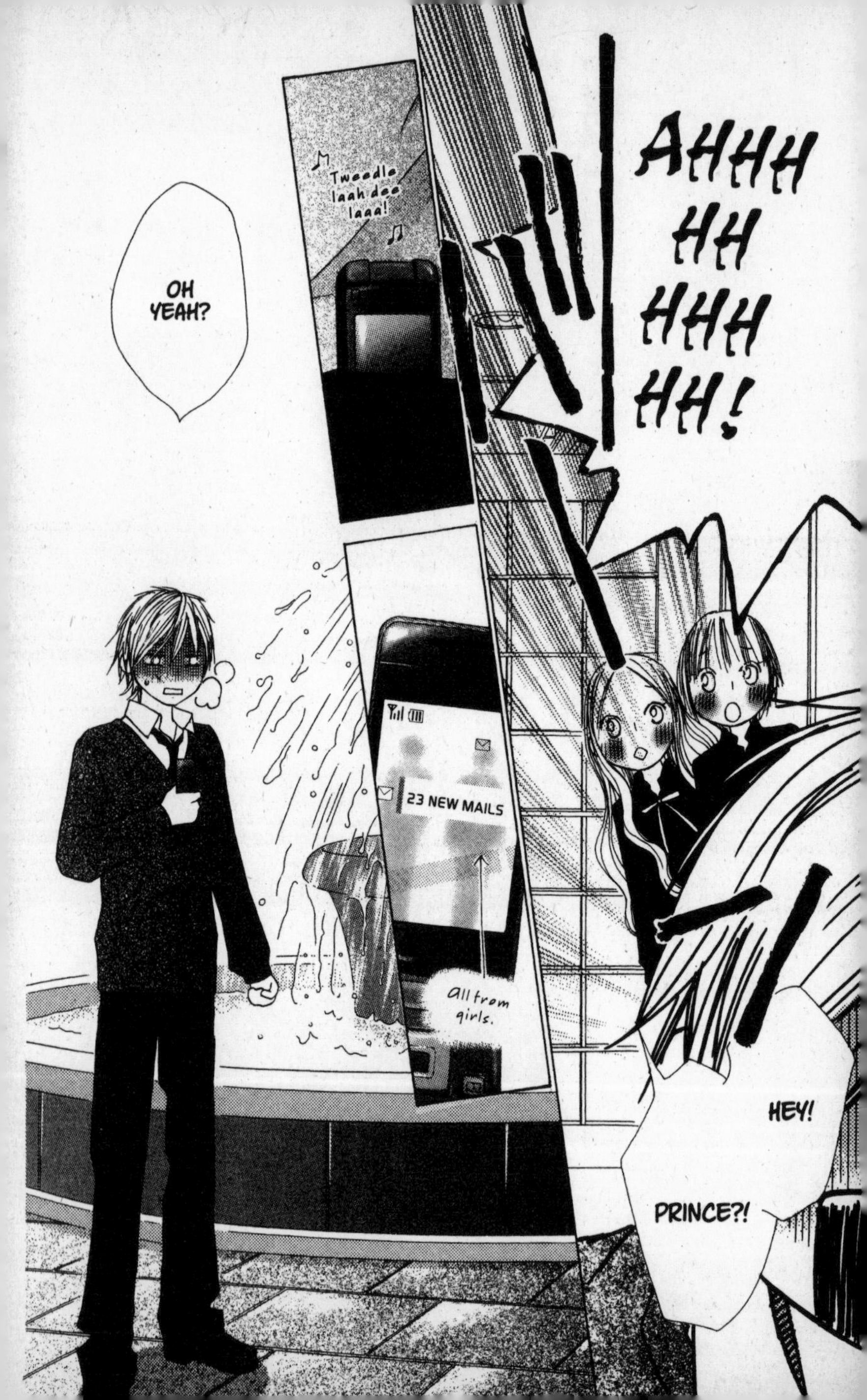
AHHHHHHHHHHH!
Tweedle laah dee laaa!
HEY!
PRINCE?!
23 NEW MAILS
all from girls.
OH YEAH?

HOW DO YOU LIKE THIS?!

☆ Please recycle your used cell-phones! ♡

IT'S FUNNY...

I HAD SO MUCH PRIDE...AND YET IT WAS CRUSHED SO EASILY.

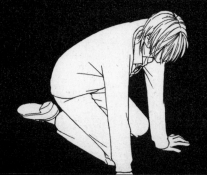

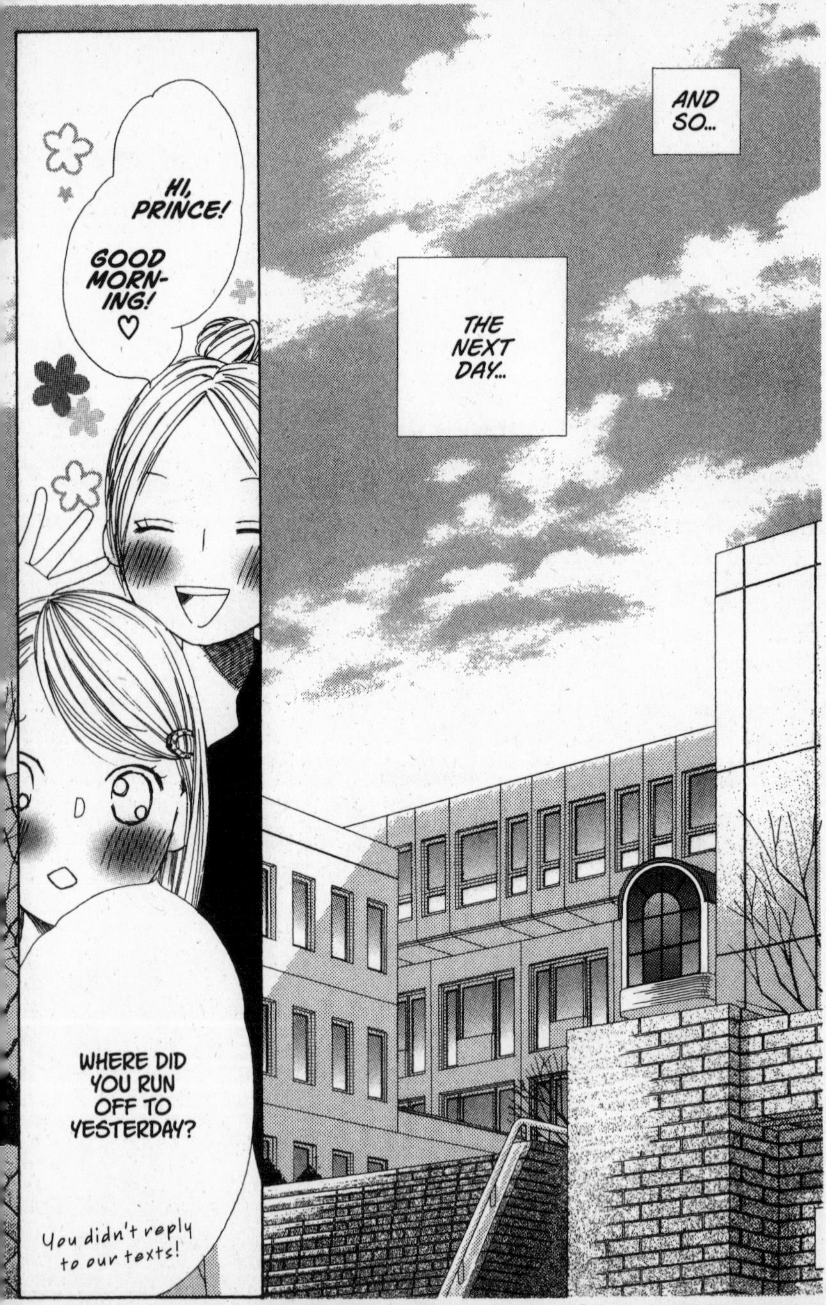
AND SO...
THE NEXT DAY...
HI, PRINCE! GOOD MORNING! ♡
WHERE DID YOU RUN OFF TO YESTERDAY?
You didn't reply to our texts!

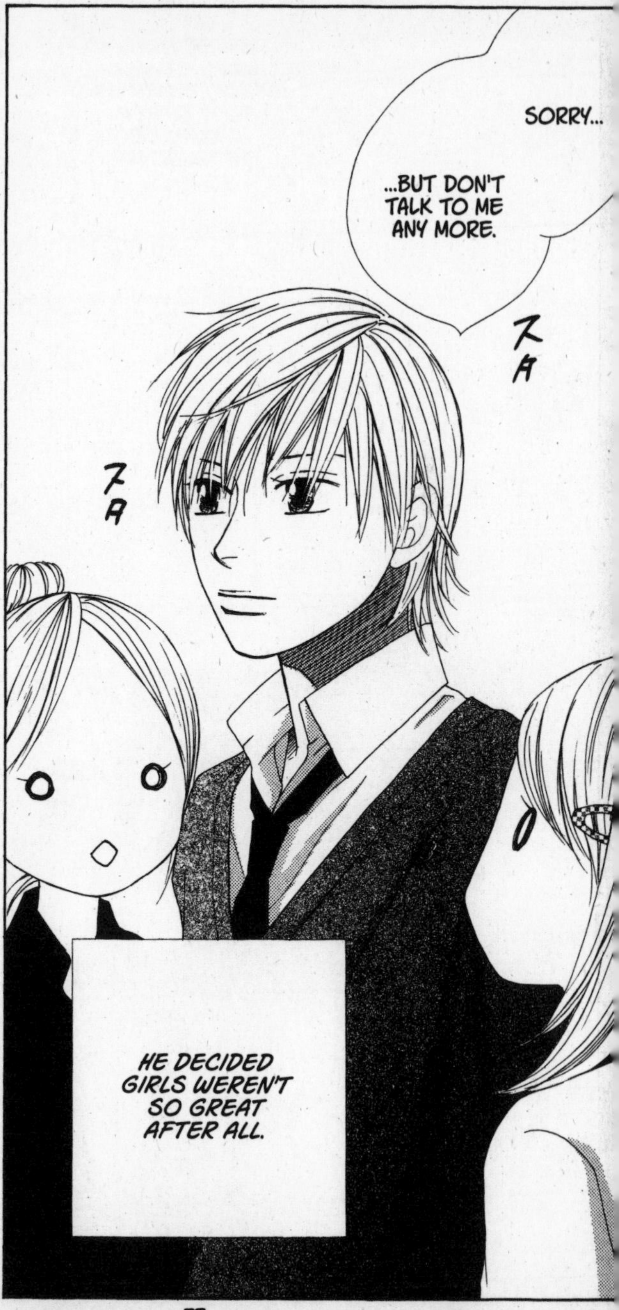
SORRY...
...BUT DON'T TALK TO ME ANY MORE.
HE DECIDED GIRLS WEREN'T SO GREAT AFTER ALL.

2

I've been eating a lot of vegetables lately.

I hate to state the obvious, but they really are good for you. My body feels great and my head has cleared up a bit, too. Even when I'm working, I try my best to cook vegetable dishes.

It's not like I didn't eat veggies before...

It seems like it works better when I cook for myself, though.

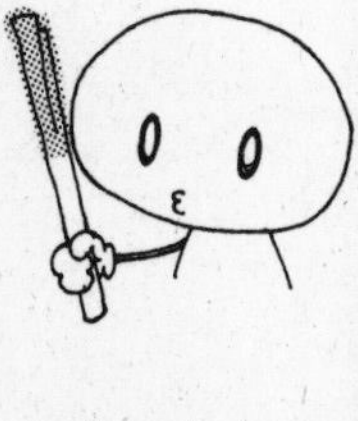

Maybe it's because I don't put any extra ingredients in.

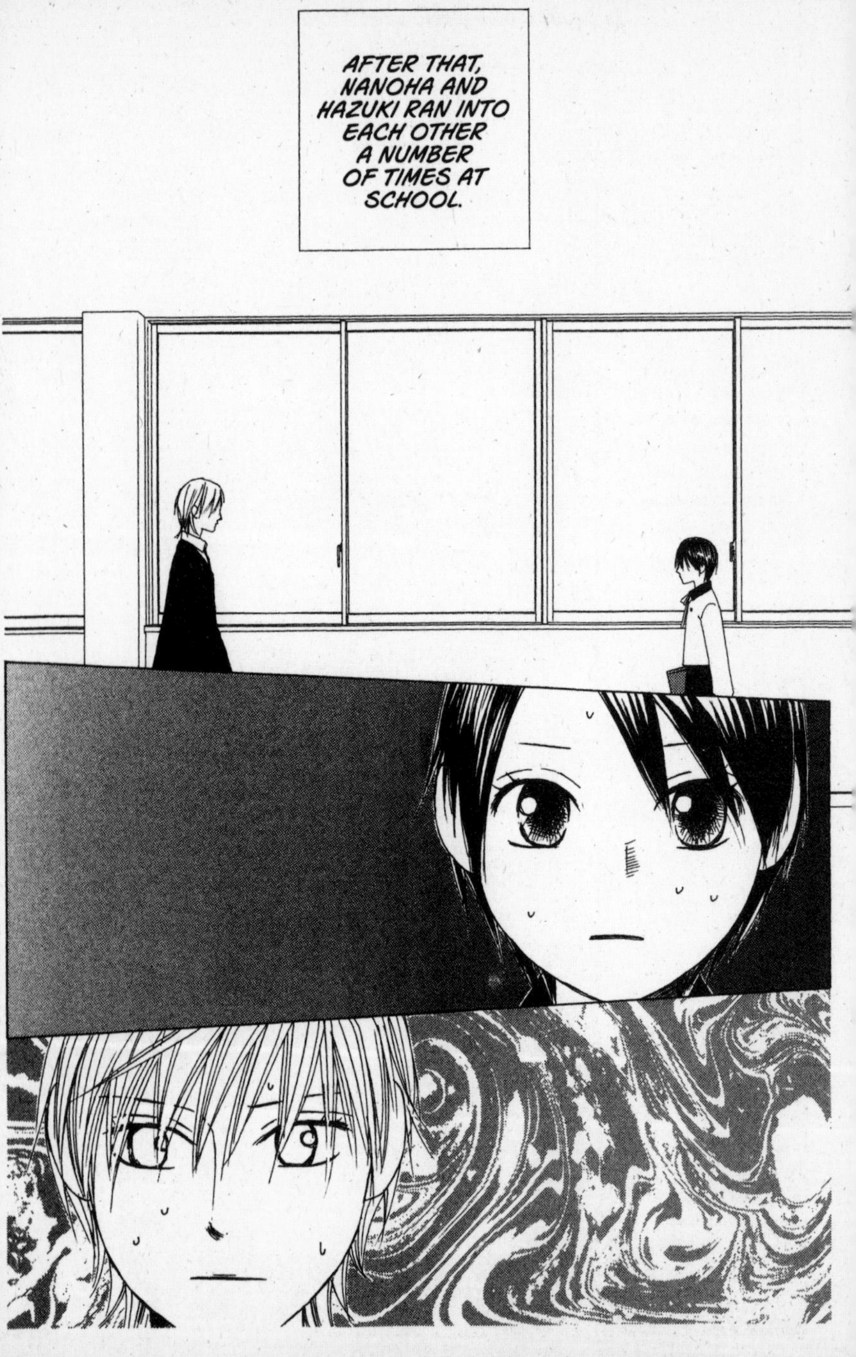
AFTER THAT, NANOHA AND HAZUKI RAN INTO EACH OTHER A NUMBER OF TIMES AT SCHOOL.

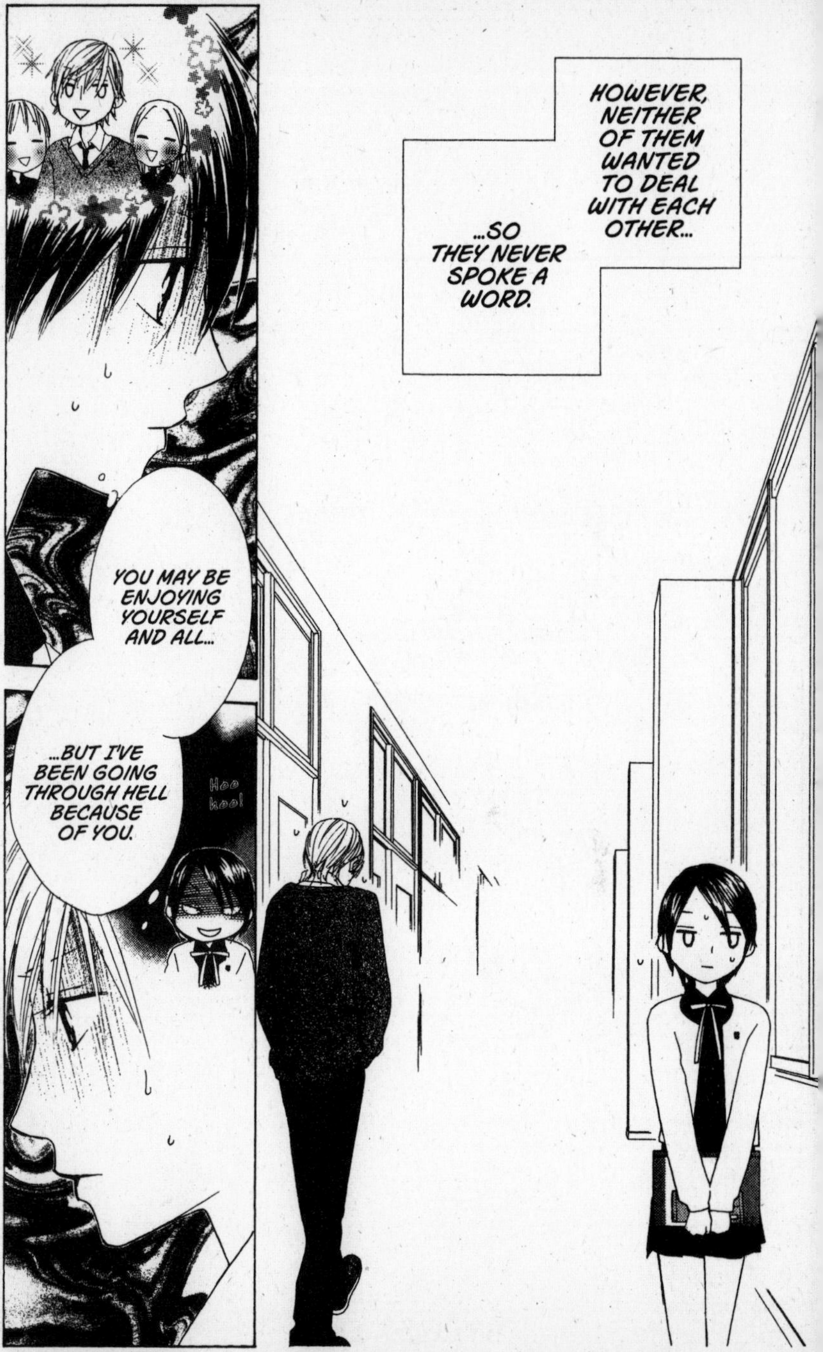
HOWEVER, NEITHER OF THEM WANTED TO DEAL WITH EACH OTHER...
...SO THEY NEVER SPOKE A WORD.
YOU MAY BE ENJOYING YOURSELF AND ALL...
...BUT I'VE BEEN GOING THROUGH HELL BECAUSE OF YOU.
Hoo hoo!

AS IT TURNED OUT...

...JANUARY WAS A MOST UNHAPPY MONTH FOR THEM BOTH.

STEP 2 / END

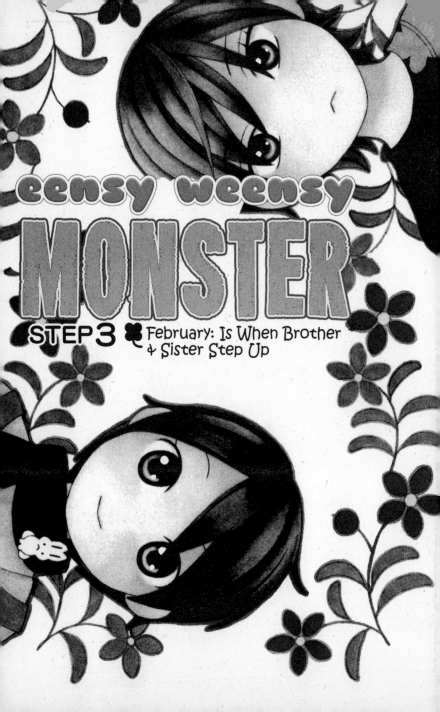

eensy weensy MONSTER

STEP 3 ❤ February: Is When Brother & Sister Step Up

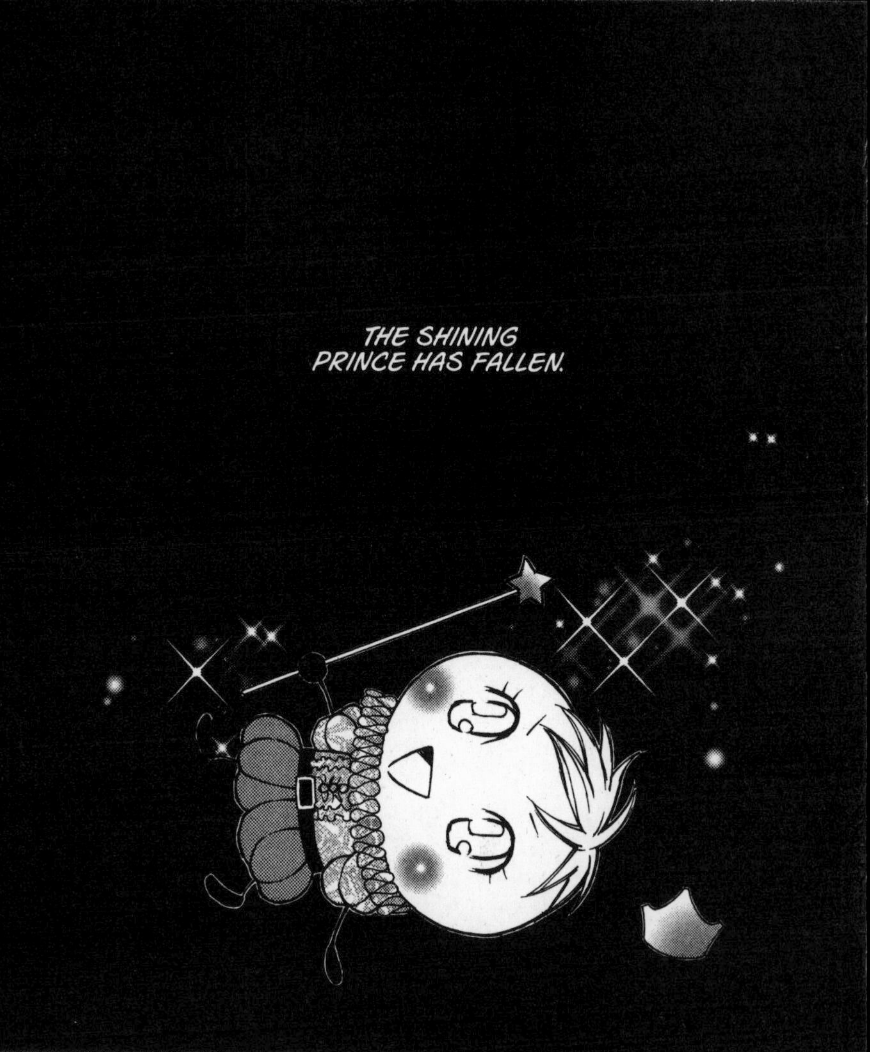
THE SHINING PRINCE HAS FALLEN.

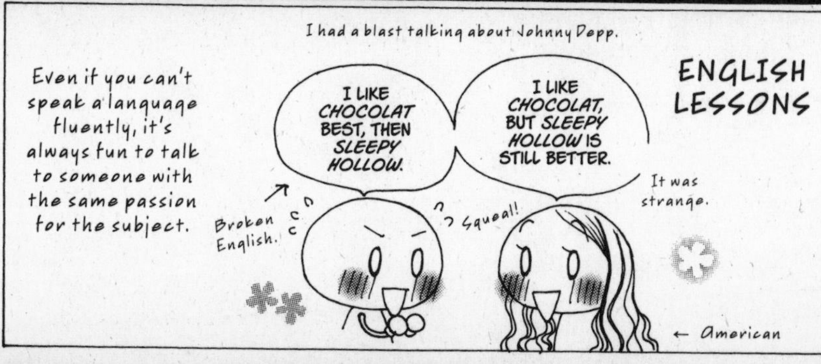
ENGLISH LESSONS
I had a blast talking about Johnny Depp.
I LIKE CHOCOLAT, BUT SLEEPY HOLLOW IS STILL BETTER.
I LIKE CHOCOLAT BEST, THEN SLEEPY HOLLOW.
It was strange.
← American
Squeal!
Broken English.
Even if you can't speak a language fluently, it's always fun to talk to someone with the same passion for the subject.

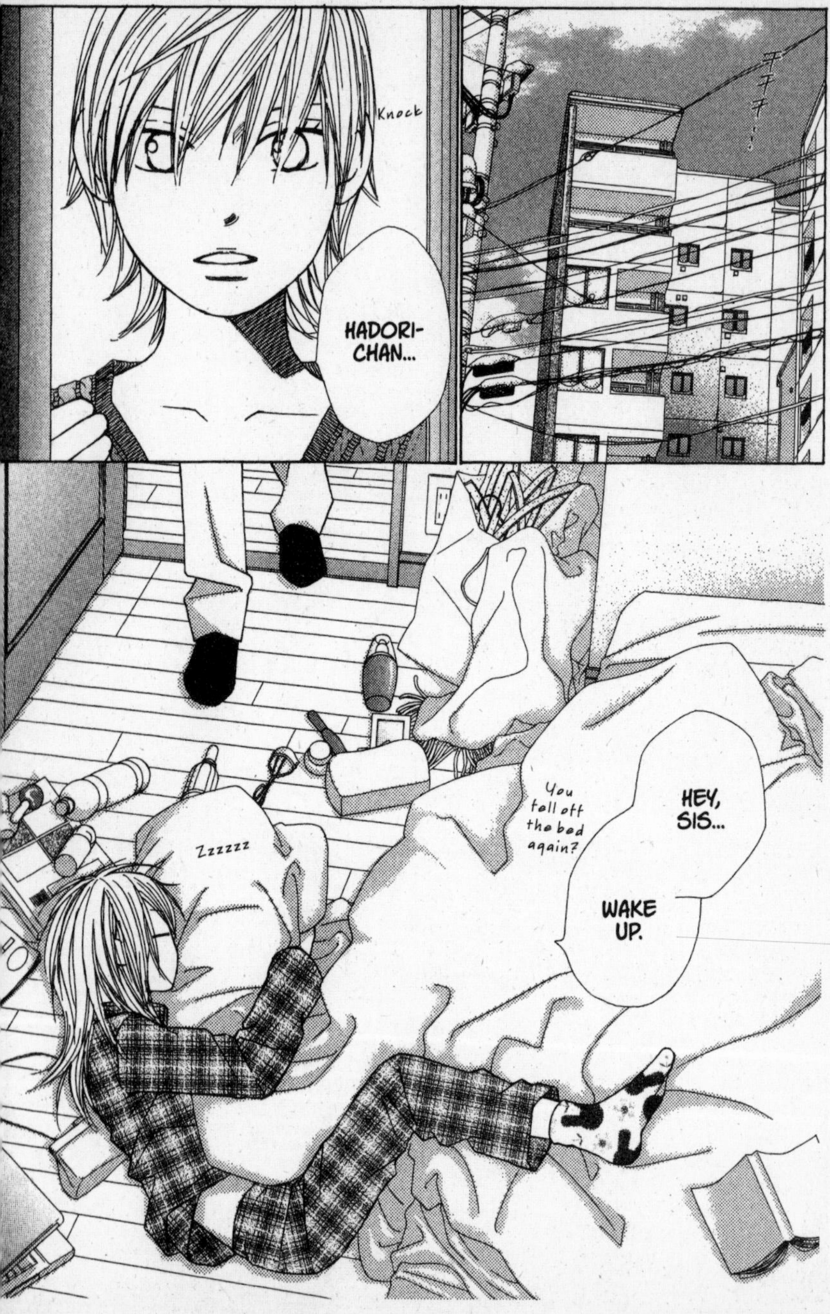
Knock
HADORI-CHAN...
HEY, SIS... WAKE UP.
You fell off the bed again?
Zzzzzz

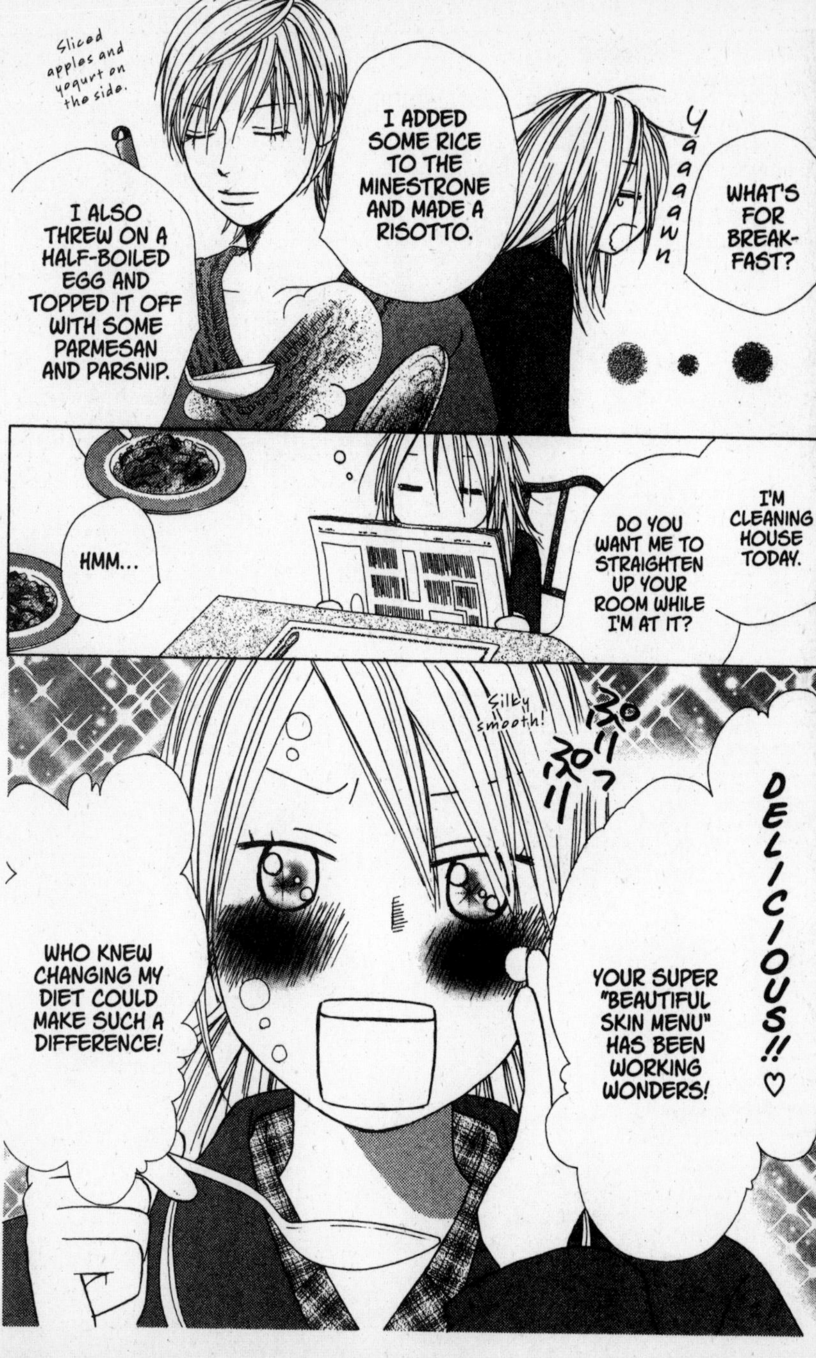
Yaaaawn
WHAT'S FOR BREAK-FAST?
...
I ADDED SOME RICE TO THE MINESTRONE AND MADE A RISOTTO.
Sliced apples and yogurt on the side.
I ALSO THREW ON A HALF-BOILED EGG AND TOPPED IT OFF WITH SOME PARMESAN AND PARSNIP.
I'M CLEANING HOUSE TODAY.
DO YOU WANT ME TO STRAIGHTEN UP YOUR ROOM WHILE I'M AT IT?
HMM...
DELICIOUS!!♡
Silky smooth!
YOUR SUPER "BEAUTIFUL SKIN MENU" HAS BEEN WORKING WONDERS!
WHO KNEW CHANGING MY DIET COULD MAKE SUCH A DIFFERENCE!

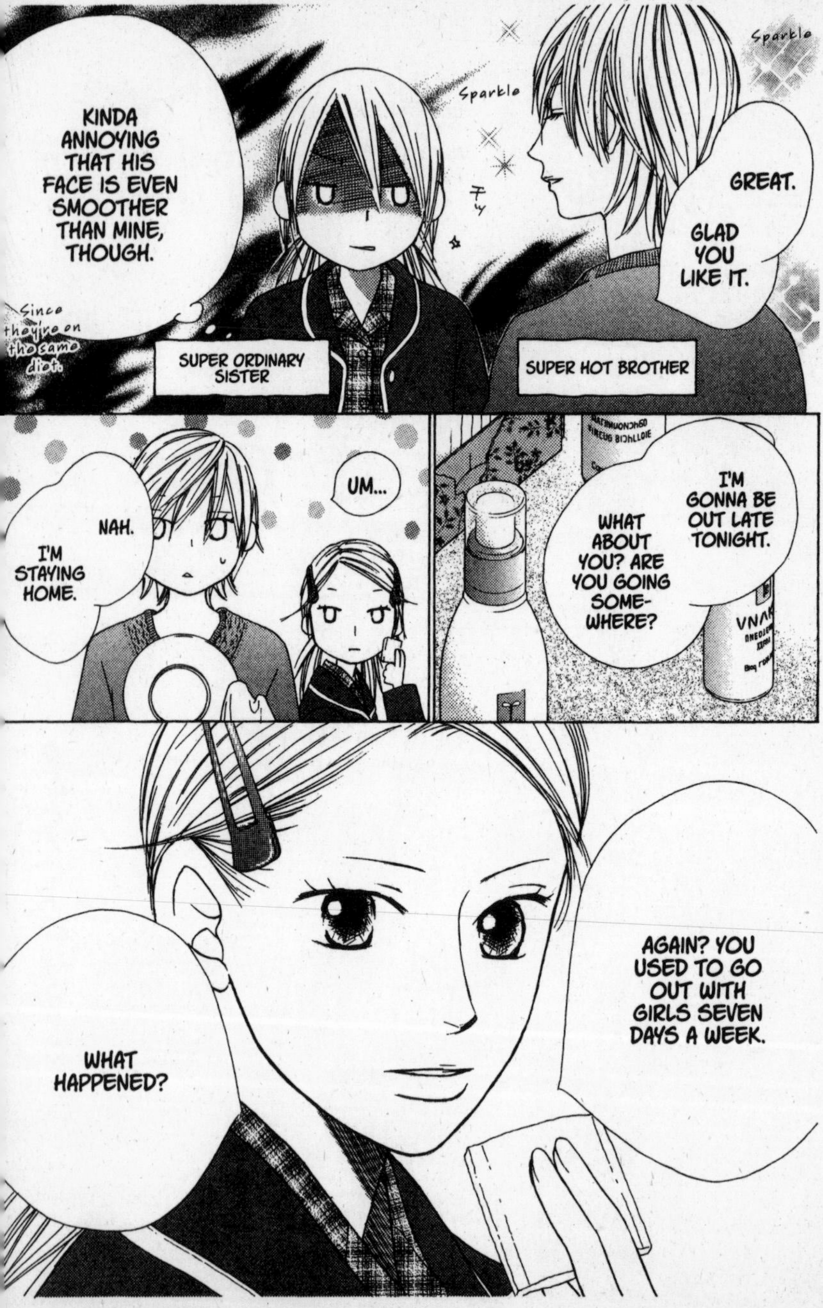
Sparkle
Sparkle
GREAT.
GLAD YOU LIKE IT.
SUPER HOT BROTHER
SUPER ORDINARY SISTER
KINDA ANNOYING THAT HIS FACE IS EVEN SMOOTHER THAN MINE, THOUGH.
Since they're on the same diet.
I'M GONNA BE OUT LATE TONIGHT.
WHAT ABOUT YOU? ARE YOU GOING SOME-WHERE?
UM...
NAH.
I'M STAYING HOME.
AGAIN? YOU USED TO GO OUT WITH GIRLS SEVEN DAYS A WEEK.
WHAT HAPPENED?

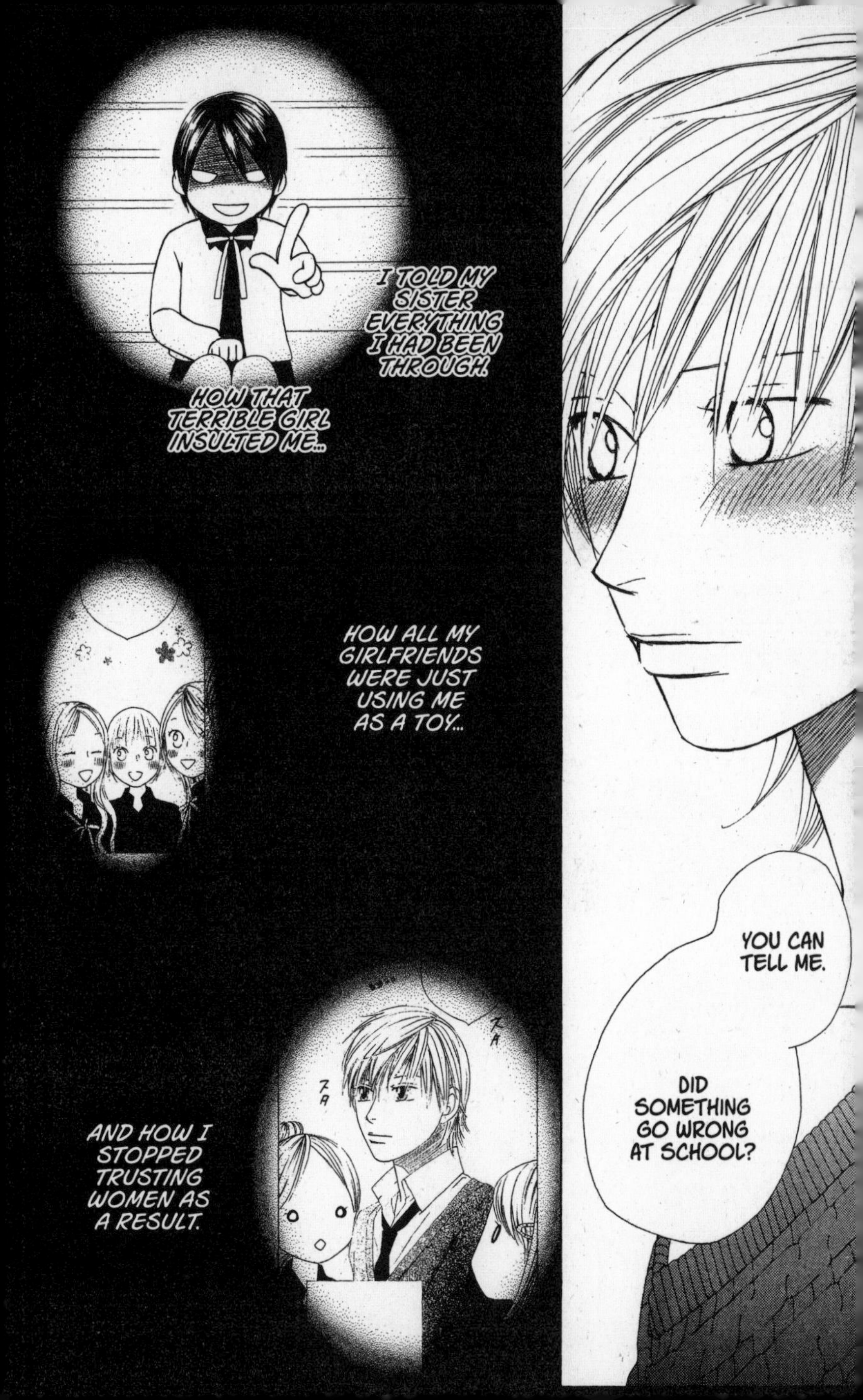
YOU CAN TELL ME.
DID SOMETHING GO WRONG AT SCHOOL?
I TOLD MY SISTER EVERYTHING I HAD BEEN THROUGH.
HOW THAT TERRIBLE GIRL INSULTED ME...
HOW ALL MY GIRLFRIENDS WERE JUST USING ME AS A TOY...
AND HOW I STOPPED TRUSTING WOMEN AS A RESULT.

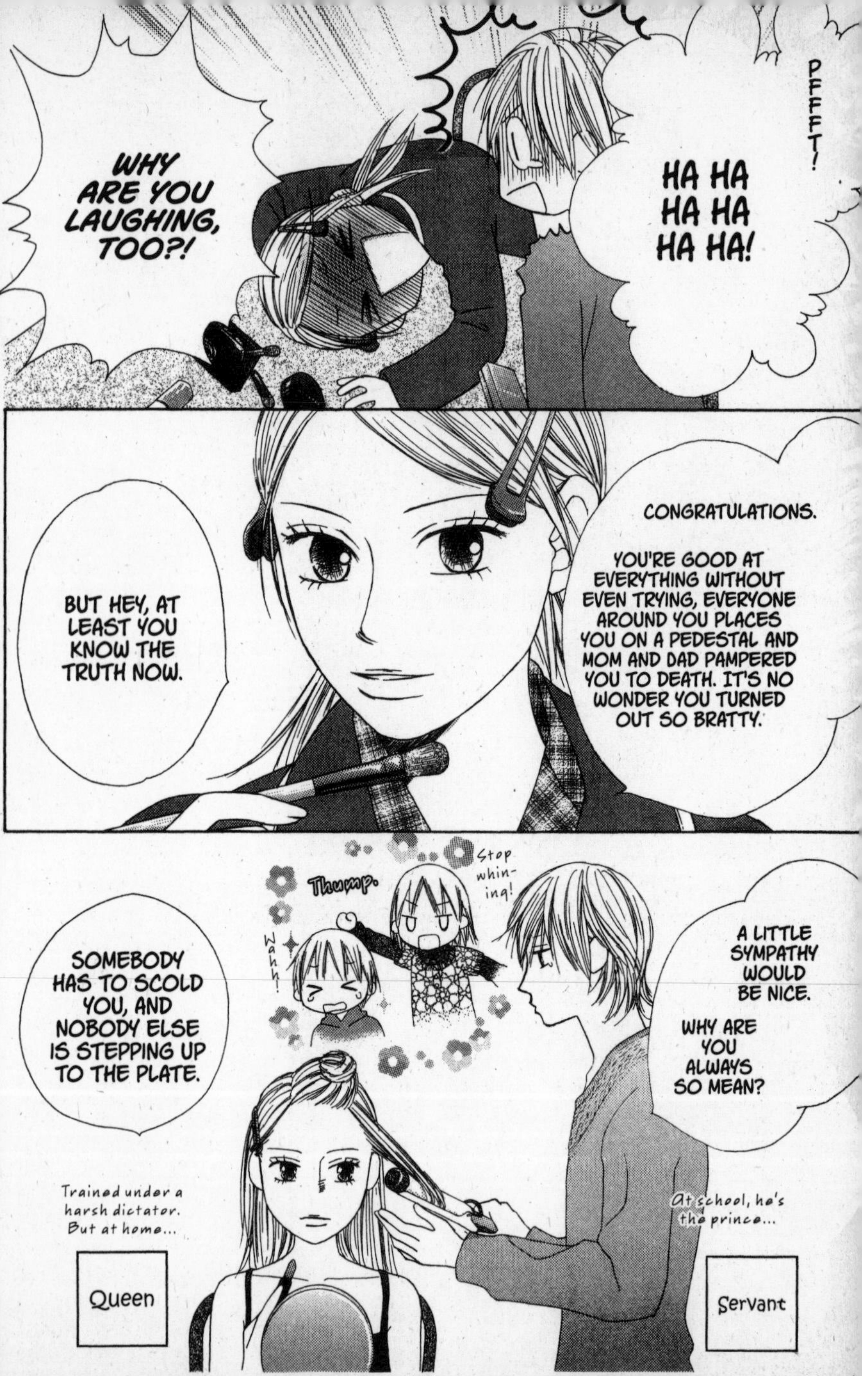
PFFFT!
HA HA HA HA HA HA!
WHY ARE YOU LAUGHING, TOO?!
CONGRATULATIONS.
YOU'RE GOOD AT EVERYTHING WITHOUT EVEN TRYING, EVERYONE AROUND YOU PLACES YOU ON A PEDESTAL AND MOM AND DAD PAMPERED YOU TO DEATH. IT'S NO WONDER YOU TURNED OUT SO BRATTY.
BUT HEY, AT LEAST YOU KNOW THE TRUTH NOW.
A LITTLE SYMPATHY WOULD BE NICE.
WHY ARE YOU ALWAYS SO MEAN?
Stop whining!
Thump.
Wahh!
SOMEBODY HAS TO SCOLD YOU, AND NOBODY ELSE IS STEPPING UP TO THE PLATE.
At school, he's the prince...
Servant
Trained under a harsh dictator. But at home...
Queen
He's even good at styling hair.

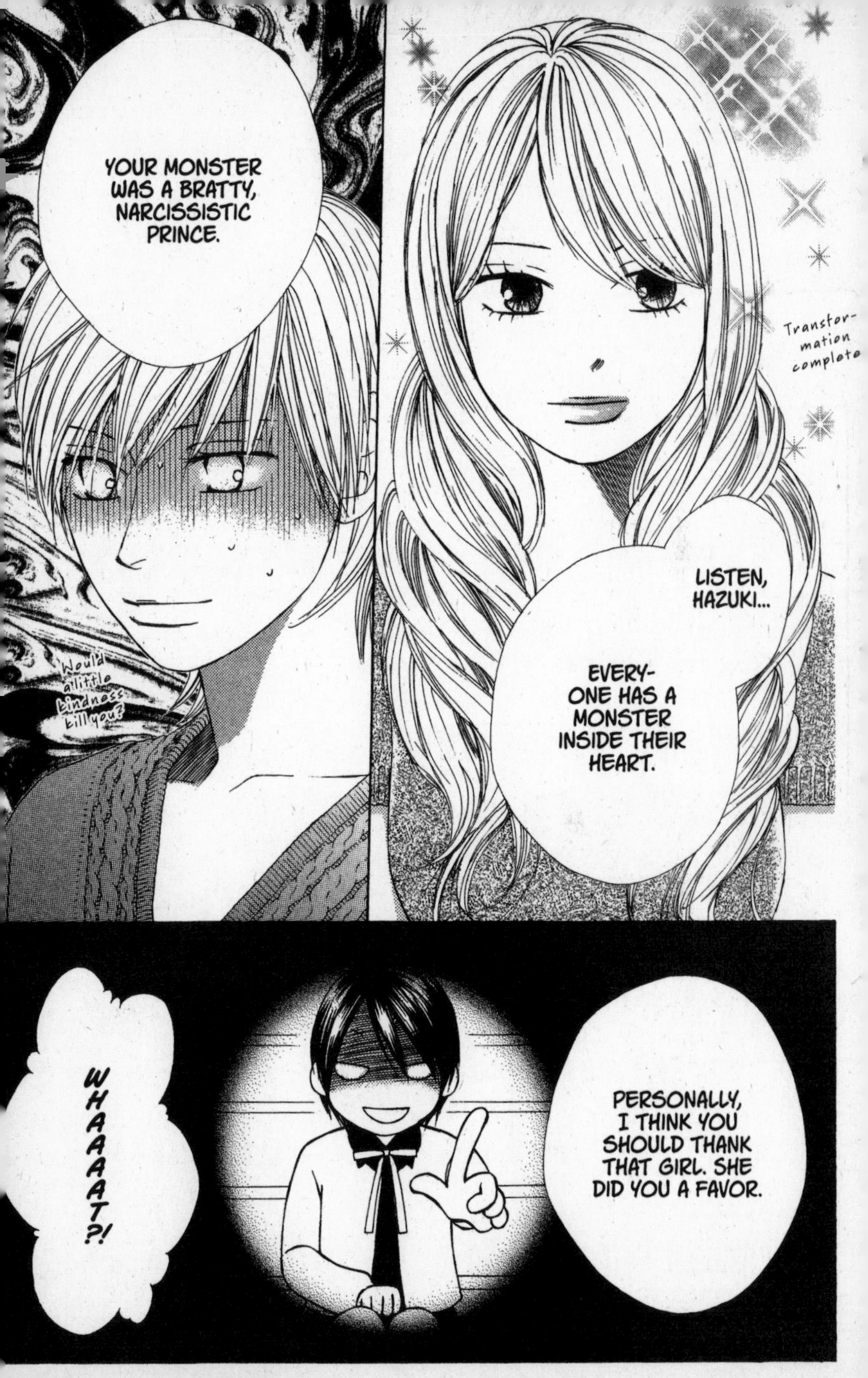
Transfor- mation complete
LISTEN, HAZUKI...
EVERY- ONE HAS A MONSTER INSIDE THEIR HEART.
YOUR MONSTER WAS A BRATTY, NARCISSISTIC PRINCE.
Would a little kindness kill you?
PERSONALLY, I THINK YOU SHOULD THANK THAT GIRL. SHE DID YOU A FAVOR.
WHAAAAAT?!

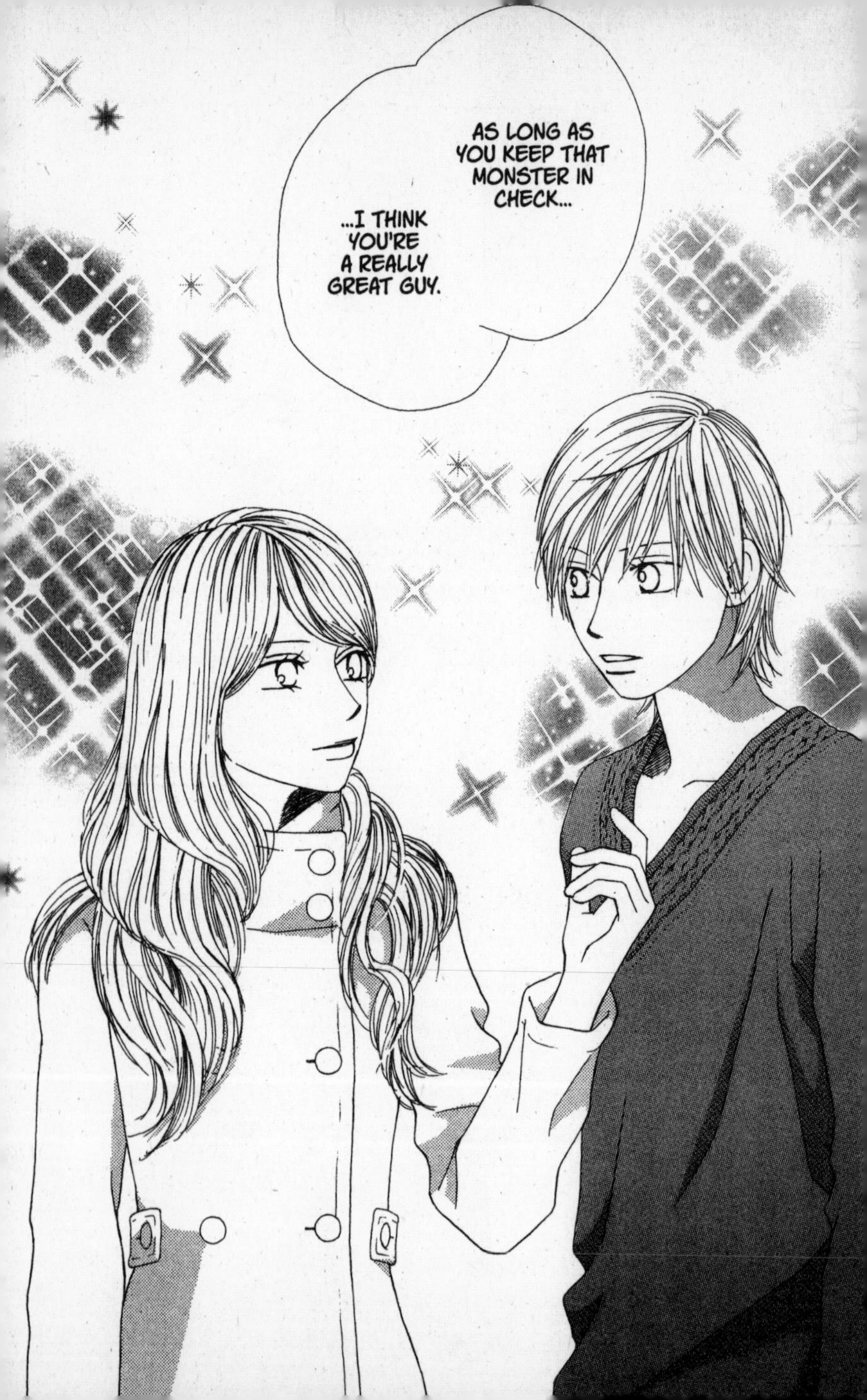
AS LONG AS YOU KEEP THAT MONSTER IN CHECK...
...I THINK YOU'RE A REALLY GREAT GUY.

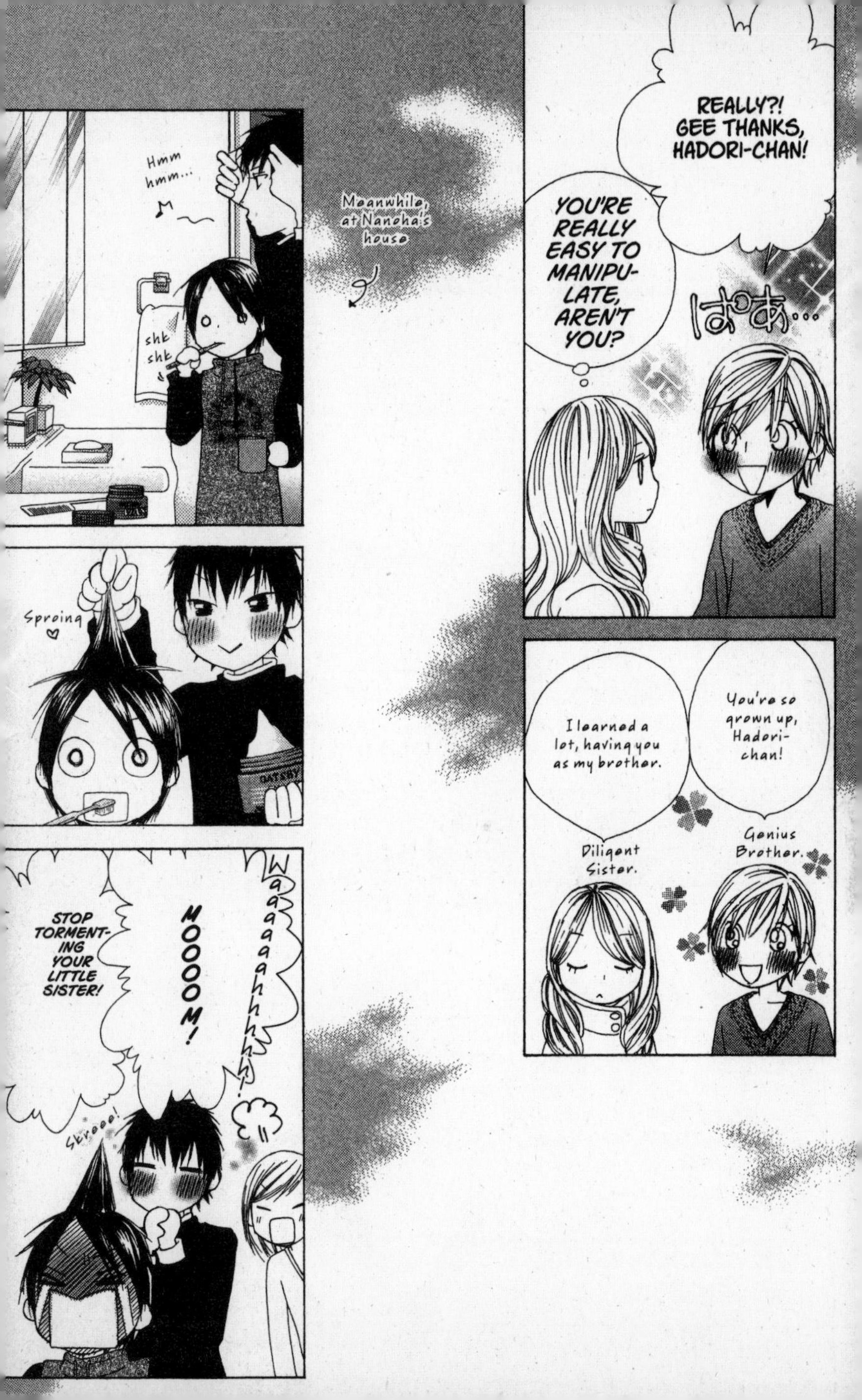
REALLY?! GEE THANKS, HADORI-CHAN!
ぱあ...
YOU'RE REALLY EASY TO MANIPU-LATE, AREN'T YOU?
You're so grown up, Hadori-chan!
I learned a lot, having you as my brother.
Genius Brother.
Diligent Sister.
Meanwhile, at Nanoha's house
Hmm hmm... ♪
shk shk
Sproing ♡
Waaaaaaaaahhhhhh!
MOOOOOM!
STOP TORMENT-ING YOUR LITTLE SISTER!
Skreee!

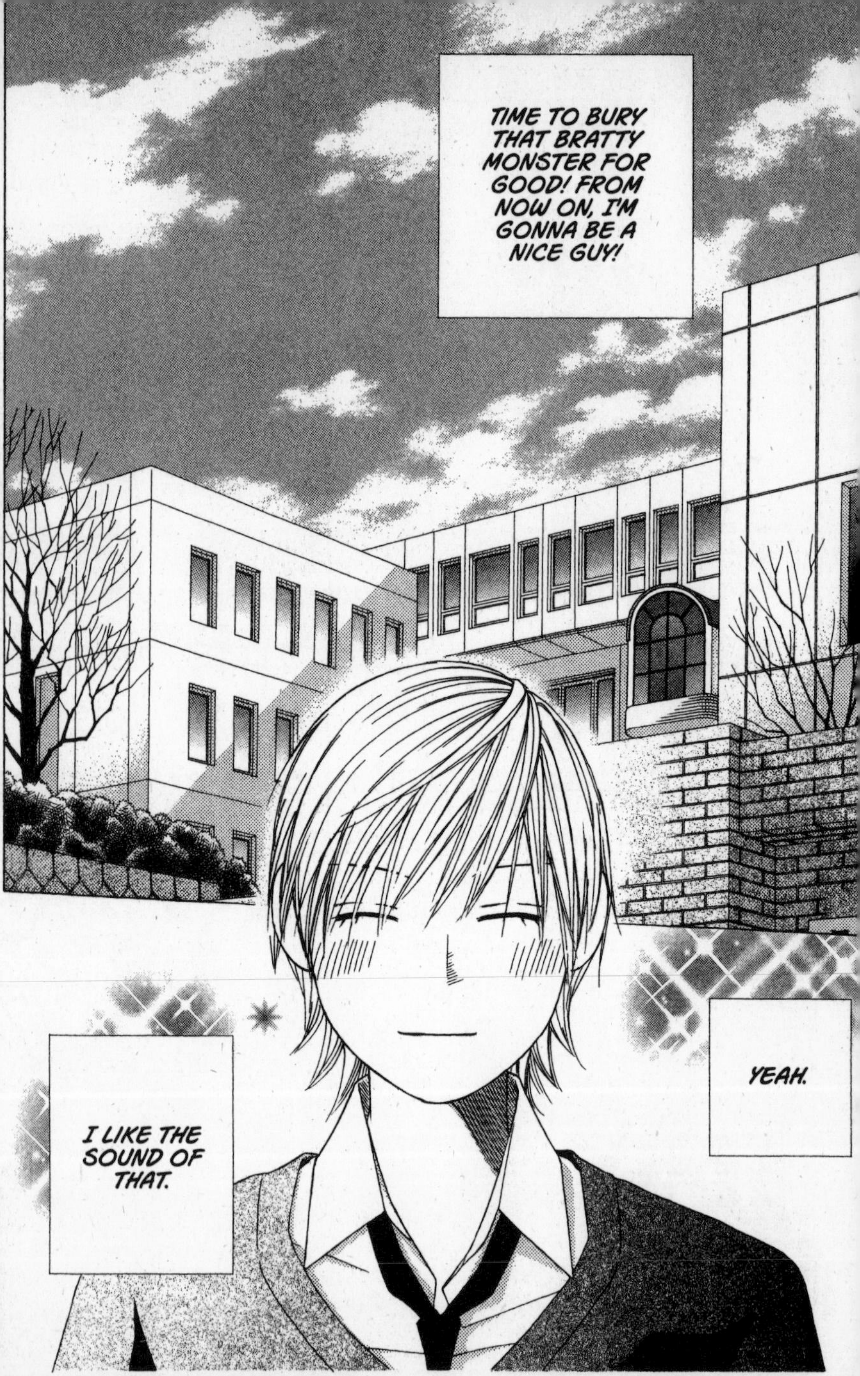
TIME TO BURY THAT BRATTY MONSTER FOR GOOD! FROM NOW ON, I'M GONNA BE A NICE GUY!
YEAH.
I LIKE THE SOUND OF THAT.

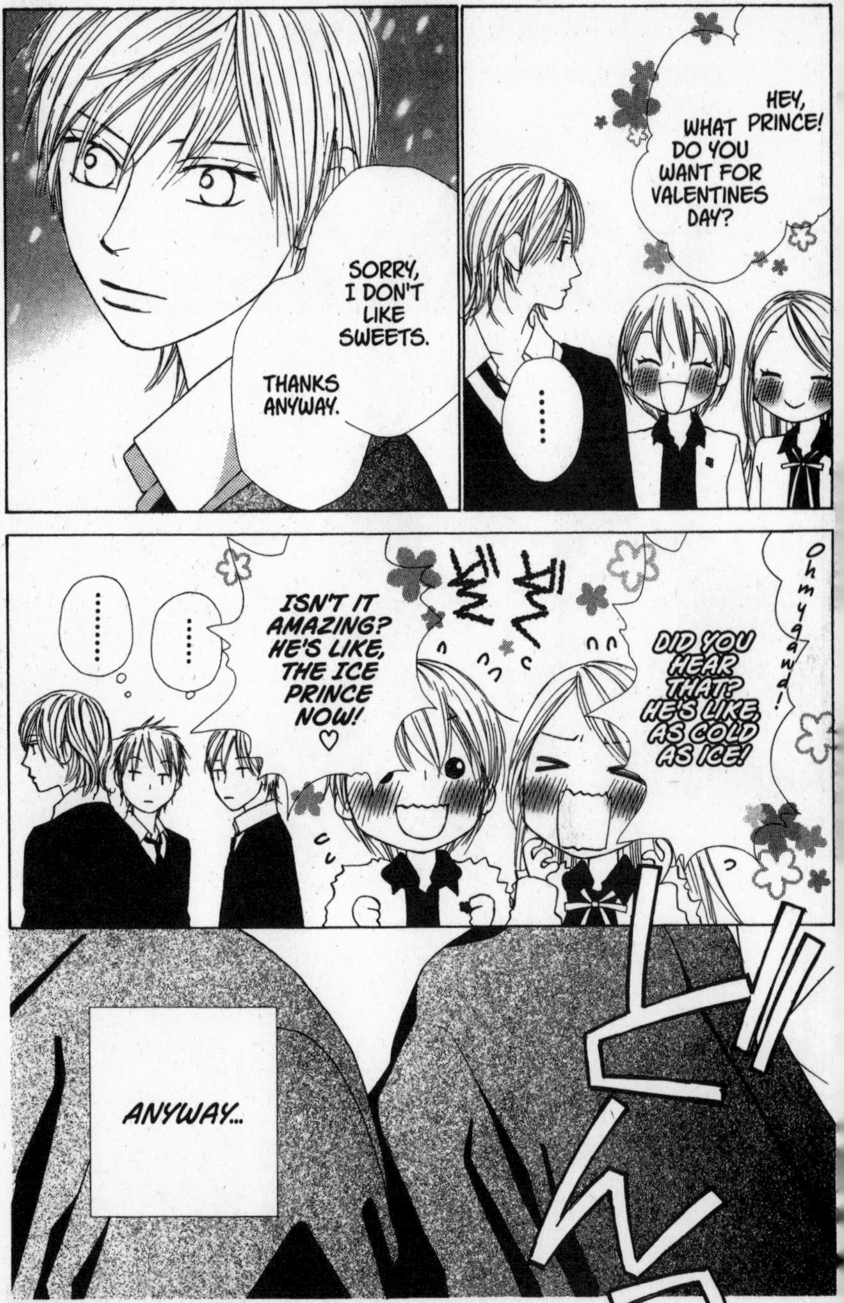
HEY, PRINCE! WHAT DO YOU WANT FOR VALENTINES DAY?
......
SORRY, I DON'T LIKE SWEETS.
THANKS ANYWAY.
Ohmygawd!
DID YOU HEAR THAT? HE'S LIKE, AS COLD AS ICE!
ISN'T IT AMAZING? HE'S LIKE, THE ICE PRINCE NOW! ♡
......
....
ANYWAY...

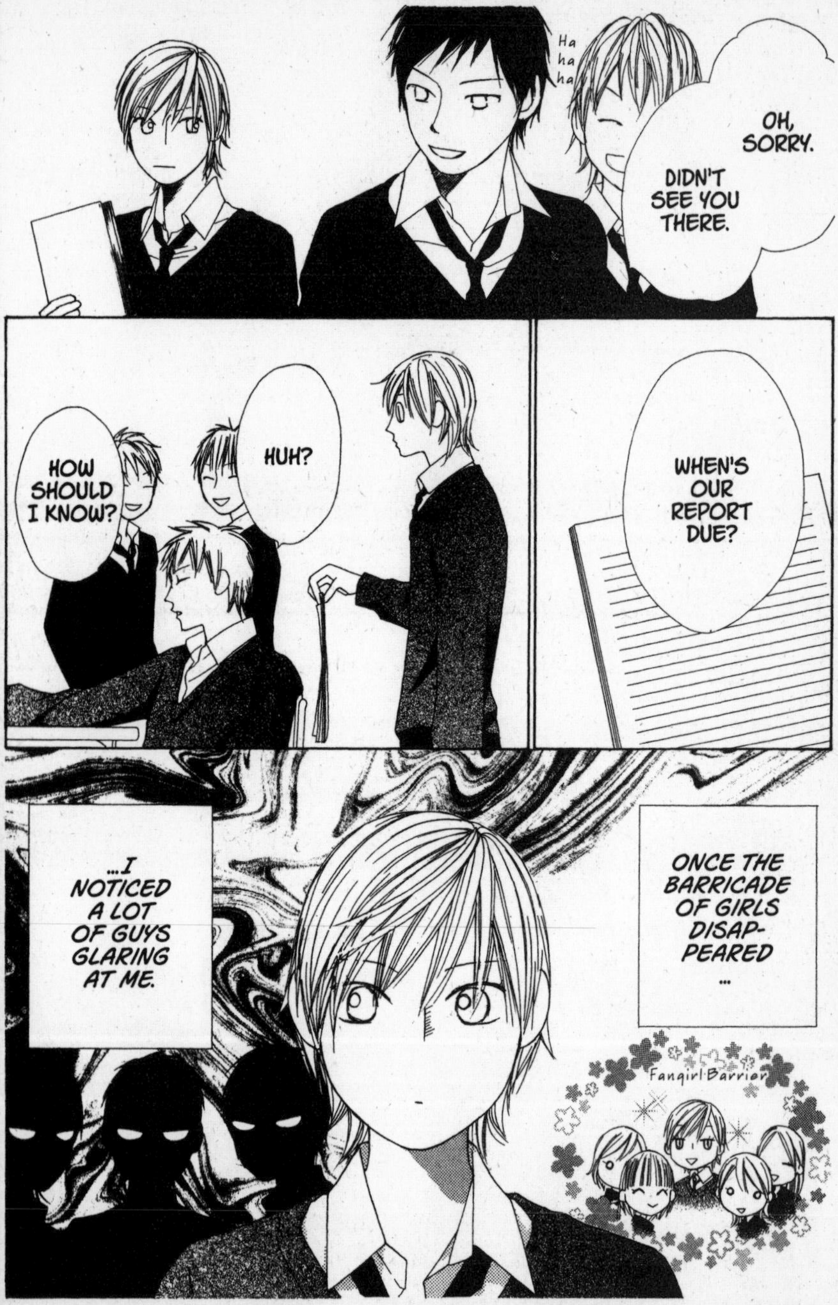
Ha ha ha
OH, SORRY.
DIDN'T SEE YOU THERE.
WHEN'S OUR REPORT DUE?
HUH?
HOW SHOULD I KNOW?
ONCE THE BARRICADE OF GIRLS DISAPPEARED ...
...I NOTICED A LOT OF GUYS GLARING AT ME.
Fangirl Barrier

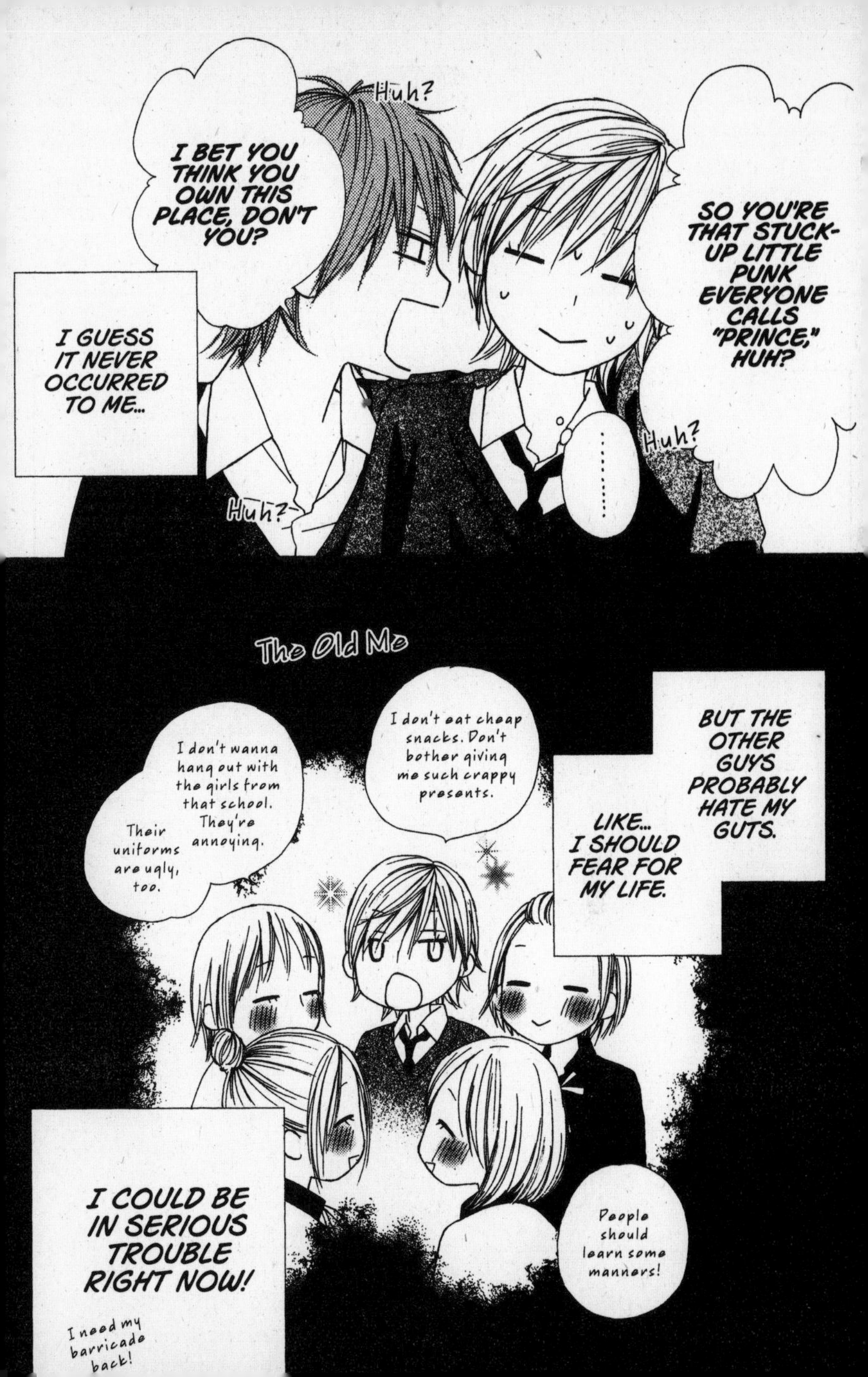
SO YOU'RE THAT STUCK-UP LITTLE PUNK EVERYONE CALLS "PRINCE," HUH?
Huh?
......
Huh?
I BET YOU THINK YOU OWN THIS PLACE, DON'T YOU?
I GUESS IT NEVER OCCURRED TO ME...
Huh?
The Old Me
BUT THE OTHER GUYS PROBABLY HATE MY GUTS.
LIKE... I SHOULD FEAR FOR MY LIFE.
I don't eat cheap snacks. Don't bother giving me such crappy presents.
I don't wanna hang out with the girls from that school. They're annoying.
Their uniforms are ugly, too.
People should learn some manners!
I COULD BE IN SERIOUS TROUBLE RIGHT NOW!
I need my barricade back!

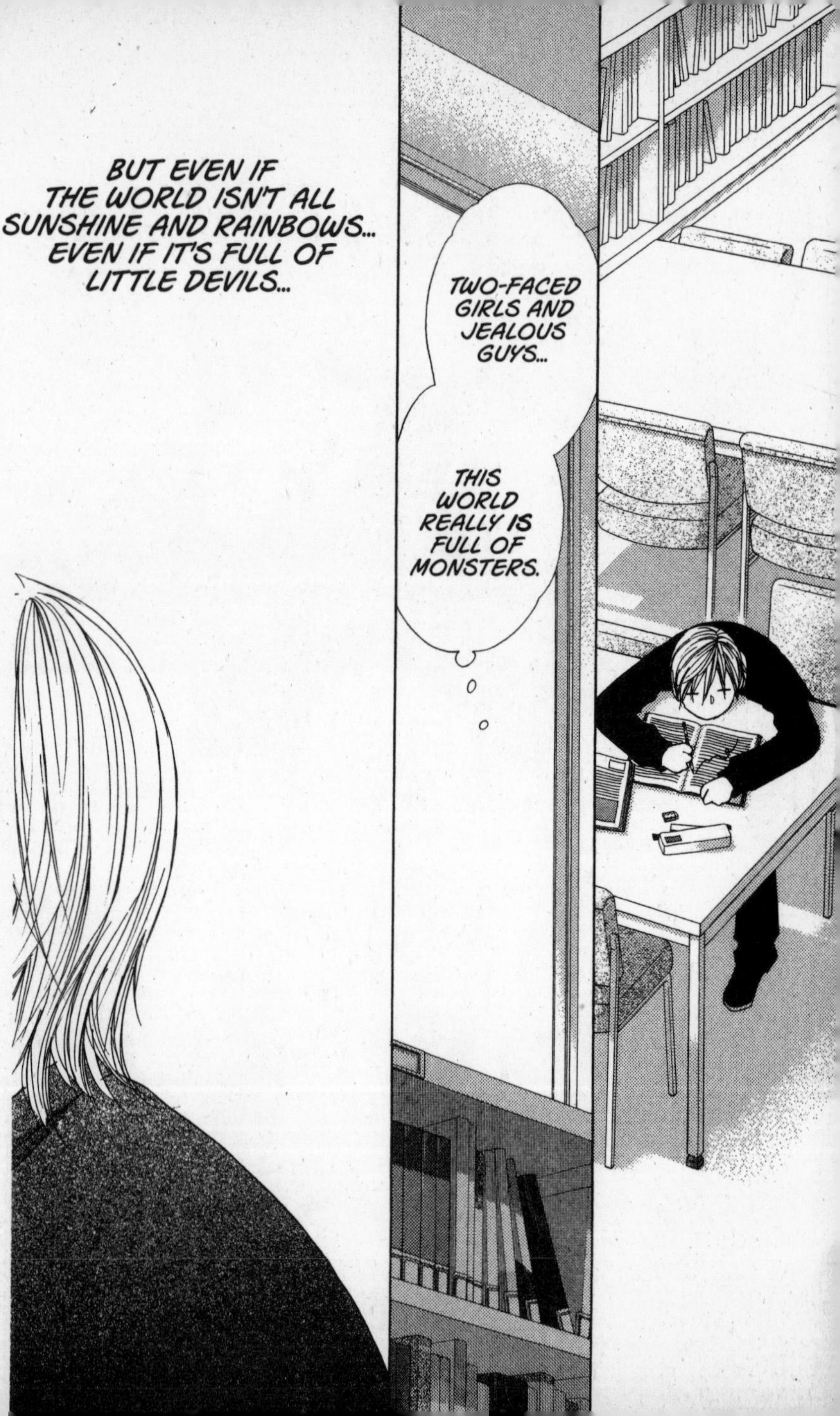
TWO-FACED GIRLS AND JEALOUS GUYS...
THIS WORLD REALLY IS FULL OF MONSTERS.
BUT EVEN IF THE WORLD ISN'T ALL SUNSHINE AND RAINBOWS... EVEN IF IT'S FULL OF LITTLE DEVILS...

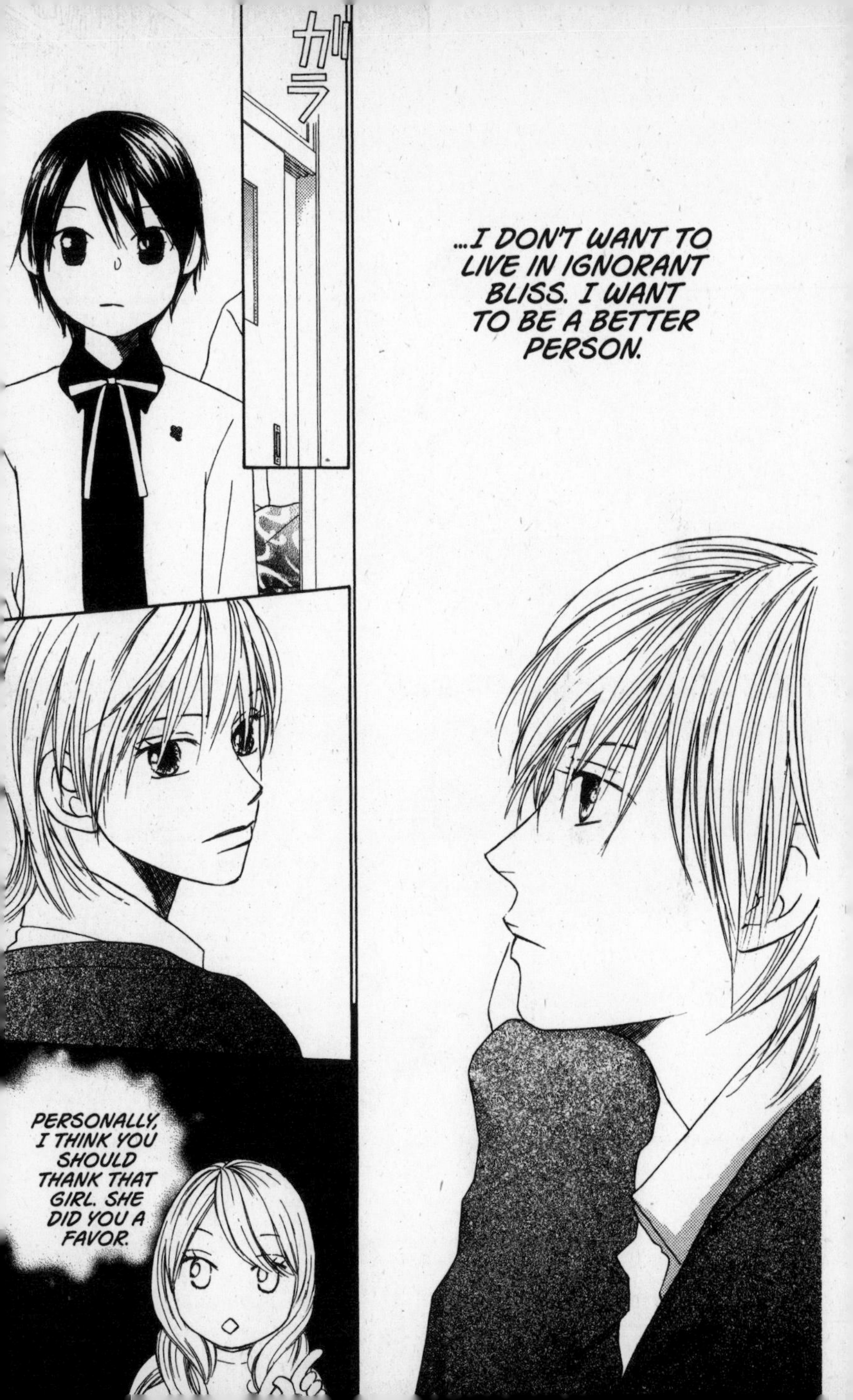
...I DON'T WANT TO LIVE IN IGNORANT BLISS. I WANT TO BE A BETTER PERSON.
ガラ
PERSONALLY, I THINK YOU SHOULD THANK THAT GIRL. SHE DID YOU A FAVOR.

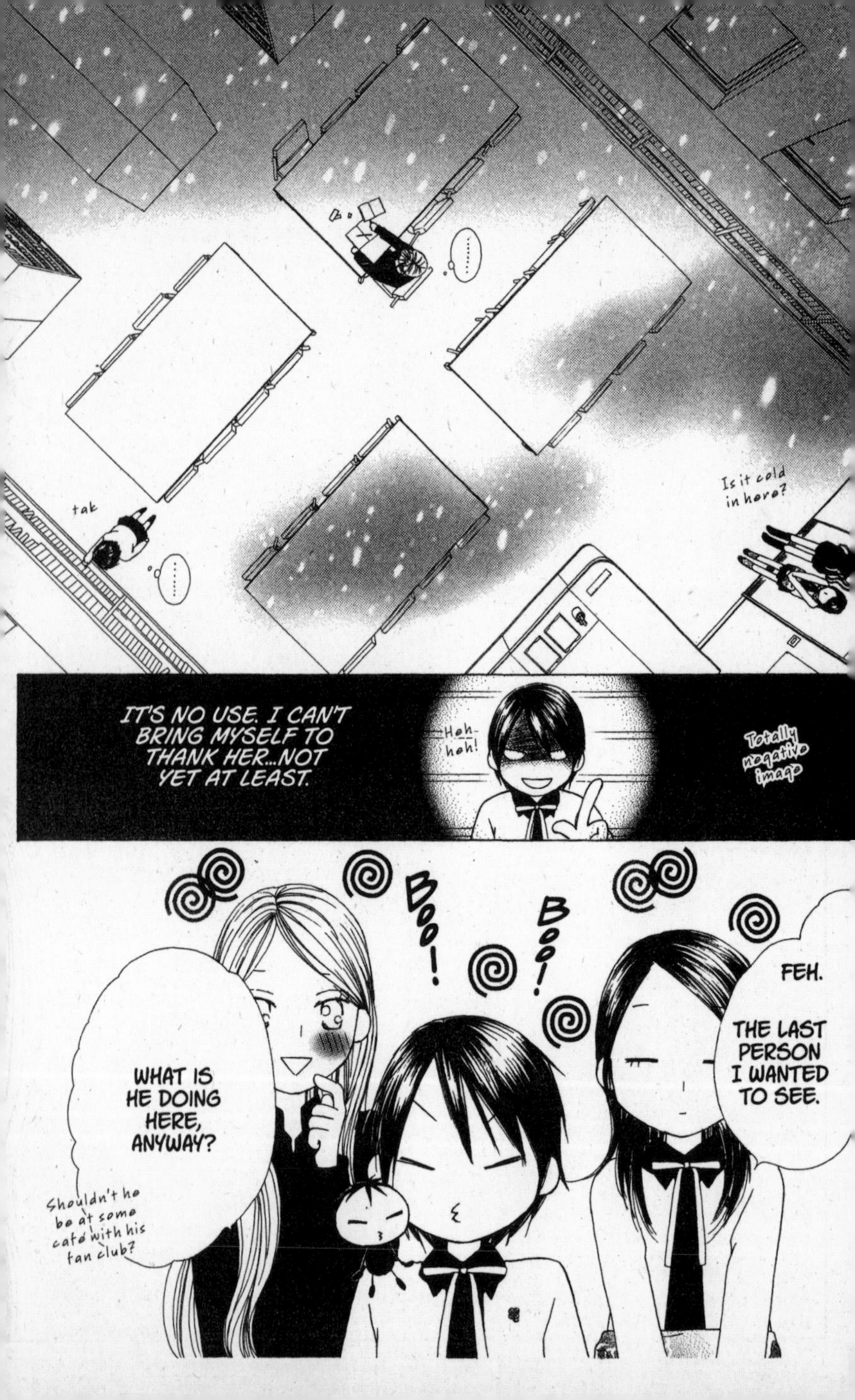
Is it cold in here?
......
tak
......
Totally negative image
Heh-heh!
IT'S NO USE. I CAN'T BRING MYSELF TO THANK HER...NOT YET AT LEAST.
FEH.
THE LAST PERSON I WANTED TO SEE.
BOO!
BOO!
WHAT IS HE DOING HERE, ANYWAY?
Shouldn't he be at some café with his fan club?

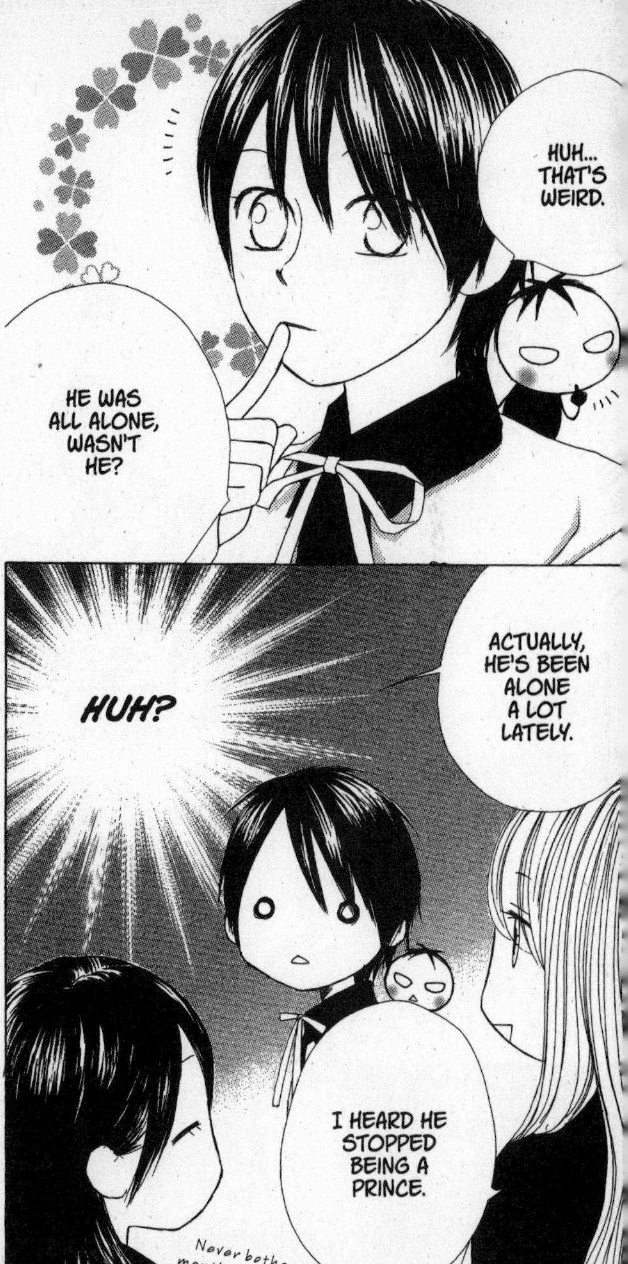
HUH... THAT'S WEIRD.
HE WAS ALL ALONE, WASN'T HE?
ACTUALLY, HE'S BEEN ALONE A LOT LATELY.
HUH?
I HEARD HE STOPPED BEING A PRINCE.
Never bothered mentioning it, since Nanoha never asked.

3

I take a half-hour break to cook during my work day.

• Just use a frying pan to grill your vegetables •

I think it tastes the best this way. Especially roots and mushrooms. Grill them until they're nice and brown. You don't even need oil and they come out really sweet! ♥

I love lotus root. It tastes great with wasabi, or citrus soy sauce.

• Boil in consomme or miso soup •

Add whatever vegetables are in season.

Keep in mind, I'm not a vegetarian. I love meat, fish, beans, seaweed... pretty much everything!

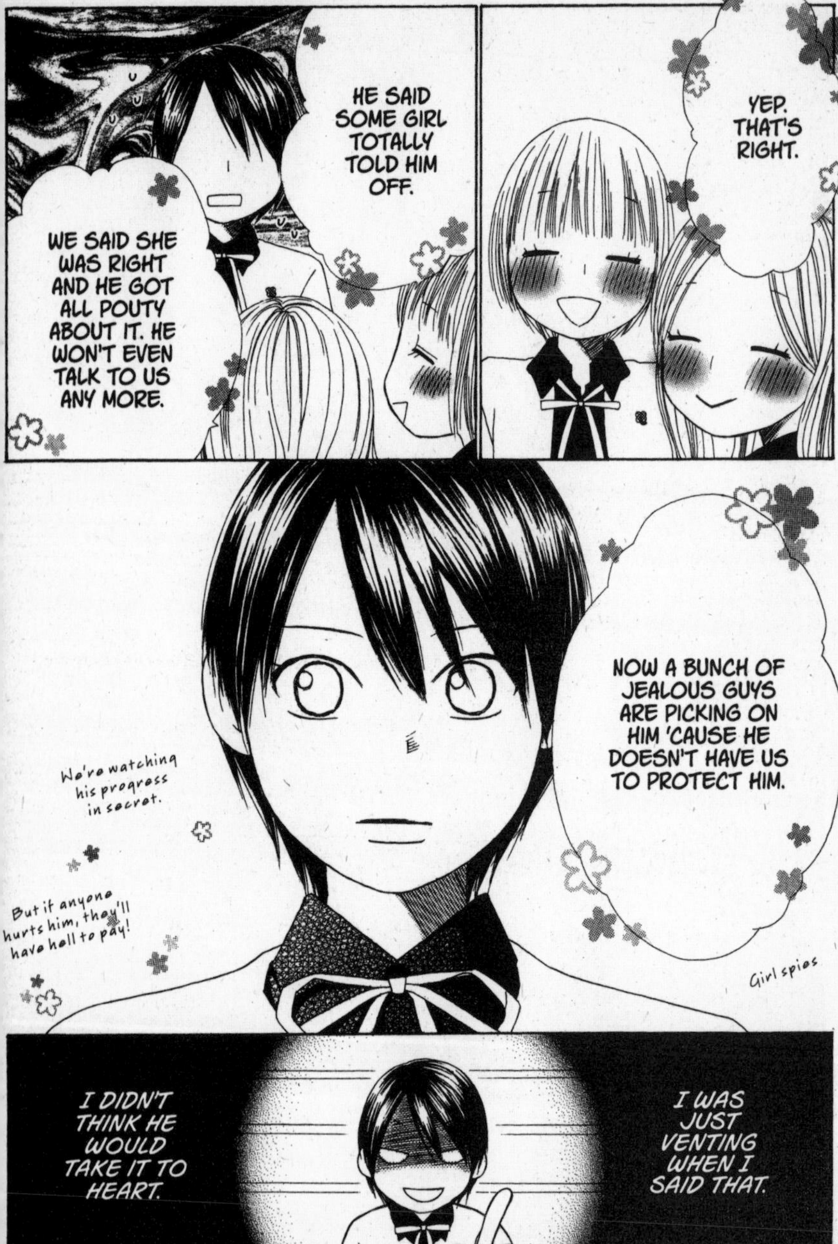
YEP. THAT'S RIGHT.
HE SAID SOME GIRL TOTALLY TOLD HIM OFF.
WE SAID SHE WAS RIGHT AND HE GOT ALL POUTY ABOUT IT. HE WON'T EVEN TALK TO US ANY MORE.
NOW A BUNCH OF JEALOUS GUYS ARE PICKING ON HIM 'CAUSE HE DOESN'T HAVE US TO PROTECT HIM.
Girl spies
We're watching his progress in secret.
But if anyone hurts him, they'll have hell to pay!
I WAS JUST VENTING WHEN I SAID THAT.
I DIDN'T THINK HE WOULD TAKE IT TO HEART.

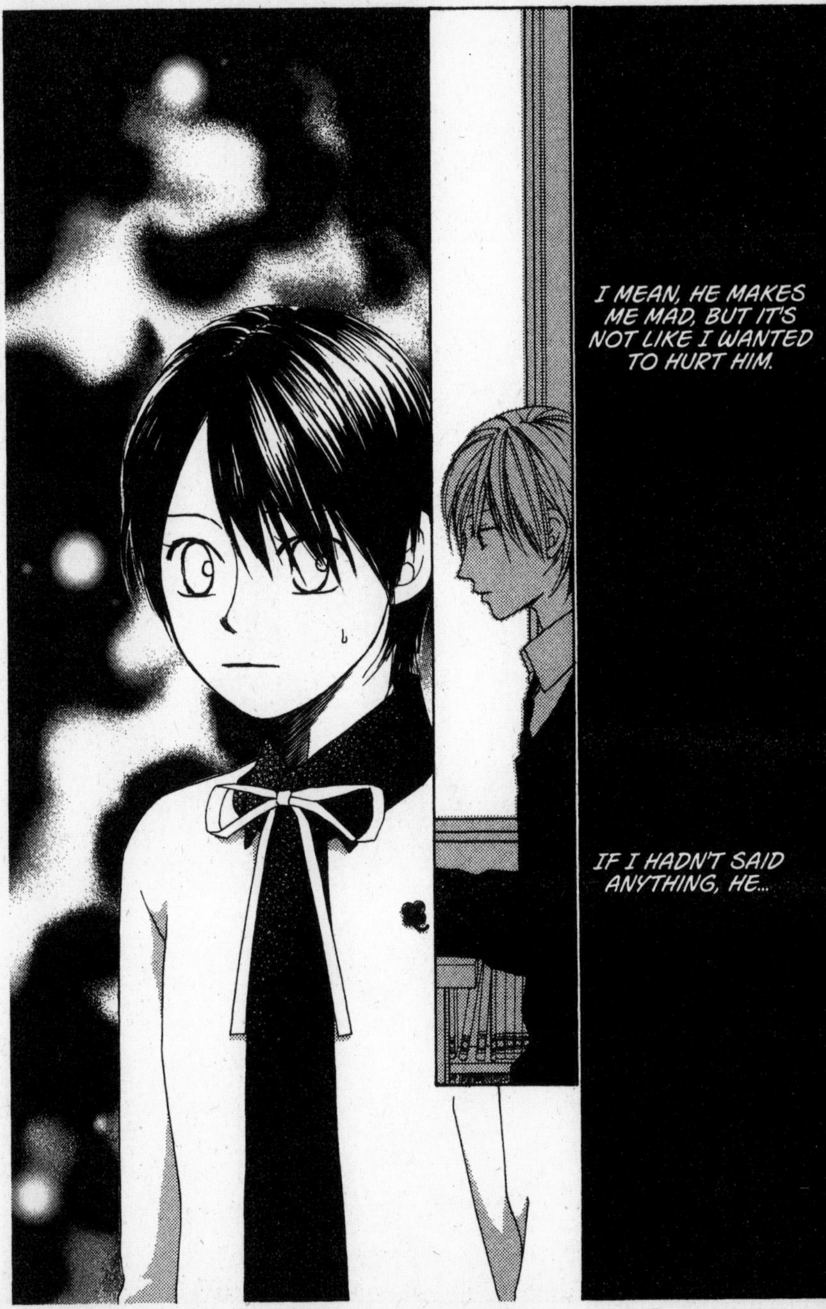
I MEAN, HE MAKES ME MAD, BUT IT'S NOT LIKE I WANTED TO HURT HIM.
IF I HADN'T SAID ANYTHING, HE...

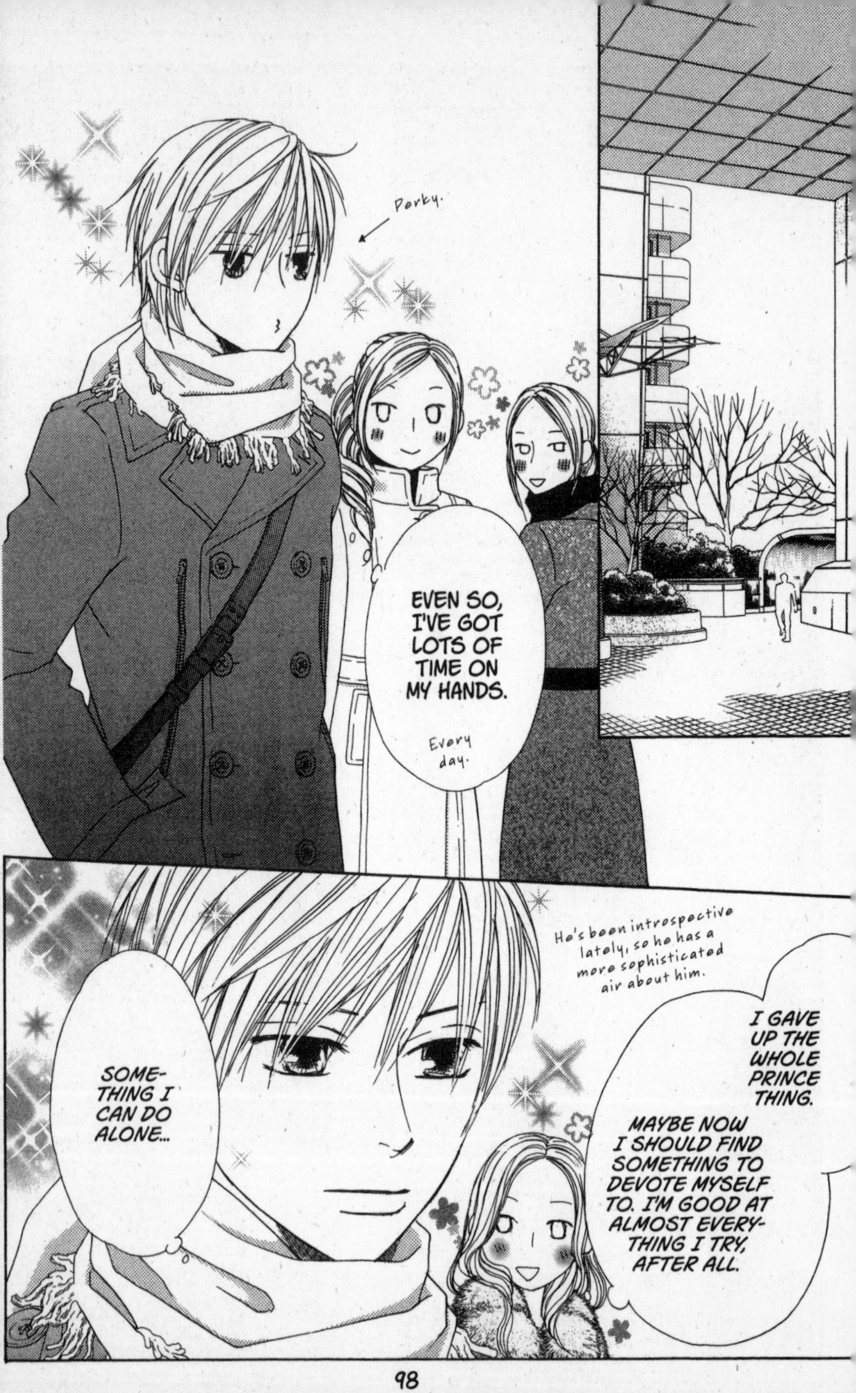
Perky.
EVEN SO, I'VE GOT LOTS OF TIME ON MY HANDS.
Every day.
I GAVE UP THE WHOLE PRINCE THING.
MAYBE NOW I SHOULD FIND SOMETHING TO DEVOTE MYSELF TO. I'M GOOD AT ALMOST EVERYTHING I TRY, AFTER ALL.
He's been introspective lately, so he has a more sophisticated air about him.
SOMETHING I CAN DO ALONE...

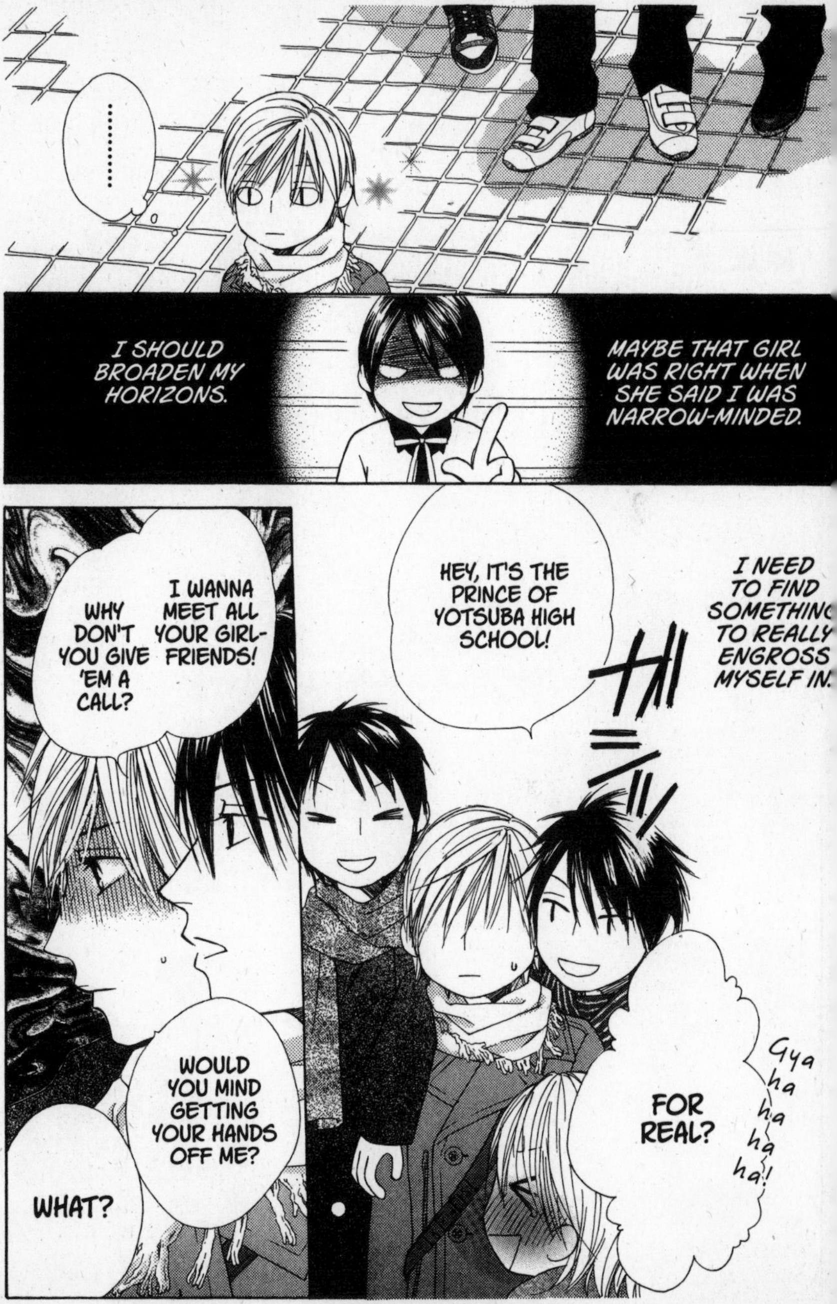

......
MAYBE THAT GIRL WAS RIGHT WHEN SHE SAID I WAS NARROW-MINDED.
I SHOULD BROADEN MY HORIZONS.
I NEED TO FIND SOMETHING TO REALLY ENGROSS MYSELF IN.
HEY, IT'S THE PRINCE OF YOTSUBA HIGH SCHOOL!
FOR REAL?
Gyahahahaha!
I WANNA MEET ALL YOUR GIRL-FRIENDS!
WHY DON'T YOU GIVE 'EM A CALL?
WOULD YOU MIND GETTING YOUR HANDS OFF ME?
WHAT?

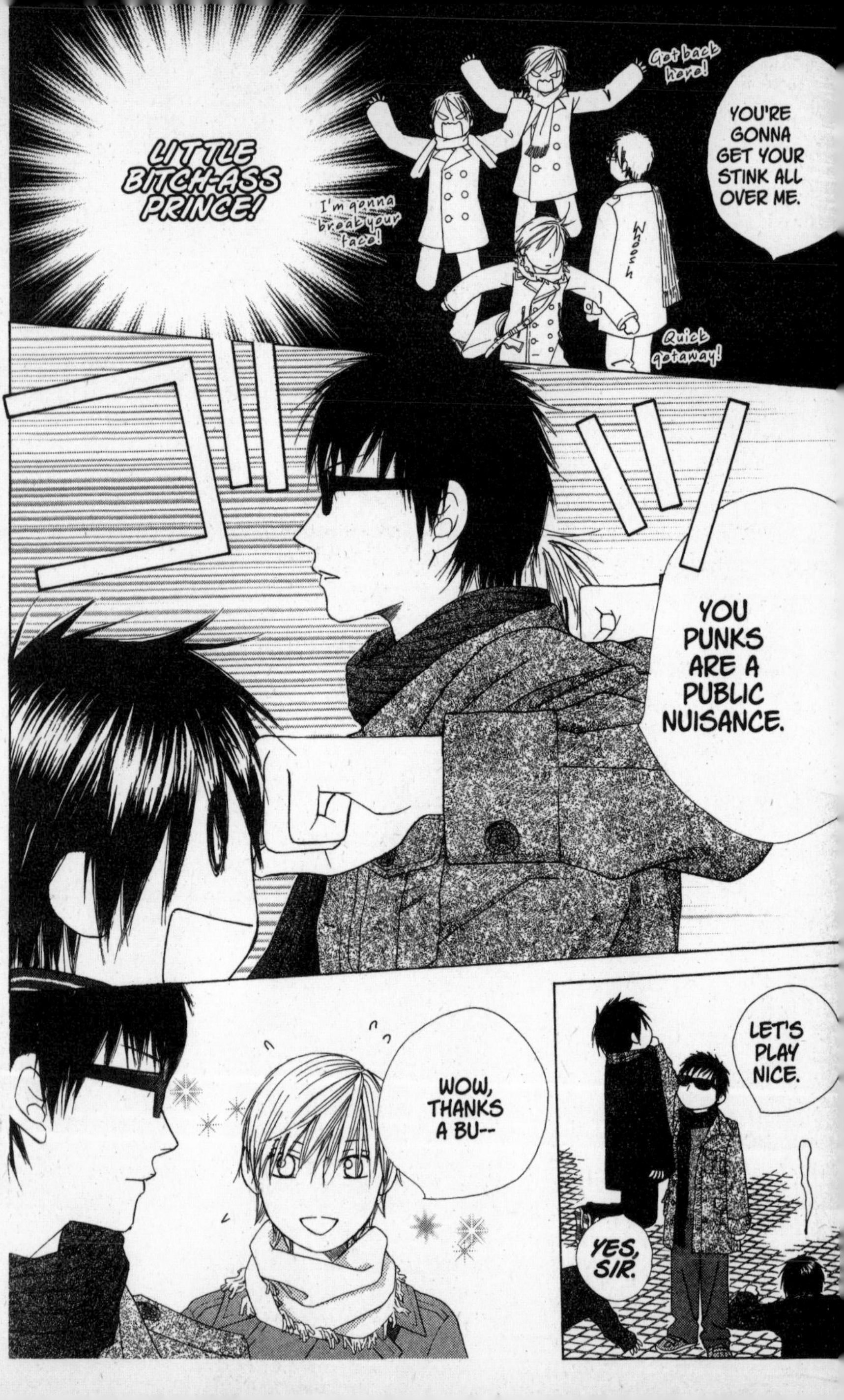

YOU'RE GONNA GET YOUR STINK ALL OVER ME.
Get back here!
Whoosh
Quick getaway!
I'm gonna break your face!
LITTLE BITCH-ASS PRINCE!
YOU PUNKS ARE A PUBLIC NUISANCE.
LET'S PLAY NICE.
YES, SIR.
WOW, THANKS A BU--

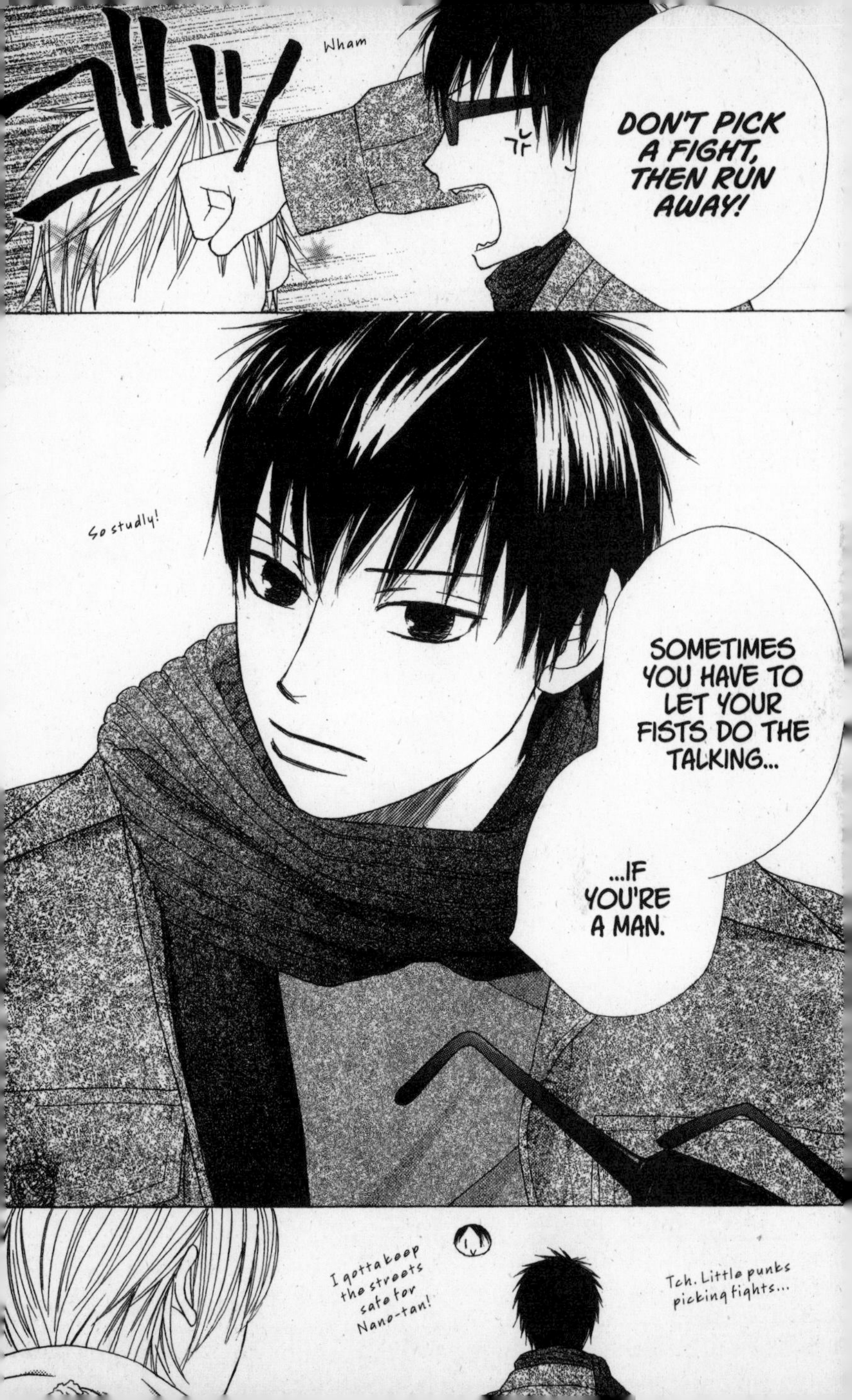
DON'T PICK A FIGHT, THEN RUN AWAY!
Wham
SOMETIMES YOU HAVE TO LET YOUR FISTS DO THE TALKING...
...IF YOU'RE A MAN.
So studly!
Tch. Little punks picking fights...
I gotta keep the streets safe for Nano-tan!

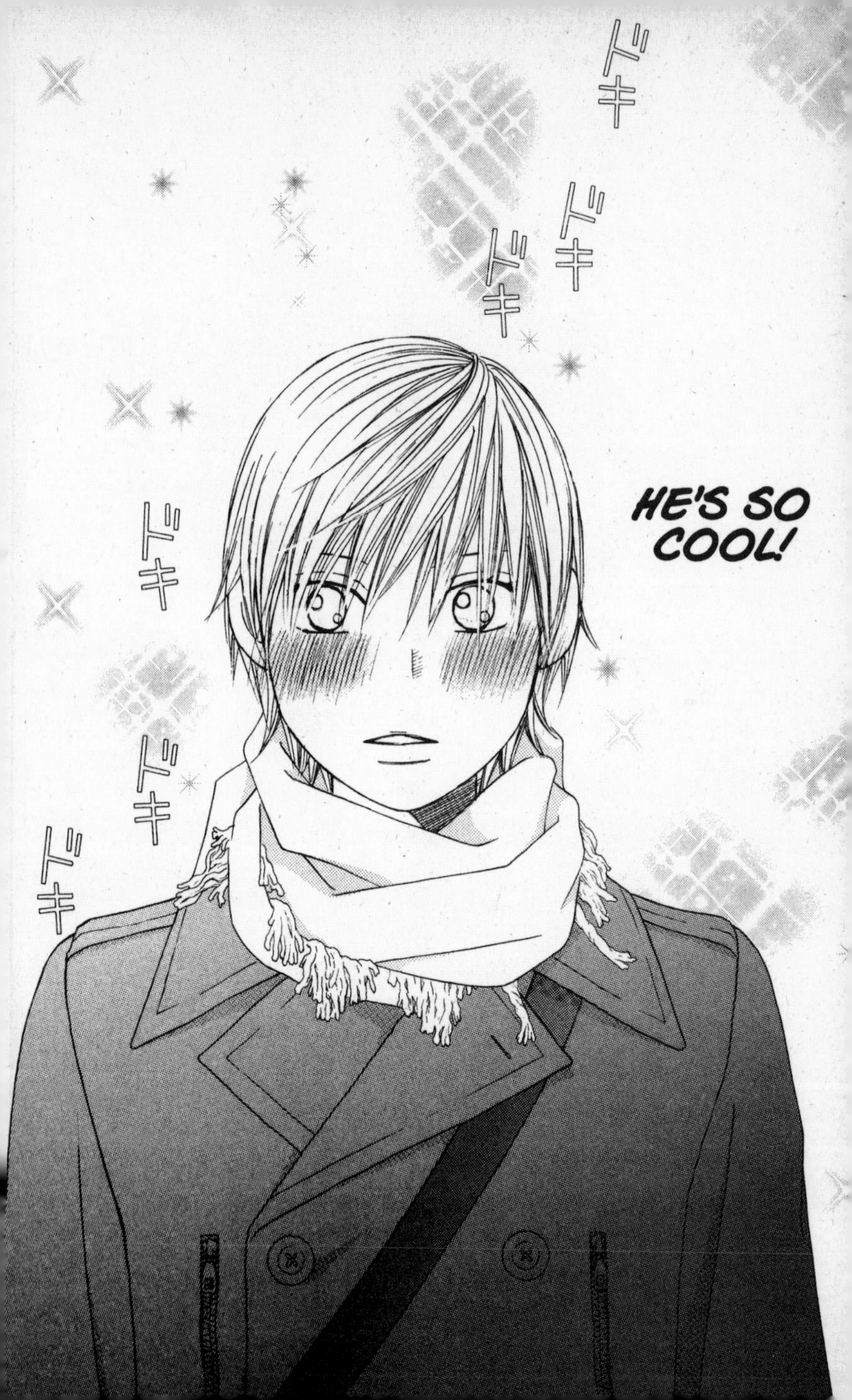
ドキ
ドキ
ドキ
HE'S SO COOL!
ドキ
ドキ
ドキ

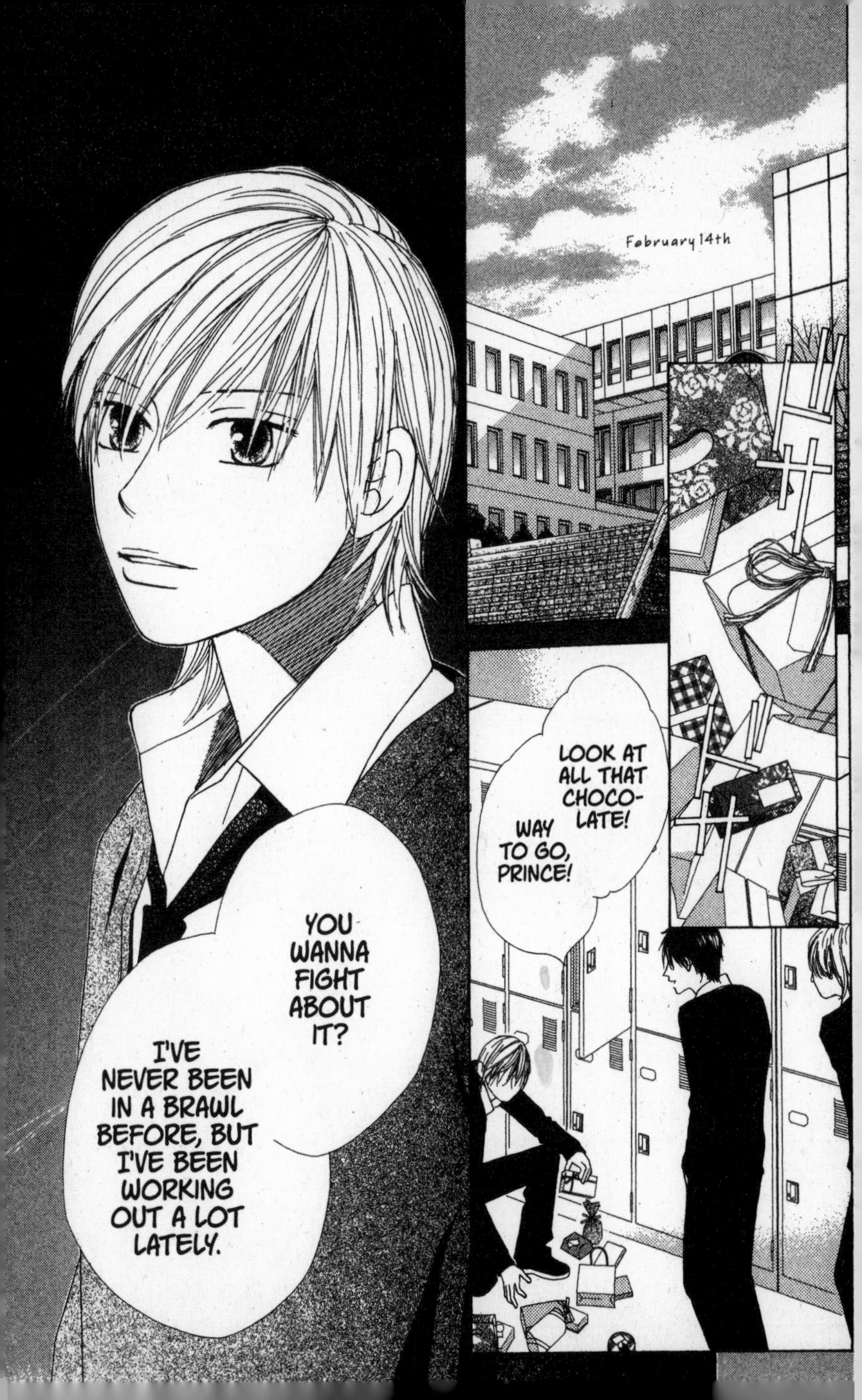
February 14th
LOOK AT ALL THAT CHOCOLATE!
WAY TO GO, PRINCE!
YOU WANNA FIGHT ABOUT IT?
I'VE NEVER BEEN IN A BRAWL BEFORE, BUT I'VE BEEN WORKING OUT A LOT LATELY.

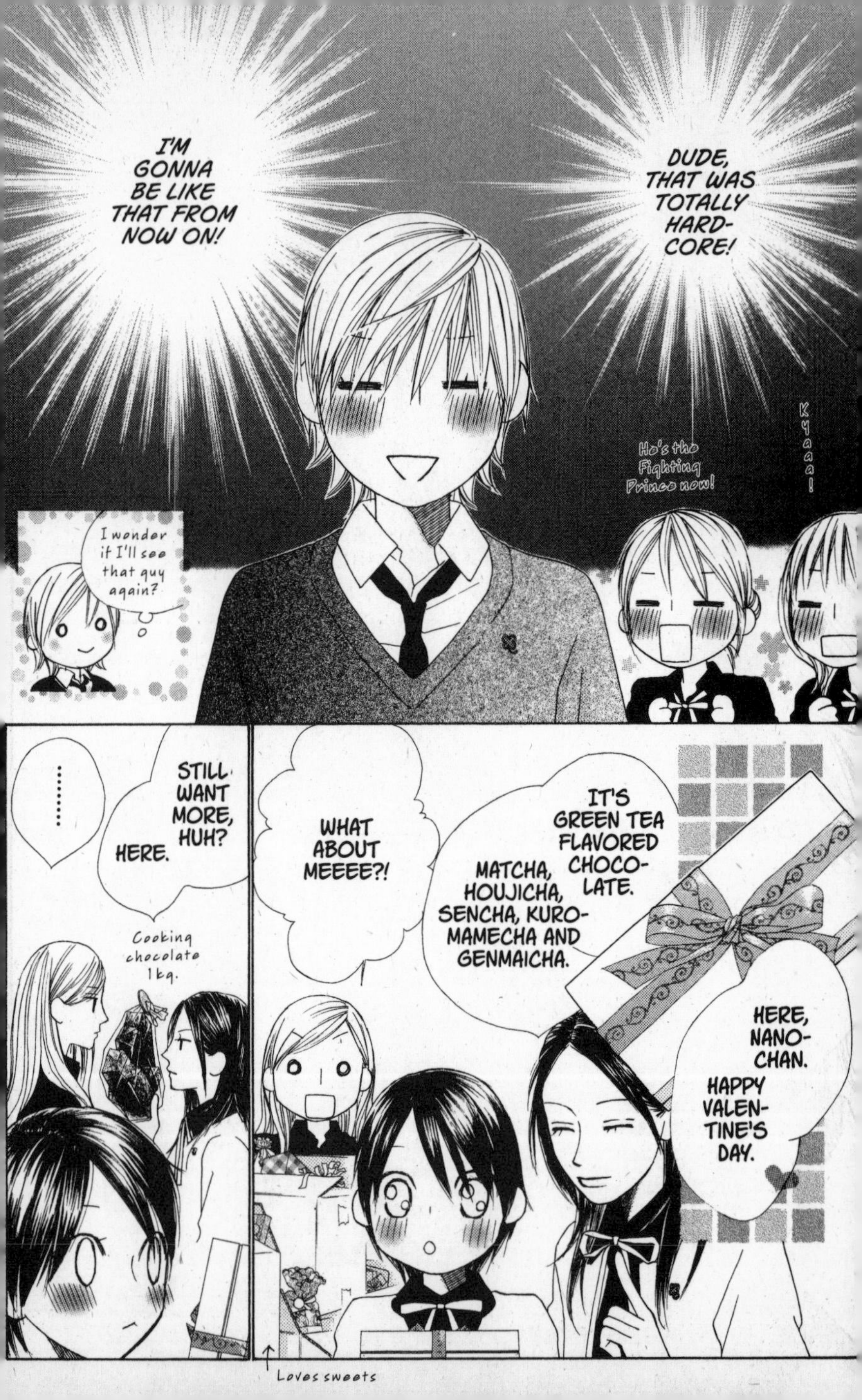
DUDE, THAT WAS TOTALLY HARD-CORE!
I'M GONNA BE LIKE THAT FROM NOW ON!
Kyaaa!
He's the Fighting Prince now!
I wonder if I'll see that guy again?
HERE, NANO-CHAN. HAPPY VALENTINE'S DAY.
IT'S GREEN TEA FLAVORED CHOCOLATE.
MATCHA, HOUJICHA, SENCHA, KURO-MAMECHA AND GENMAICHA.
WHAT ABOUT MEEEE?!
Loves sweets
STILL WANT MORE, HUH?
HERE.
......
Cooking chocolate 1kg.

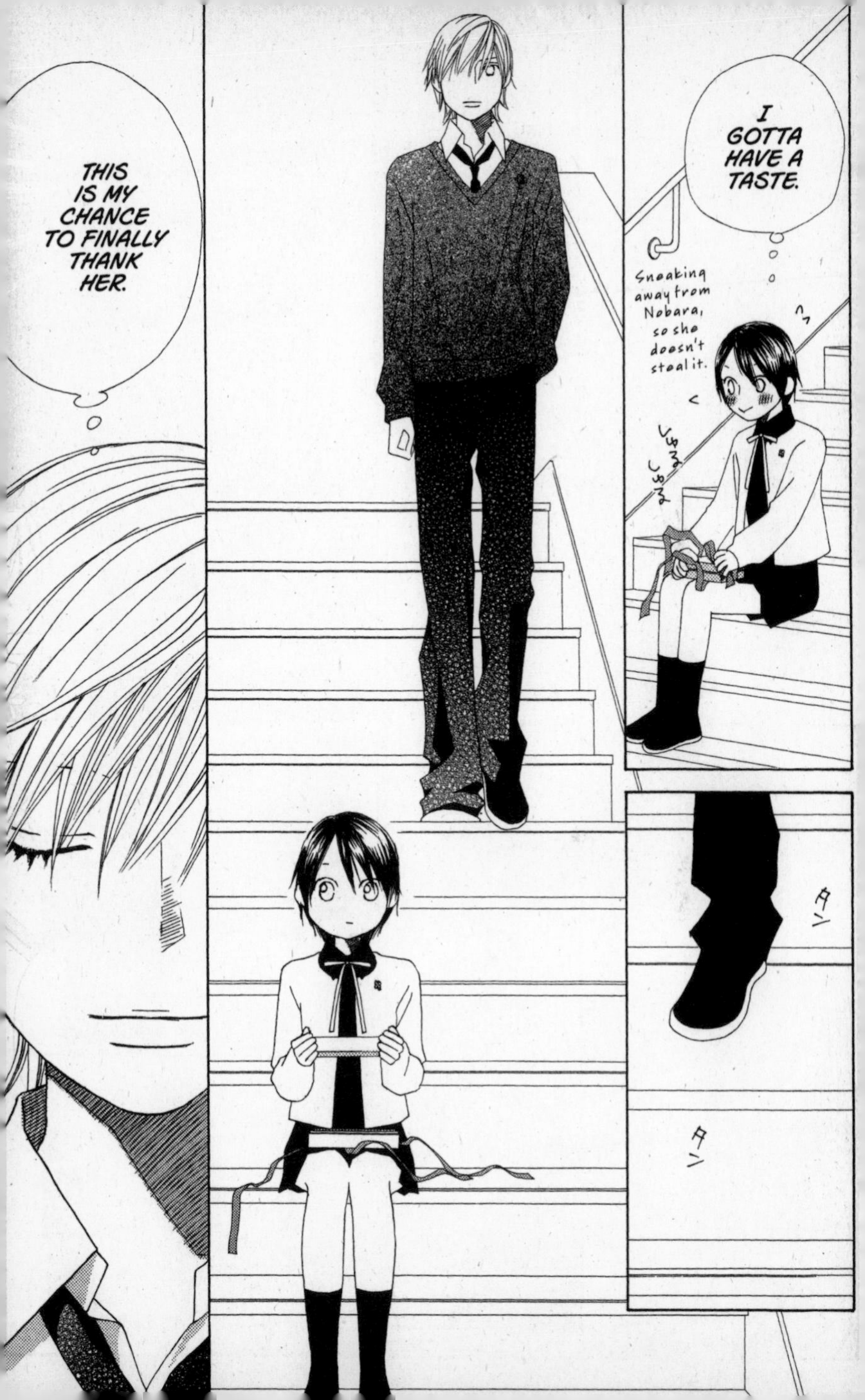
I GOTTA HAVE A TASTE.
Sneaking away from Nobara, so she doesn't steal it.
しゅる しゅる
タン
タン
THIS IS MY CHANCE TO FINALLY THANK HER.

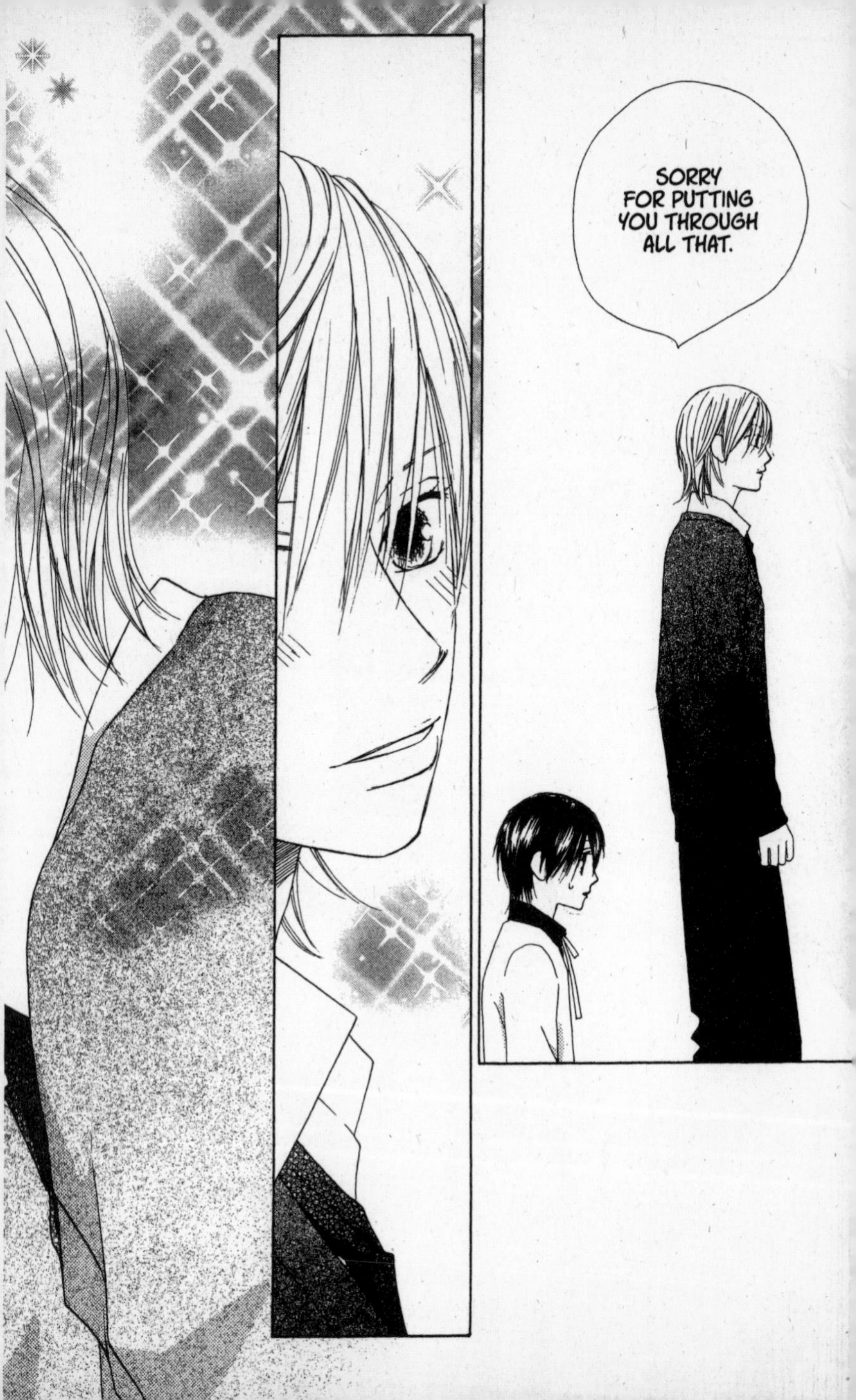
SORRY FOR PUTTING YOU THROUGH ALL THAT.

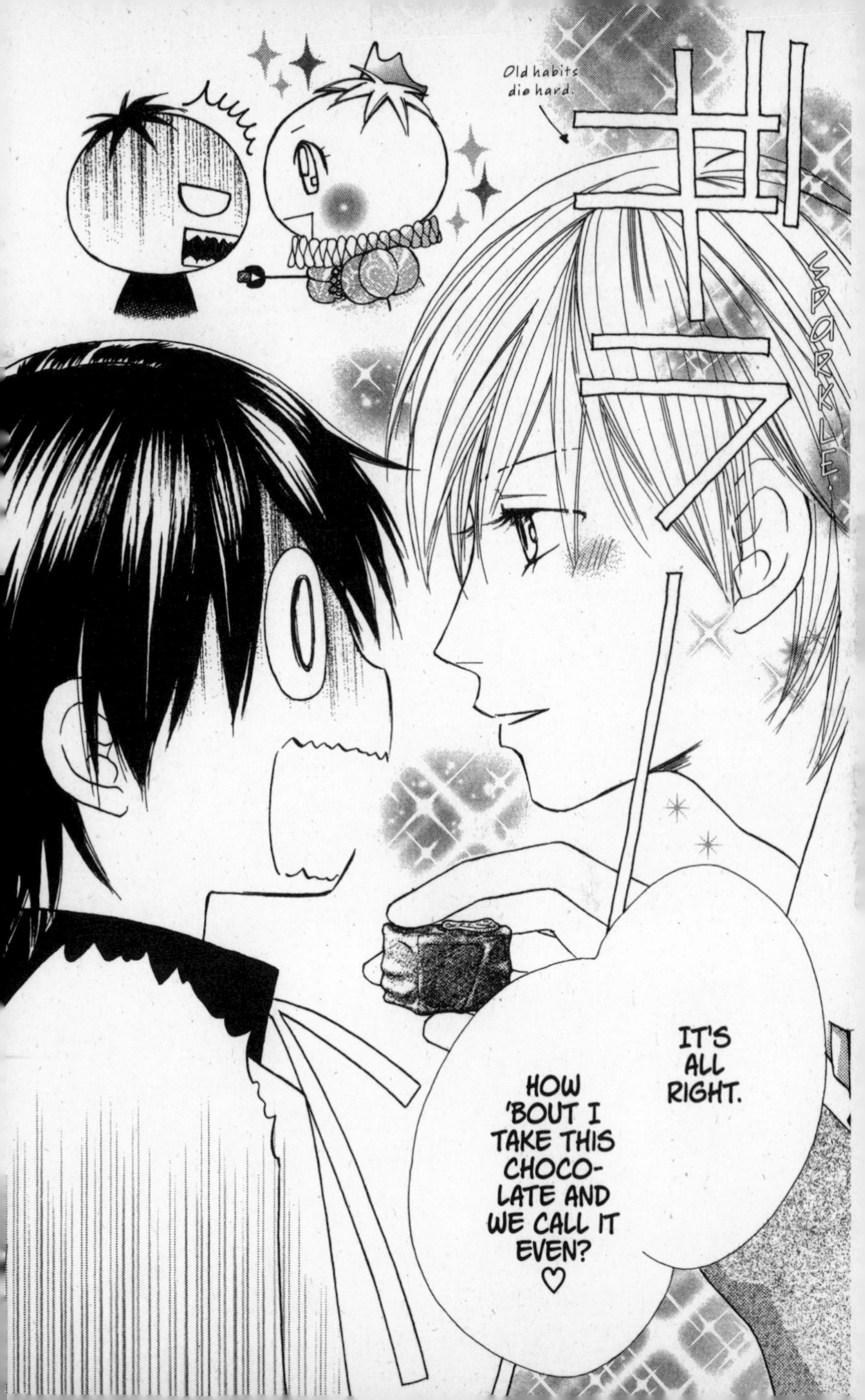
Old habits die hard.
キラ
SPARKLE
IT'S ALL RIGHT.
HOW 'BOUT I TAKE THIS CHOCO-LATE AND WE CALL IT EVEN? ♡

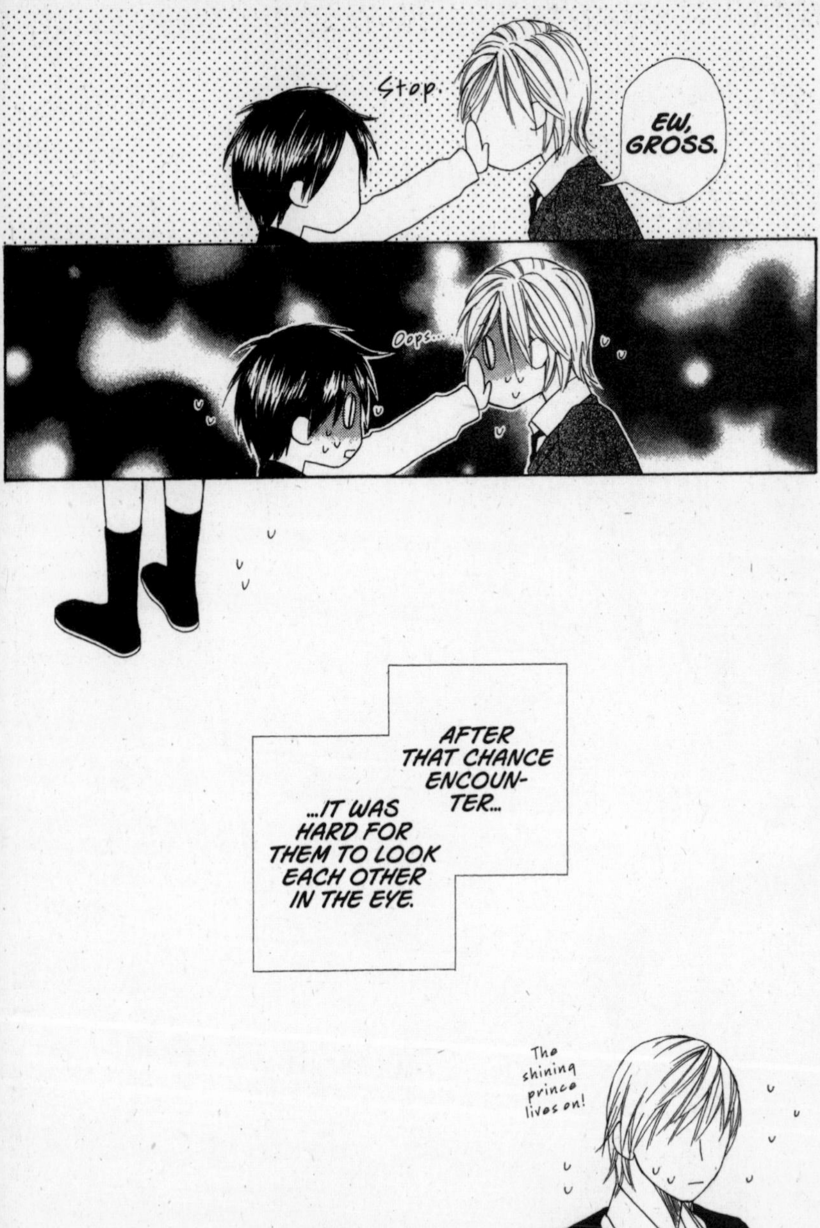
EW, GROSS.
Stop.
Oops...
AFTER THAT CHANCE ENCOUNTER...
...IT WAS HARD FOR THEM TO LOOK EACH OTHER IN THE EYE.
The shining prince lives on!

STEP 3 / END

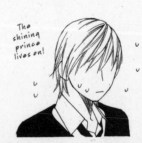

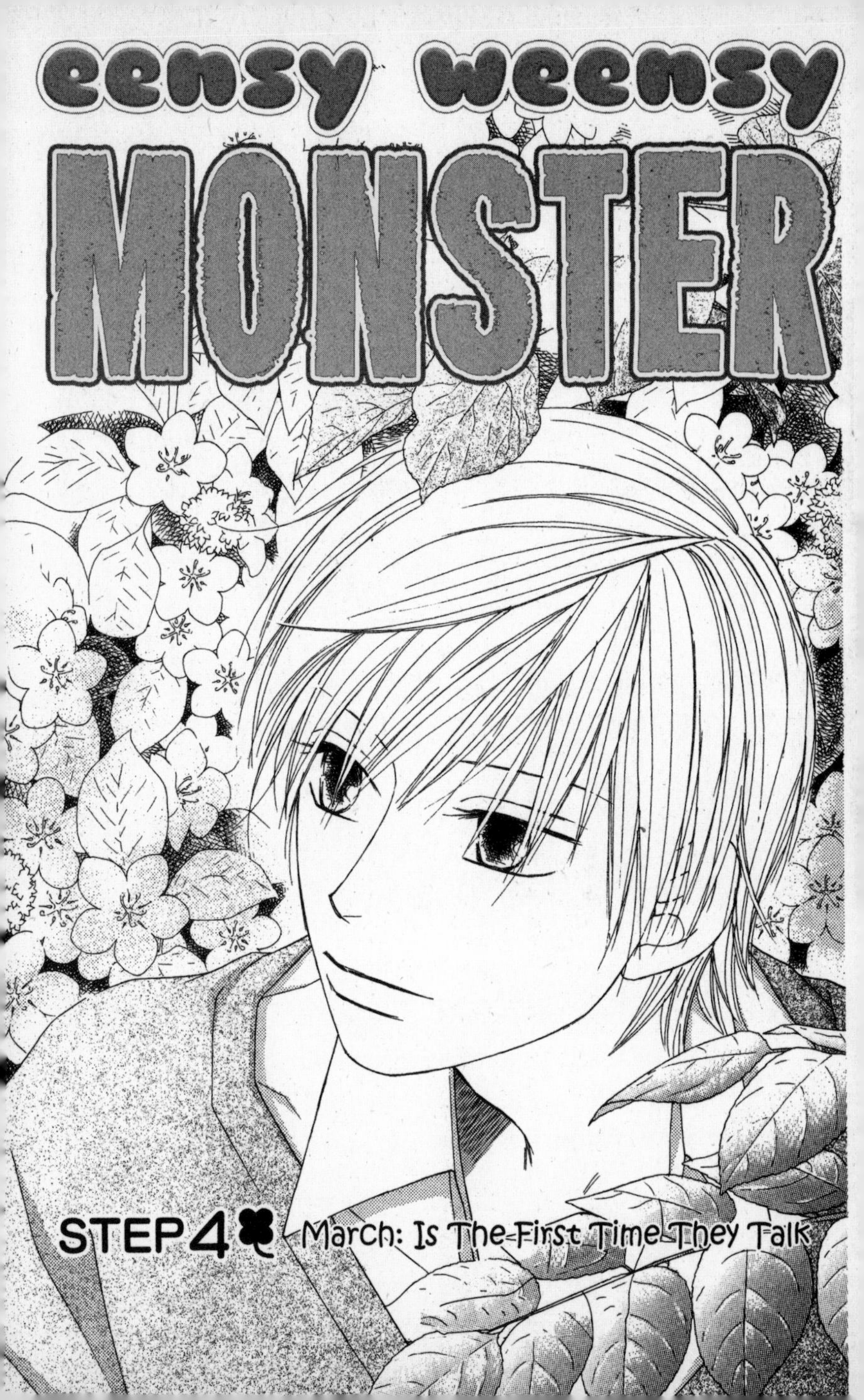
eensy weensy
MONSTER
STEP 4
March: Is The First Time They Talk

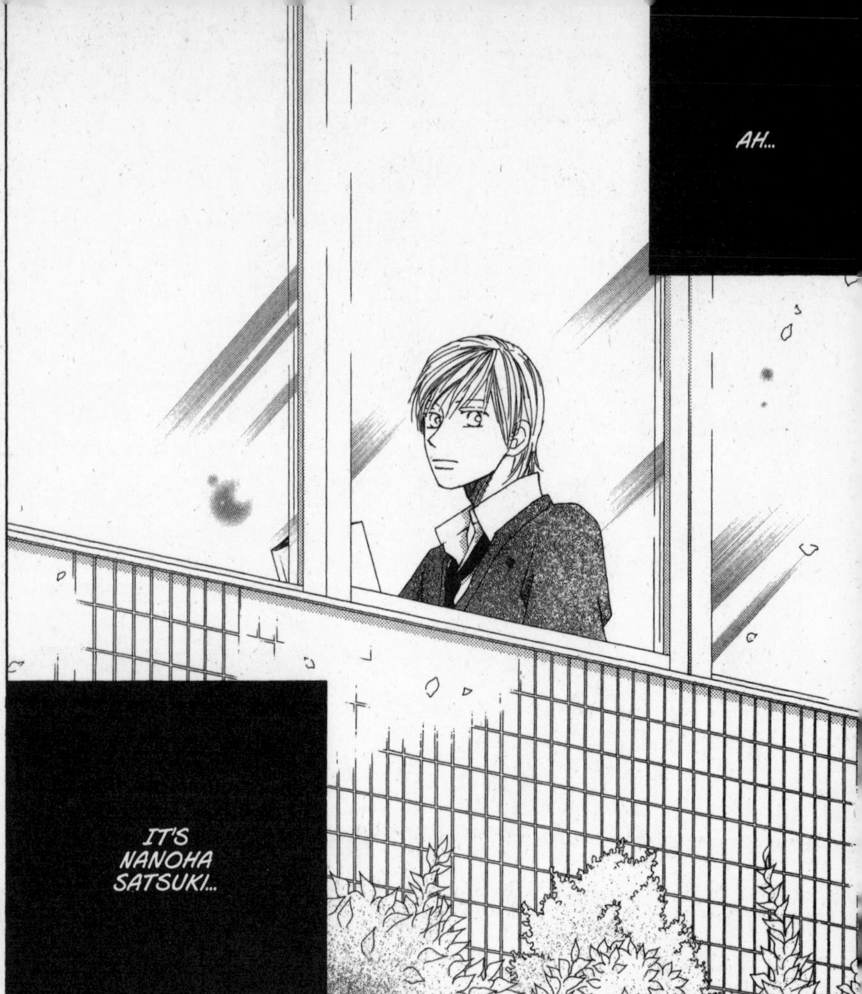
AH...
IT'S NANOHA SATSUKI...

Sumo

I really like Japanese history and culture, so naturally I'm a fan of kabuki and judo. It was only a matter of time before I got into sumo as well.

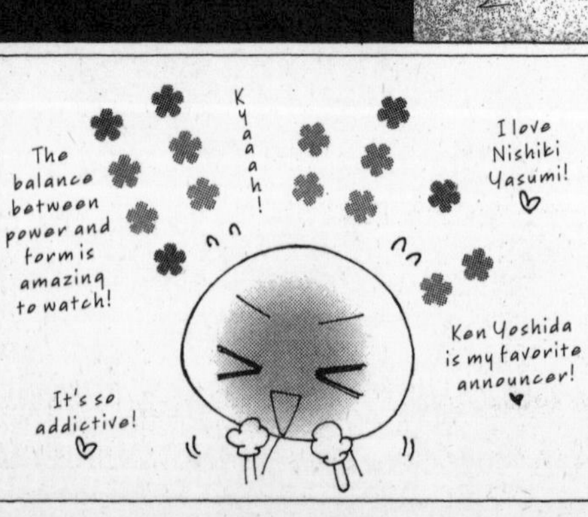
I love Nishiki Yasumi!
Ken Yoshida is my favorite announcer!
Kyaaah!
The balance between power and form is amazing to watch!
It's so addictive!

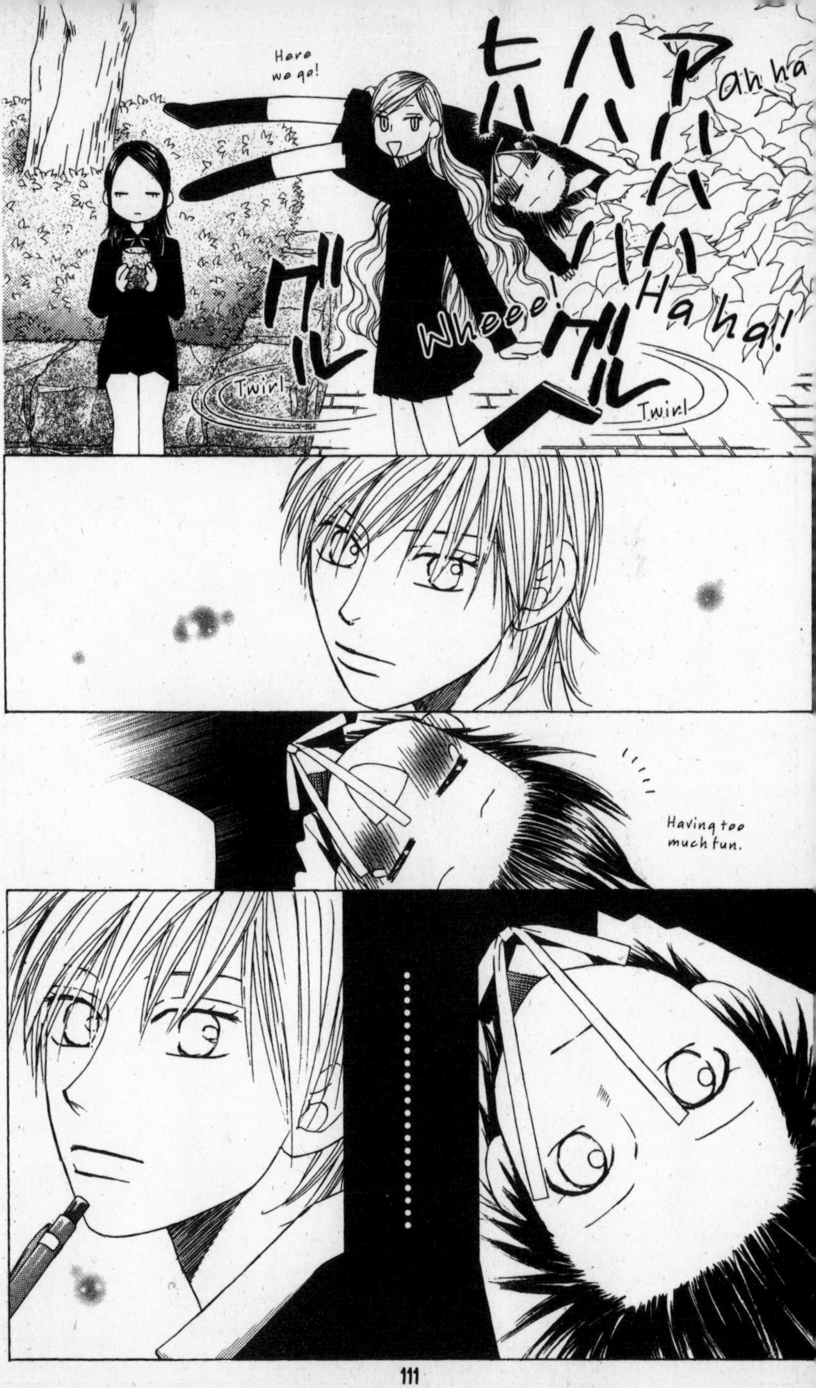
Ah ha
Ha ha!
Wheeee!
Here we go!
Twirl
Twirl
Having too much fun.

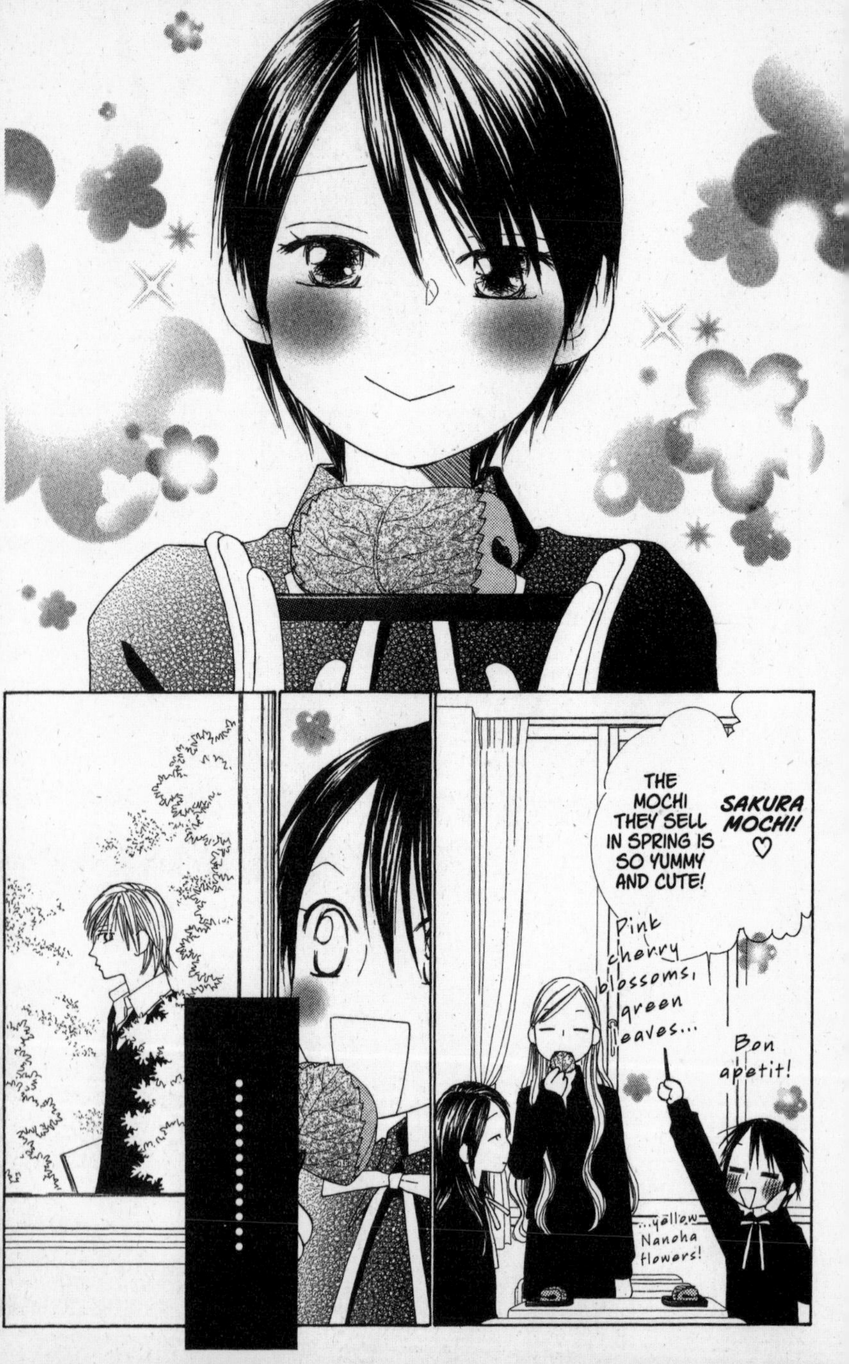
SAKURA MOCHI! ♡
THE MOCHI THEY SELL IN SPRING IS SO YUMMY AND CUTE!
Pink cherry blossoms, green leaves...
...yellow Nanoha flowers!
Bon apetit!
....

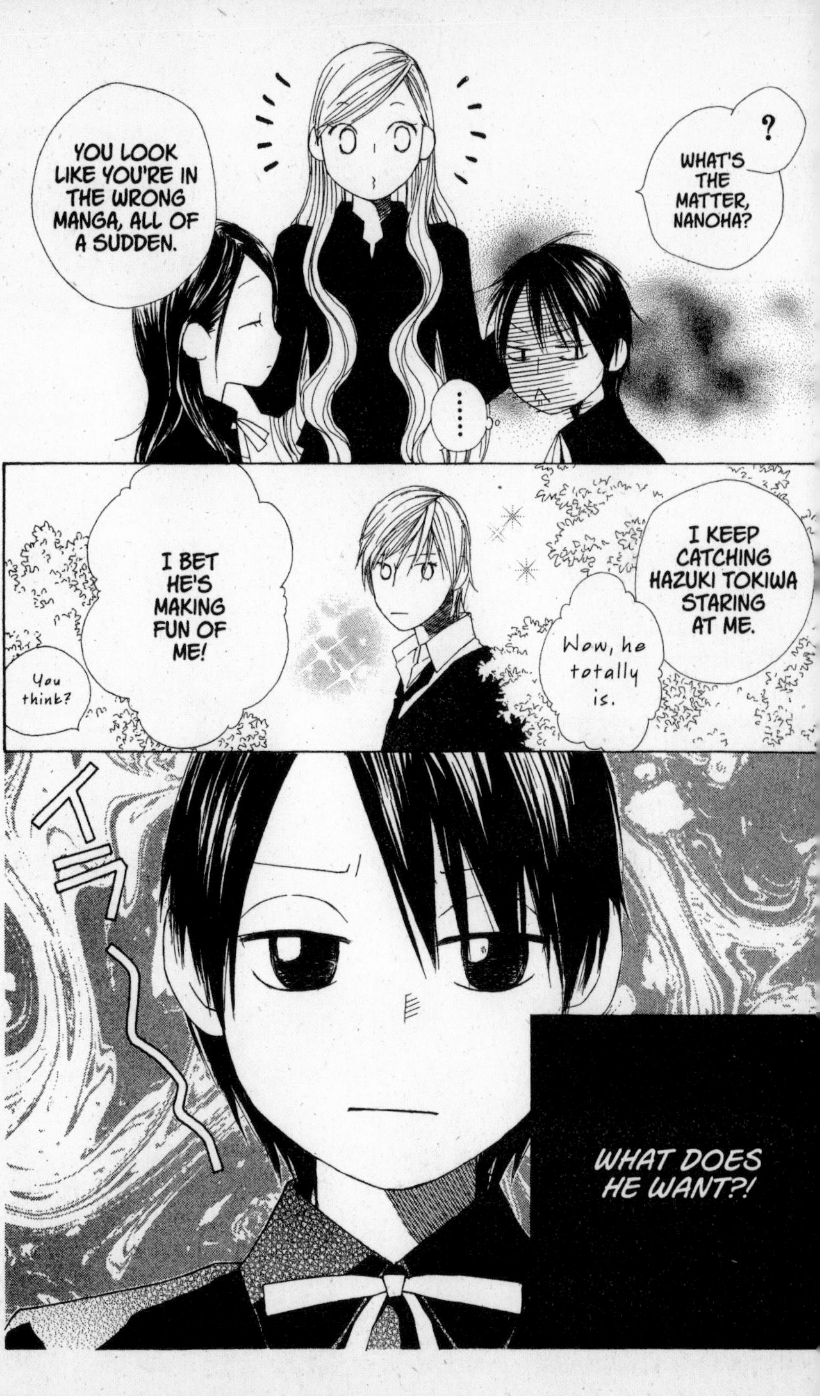
?
WHAT'S THE MATTER, NANOHA?
...
YOU LOOK LIKE YOU'RE IN THE WRONG MANGA, ALL OF A SUDDEN.
I KEEP CATCHING HAZUKI TOKIWA STARING AT ME.
Wow, he totally is.
I BET HE'S MAKING FUN OF ME!
You think?
イラ
WHAT DOES HE WANT?!

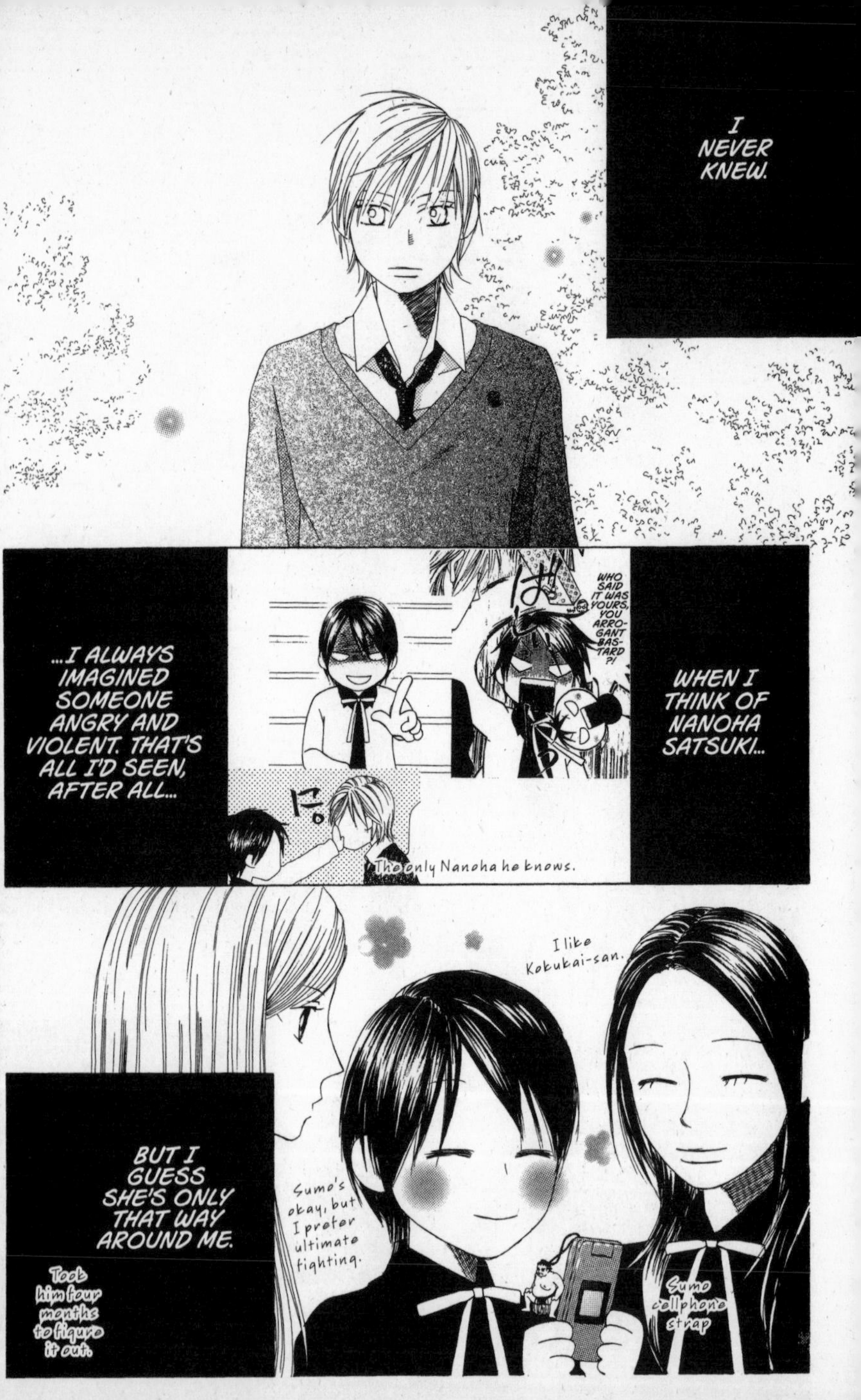
I NEVER KNEW.
WHEN I THINK OF NANOHA SATSUKI...
WHO SAID IT WAS YOURS, YOU ARROGANT BASTARD?!
The only Nanoha he knows.
...I ALWAYS IMAGINED SOMEONE ANGRY AND VIOLENT. THAT'S ALL I'D SEEN, AFTER ALL...
I like Kokukai-san.
Sumo cellphone strap
Sumo's okay, but I prefer ultimate fighting.
BUT I GUESS SHE'S ONLY THAT WAY AROUND ME.
Took him four months to figure it out.

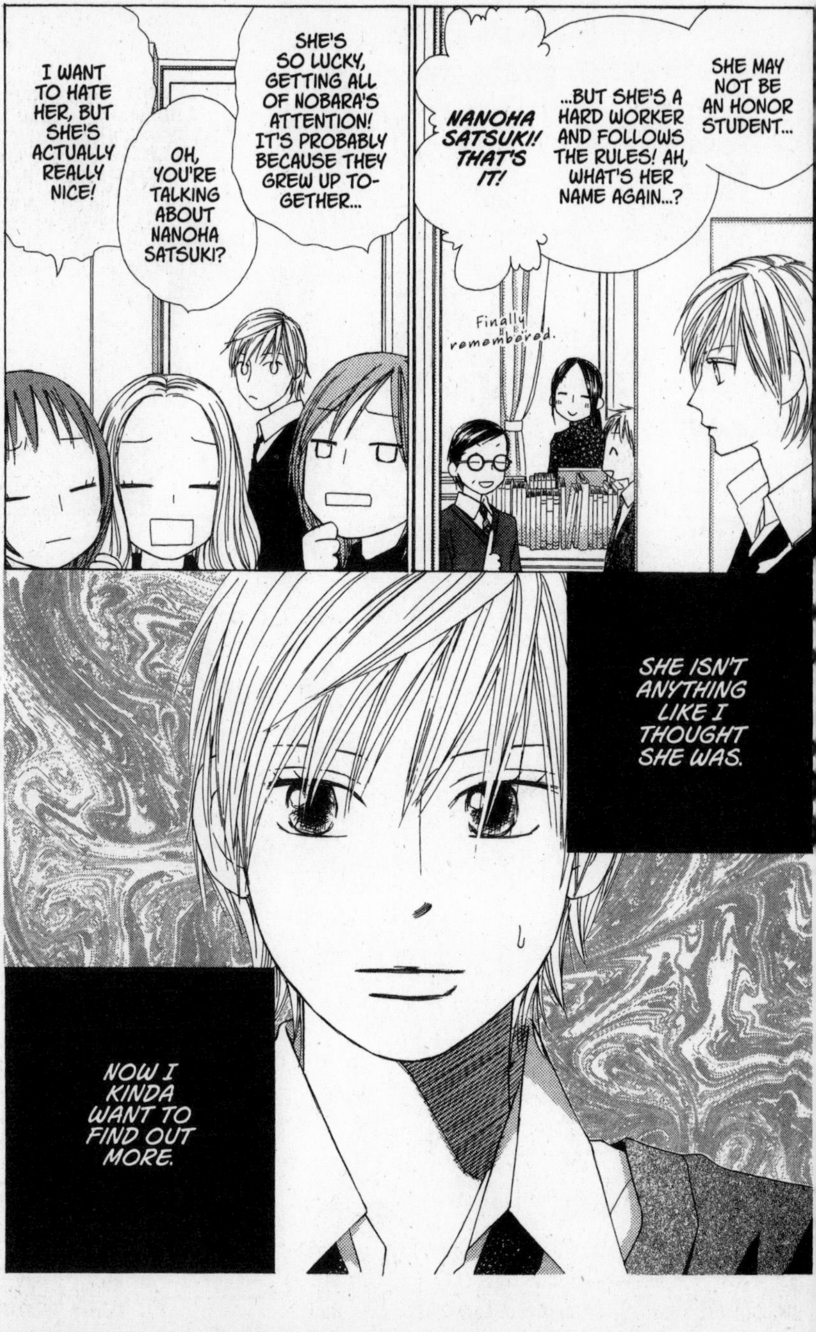
SHE MAY NOT BE AN HONOR STUDENT...
...BUT SHE'S A HARD WORKER AND FOLLOWS THE RULES! AH, WHAT'S HER NAME AGAIN...?
NANOHA SATSUKI!! THAT'S IT!
Finally remembered.
SHE'S SO LUCKY, GETTING ALL OF NOBARA'S ATTENTION! IT'S PROBABLY BECAUSE THEY GREW UP TO-GETHER...
I WANT TO HATE HER, BUT SHE'S ACTUALLY REALLY NICE!
OH, YOU'RE TALKING ABOUT NANOHA SATSUKI?
SHE ISN'T ANYTHING LIKE I THOUGHT SHE WAS.
NOW I KINDA WANT TO FIND OUT MORE.

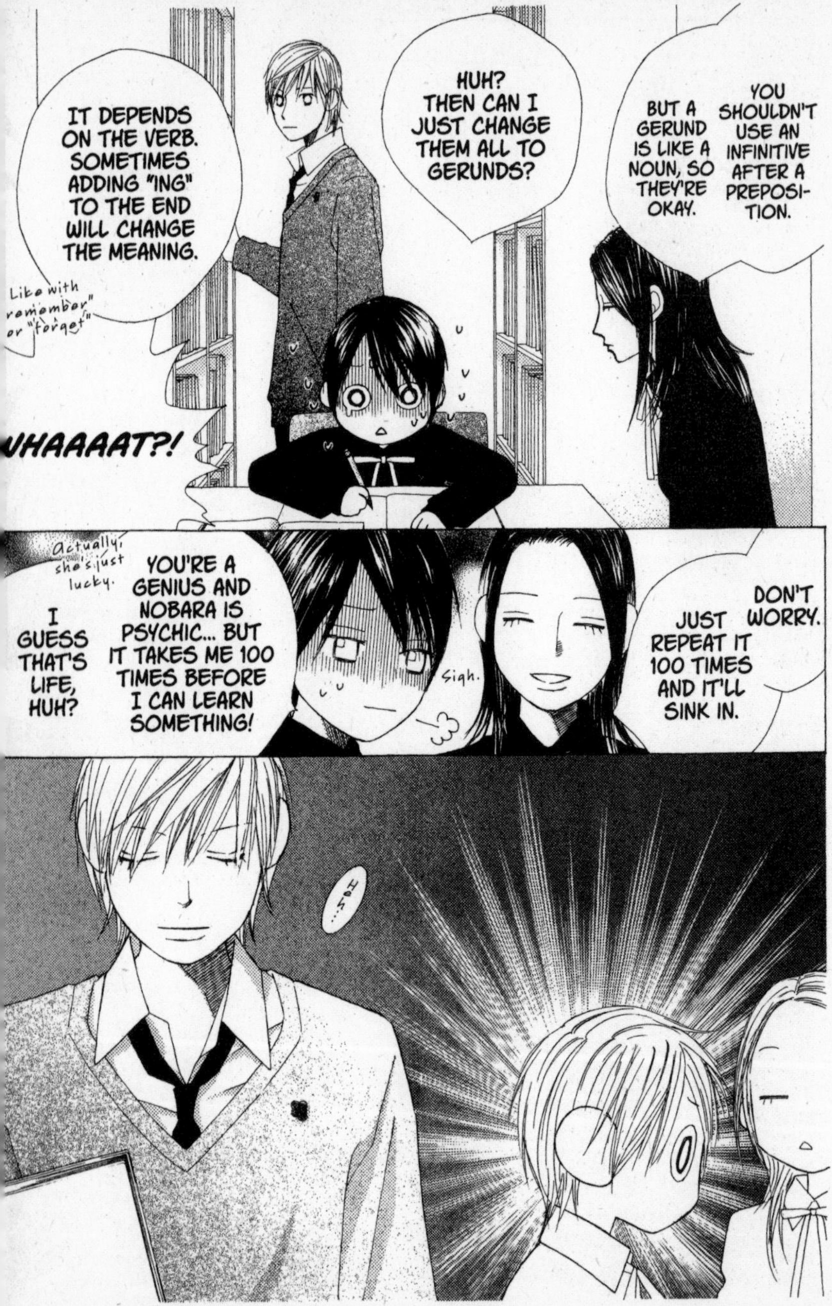
YOU SHOULDN'T USE AN INFINITIVE AFTER A PREPOSITION.
BUT A GERUND IS LIKE A NOUN, SO THEY'RE OKAY.
HUH? THEN CAN I JUST CHANGE THEM ALL TO GERUNDS?
IT DEPENDS ON THE VERB. SOMETIMES ADDING "ING" TO THE END WILL CHANGE THE MEANING.
Like with "remember" or "forget"
WHAAAAT?!
DON'T WORRY.
JUST REPEAT IT 100 TIMES AND IT'LL SINK IN.
Sigh.
YOU'RE A GENIUS AND NOBARA IS PSYCHIC... BUT IT TAKES ME 100 TIMES BEFORE I CAN LEARN SOMETHING!
Actually, she's just lucky.
I GUESS THAT'S LIFE, HUH?
Heh...

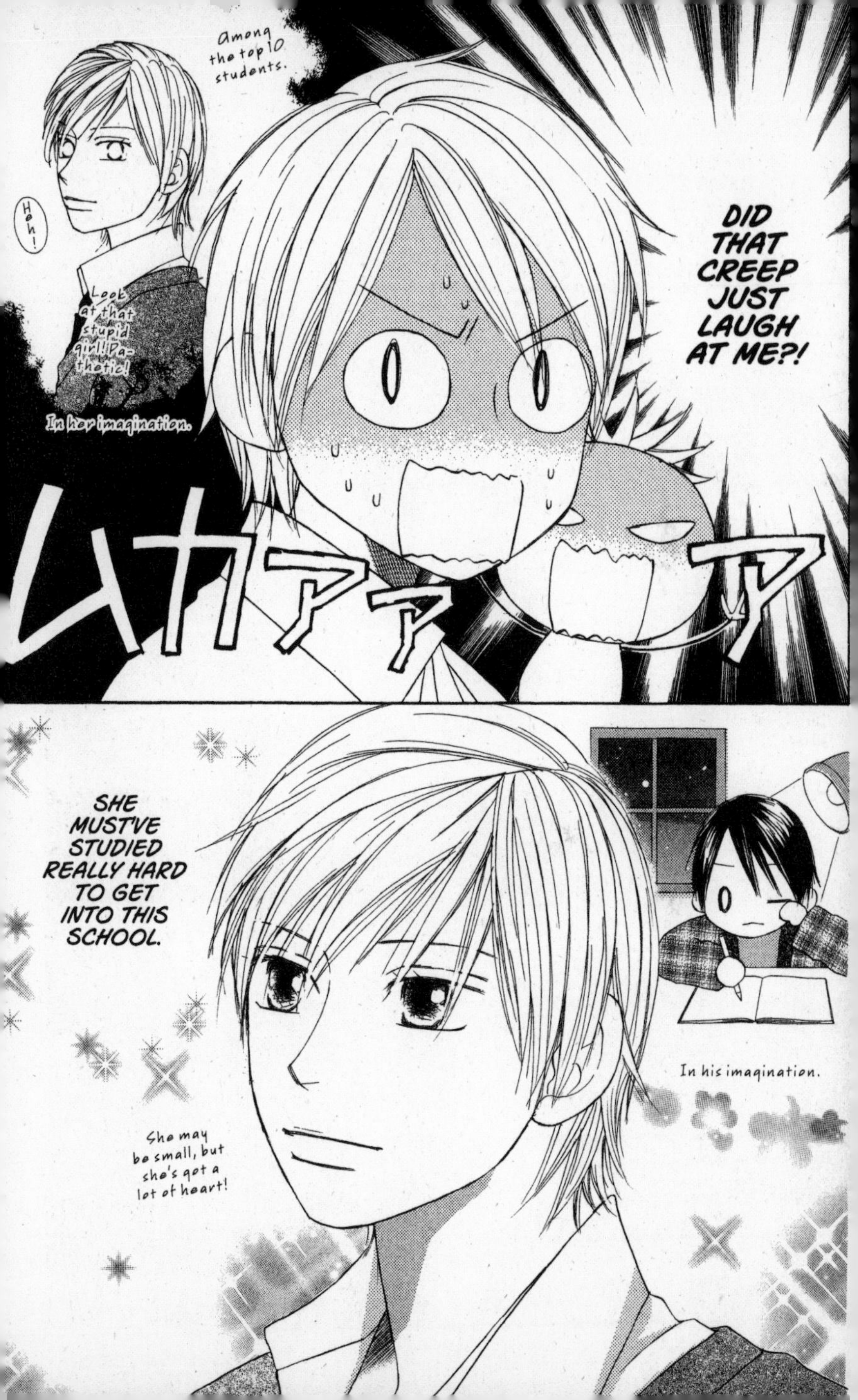
DID THAT CREEP JUST LAUGH AT ME?!
Among the top 10 students.
Heh!
Look at that stupid girl! Pa-thetic!
In her imagination.
ムカァァァ
In his imagination.
SHE MUST'VE STUDIED REALLY HARD TO GET INTO THIS SCHOOL.
She may be small, but she's got a lot of heart!

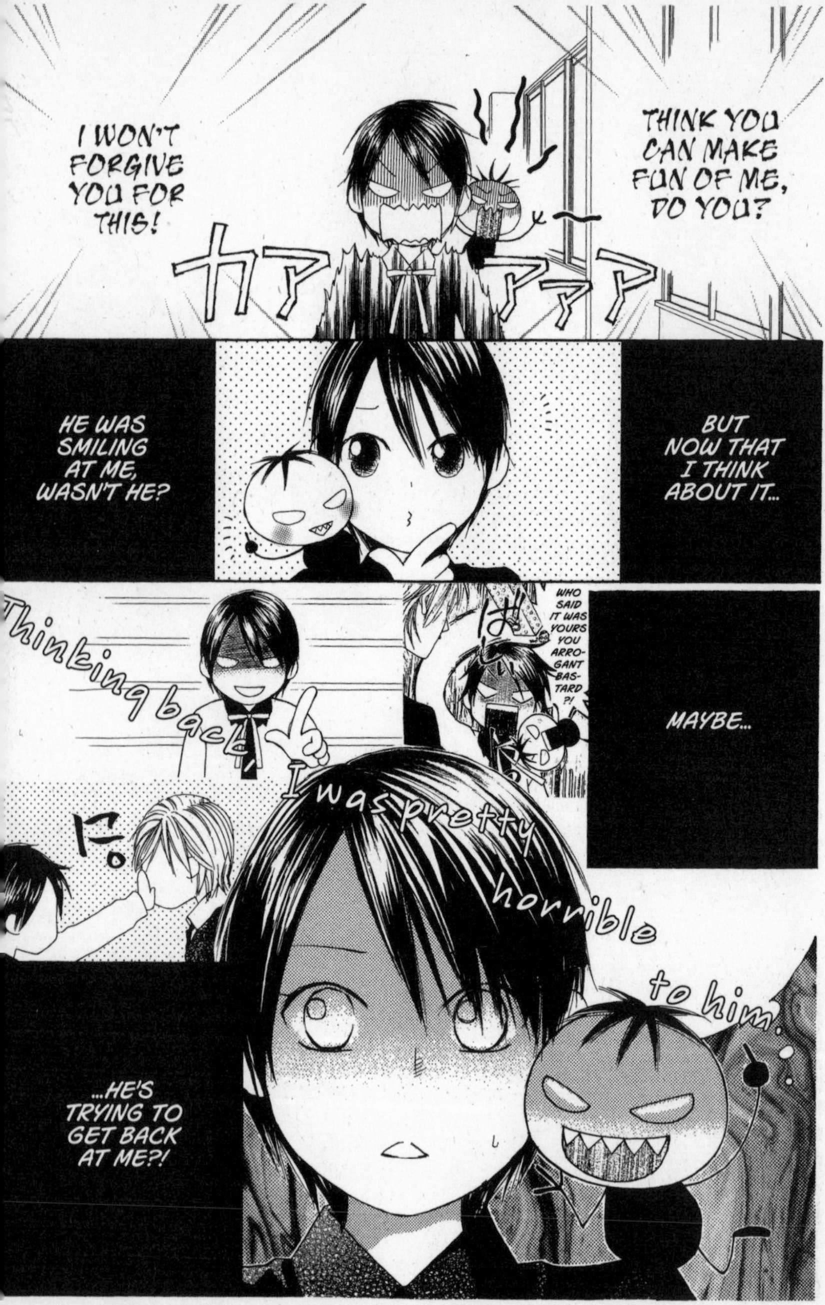
THINK YOU CAN MAKE FUN OF ME, DO YOU?
I WON'T FORGIVE YOU FOR THIS!
カァァァァ
BUT NOW THAT I THINK ABOUT IT...
HE WAS SMILING AT ME, WASN'T HE?
MAYBE...
WHO SAID IT WAS YOURS YOU ARROGANT BASTARD?!
は
Thinking back, I was pretty horrible to him.
に
...HE'S TRYING TO GET BACK AT ME?!

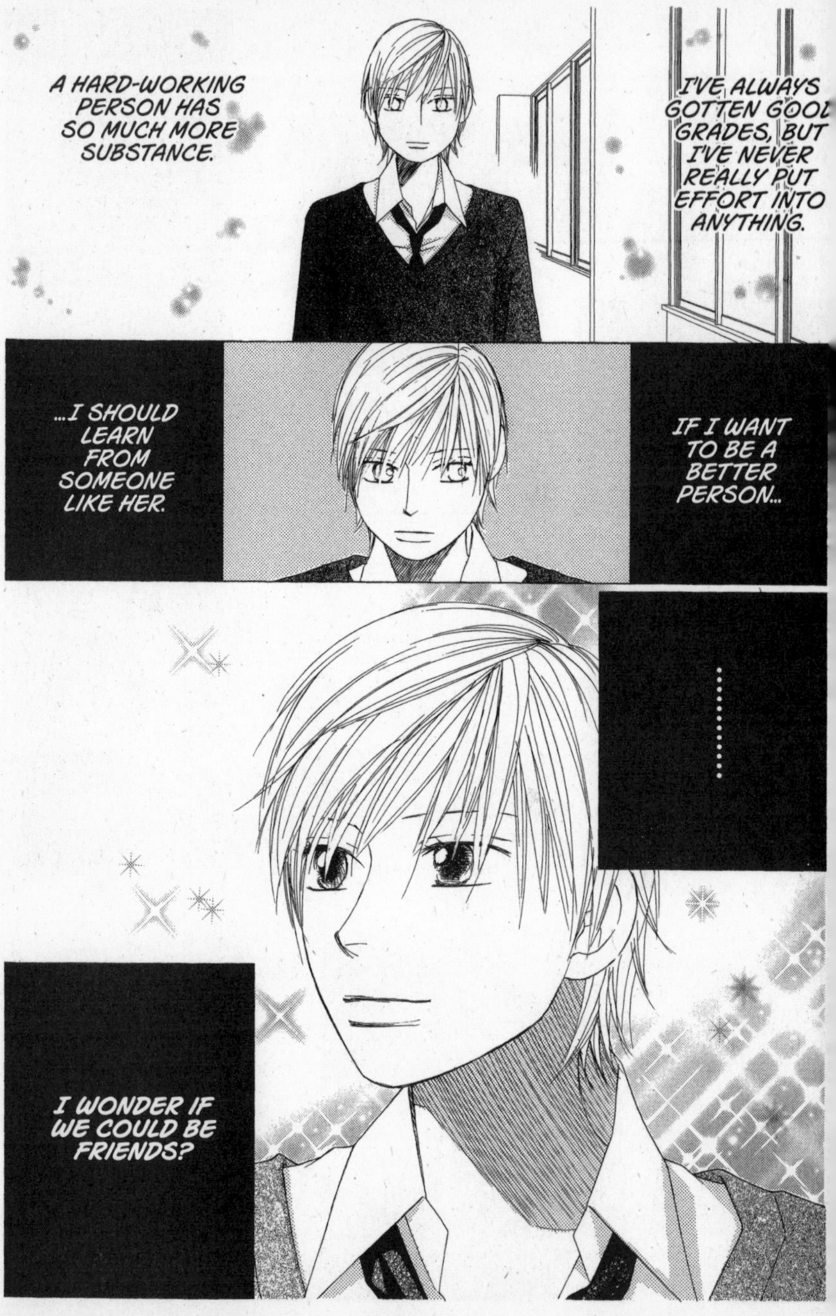
I'VE ALWAYS GOTTEN GOOD GRADES, BUT I'VE NEVER REALLY PUT EFFORT INTO ANYTHING.
A HARD-WORKING PERSON HAS SO MUCH MORE SUBSTANCE.
IF I WANT TO BE A BETTER PERSON...
...I SHOULD LEARN FROM SOMEONE LIKE HER.
....
I WONDER IF WE COULD BE FRIENDS?

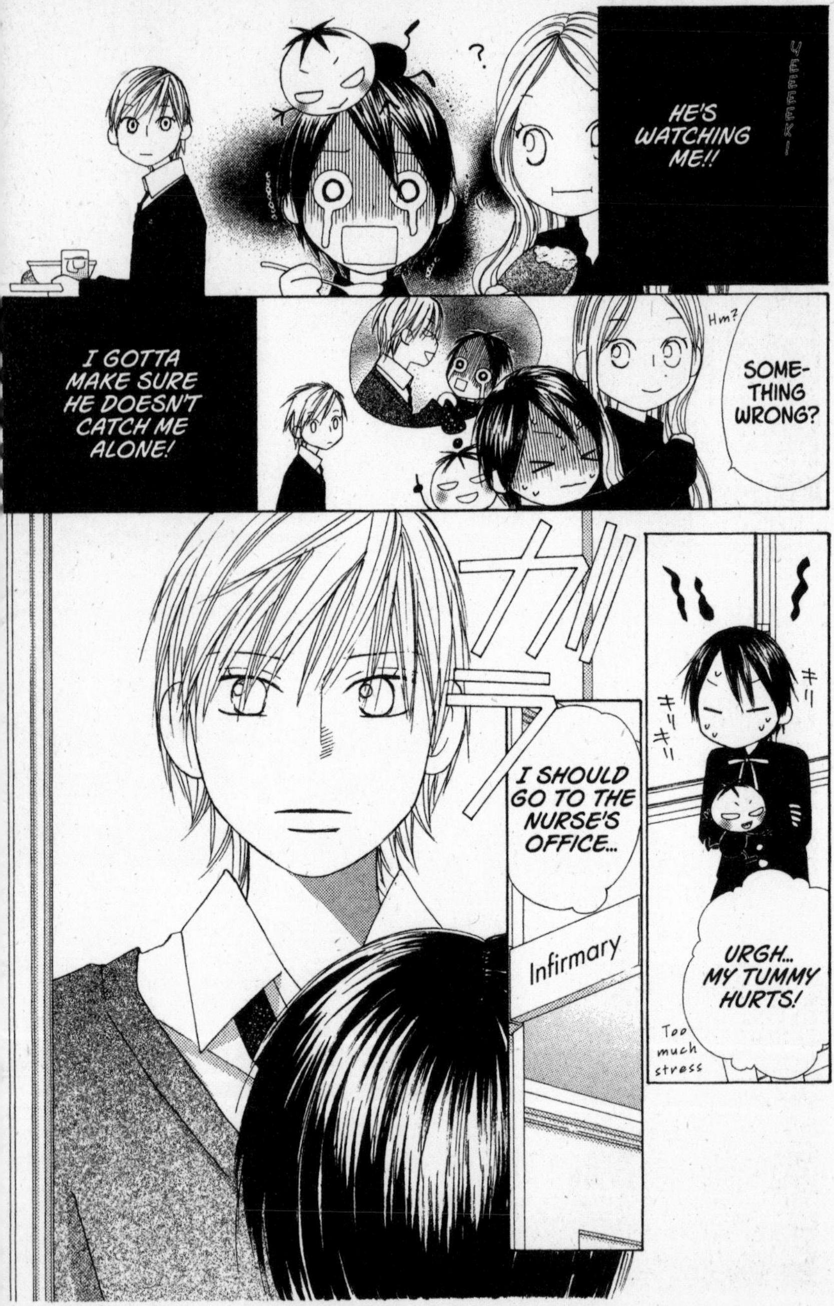
WEEEEEK!
HE'S WATCHING ME!!
Hm?
SOME-THING WRONG?
I GOTTA MAKE SURE HE DOESN'T CATCH ME ALONE!
キリ キリキリ
URGH... MY TUMMY HURTS!
Too much stress
ガラ
I SHOULD GO TO THE NURSE'S OFFICE...
Infirmary

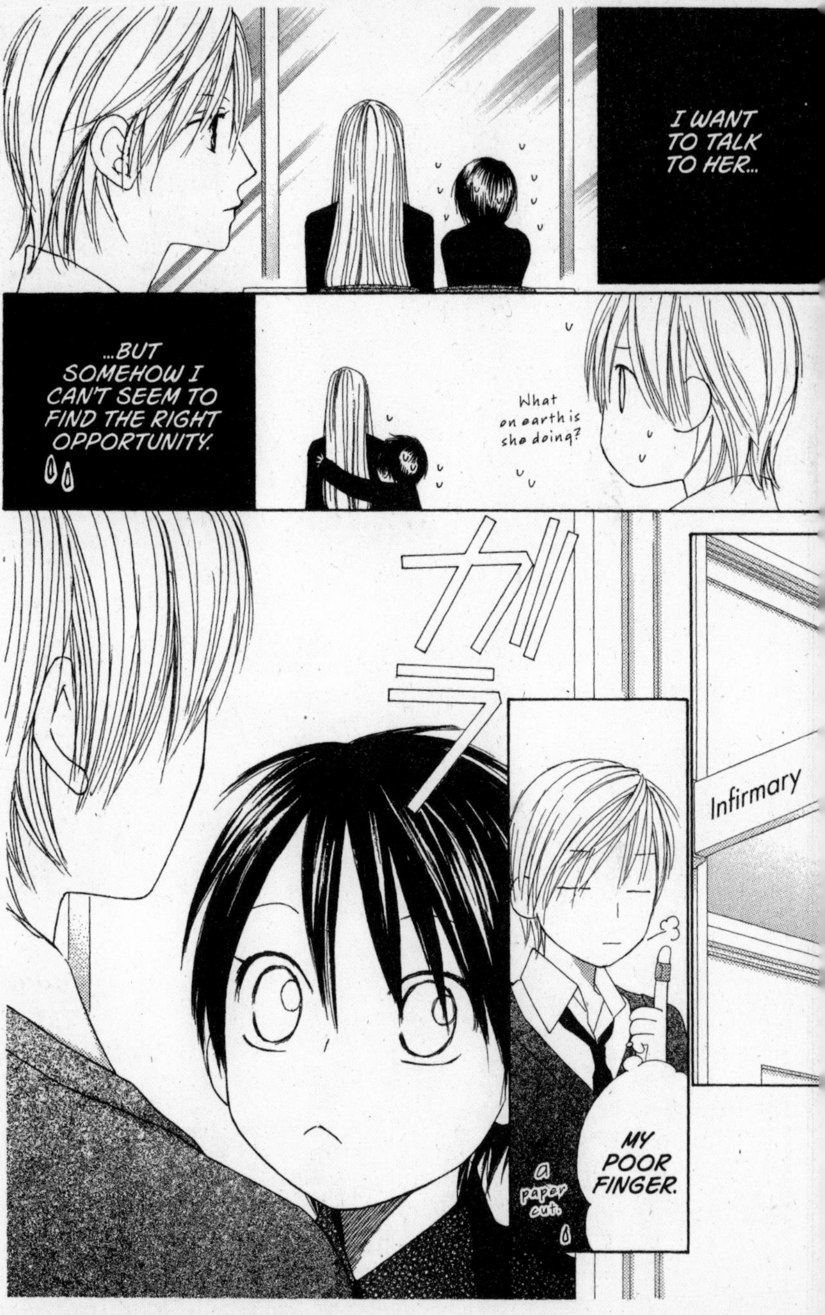
I WANT TO TALK TO HER...
What on earth is she doing?
...BUT SOMEHOW I CAN'T SEEM TO FIND THE RIGHT OPPORTUNITY.
カラ
Infirmary
MY POOR FINGER.
a paper cut.

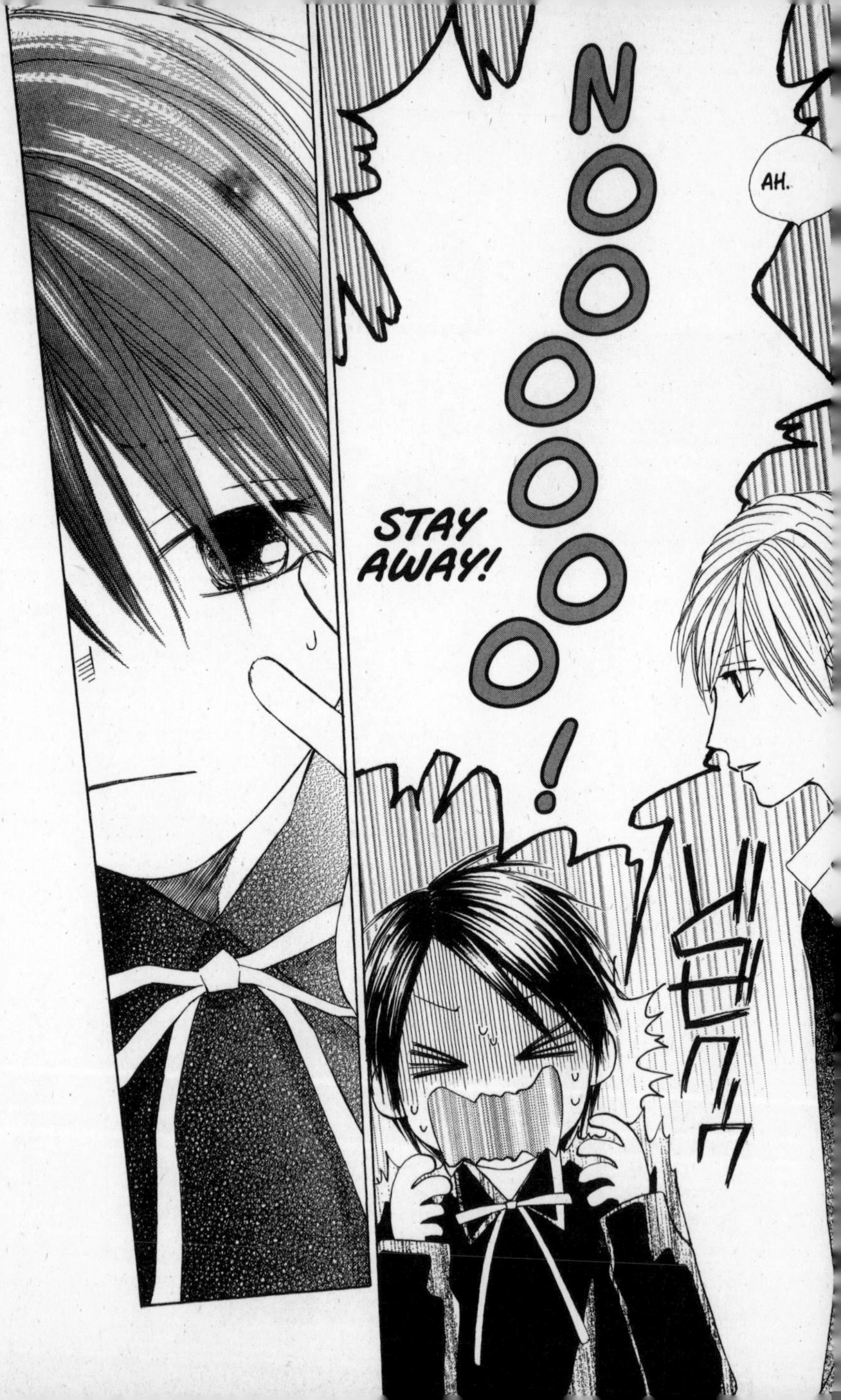
AH.
NOOOOOOOO!
STAY AWAY!

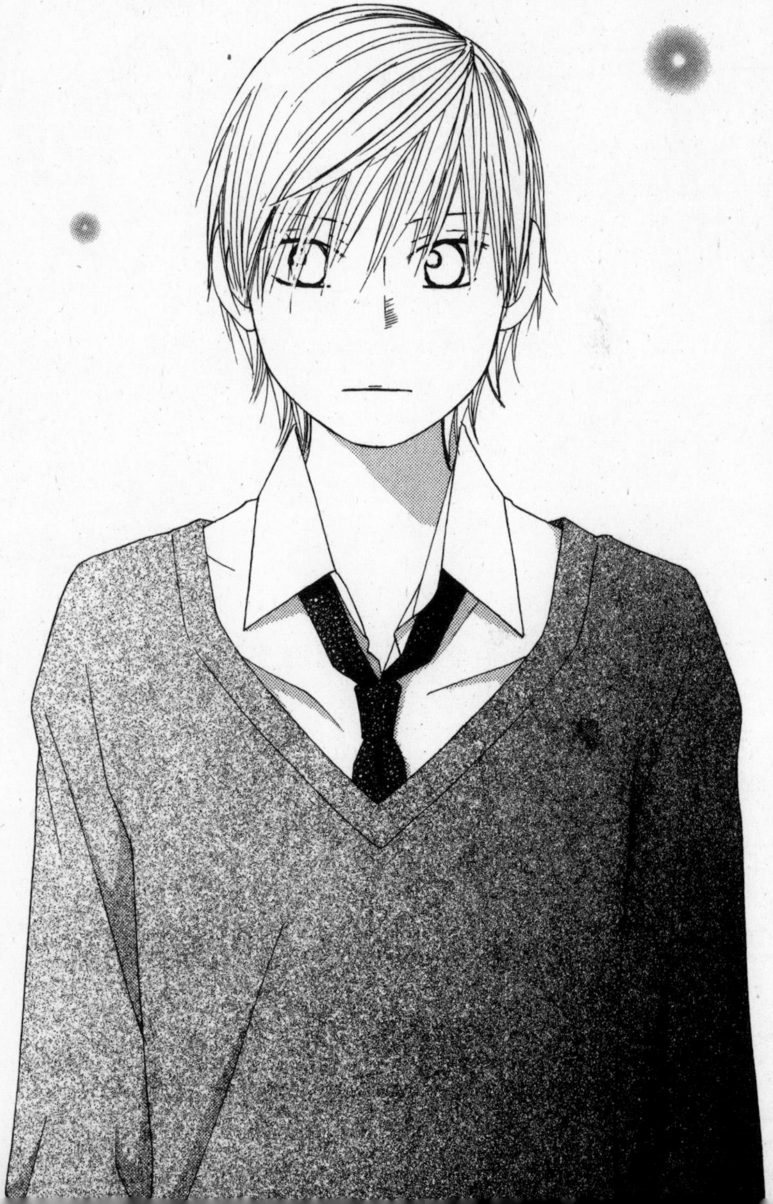

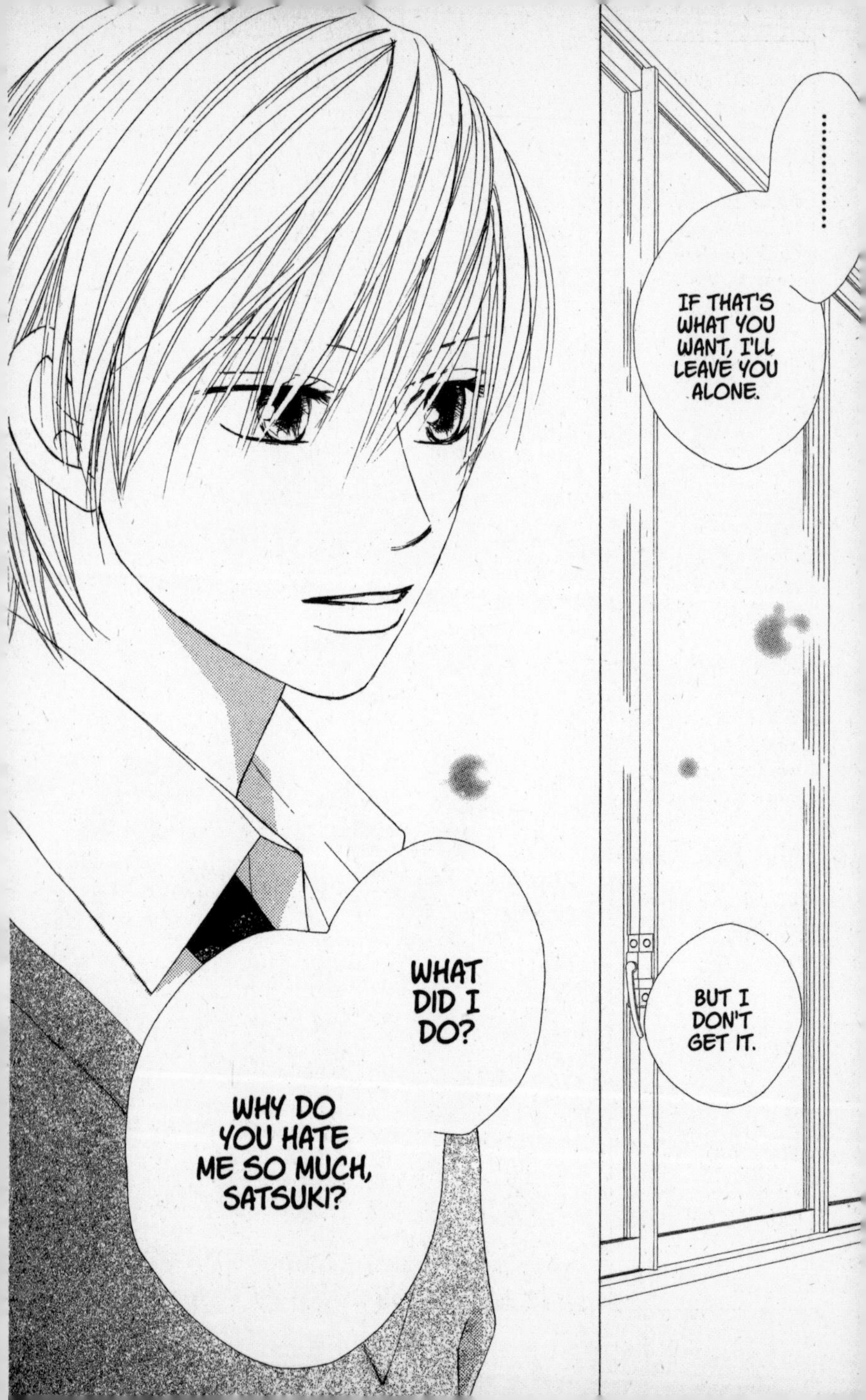
......
IF THAT'S WHAT YOU WANT, I'LL LEAVE YOU ALONE.
BUT I DON'T GET IT.
WHAT DID I DO?
WHY DO YOU HATE ME SO MUCH, SATSUKI?

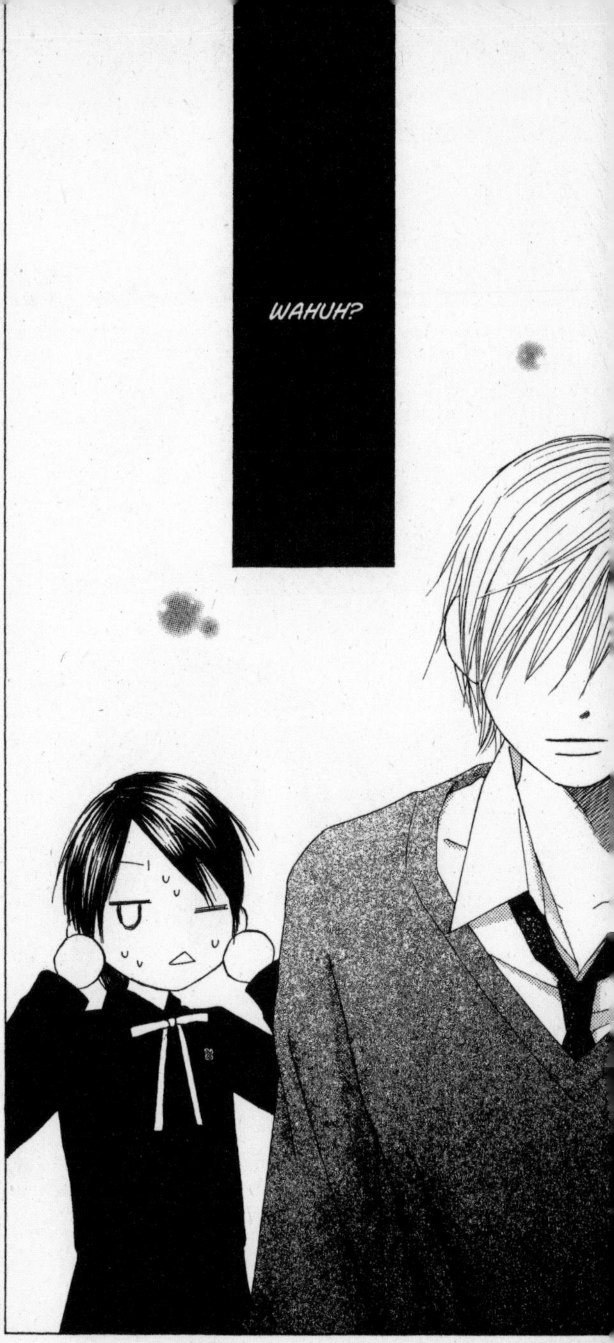
WAHUH?

4

I was trying to eat more to improve my health, but it backfired and I started getting fat.

Over ate

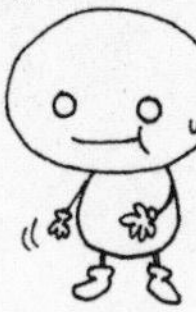

On the upside, I seem to have more energy now, so I'm going to start exercising!

My goal is to swim 100m with the crawl stroke.

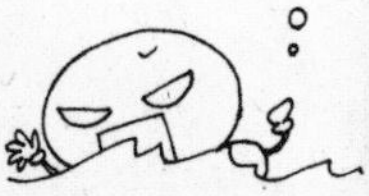

Back in high school, I could swim 75m, but I can only do 25 now...

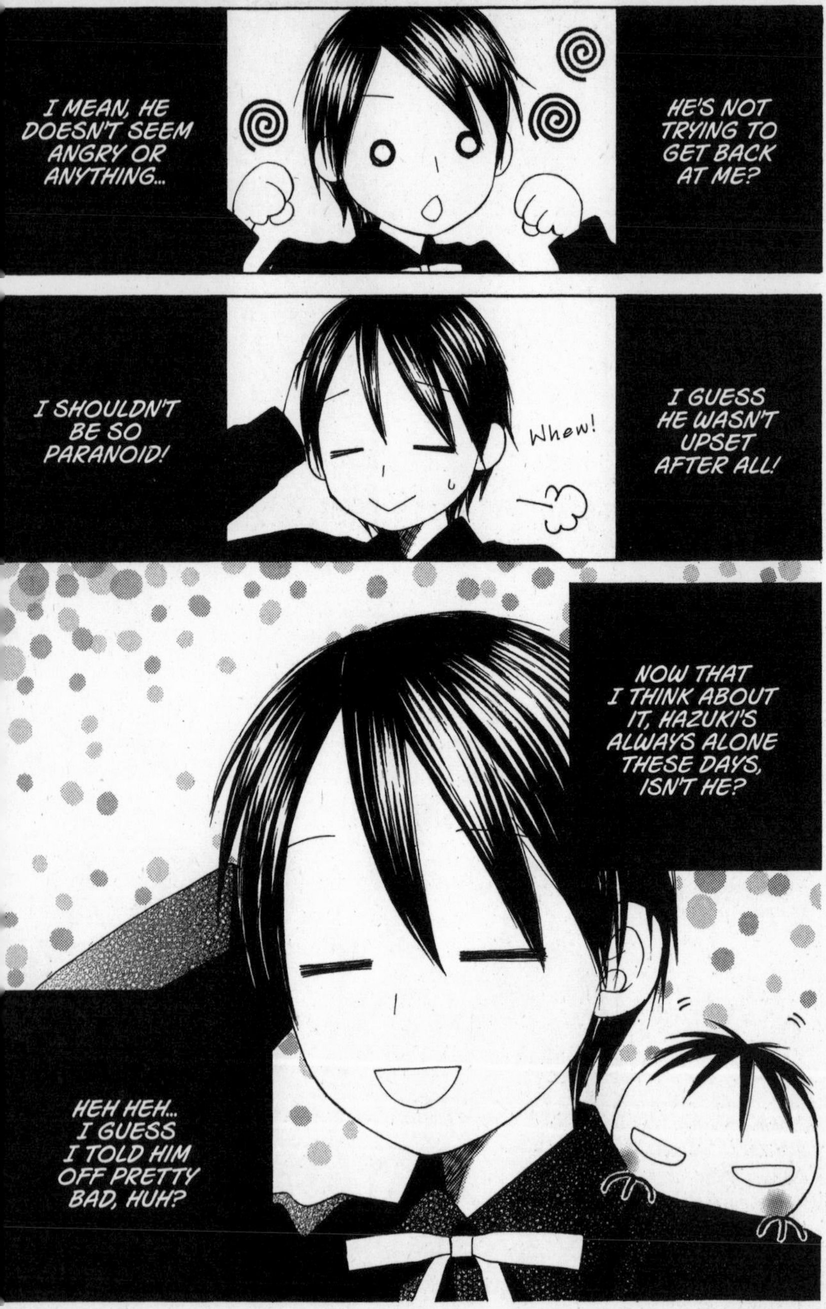
HE'S NOT TRYING TO GET BACK AT ME?
I MEAN, HE DOESN'T SEEM ANGRY OR ANYTHING...
I GUESS HE WASN'T UPSET AFTER ALL!
Whew!
I SHOULDN'T BE SO PARANOID!
NOW THAT I THINK ABOUT IT, HAZUKI'S ALWAYS ALONE THESE DAYS, ISN'T HE?
HEH HEH... I GUESS I TOLD HIM OFF PRETTY BAD, HUH?

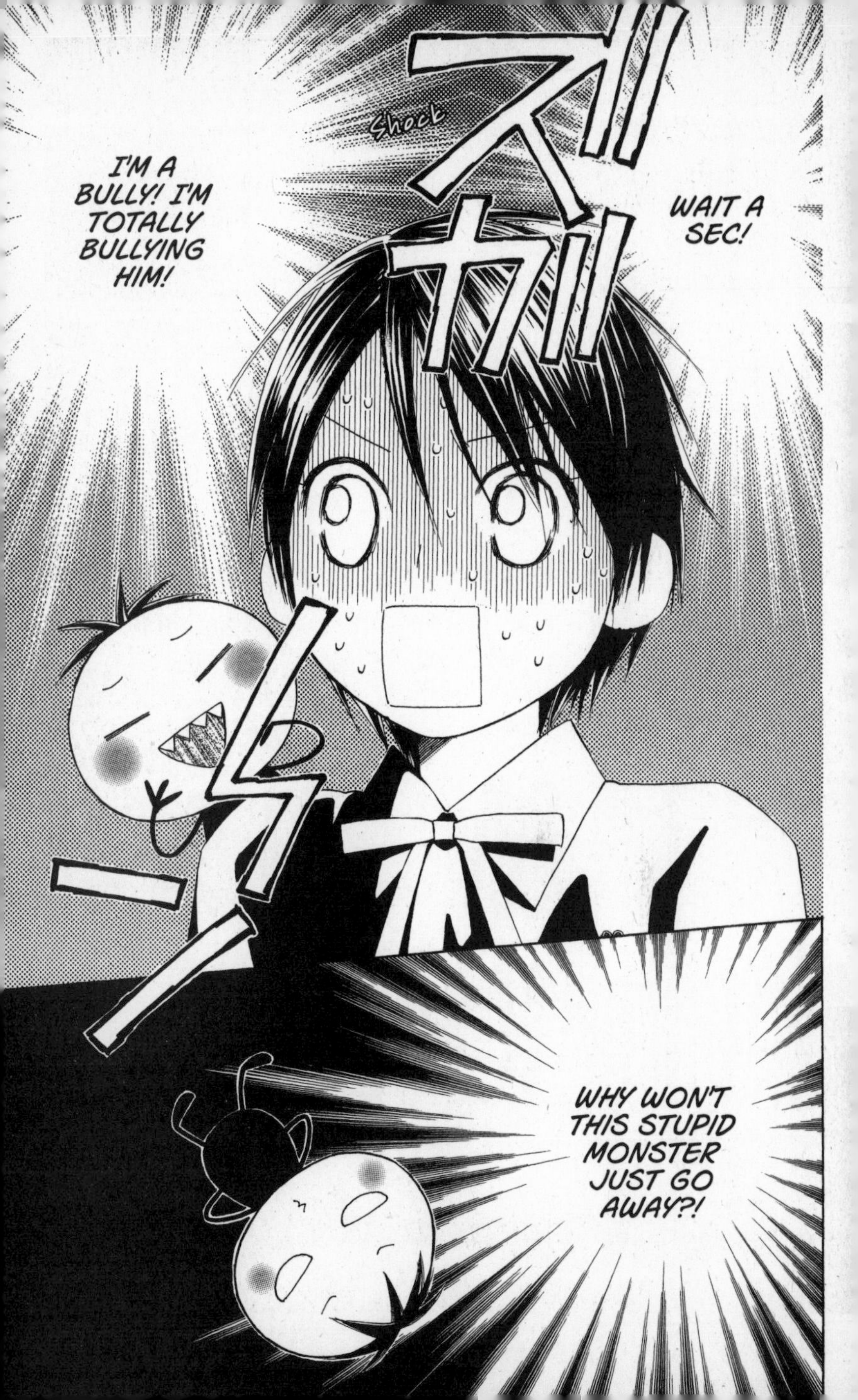
WAIT A SEC!
Shock
I'M A BULLY! I'M TOTALLY BULLYING HIM!
WHY WON'T THIS STUPID MONSTER JUST GO AWAY?!

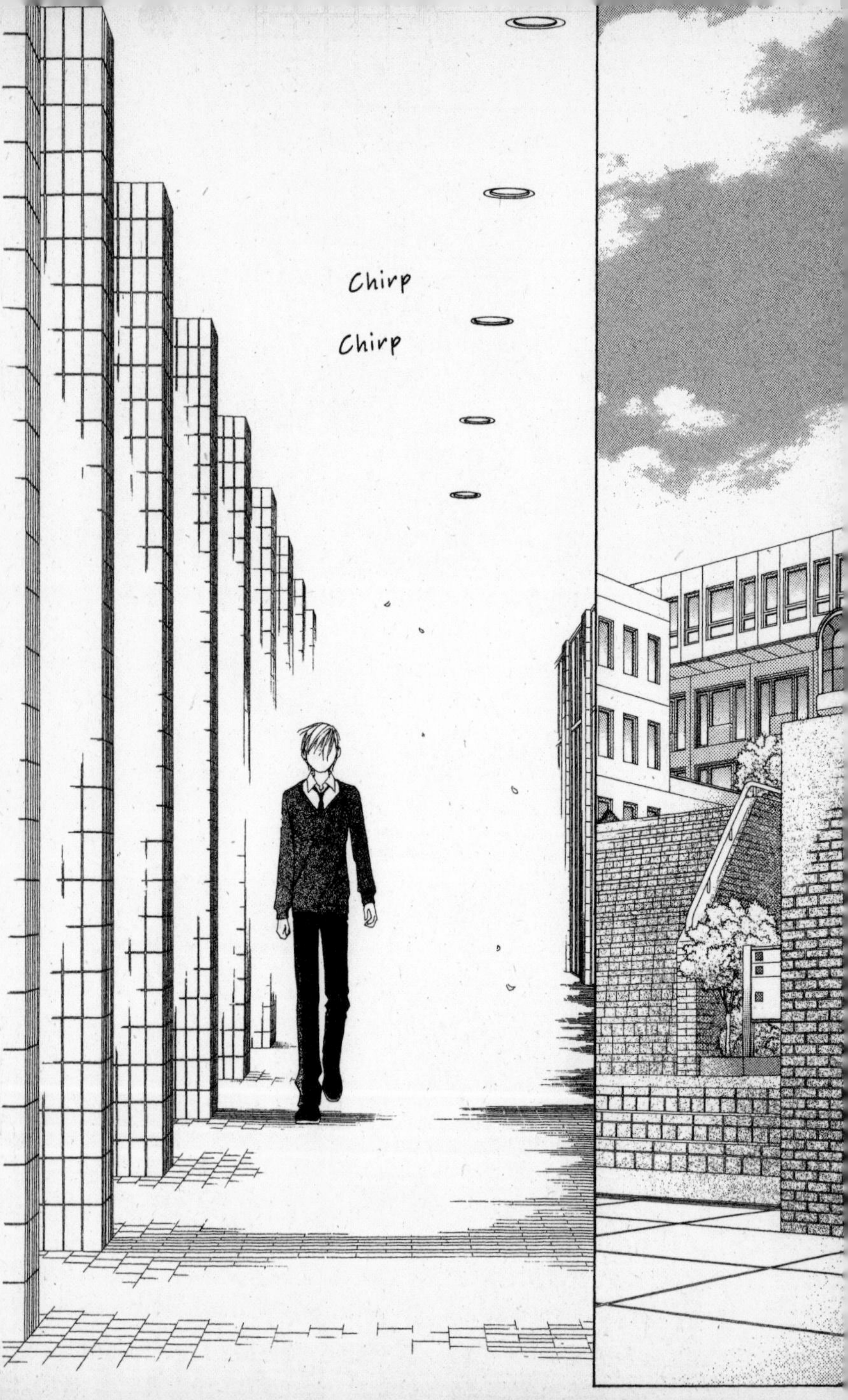
Chirp
Chirp

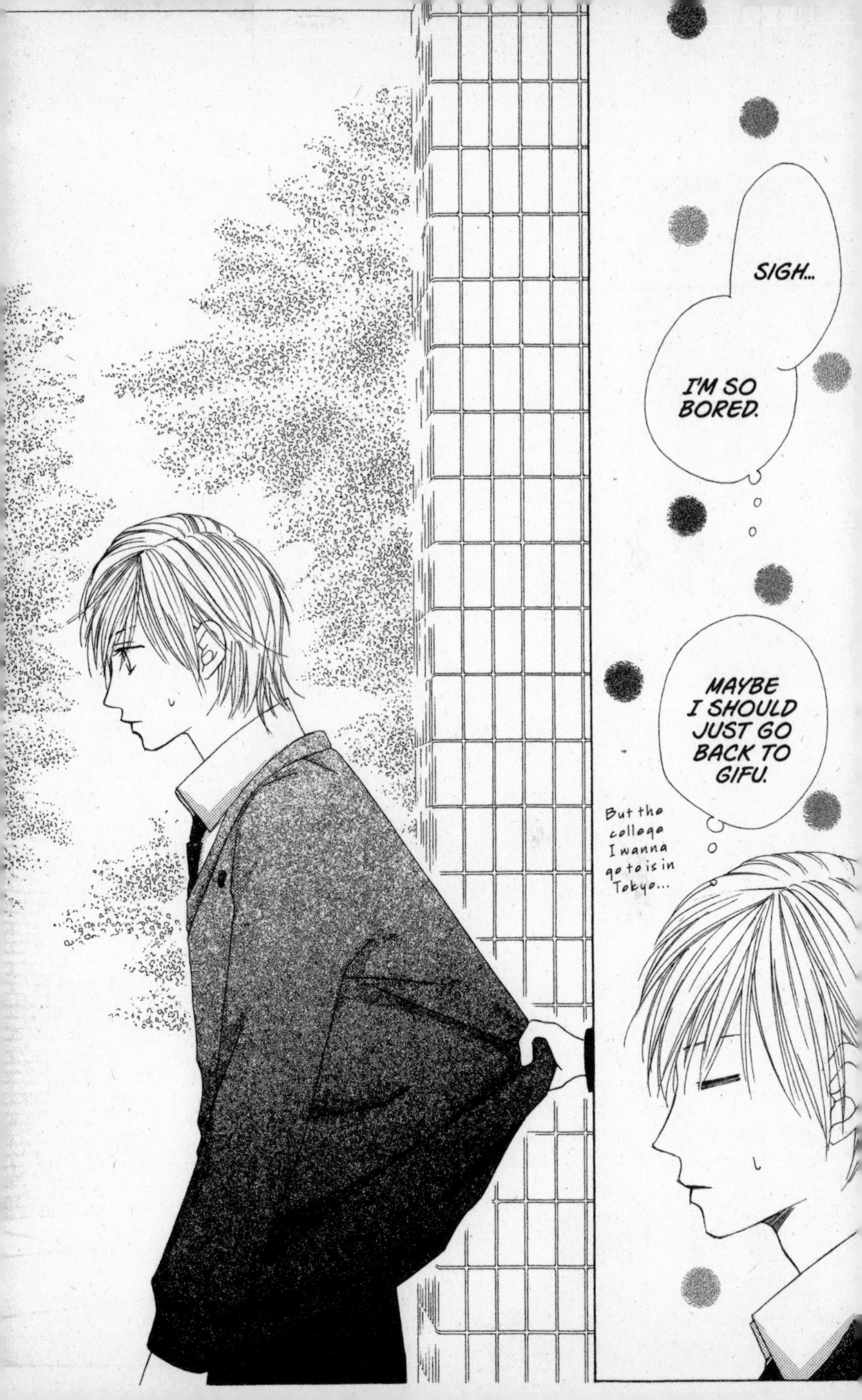
SIGH...
I'M SO BORED.
MAYBE I SHOULD JUST GO BACK TO GIFU.
But the college I wanna go to is in Tokyo...

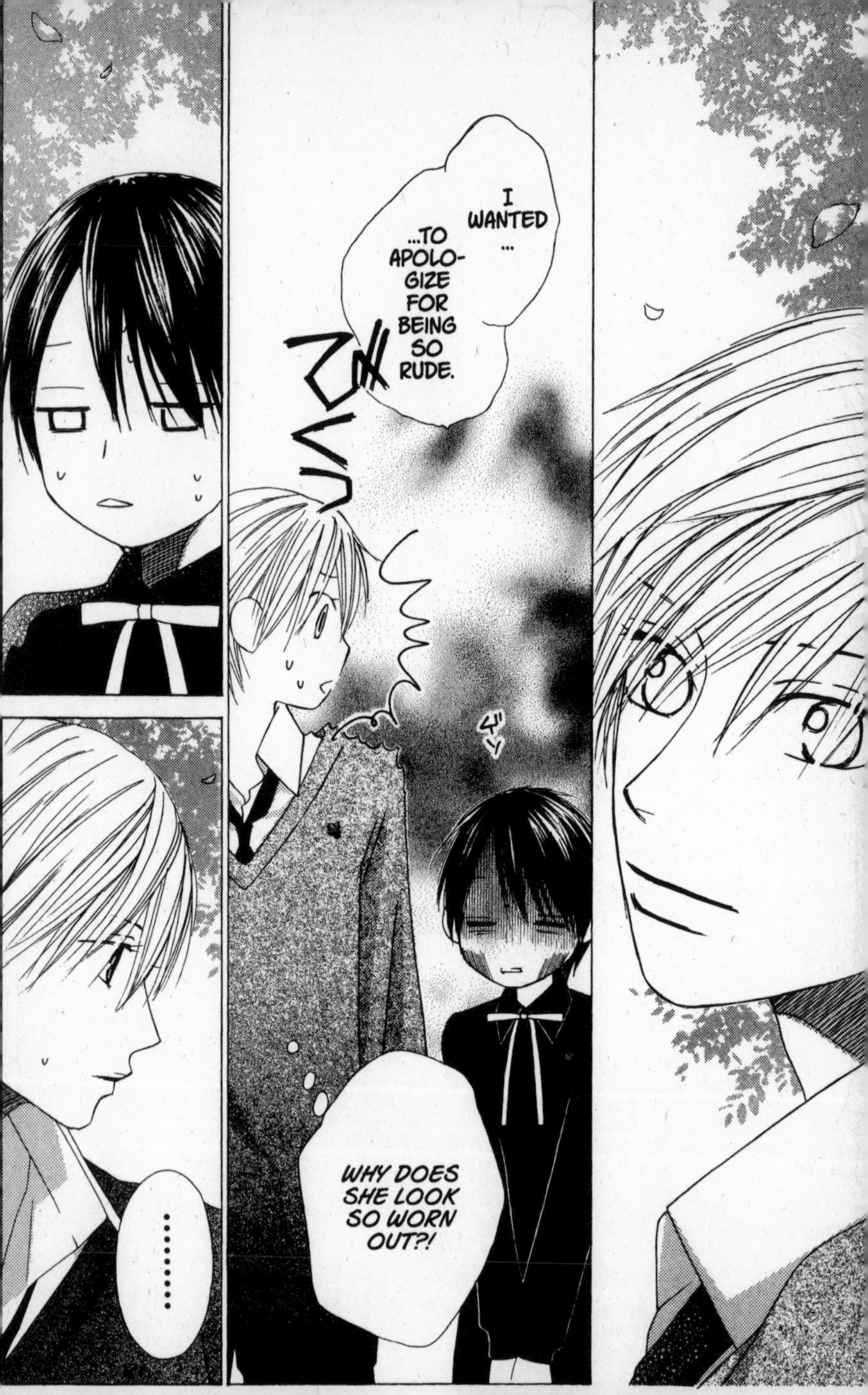
I WANTED ...
...TO APOLO-GIZE FOR BEING SO RUDE.
WHY DOES SHE LOOK SO WORN OUT?!
....

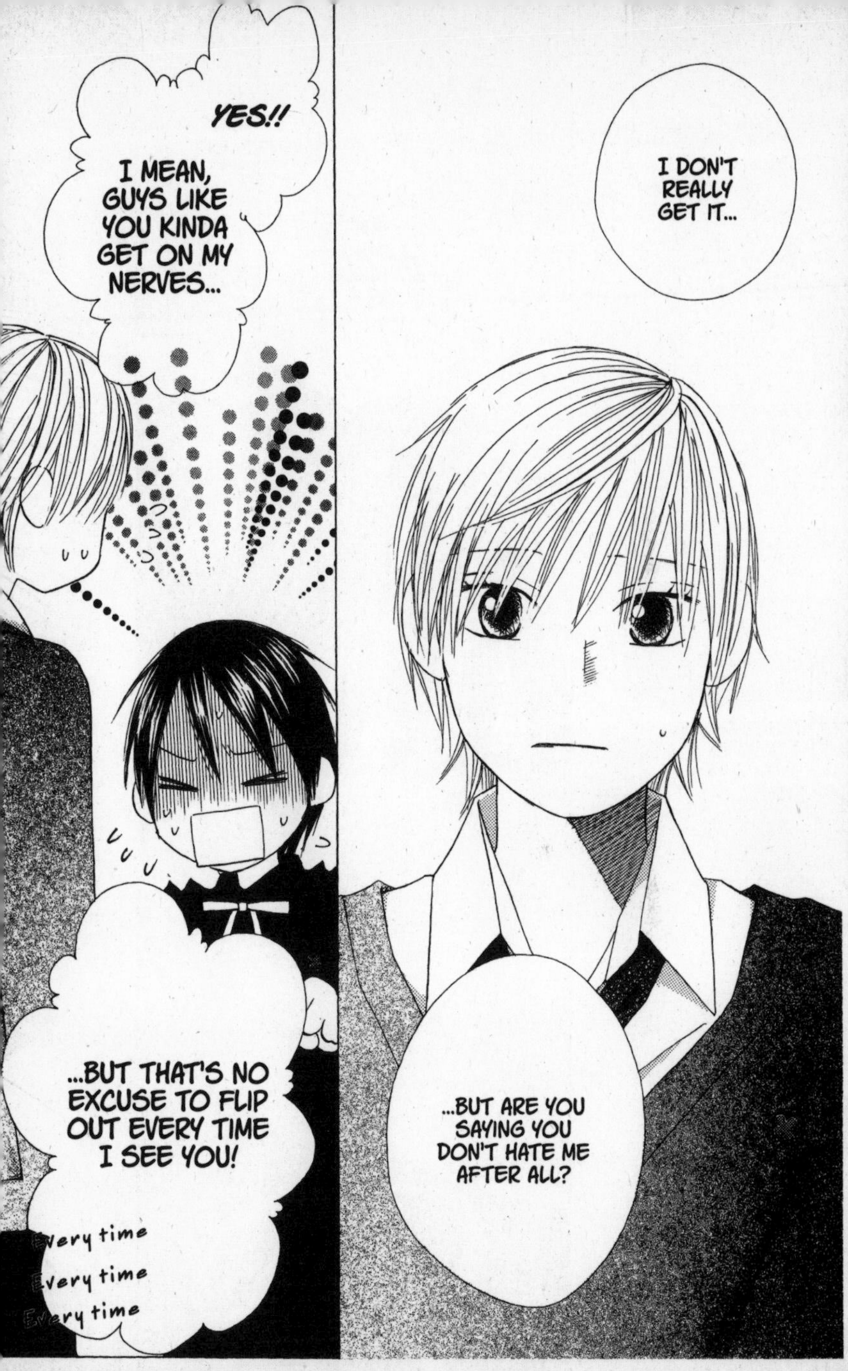
I DON'T REALLY GET IT...
...BUT ARE YOU SAYING YOU DON'T HATE ME AFTER ALL?
YES!!
I MEAN, GUYS LIKE YOU KINDA GET ON MY NERVES...
...BUT THAT'S NO EXCUSE TO FLIP OUT EVERY TIME I SEE YOU!
Every time
Every time
Every time

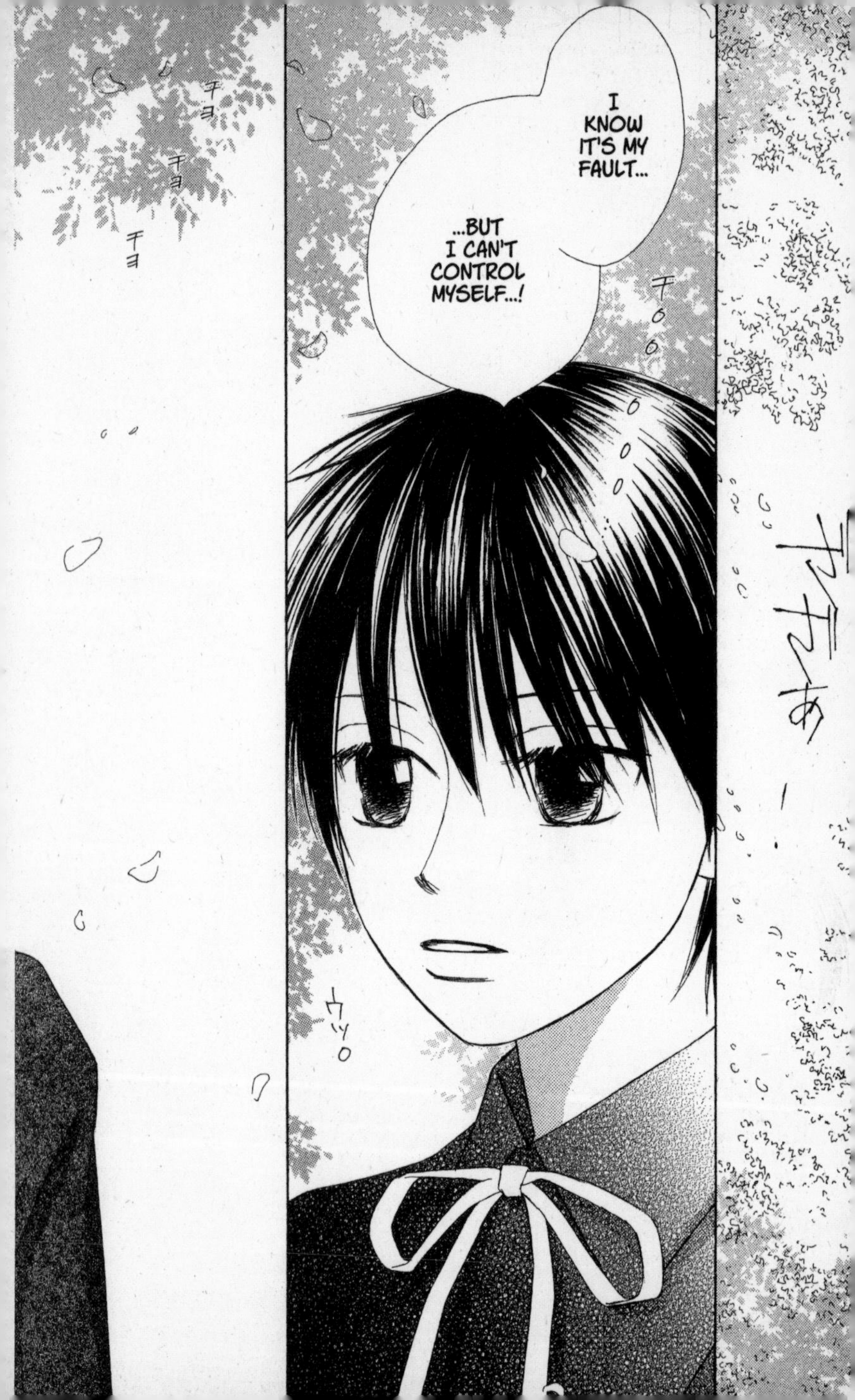
I KNOW IT'S MY FAULT...
...BUT I CAN'T CONTROL MYSELF...!

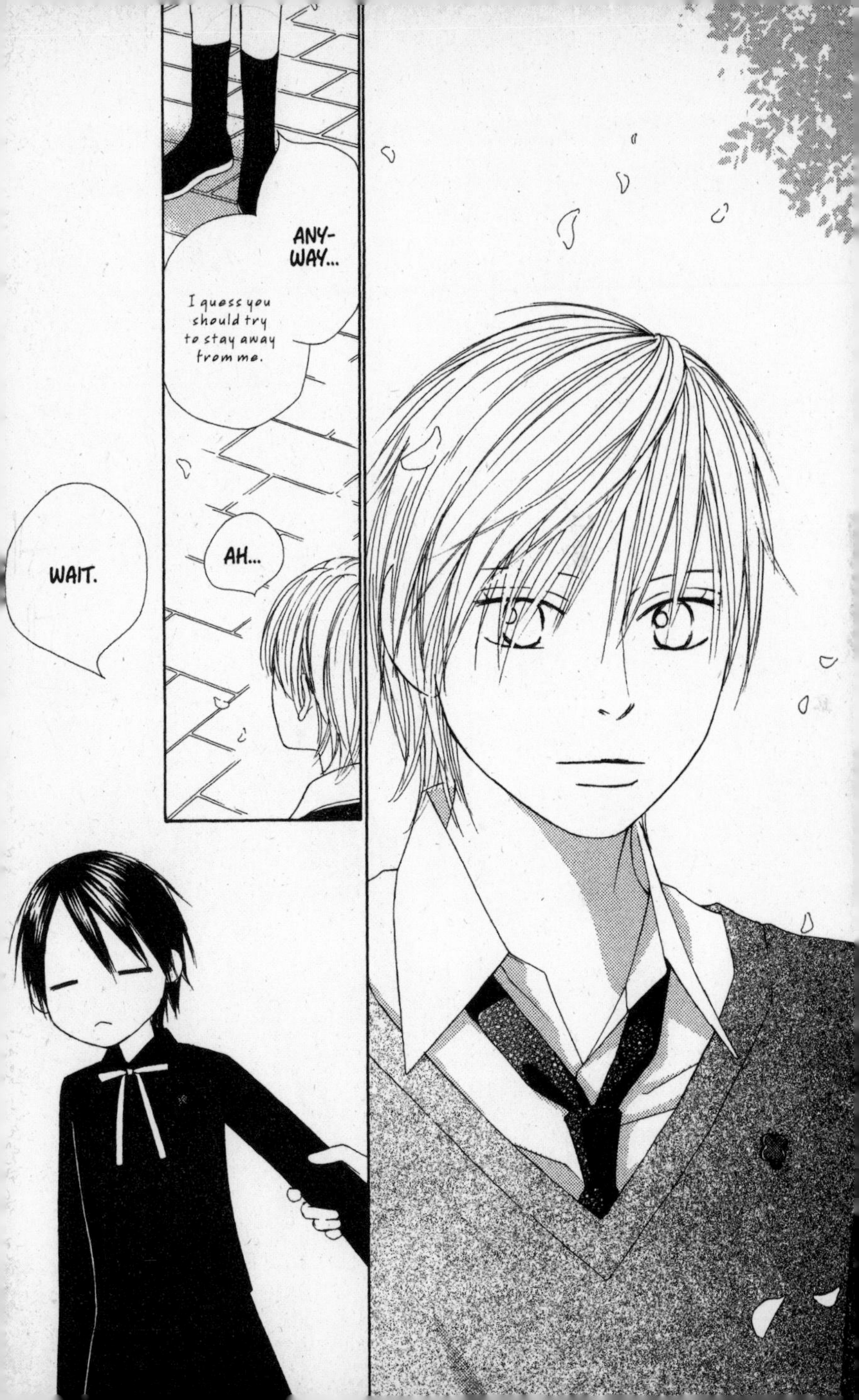
ANY-WAY...
I guess you should try to stay away from me.
AH...
WAIT.

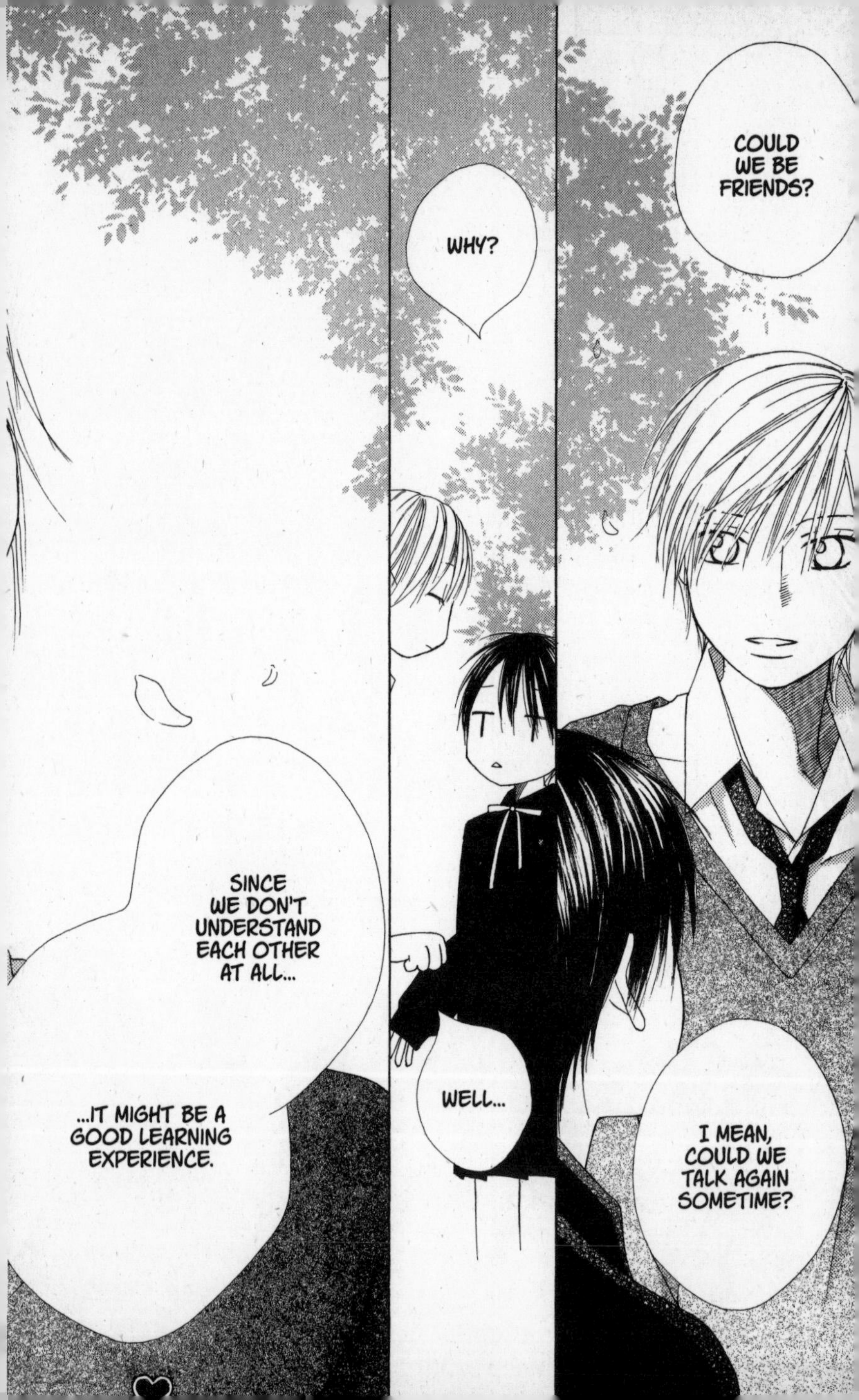
COULD WE BE FRIENDS?
I MEAN, COULD WE TALK AGAIN SOMETIME?
WHY?
WELL...
SINCE WE DON'T UNDERSTAND EACH OTHER AT ALL...
...IT MIGHT BE A GOOD LEARNING EXPERIENCE.

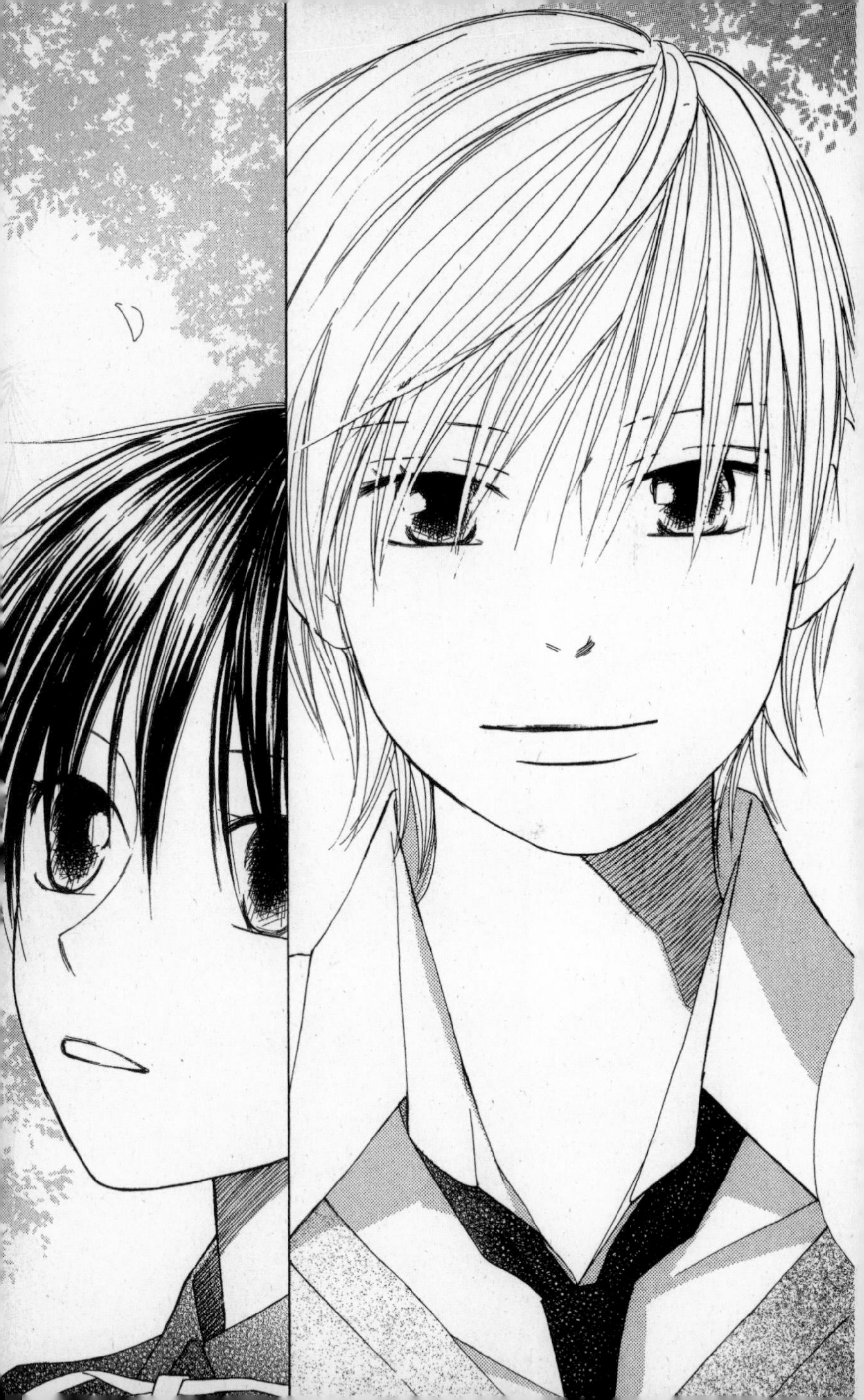

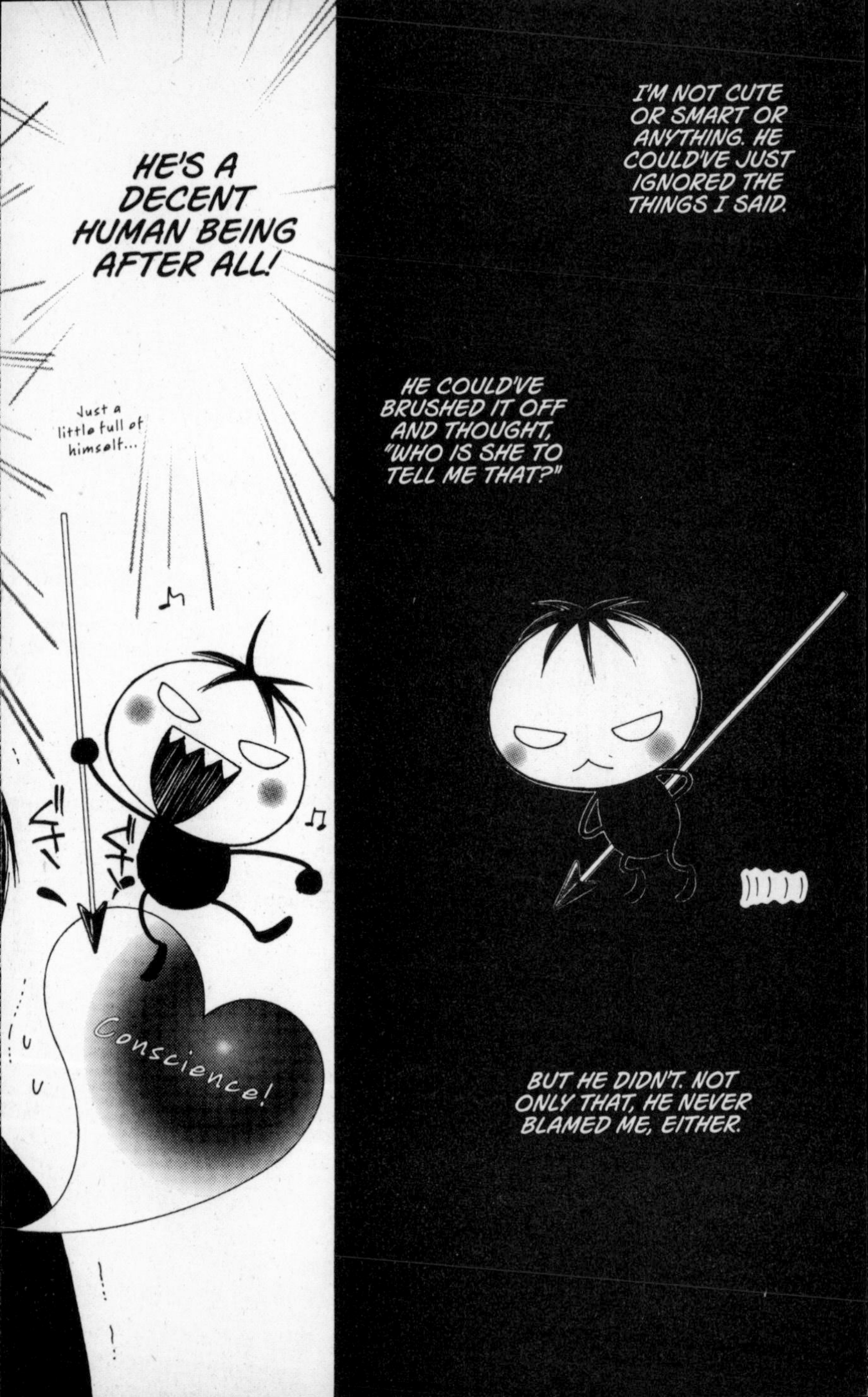
I'M NOT CUTE OR SMART OR ANYTHING. HE COULD'VE JUST IGNORED THE THINGS I SAID.
HE COULD'VE BRUSHED IT OFF AND THOUGHT, "WHO IS SHE TO TELL ME THAT?"
BUT HE DIDN'T. NOT ONLY THAT, HE NEVER BLAMED ME, EITHER.
HE'S A DECENT HUMAN BEING AFTER ALL!
Just a little full of himself...
Conscience!

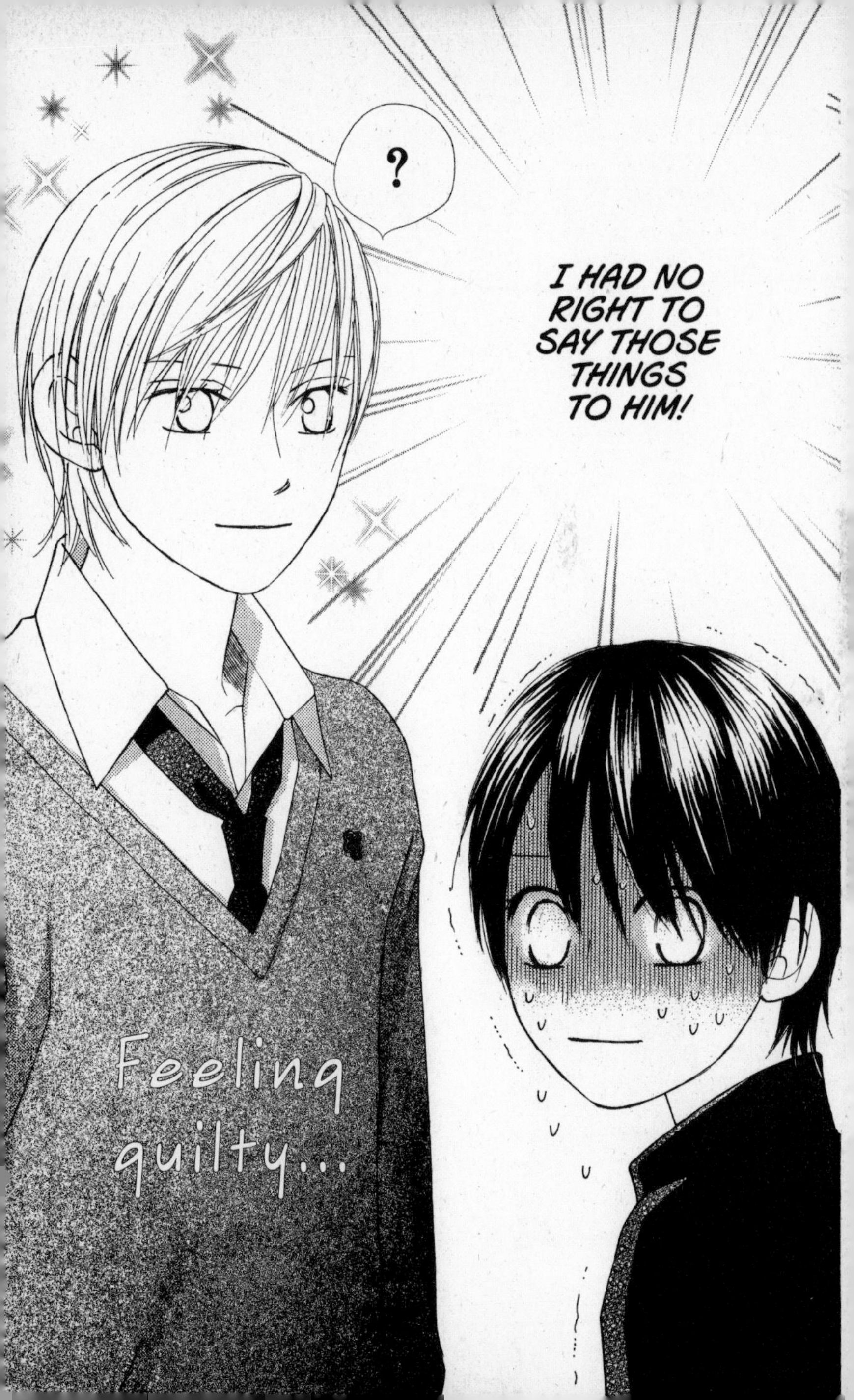
I HAD NO RIGHT TO SAY THOSE THINGS TO HIM!
?
Feeling guilty...

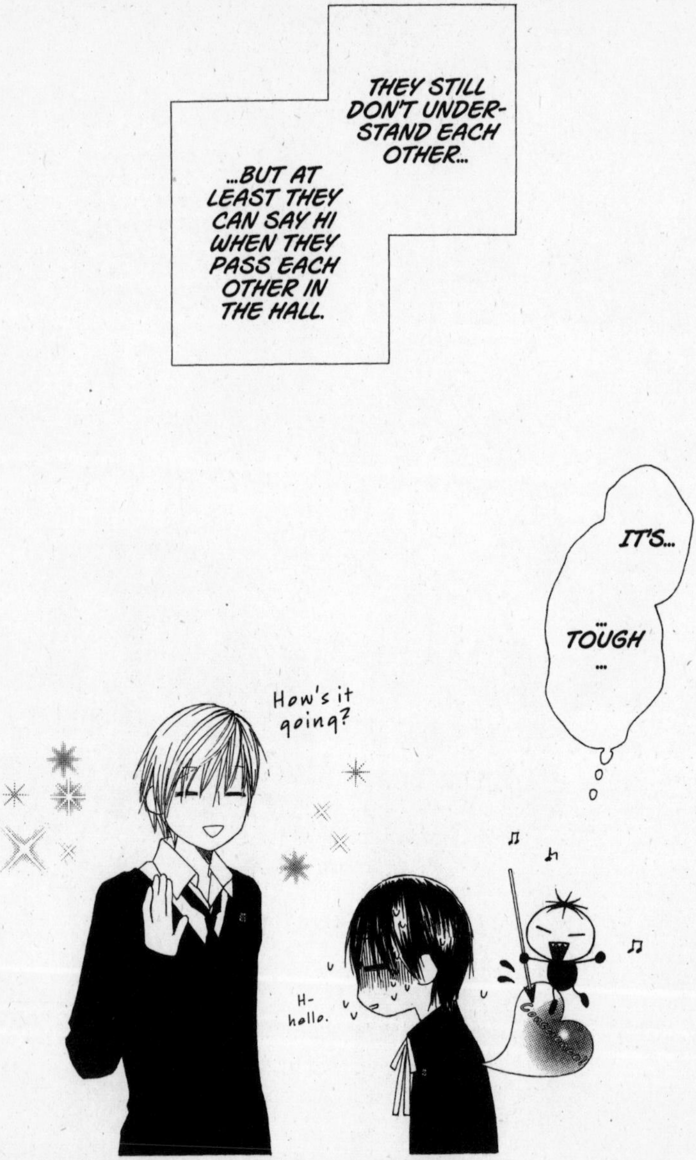
THEY STILL DON'T UNDER-STAND EACH OTHER...
...BUT AT LEAST THEY CAN SAY HI WHEN THEY PASS EACH OTHER IN THE HALL.
IT'S...
...TOUGH...
How's it going?
H- hello.

STEP 4 / END

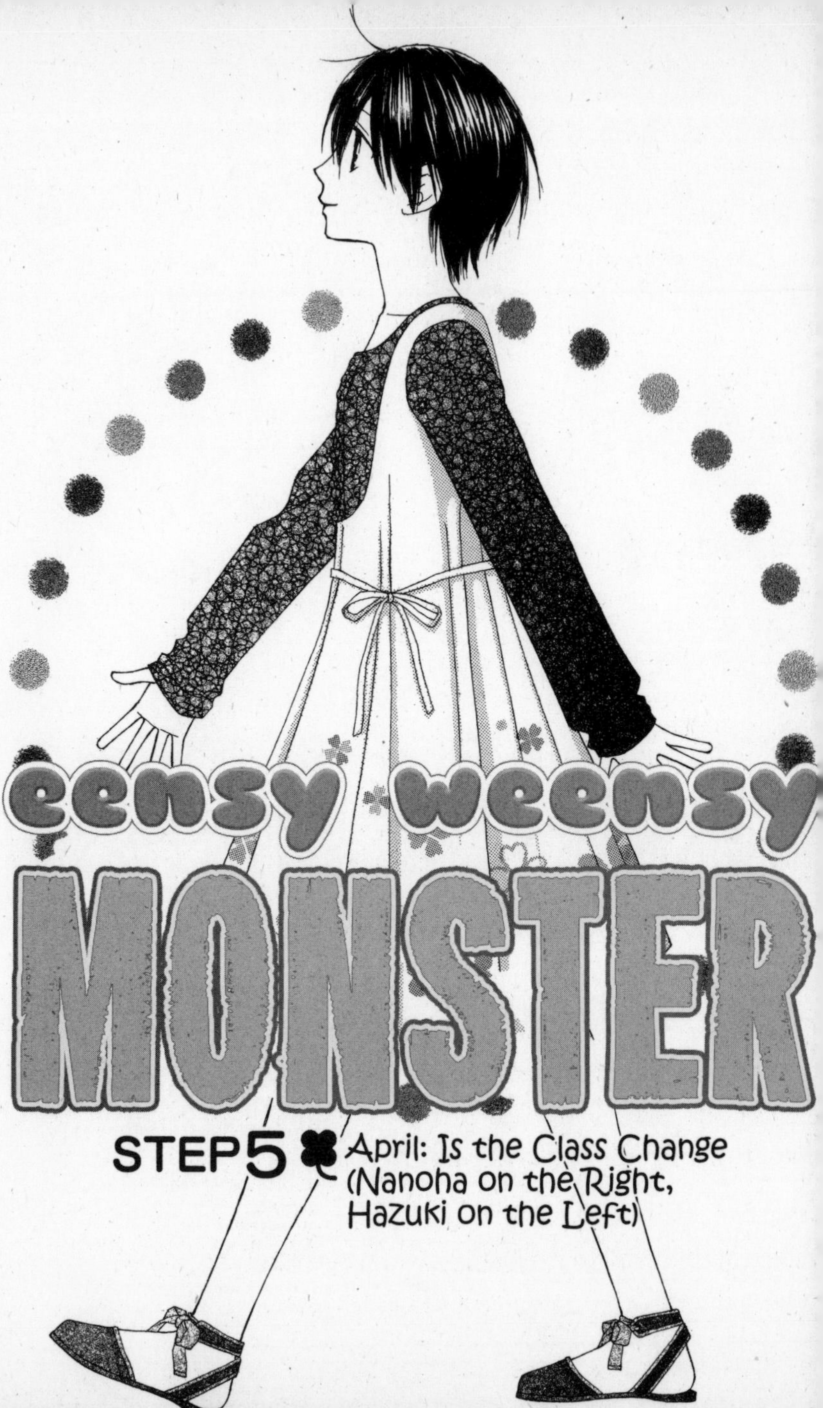
eensy weensy
MONSTER
STEP 5
April: Is the Class Change
(Nanoha on the Right,
Hazuki on the Left)

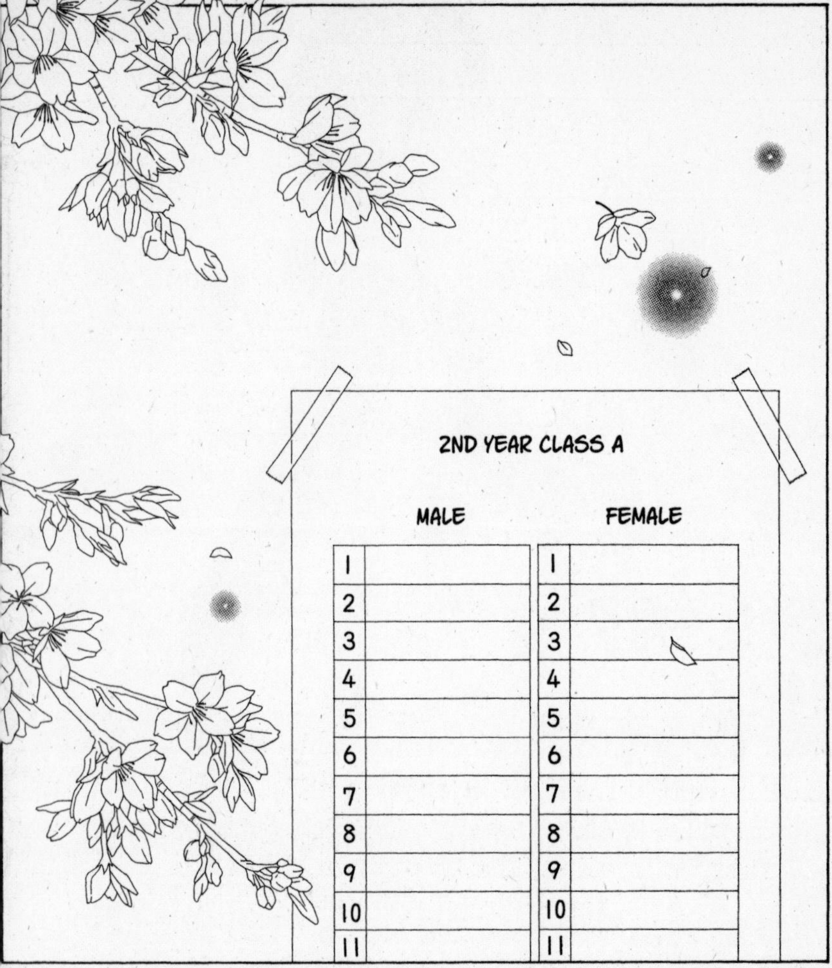
2ND YEAR CLASS A
MALE
FEMALE
1 2 3 4 5 6 7 8 9 10 11
1 2 3 4 5 6 7 8 9 10 11

SUMO

The kabuki theater is an enchanting place but the Ryogoku Kokugikan (known for sumo wrestling) is also really interesting!

Old, young, male, female, foreigners and locals all come together to watch the match and eat snacks. No matter who you are, you can feel at home there.

Their famous yakitori is really tasty!

Please go visit if you have the chance!

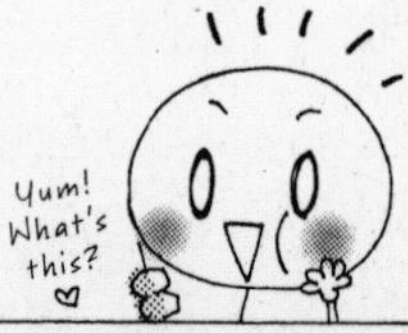
Yum! What's this?

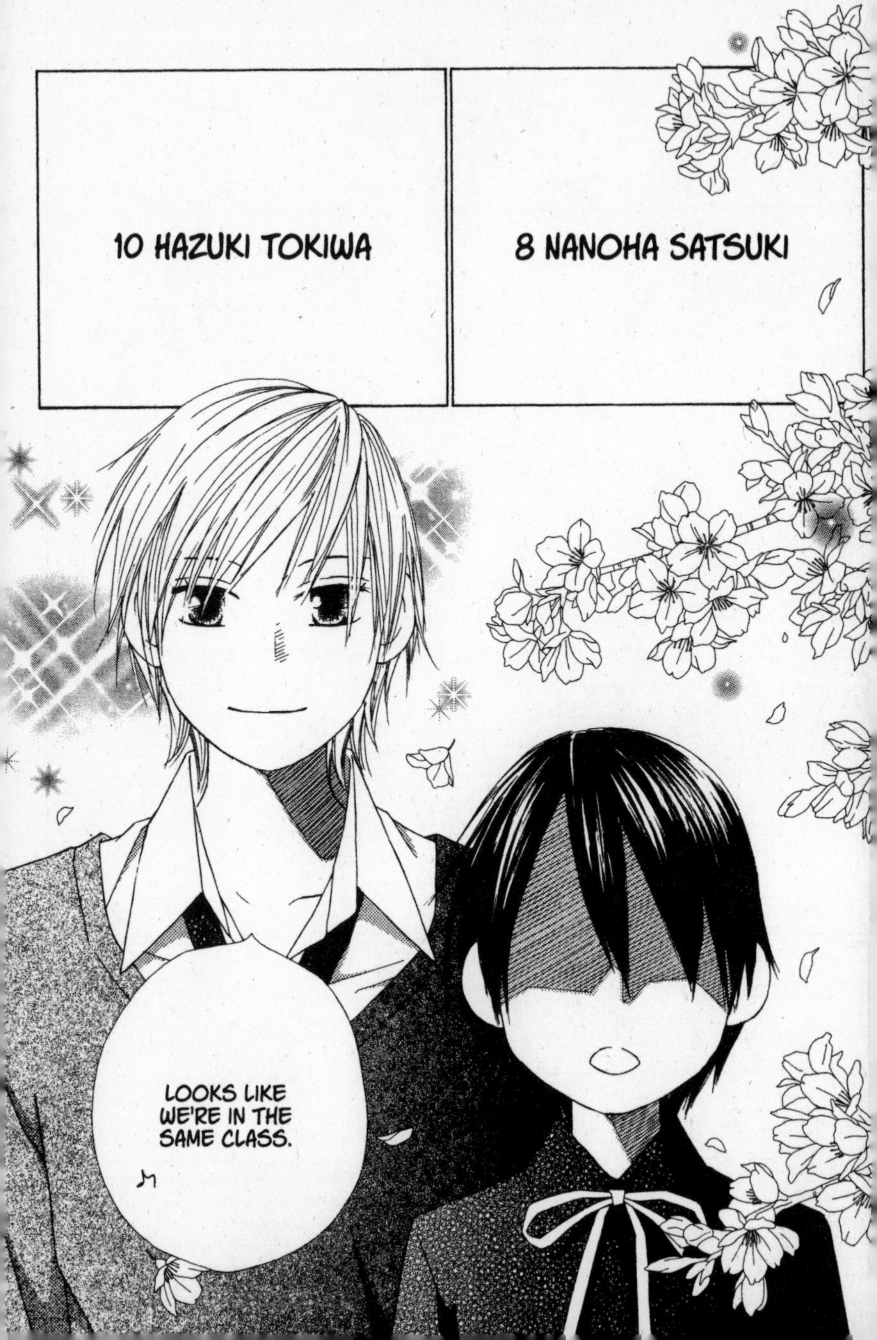
8 NANOHA SATSUKI
10 HAZUKI TOKIWA
LOOKS LIKE WE'RE IN THE SAME CLASS.

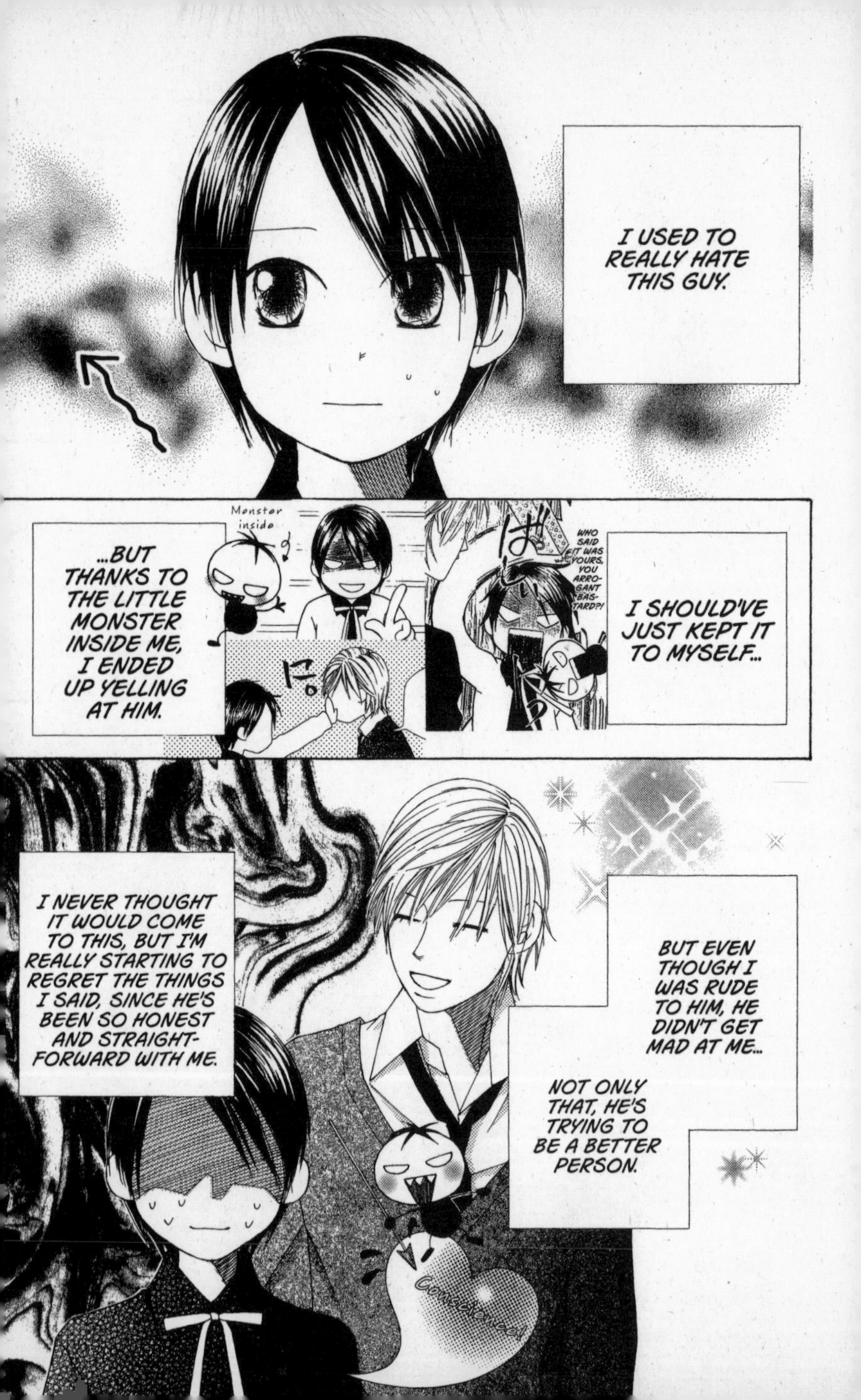

I USED TO REALLY HATE THIS GUY.
WHO SAID IT WAS YOURS, YOU ARROGANT BASTARD?!
I SHOULD'VE JUST KEPT IT TO MYSELF...
Monster inside
...BUT THANKS TO THE LITTLE MONSTER INSIDE ME, I ENDED UP YELLING AT HIM.
BUT EVEN THOUGH I WAS RUDE TO HIM, HE DIDN'T GET MAD AT ME...
NOT ONLY THAT, HE'S TRYING TO BE A BETTER PERSON.
I NEVER THOUGHT IT WOULD COME TO THIS, BUT I'M REALLY STARTING TO REGRET THE THINGS I SAID, SINCE HE'S BEEN SO HONEST AND STRAIGHTFORWARD WITH ME.
Conscience

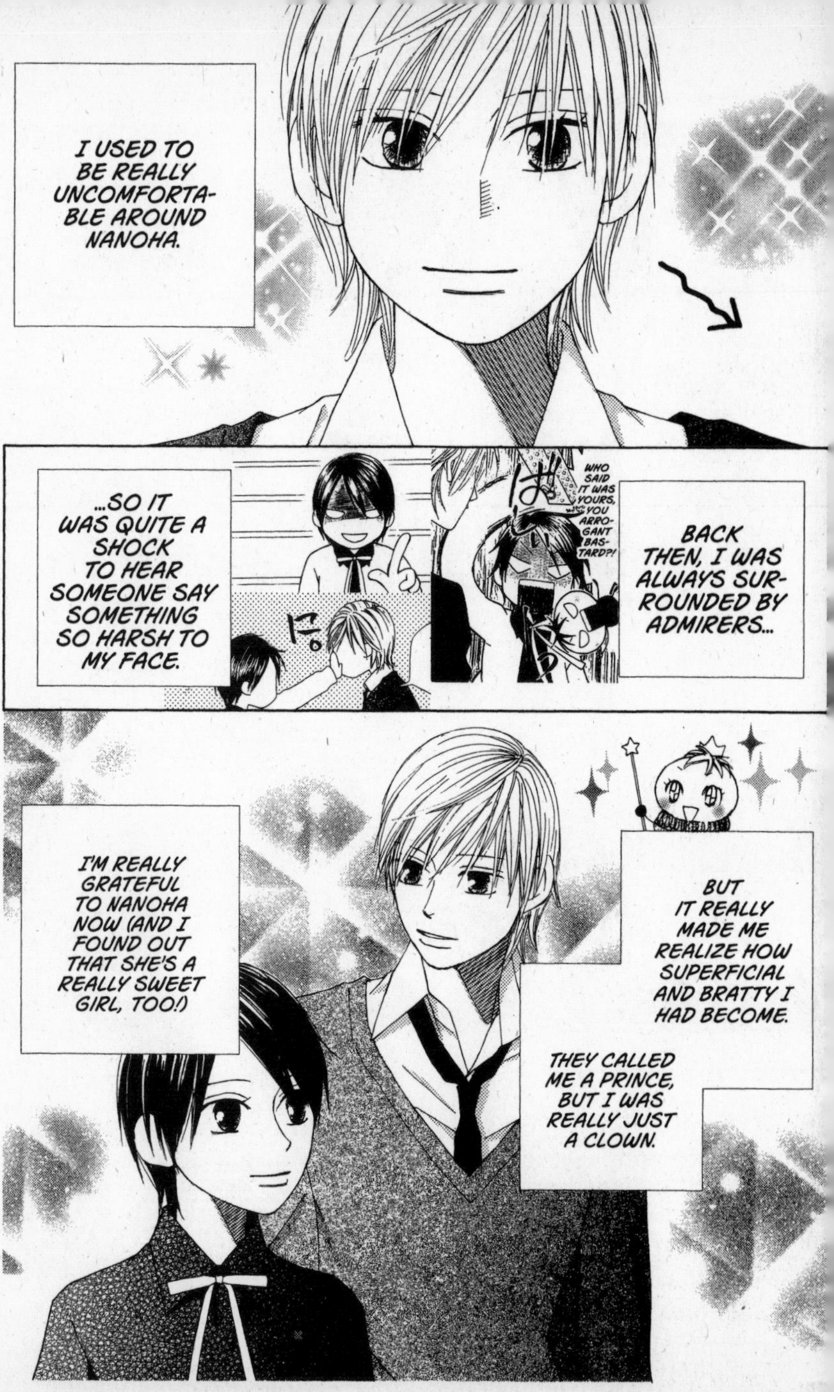
I USED TO BE REALLY UNCOMFORTA-BLE AROUND NANOHA.
BACK THEN, I WAS ALWAYS SUR-ROUNDED BY ADMIRERS...
WHO SAID IT WAS YOURS, YOU ARRO-GANT BAS-TARD?!
...SO IT WAS QUITE A SHOCK TO HEAR SOMEONE SAY SOMETHING SO HARSH TO MY FACE.
BUT IT REALLY MADE ME REALIZE HOW SUPERFICIAL AND BRATTY I HAD BECOME.
THEY CALLED ME A PRINCE, BUT I WAS REALLY JUST A CLOWN.
I'M REALLY GRATEFUL TO NANOHA NOW (AND I FOUND OUT THAT SHE'S A REALLY SWEET GIRL, TOO!)

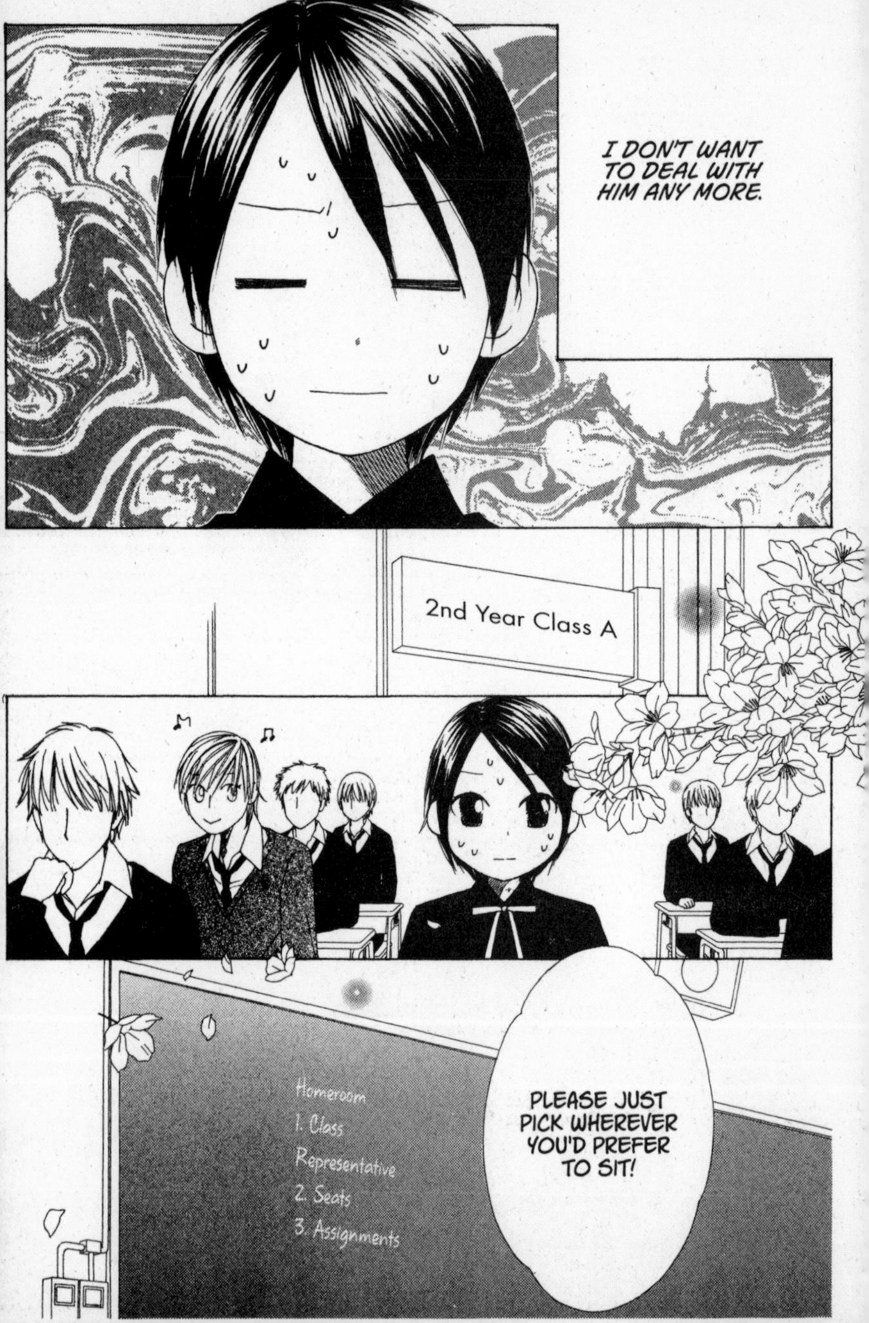
I DON'T WANT TO DEAL WITH HIM ANY MORE.
2nd Year Class A
PLEASE JUST PICK WHEREVER YOU'D PREFER TO SIT!
Homeroom
1. Class Representative
2. Seats
3. Assignments

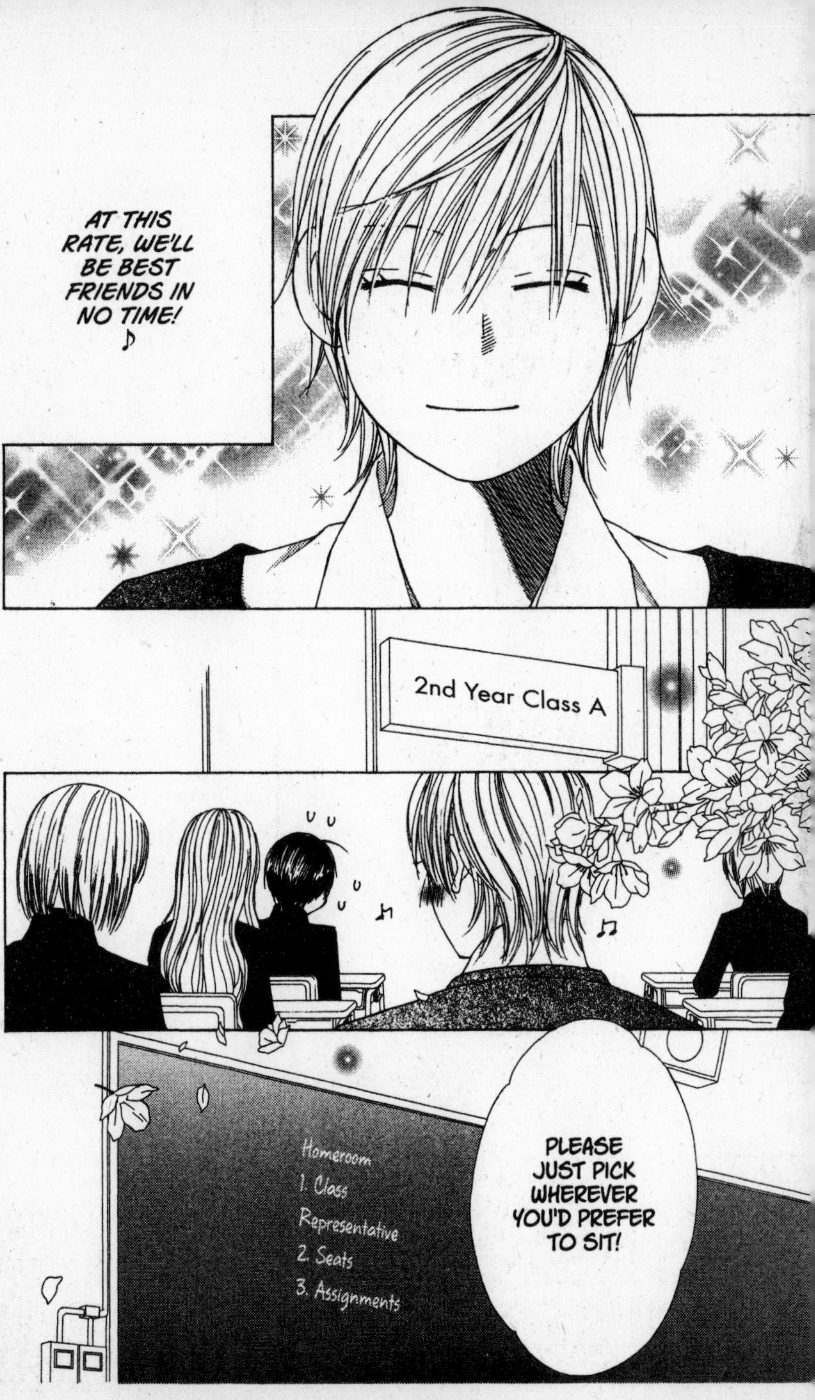
AT THIS RATE, WE'LL BE BEST FRIENDS IN NO TIME! ♪
2nd Year Class A
PLEASE JUST PICK WHEREVER YOU'D PREFER TO SIT!
Homeroom
1. Class Representative
2. Seats
3. Assignments

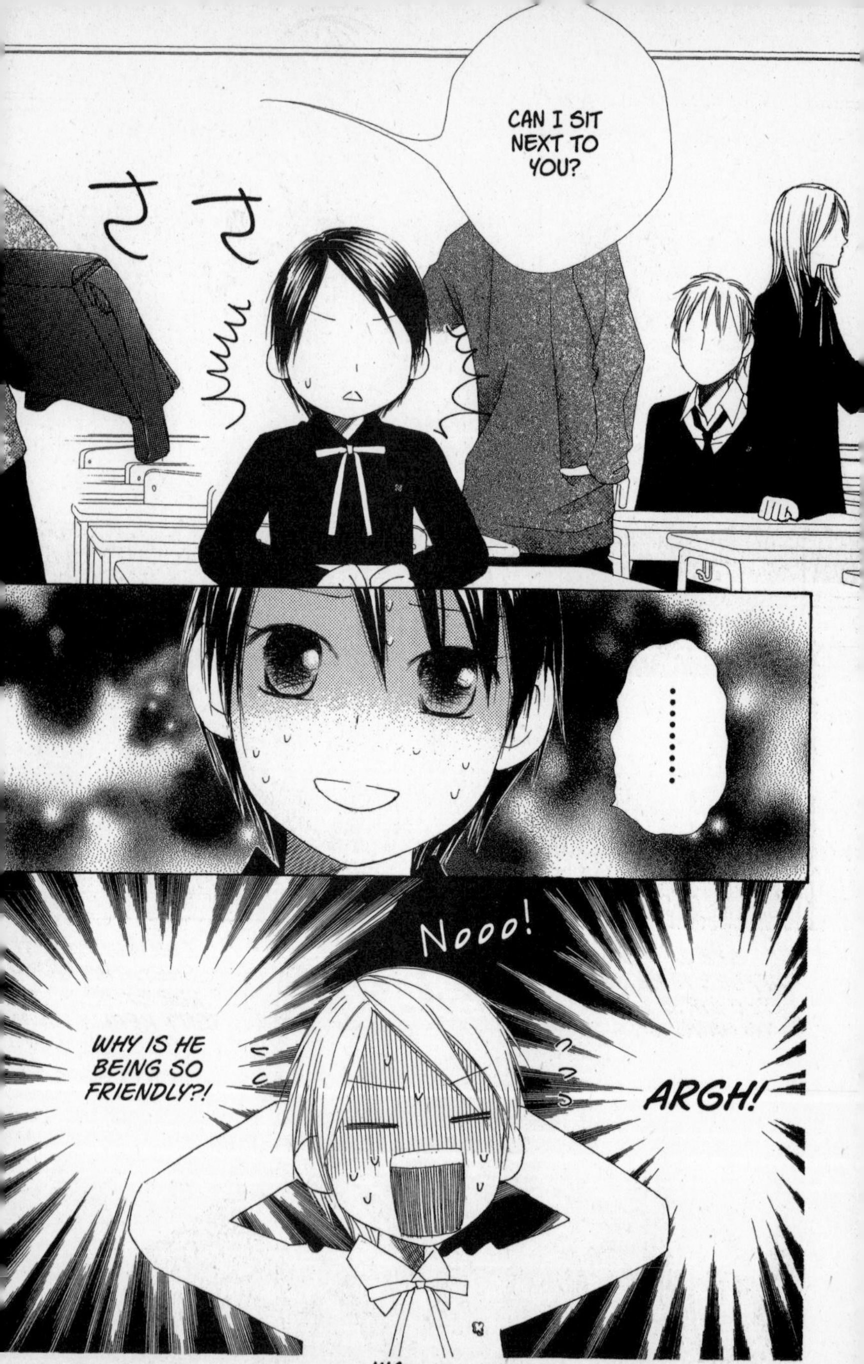

CAN I SIT NEXT TO YOU?
さ さ
....
Nooo!
ARGH!
WHY IS HE BEING SO FRIENDLY?!

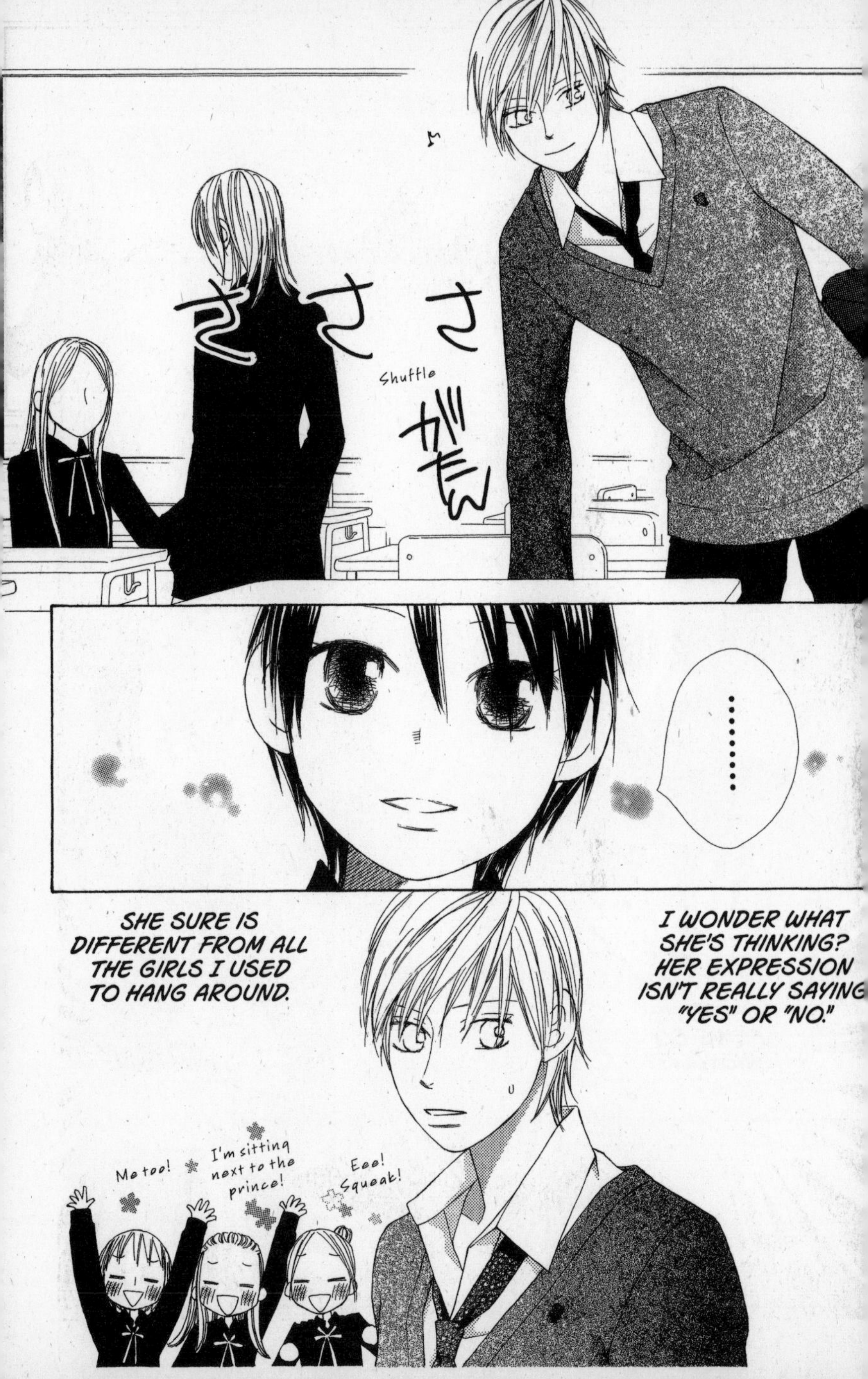
さささ
Shuffle
がたん
......
I WONDER WHAT SHE'S THINKING? HER EXPRESSION ISN'T REALLY SAYING "YES" OR "NO."
SHE SURE IS DIFFERENT FROM ALL THE GIRLS I USED TO HANG AROUND.
Eee! Squeak!
I'm sitting next to the prince!
Me too!

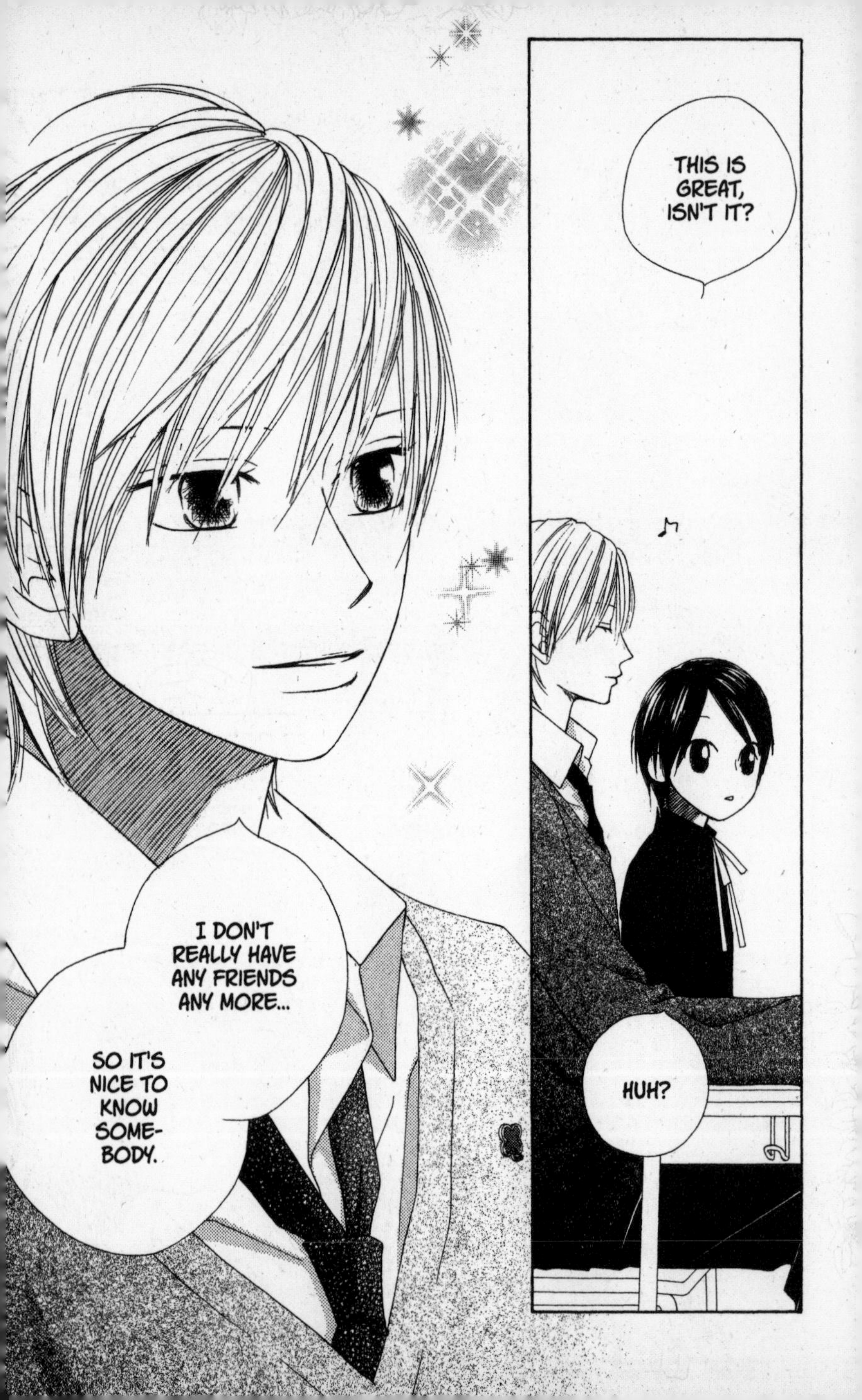
THIS IS GREAT, ISN'T IT?
HUH?
I DON'T REALLY HAVE ANY FRIENDS ANY MORE...
SO IT'S NICE TO KNOW SOME-BODY.

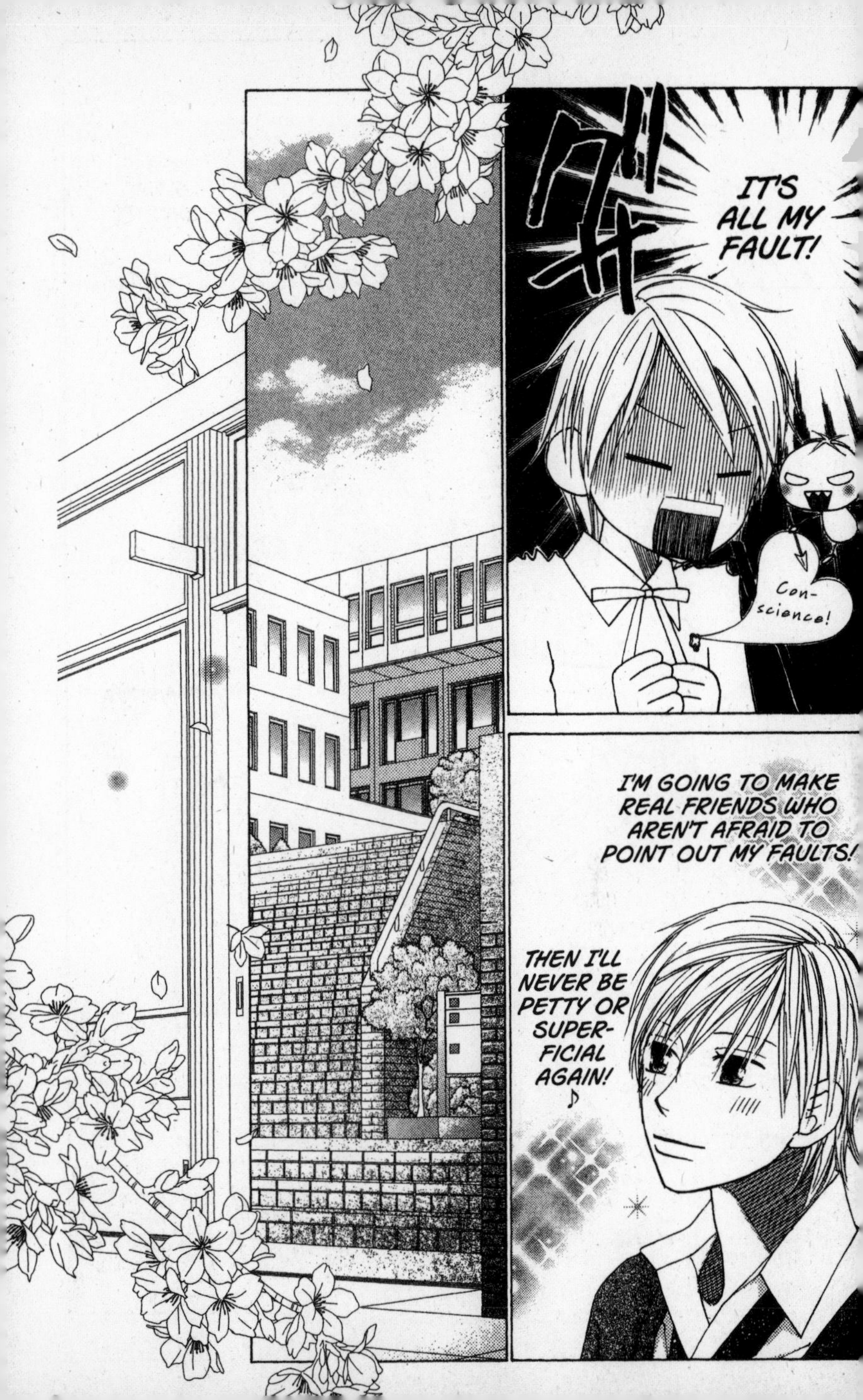
IT'S ALL MY FAULT!
Con-science!
I'M GOING TO MAKE REAL FRIENDS WHO AREN'T AFRAID TO POINT OUT MY FAULTS!
THEN I'LL NEVER BE PETTY OR SUPER-FICIAL AGAIN! ♪

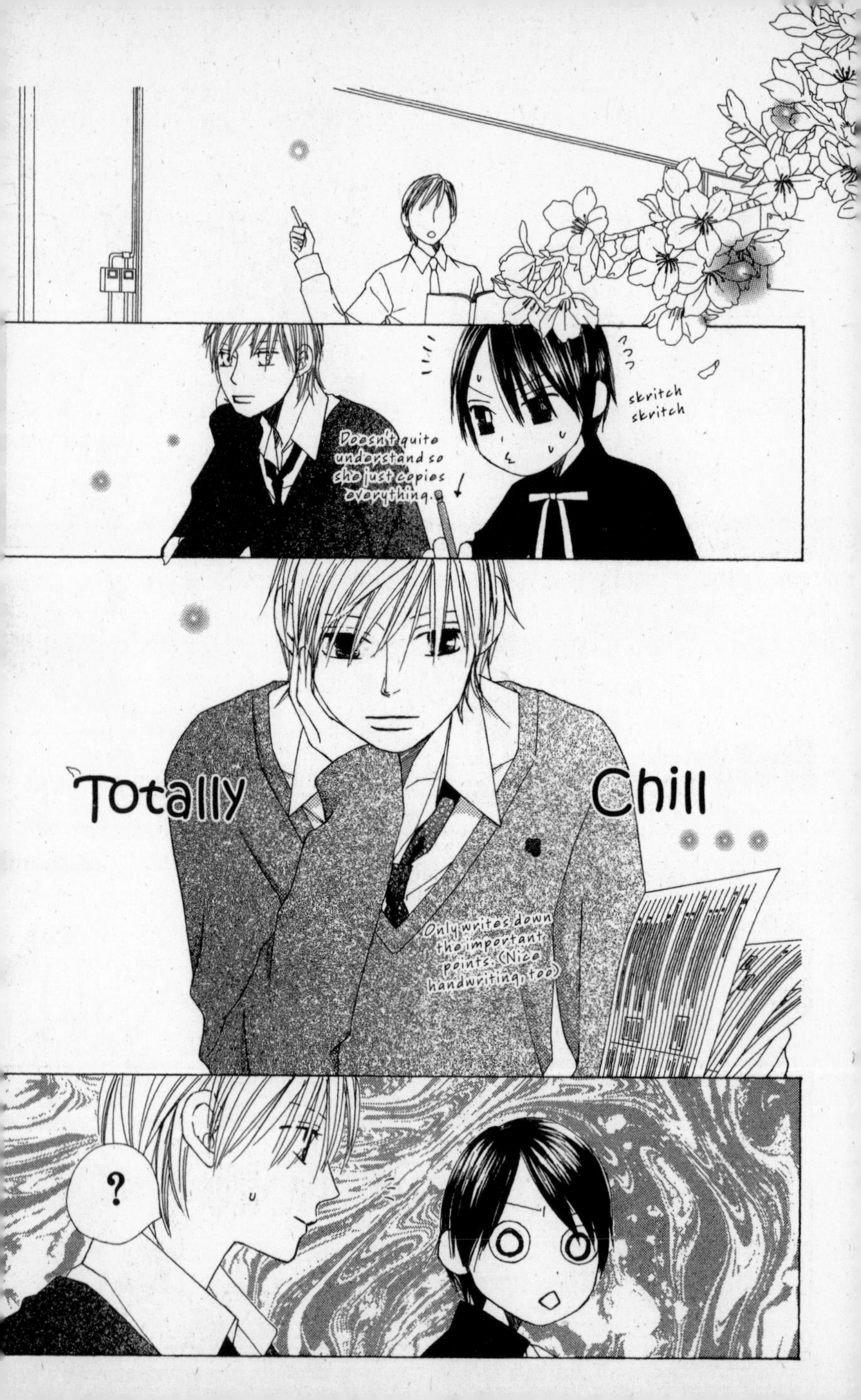
skritch skritch
Doesn't quite understand so she just copies everything.
Totally Chill
Only writes down the important points. (Nice handwriting, too)
?

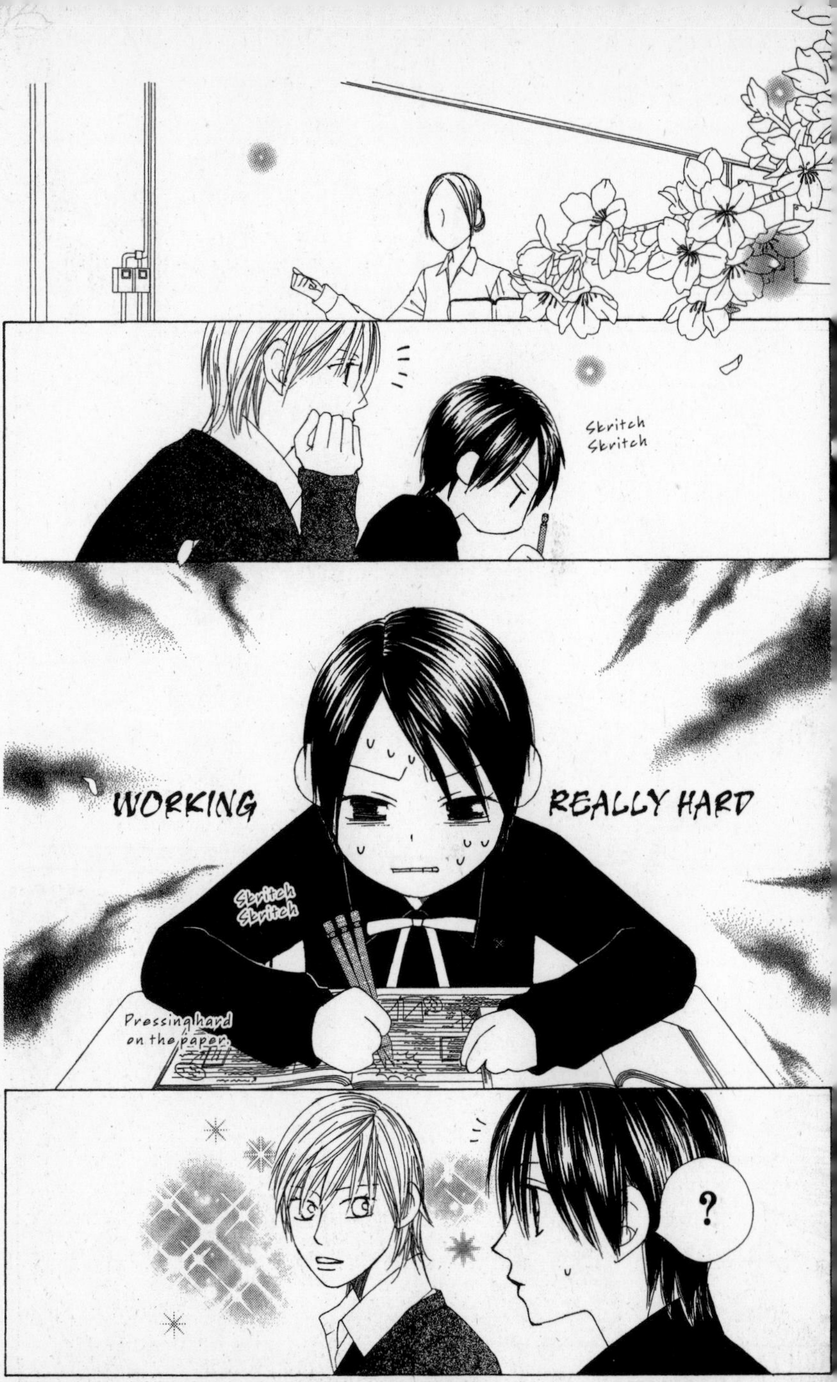
Skritch
Skritch
WORKING
REALLY HARD
Skritch
Skritch
Pressing hard
on the paper.
?

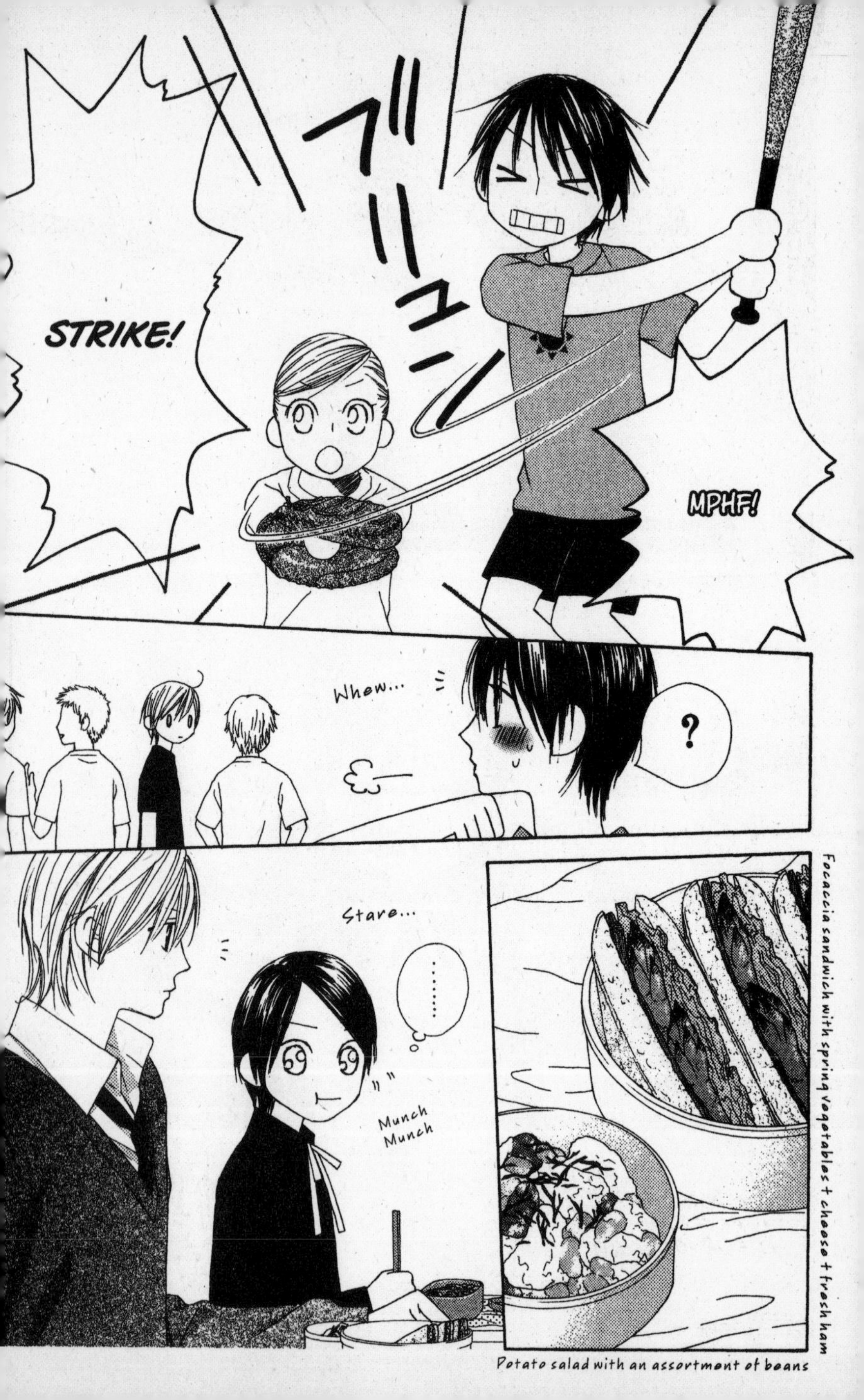
MPHF!
ブリュン
STRIKE!
?
Whew...
Focaccia sandwich with spring vegetables + cheese + fresh ham
Potato salad with an assortment of beans
....
Stare...
Munch
Munch

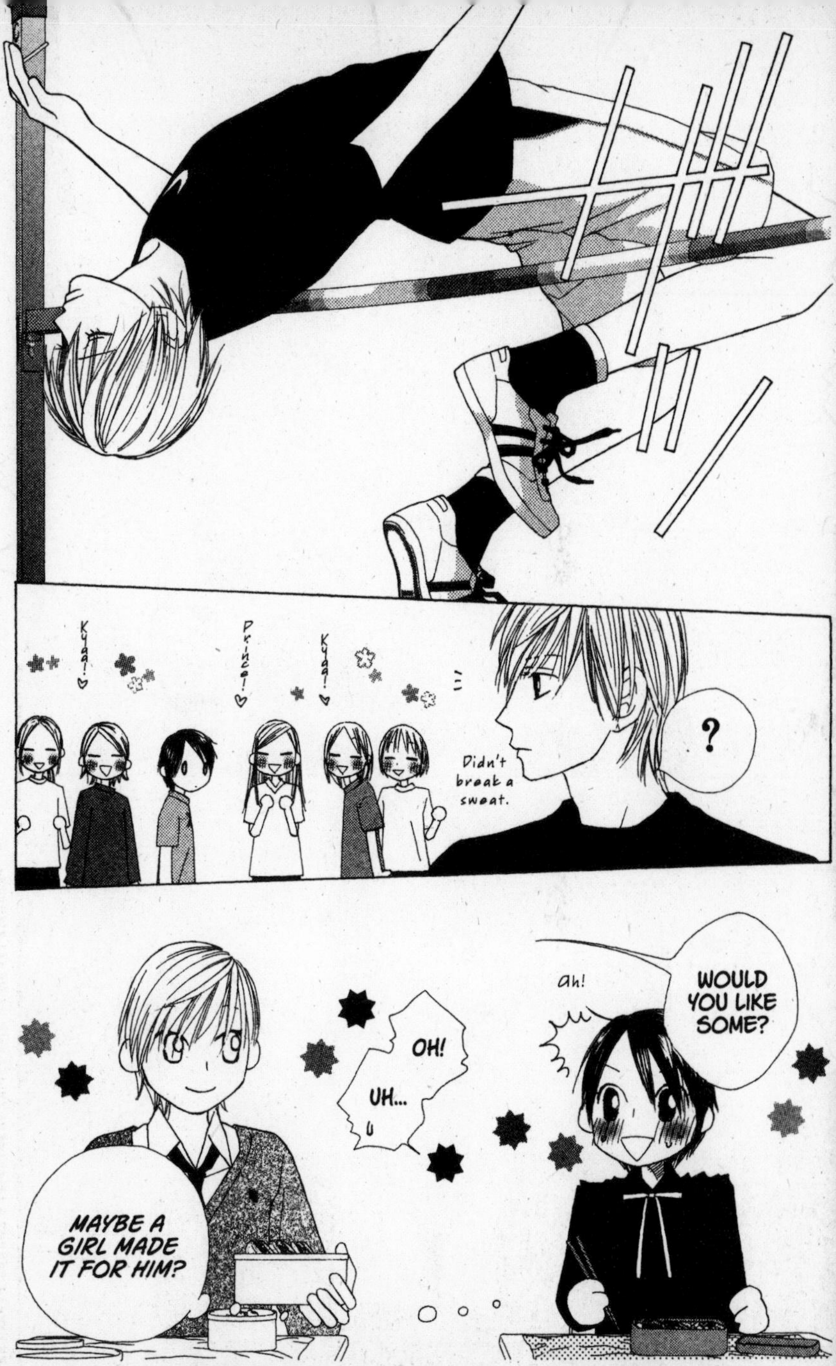
?
Didn't break a sweat.
Kyaa!♡
Prince!♡
Kyaa!♡
WOULD YOU LIKE SOME?
ah!
OH!
UH...
MAYBE A GIRL MADE IT FOR HIM?

Made it himself.

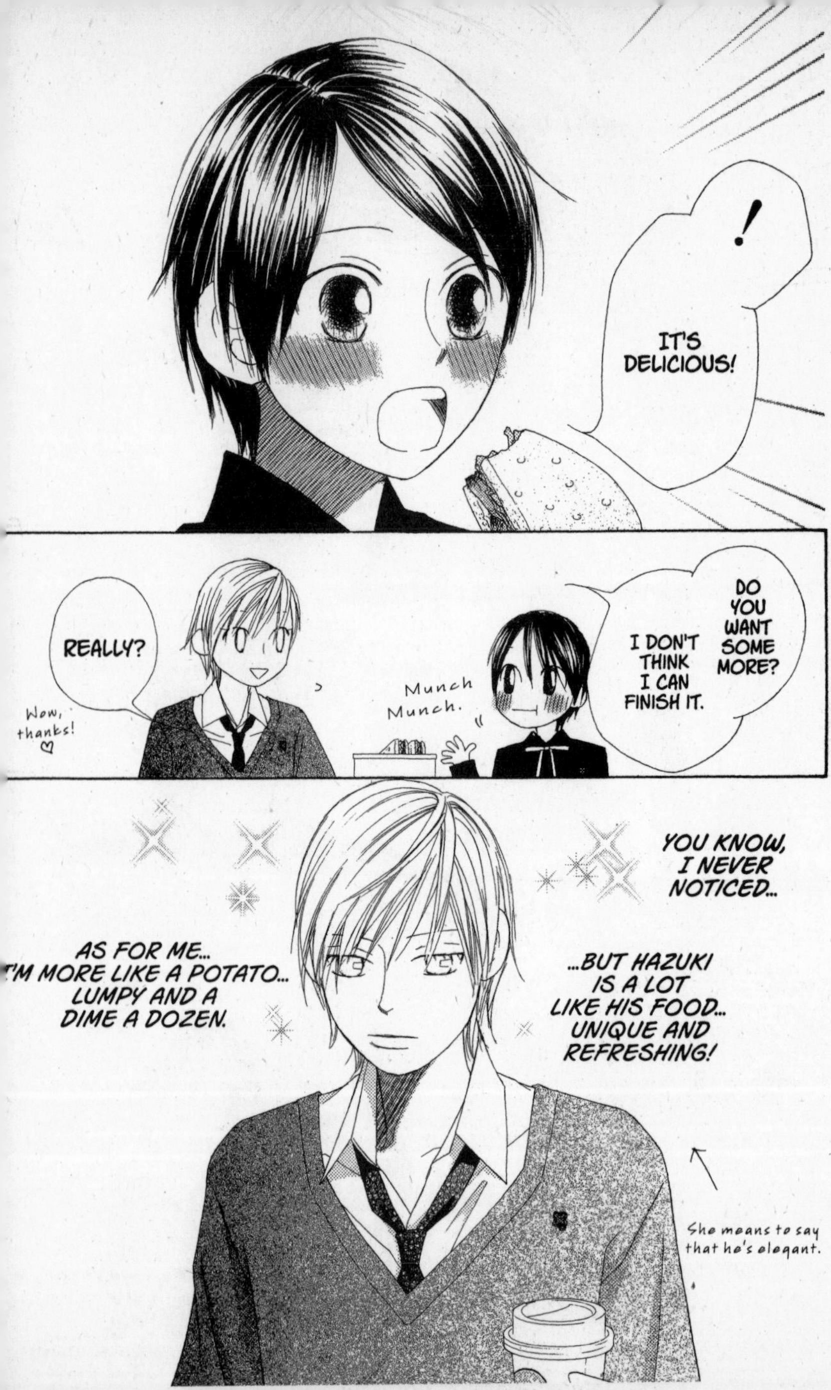
!
IT'S DELICIOUS!
DO YOU WANT SOME MORE?
I DON'T THINK I CAN FINISH IT.
Munch Munch.
REALLY?
Wow, thanks! ♡
YOU KNOW, I NEVER NOTICED...
...BUT HAZUKI IS A LOT LIKE HIS FOOD... UNIQUE AND REFRESHING!
AS FOR ME... I'M MORE LIKE A POTATO... LUMPY AND A DIME A DOZEN.
She means to say that he's elegant.

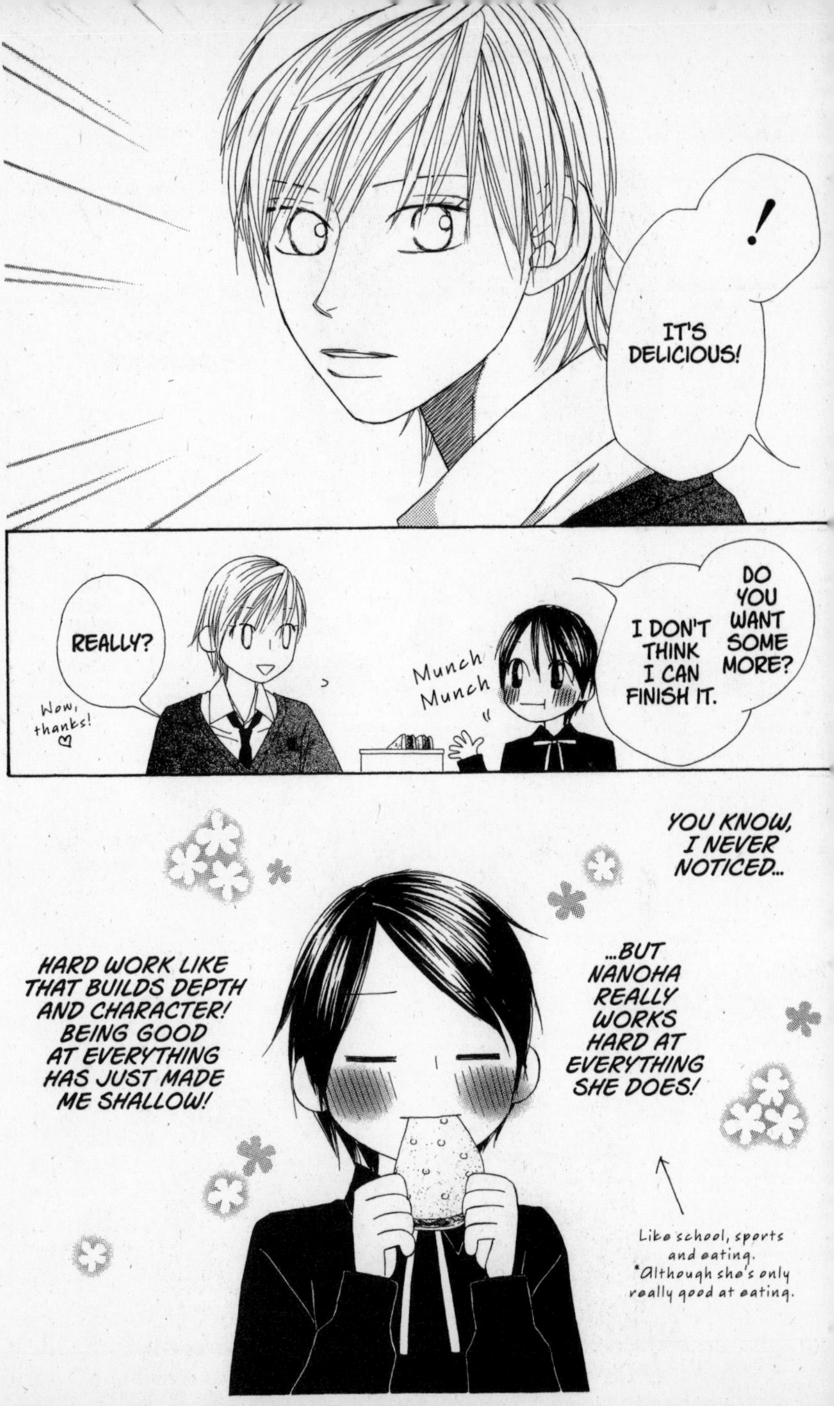
!
IT'S DELICIOUS!
DO YOU WANT SOME MORE?
I DON'T THINK I CAN FINISH IT.
Munch Munch
REALLY?
Wow, thanks! ♡
YOU KNOW, I NEVER NOTICED...
...BUT NANOHA REALLY WORKS HARD AT EVERYTHING SHE DOES!
Like school, sports and eating.
*Although she's only really good at eating.
HARD WORK LIKE THAT BUILDS DEPTH AND CHARACTER! BEING GOOD AT EVERYTHING HAS JUST MADE ME SHALLOW!

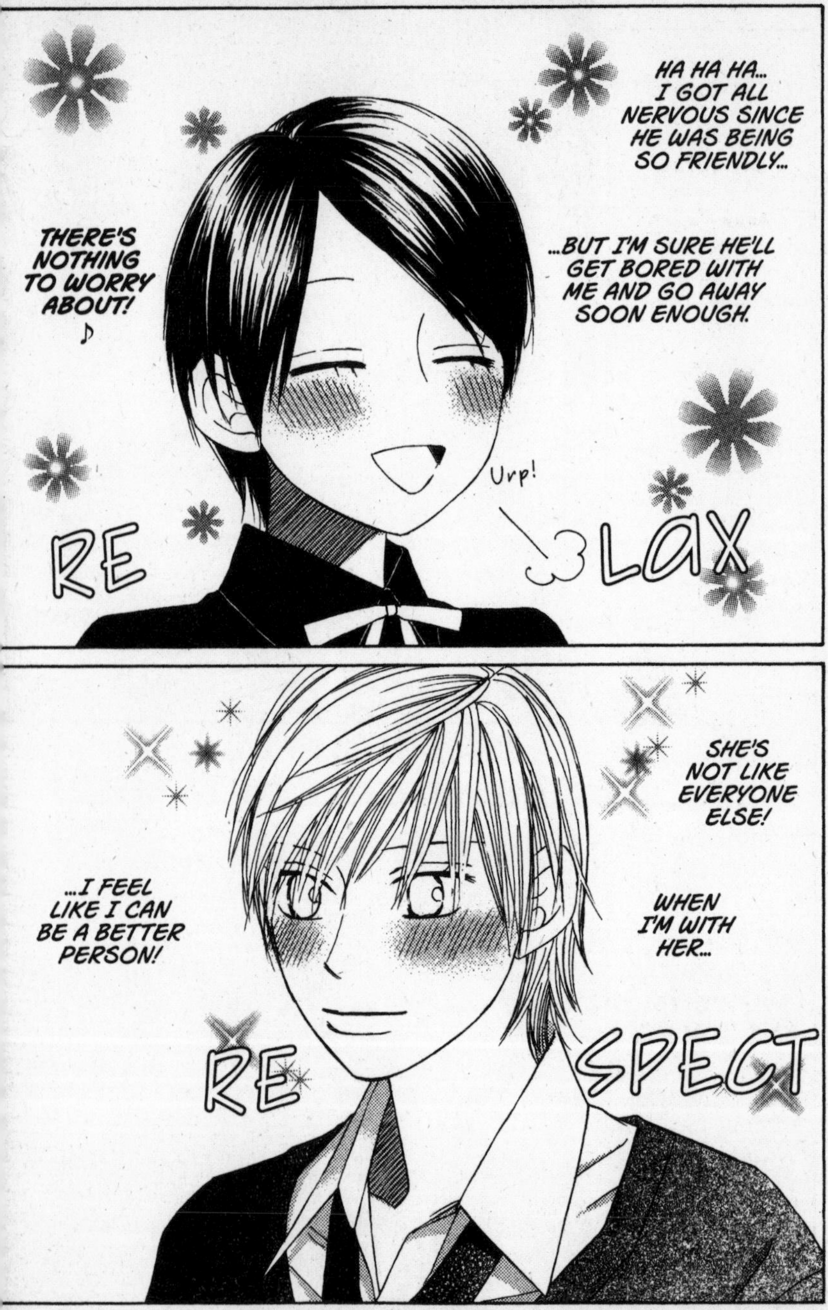
HA HA HA... I GOT ALL NERVOUS SINCE HE WAS BEING SO FRIENDLY...
...BUT I'M SURE HE'LL GET BORED WITH ME AND GO AWAY SOON ENOUGH.
THERE'S NOTHING TO WORRY ABOUT! ♪
Urp!
RE LAX
SHE'S NOT LIKE EVERYONE ELSE!
WHEN I'M WITH HER...
...I FEEL LIKE I CAN BE A BETTER PERSON!
RE SPECT

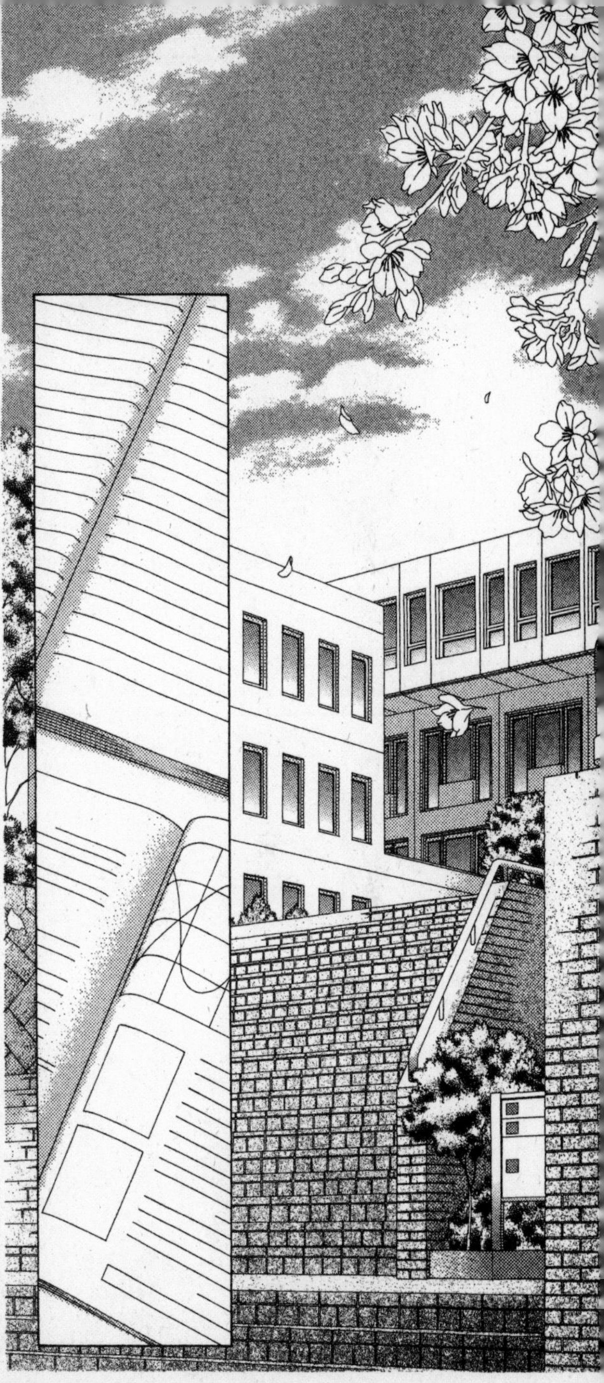

5
Cleaning

I cleaned a lot while I was off from work. Or rather, I threw away a lot.

Every time I decide to throw something away, it feels like I'm jumping off a cliff. No turning back! Still, I feel better when my place is nice and neat.

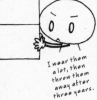

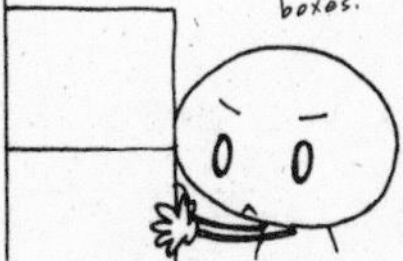
Keep only enough clothes to fit in these boxes.
I wear them a lot, then throw them away after three years.

If it's not in my line of vision, then it belongs in the trash!

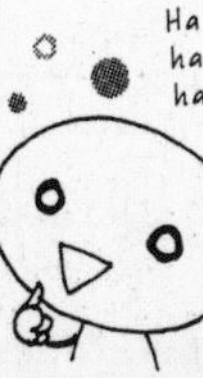
Now that I stopped spending so much money on junk, maybe I should travel more.
Ha ha ha

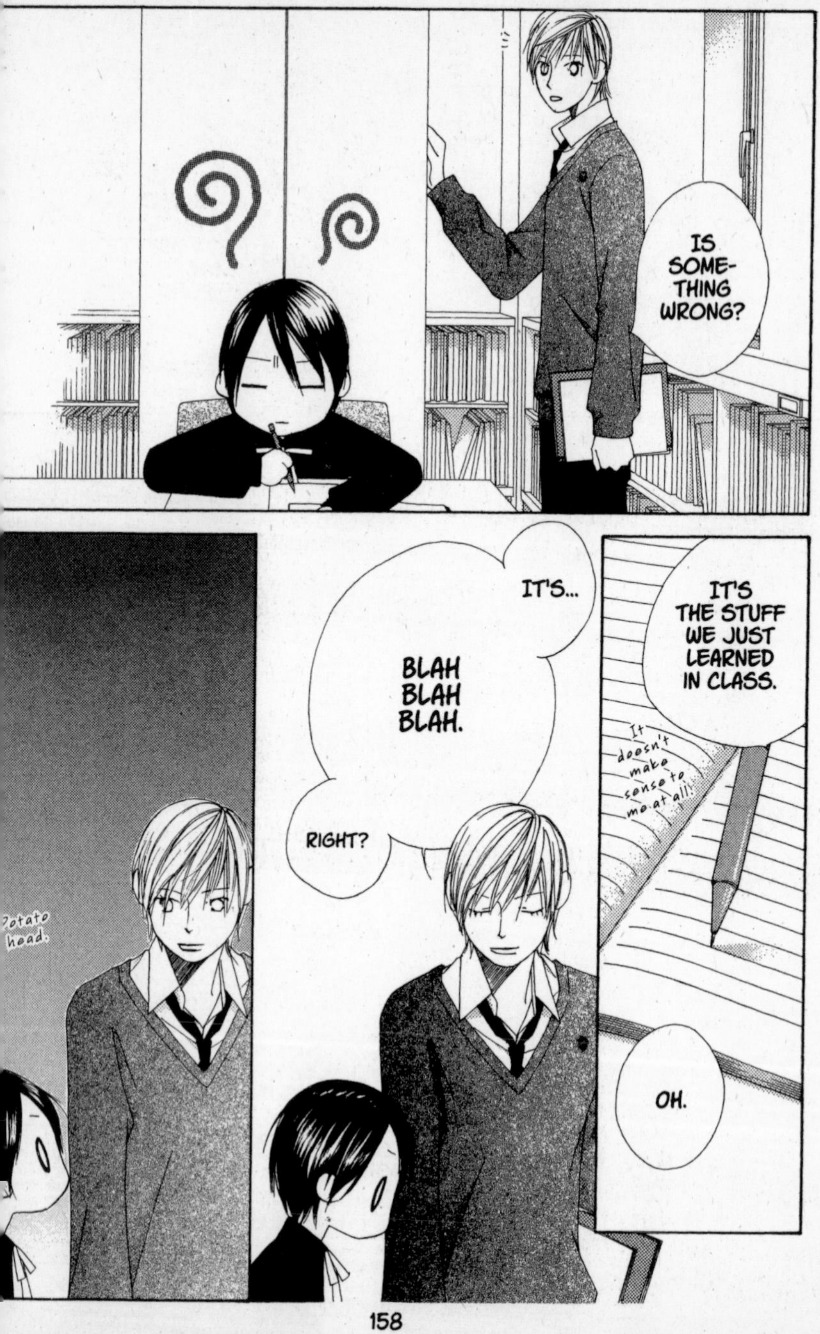
IS SOMETHING-THING WRONG?
IT'S THE STUFF WE JUST LEARNED IN CLASS.
It doesn't make sense to me at all!
OH.
IT'S...
BLAH BLAH BLAH.
RIGHT?
Potato head.

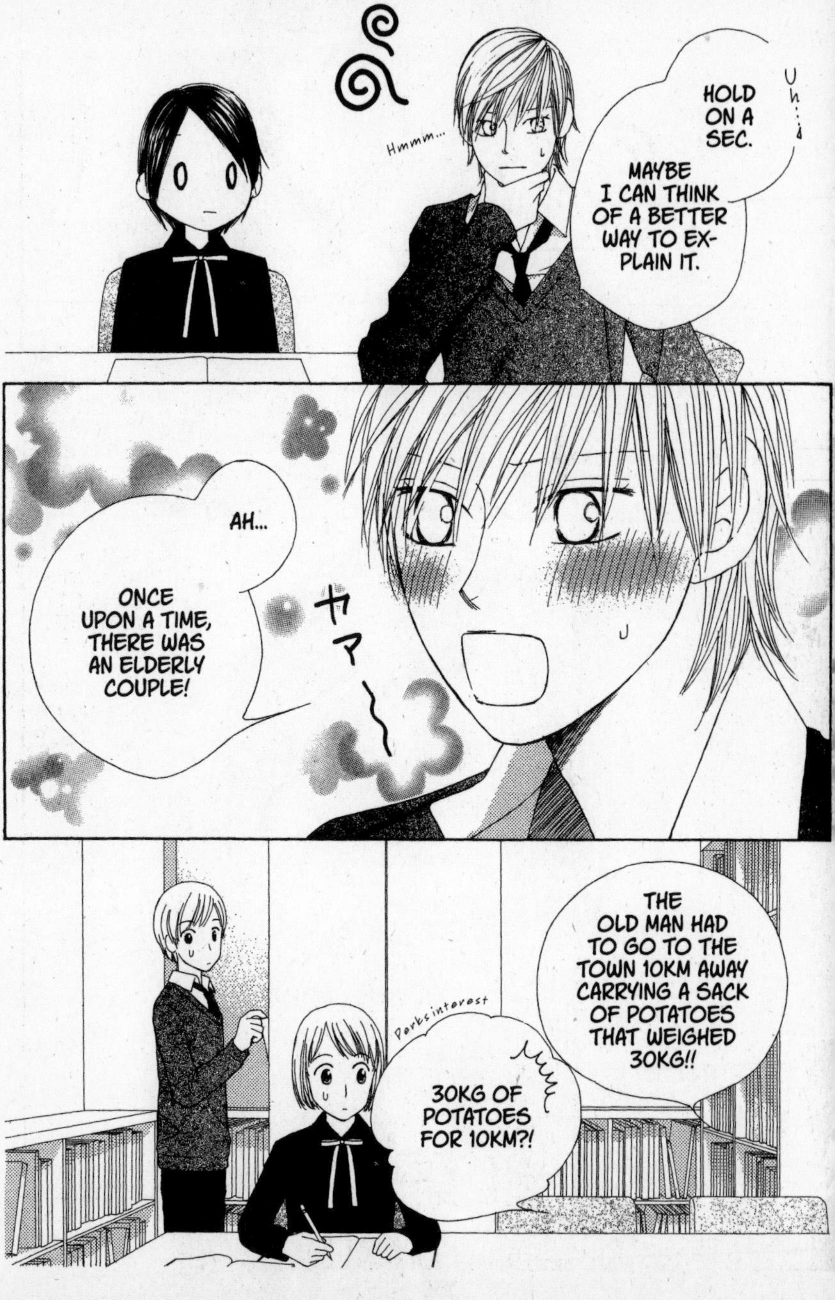
Uh...
HOLD ON A SEC.
MAYBE I CAN THINK OF A BETTER WAY TO EX-PLAIN IT.
Hmmm...
ヤァ～
AH...
ONCE UPON A TIME, THERE WAS AN ELDERLY COUPLE!
THE OLD MAN HAD TO GO TO THE TOWN 10KM AWAY CARRYING A SACK OF POTATOES THAT WEIGHED 30KG!!
Perks interest
30KG OF POTATOES FOR 10KM?!

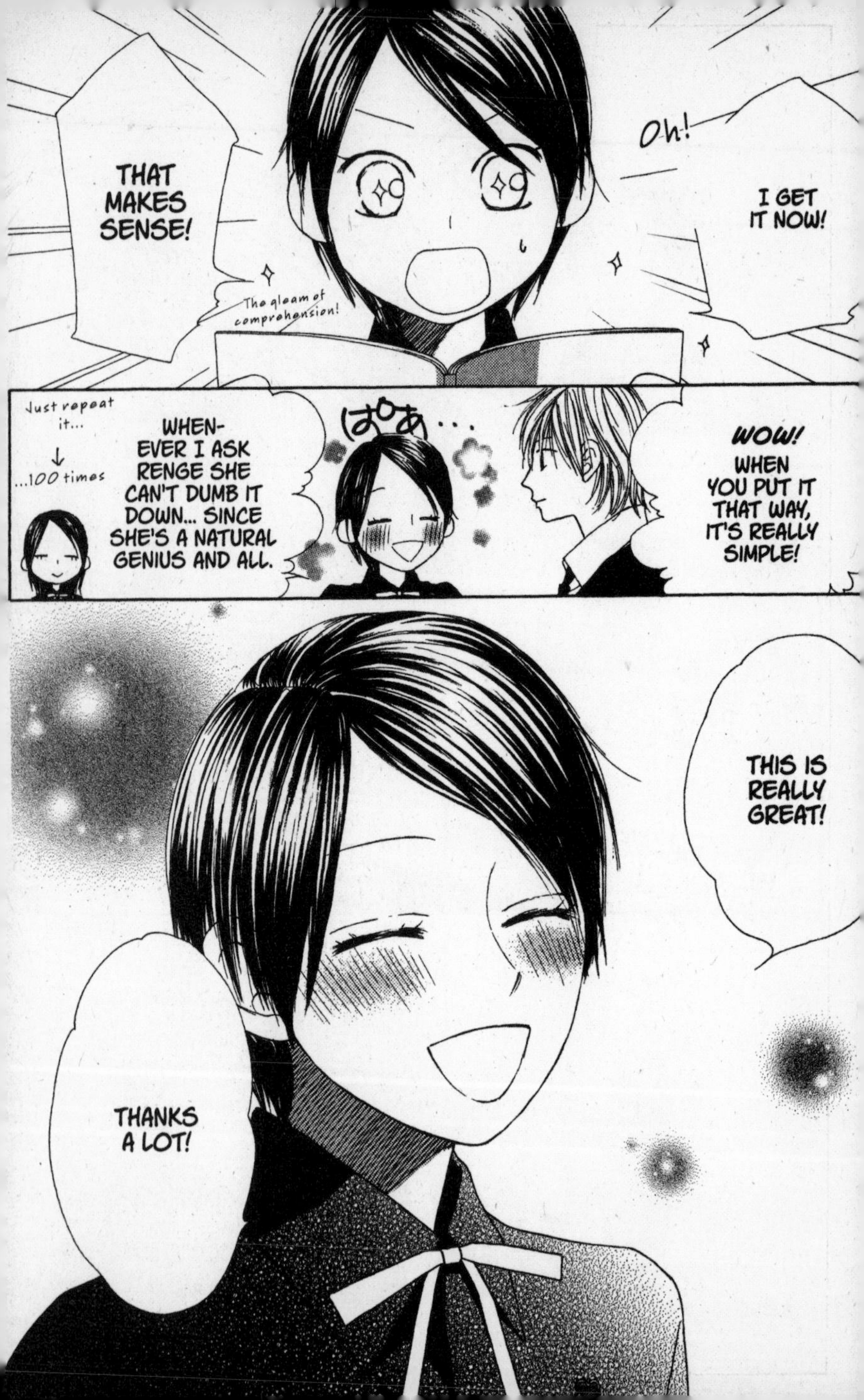
Oh!
I GET IT NOW!
THAT MAKES SENSE!
The gleam of comprehension!
WOW! WHEN YOU PUT IT THAT WAY, IT'S REALLY SIMPLE!
ぱあ…
WHEN-EVER I ASK RENGE SHE CAN'T DUMB IT DOWN... SINCE SHE'S A NATURAL GENIUS AND ALL.
Just repeat it... ↓ ...100 times
THIS IS REALLY GREAT!
THANKS A LOT!

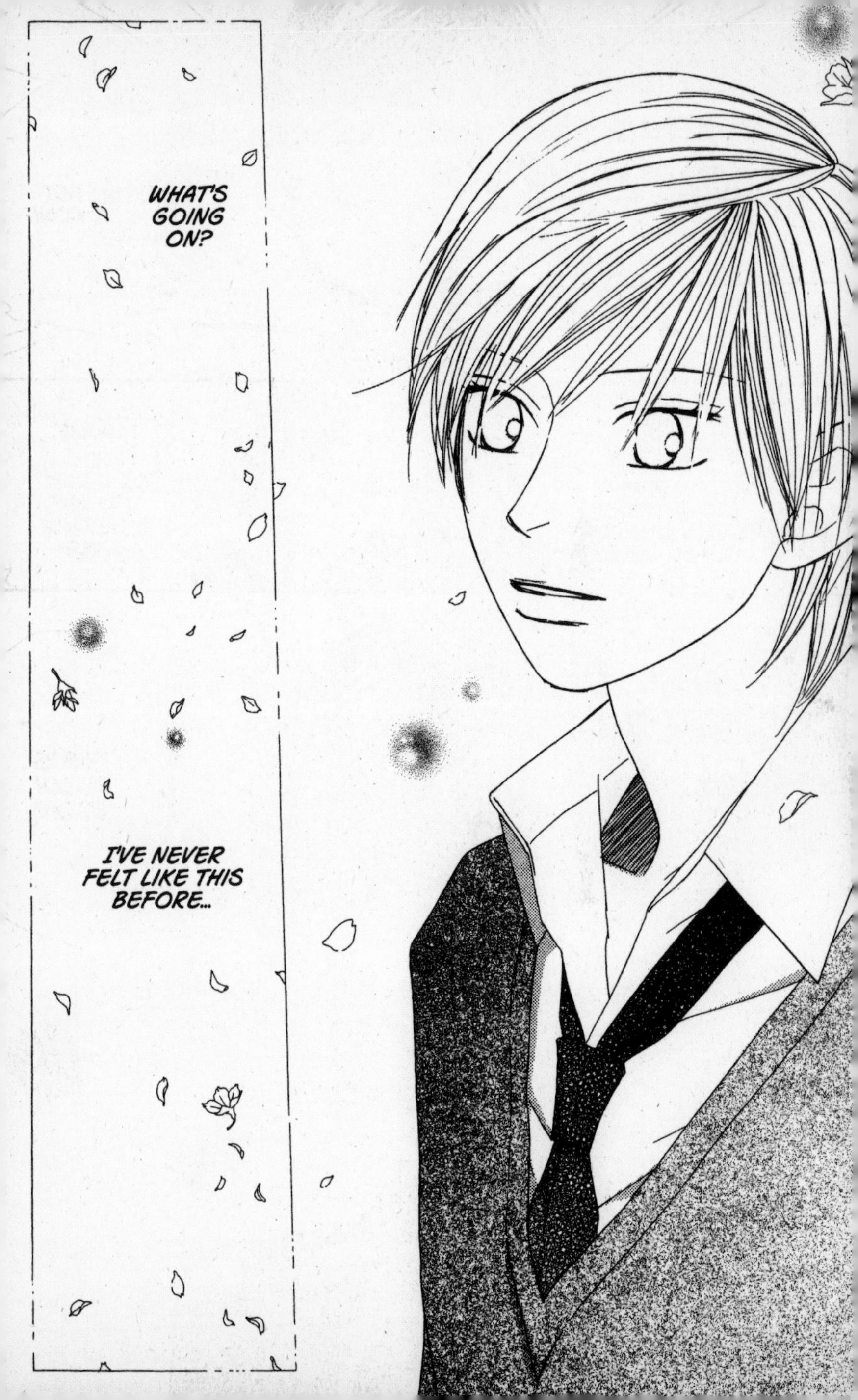
WHAT'S GOING ON?
I'VE NEVER FELT LIKE THIS BEFORE...

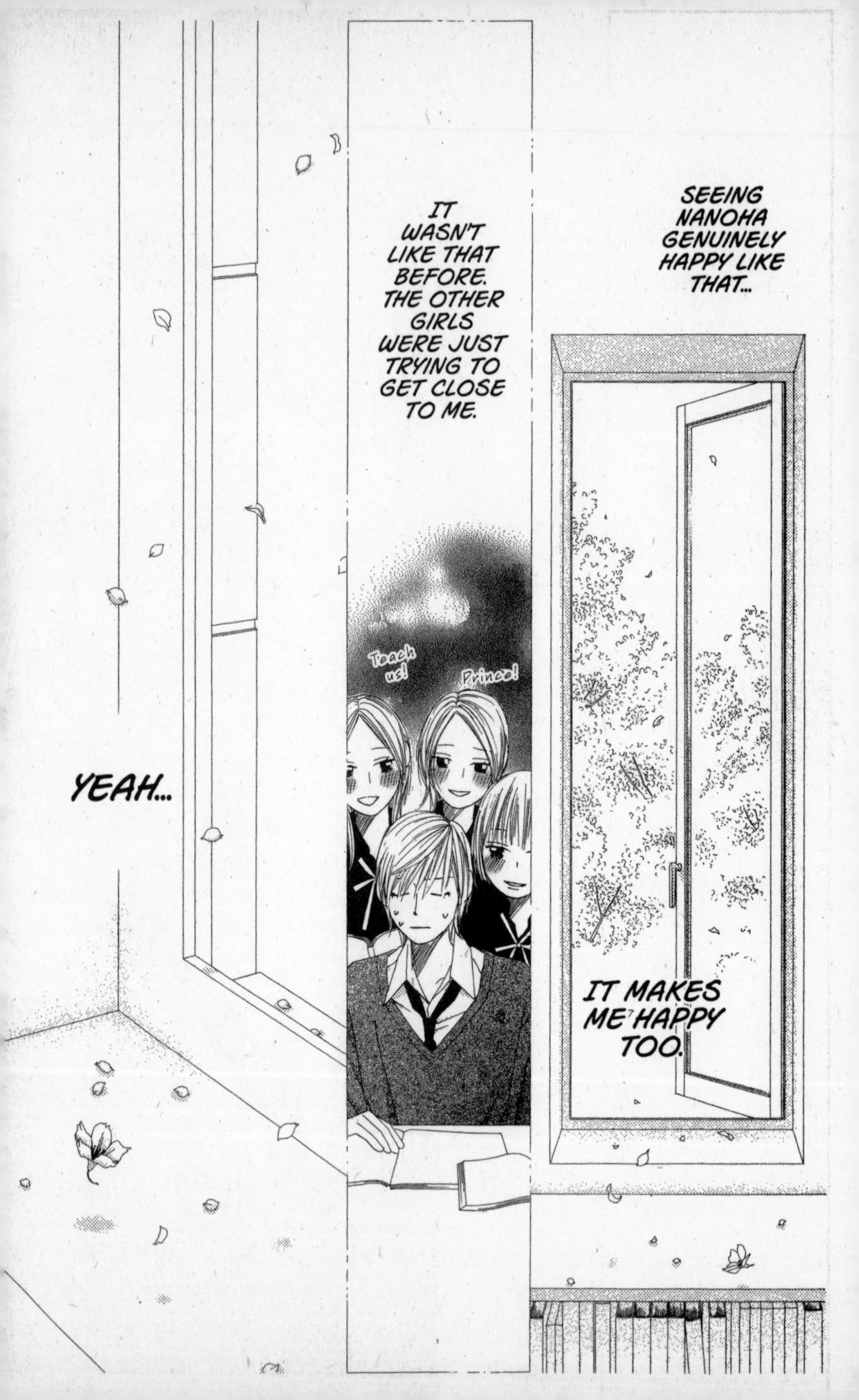
SEEING NANOHA GENUINELY HAPPY LIKE THAT...
IT MAKES ME HAPPY TOO.
IT WASN'T LIKE THAT BEFORE. THE OTHER GIRLS WERE JUST TRYING TO GET CLOSE TO ME.
Prince!
Teach us!
YEAH...

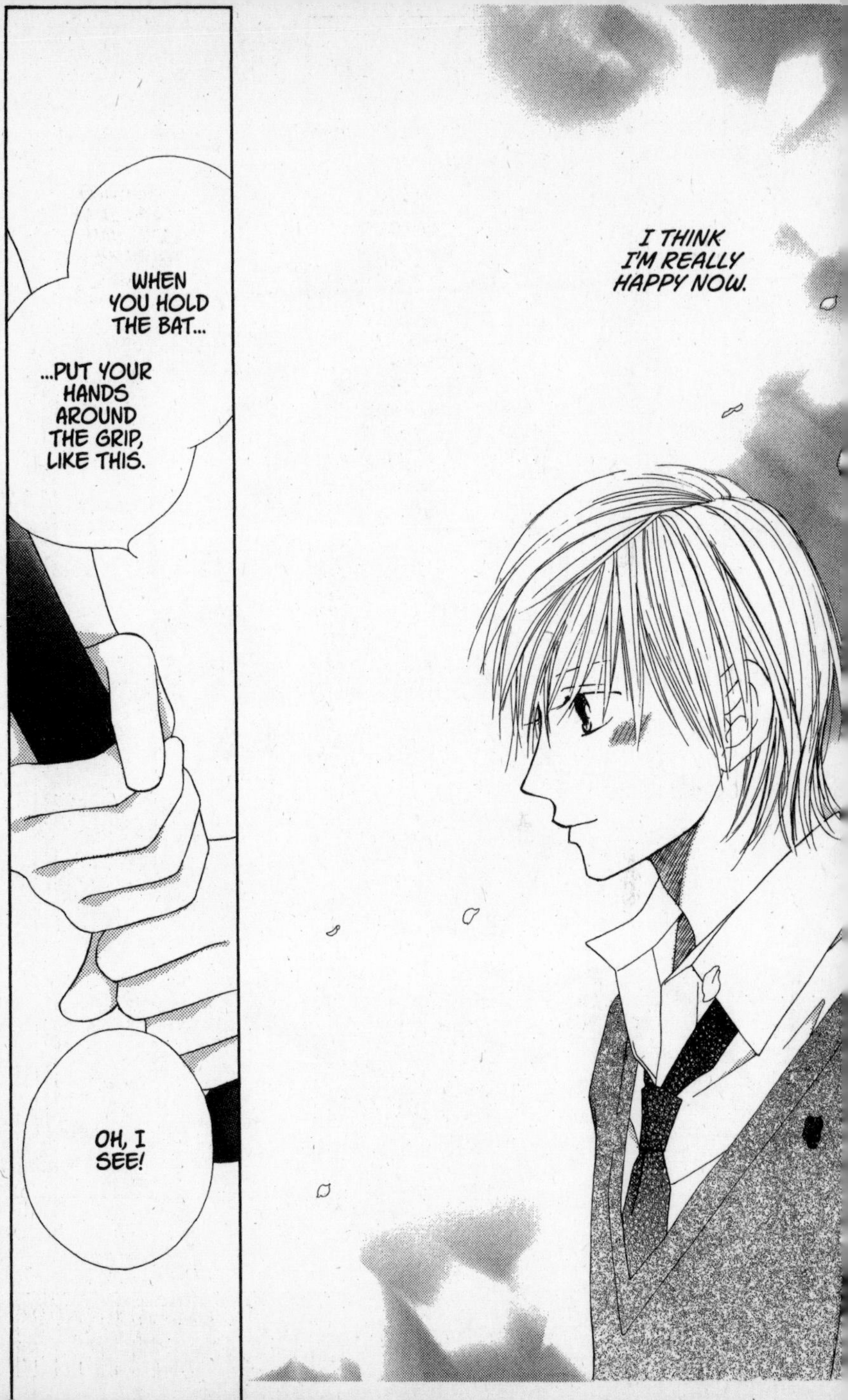
I THINK I'M REALLY HAPPY NOW.
WHEN YOU HOLD THE BAT...
...PUT YOUR HANDS AROUND THE GRIP, LIKE THIS.
OH, I SEE!

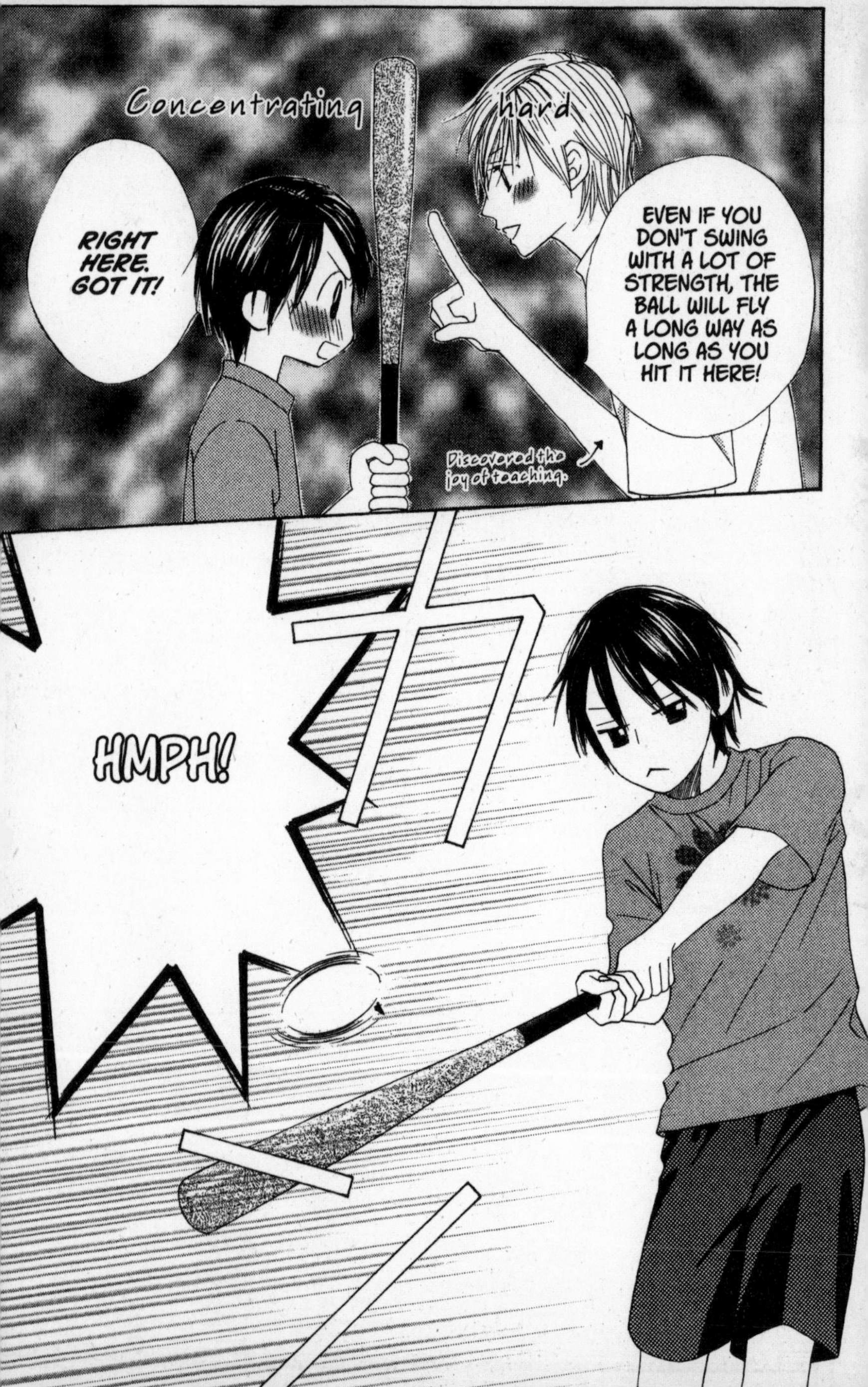

Concentrating hard
EVEN IF YOU DON'T SWING WITH A LOT OF STRENGTH, THE BALL WILL FLY A LONG WAY AS LONG AS YOU HIT IT HERE!
Discovered the joy of teaching.
RIGHT HERE. GOT IT!
HMPH!

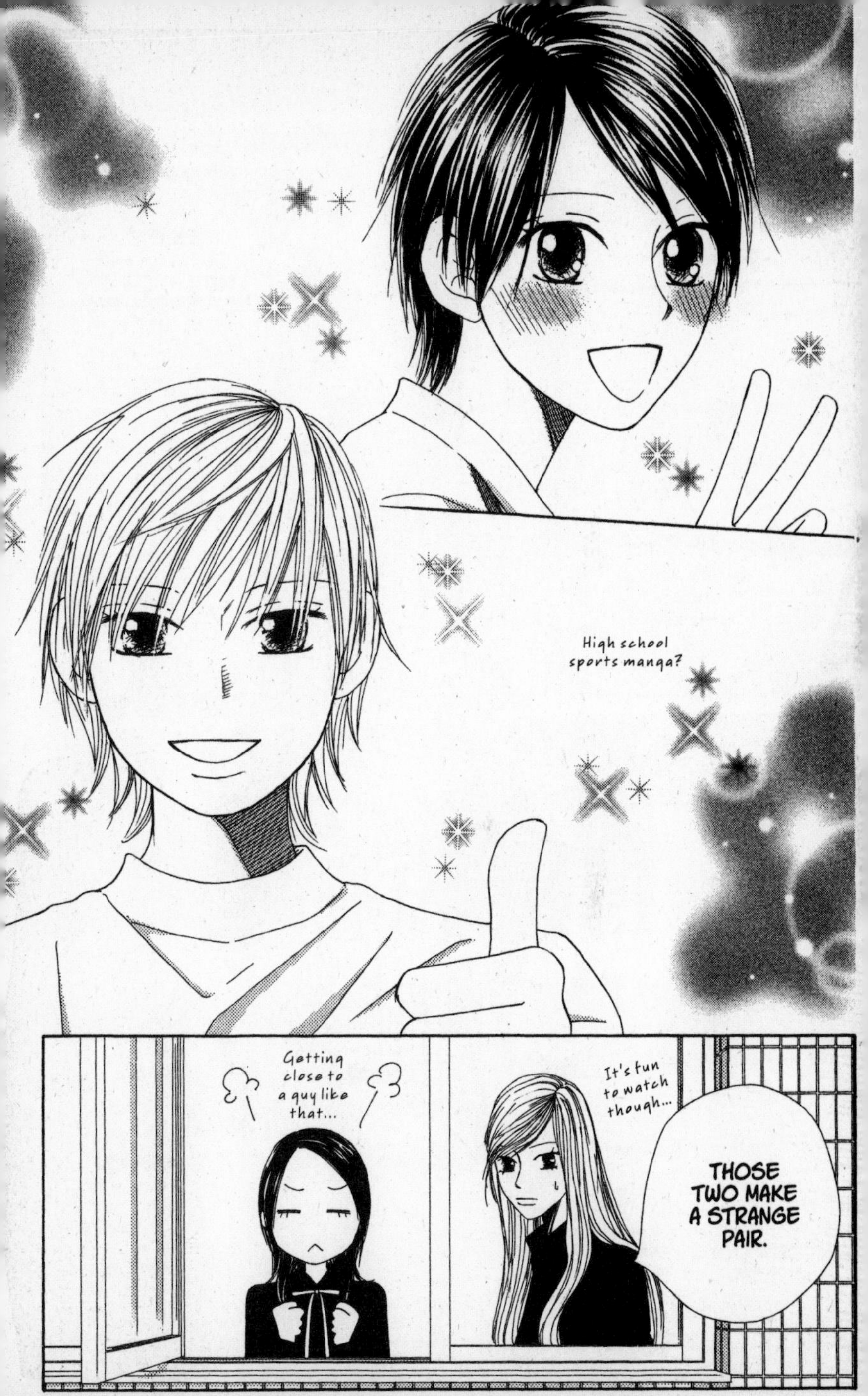
High school sports manga?
THOSE TWO MAKE A STRANGE PAIR.
It's fun to watch though...
Getting close to a guy like that...

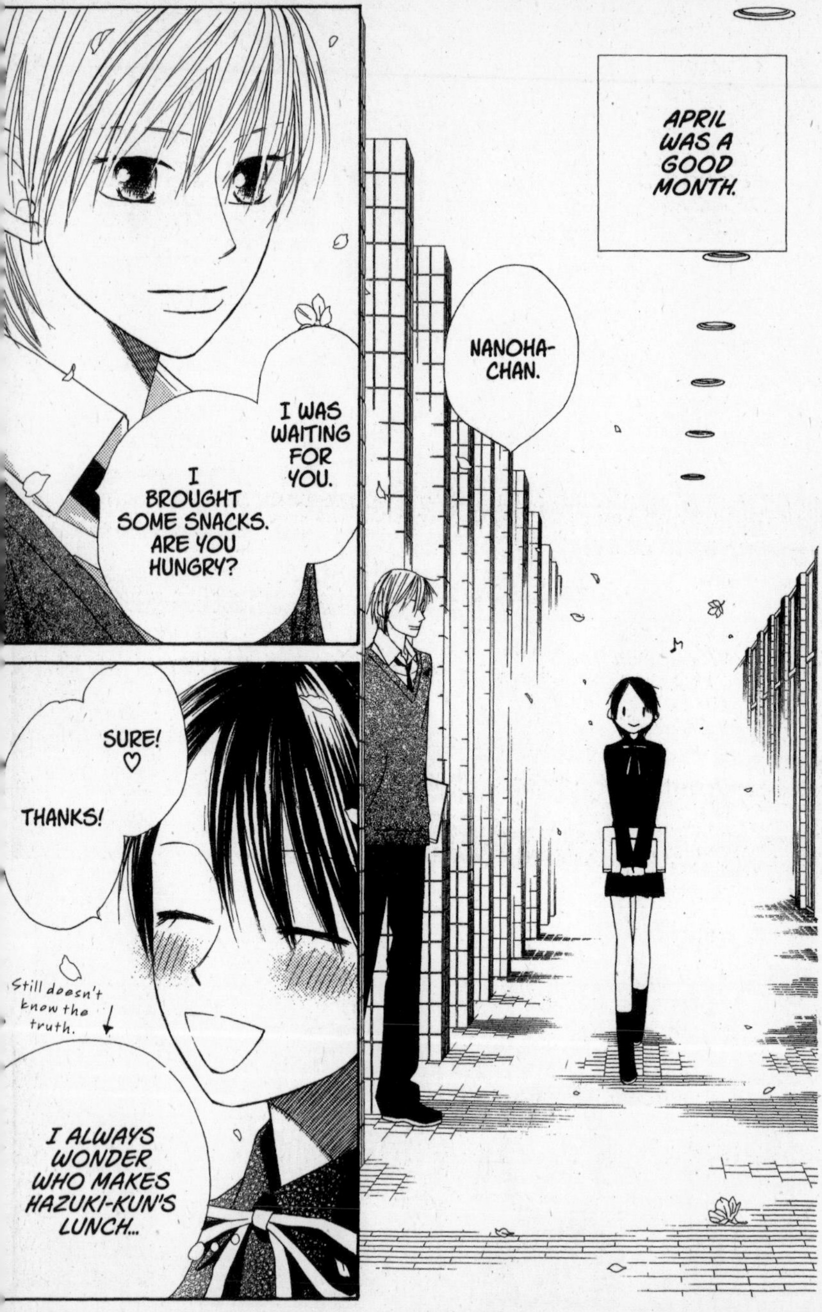
APRIL WAS A GOOD MONTH.
NANOHA-CHAN.
I WAS WAITING FOR YOU.
I BROUGHT SOME SNACKS. ARE YOU HUNGRY?
SURE! ♡
THANKS!
Still doesn't know the truth.
I ALWAYS WONDER WHO MAKES HAZUKI-KUN'S LUNCH...

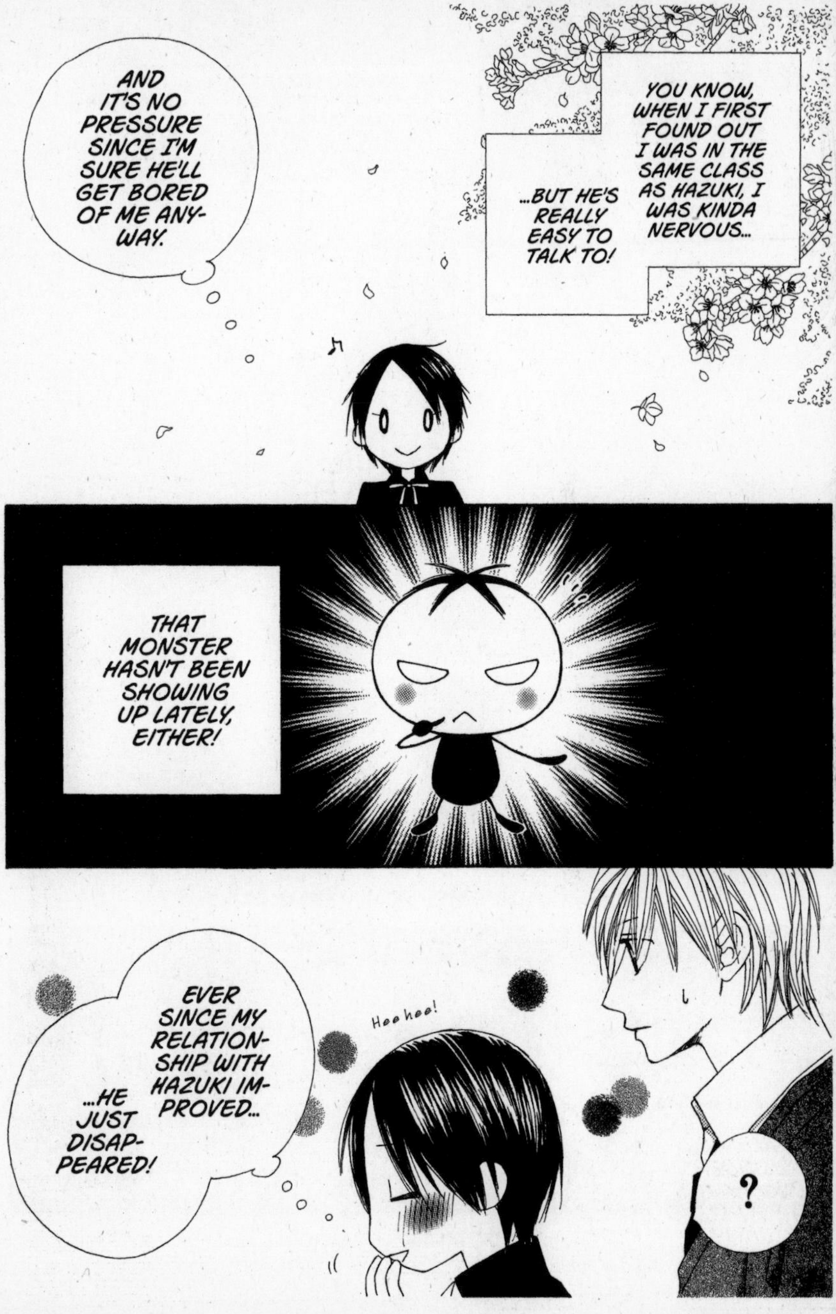
YOU KNOW, WHEN I FIRST FOUND OUT I WAS IN THE SAME CLASS AS HAZUKI, I WAS KINDA NERVOUS...
...BUT HE'S REALLY EASY TO TALK TO!
AND IT'S NO PRESSURE SINCE I'M SURE HE'LL GET BORED OF ME ANY-WAY.
THAT MONSTER HASN'T BEEN SHOWING UP LATELY, EITHER!
EVER SINCE MY RELATION-SHIP WITH HAZUKI IM-PROVED...
...HE JUST DISAP-PEARED!
Hee hee!
?

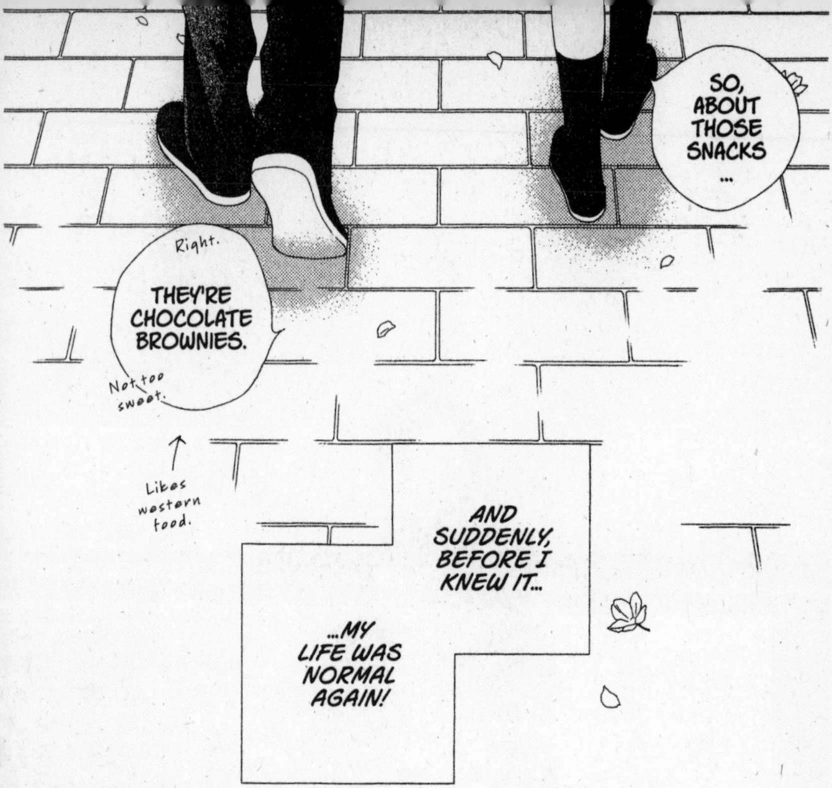
SO, ABOUT THOSE SNACKS ...
Right.
THEY'RE CHOCOLATE BROWNIES.
Not too sweet.
Likes western food.
AND SUDDENLY, BEFORE I KNEW IT...
...MY LIFE WAS NORMAL AGAIN!

EENSY WEENSY MONSTER <END>

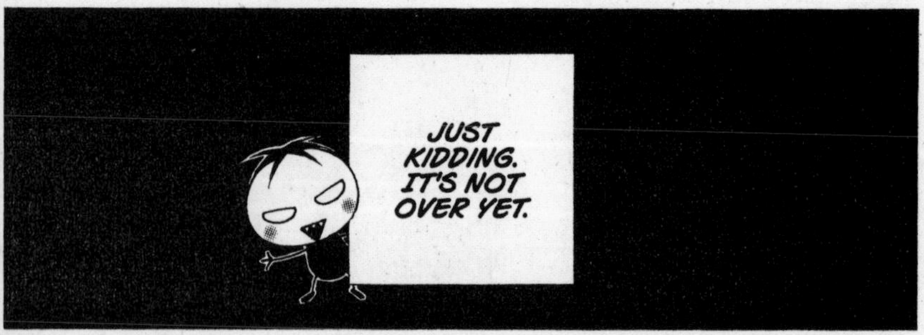
JUST KIDDING. IT'S NOT OVER YET.

STEP 5 / END

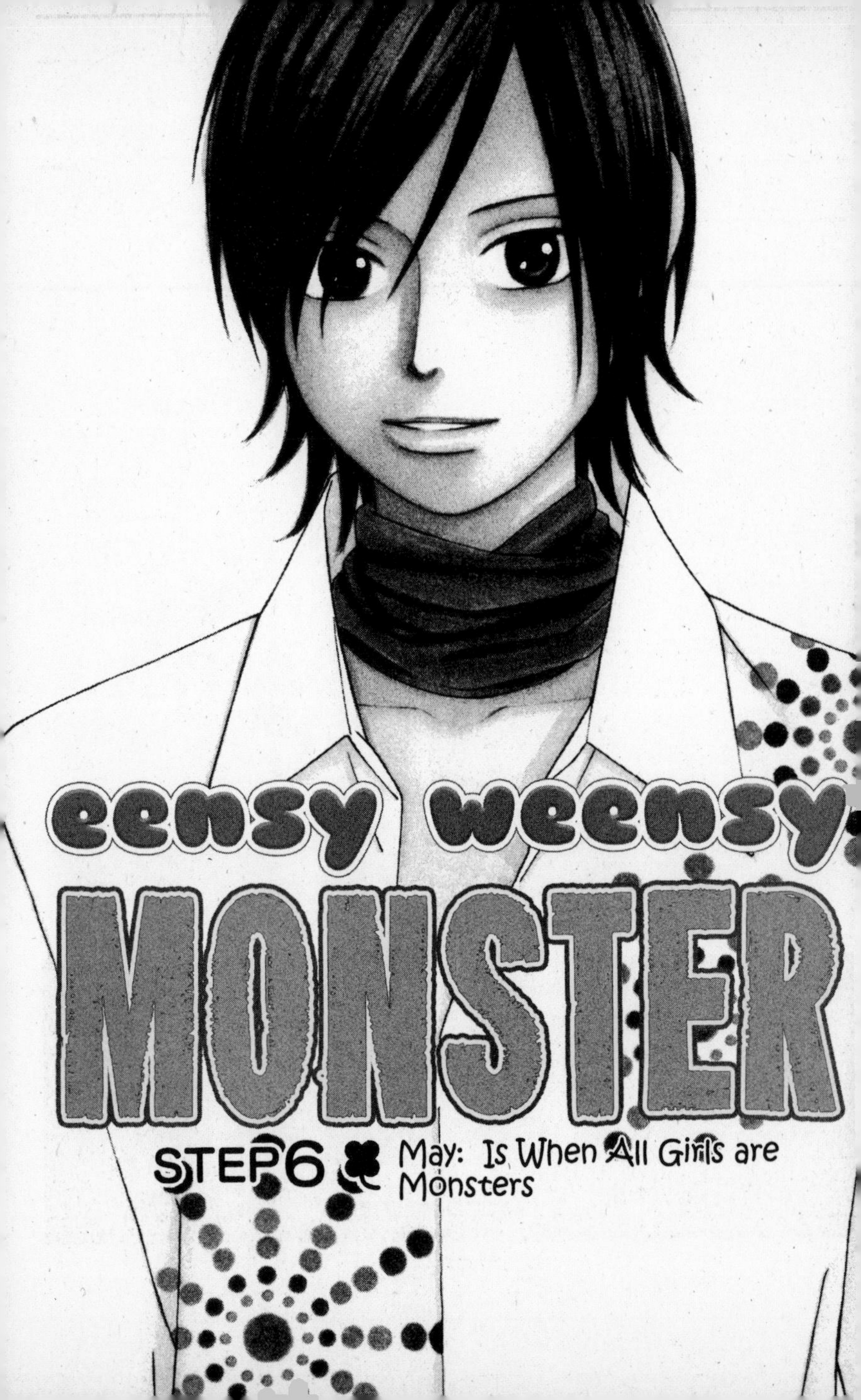
eensy weensy
MONSTER
STEP 6
May: Is When All Girls are Monsters

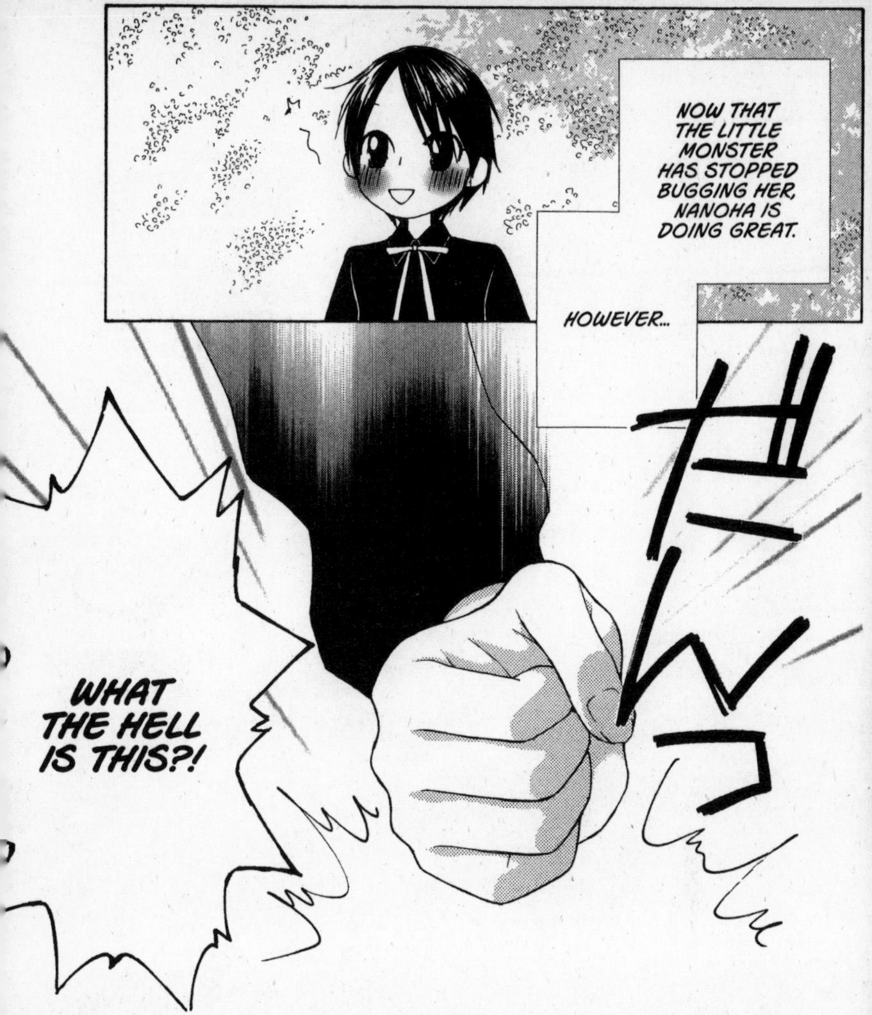

NOW THAT THE LITTLE MONSTER HAS STOPPED BUGGING HER, NANOHA IS DOING GREAT.
HOWEVER...
WHAT THE HELL IS THIS?!

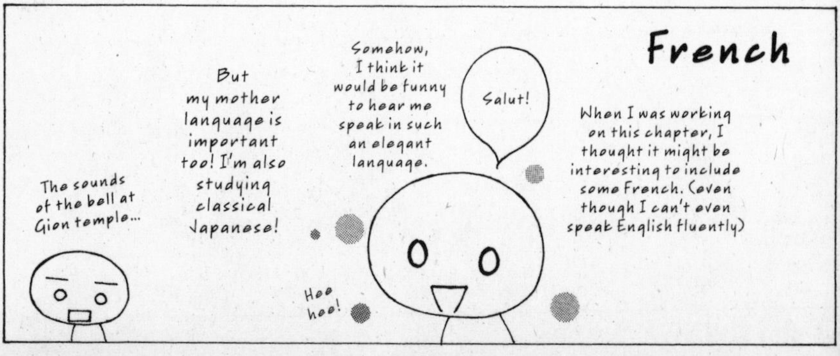

French
When I was working on this chapter, I thought it might be interesting to include some French. (even though I can't even speak English fluently)
Salut!
Somehow, I think it would be funny to hear me speak in such an elegant language.
Hee hee!
But my mother language is important too! I'm also studying classical Japanese!
The sounds of the bell at Gion temple...

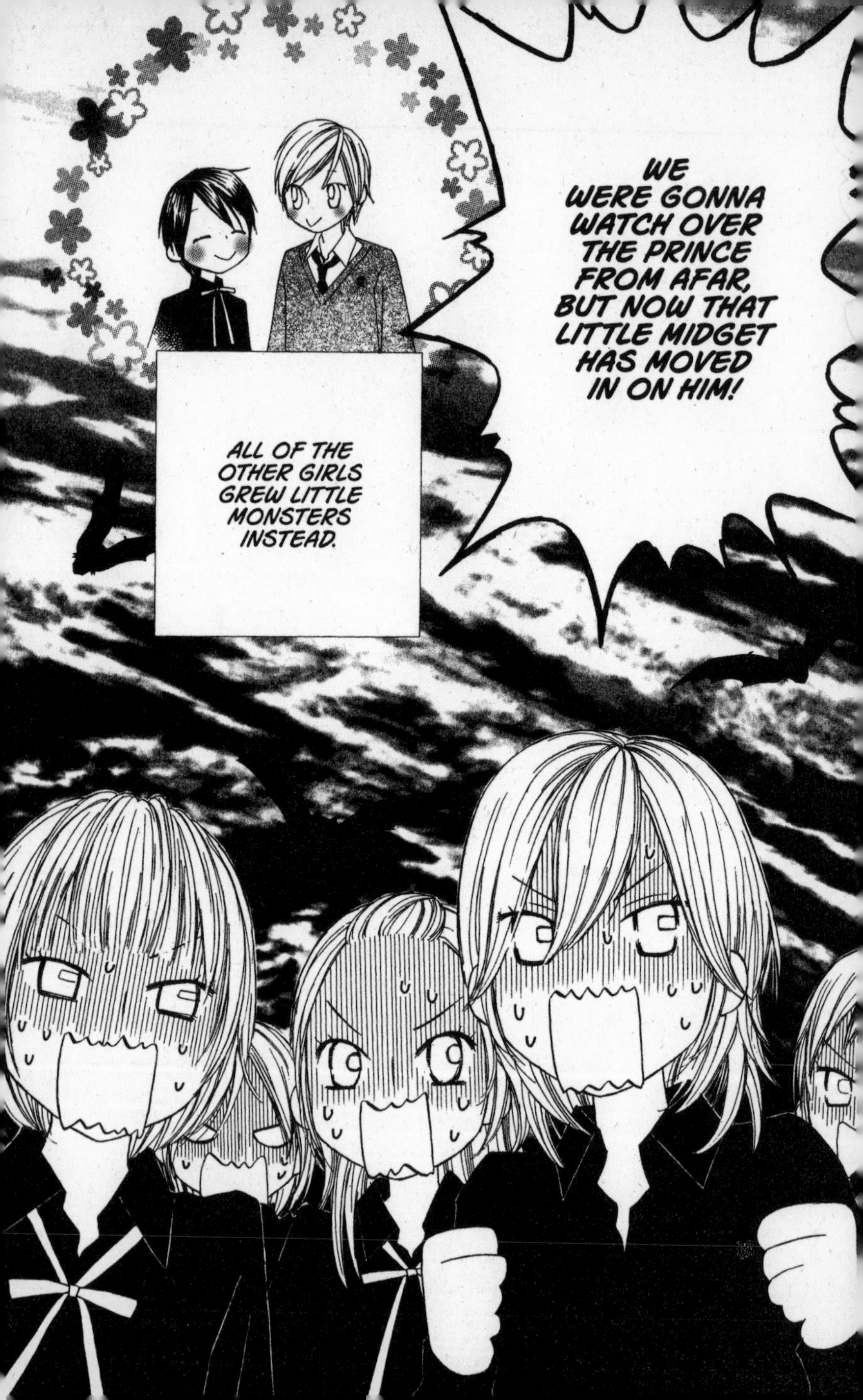
WE WERE GONNA WATCH OVER THE PRINCE FROM AFAR, BUT NOW THAT LITTLE MIDGET HAS MOVED IN ON HIM!
ALL OF THE OTHER GIRLS GREW LITTLE MONSTERS INSTEAD.

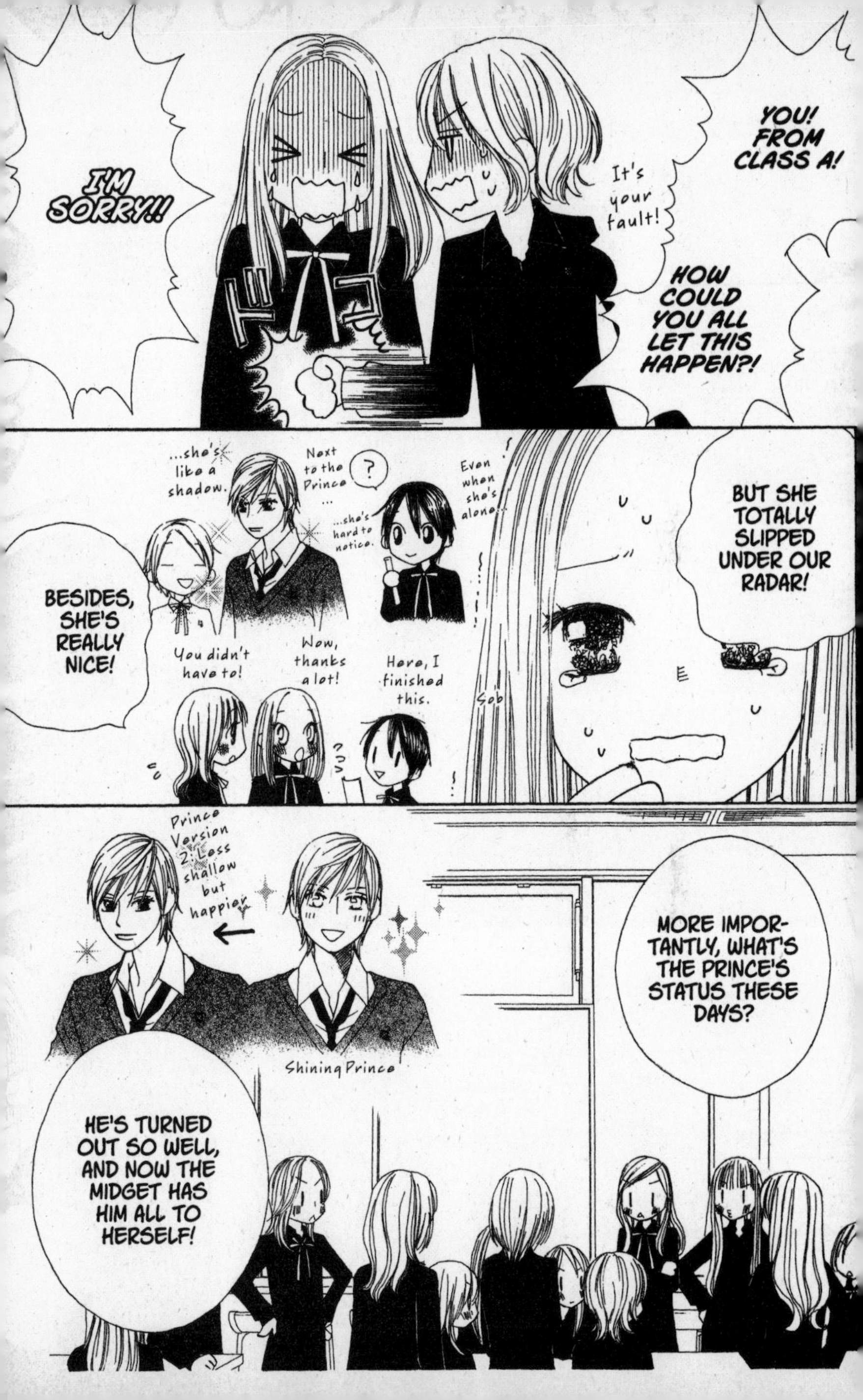
YOU! FROM CLASS A!
HOW COULD YOU ALL LET THIS HAPPEN?!
It's your fault!
I'M SORRY!!
BUT SHE TOTALLY SLIPPED UNDER OUR RADAR!
Sob
Even when she's alone...
Next to the Prince...
...she's hard to notice.
...she's like a shadow.
BESIDES, SHE'S REALLY NICE!
Here, I finished this.
Wow, thanks a lot!
You didn't have to!
MORE IMPORTANTLY, WHAT'S THE PRINCE'S STATUS THESE DAYS?
Prince Version 2: Less shallow but happier
Shining Prince
HE'S TURNED OUT SO WELL, AND NOW THE MIDGET HAS HIM ALL TO HERSELF!

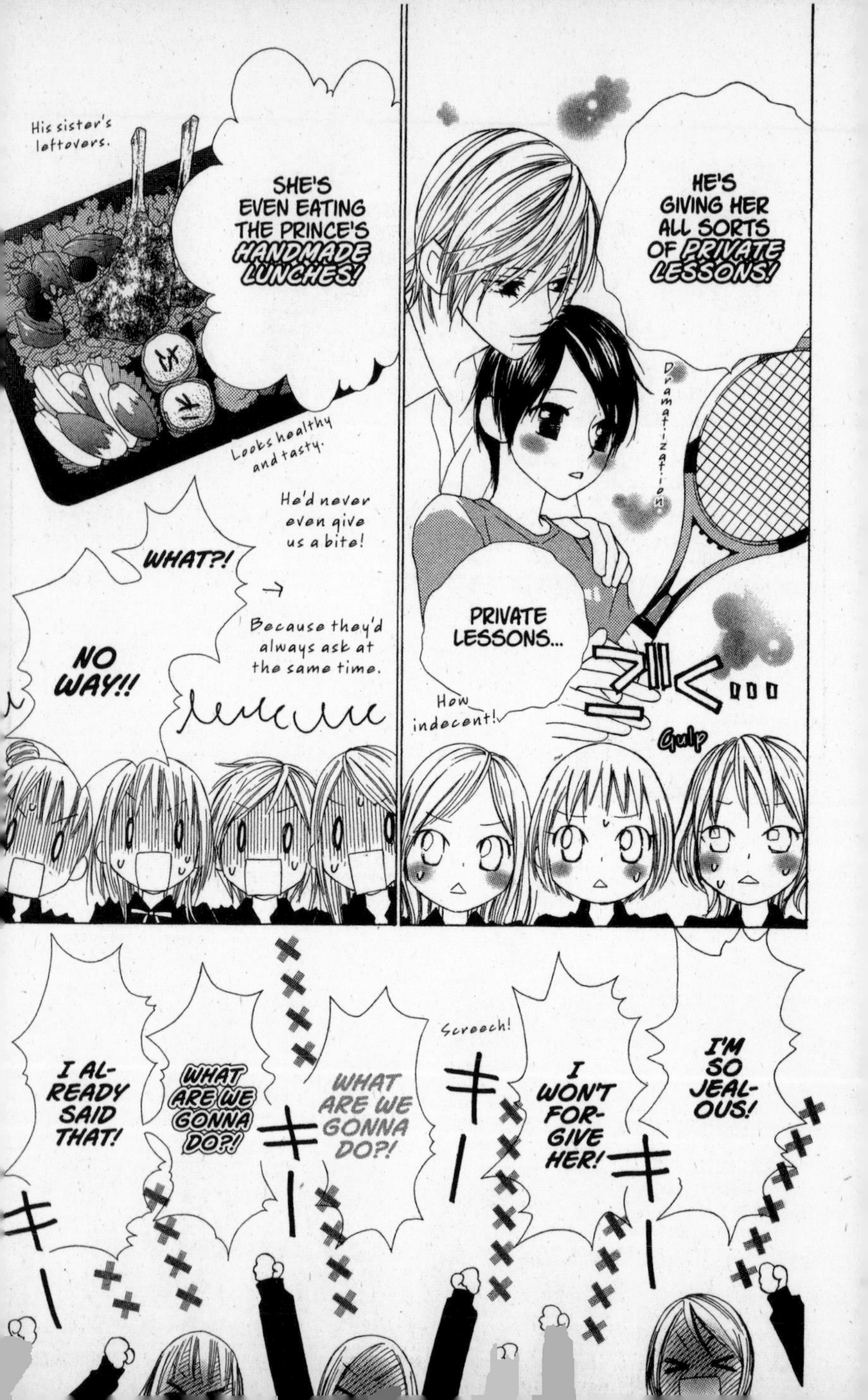
HE'S GIVING HER ALL SORTS OF PRIVATE LESSONS!
Dramatization
PRIVATE LESSONS...
How indecent!
Gulp
His sister's leftovers.
SHE'S EVEN EATING THE PRINCE'S HANDMADE LUNCHES!
Looks healthy and tasty.
He'd never even give us a bite!
→
Because they'd always ask at the same time.
WHAT?!
NO WAY!!
I'M SO JEAL-OUS!
I WON'T FOR-GIVE HER!
Screech!
WHAT ARE WE GONNA DO?!
WHAT ARE WE GONNA DO?!
I AL-READY SAID THAT!

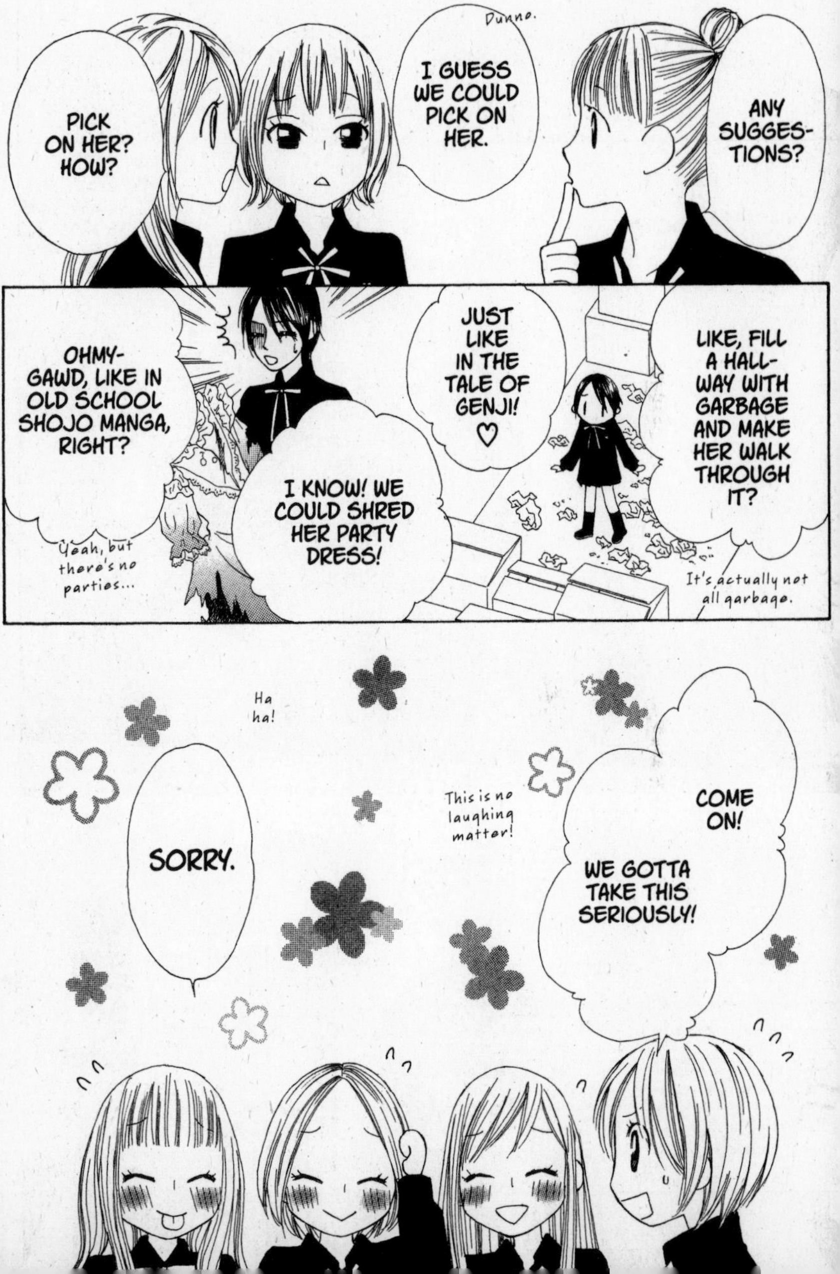
ANY SUGGES-TIONS?
Dunno.
I GUESS WE COULD PICK ON HER.
PICK ON HER? HOW?
LIKE, FILL A HALL-WAY WITH GARBAGE AND MAKE HER WALK THROUGH IT?
It's actually not all garbage.
JUST LIKE IN THE TALE OF GENJI! ♡
OHMY-GAWD, LIKE IN OLD SCHOOL SHOJO MANGA, RIGHT?
I KNOW! WE COULD SHRED HER PARTY DRESS!
Yeah, but there's no parties...
COME ON!
WE GOTTA TAKE THIS SERIOUSLY!
This is no laughing matter!
Ha ha!
SORRY.

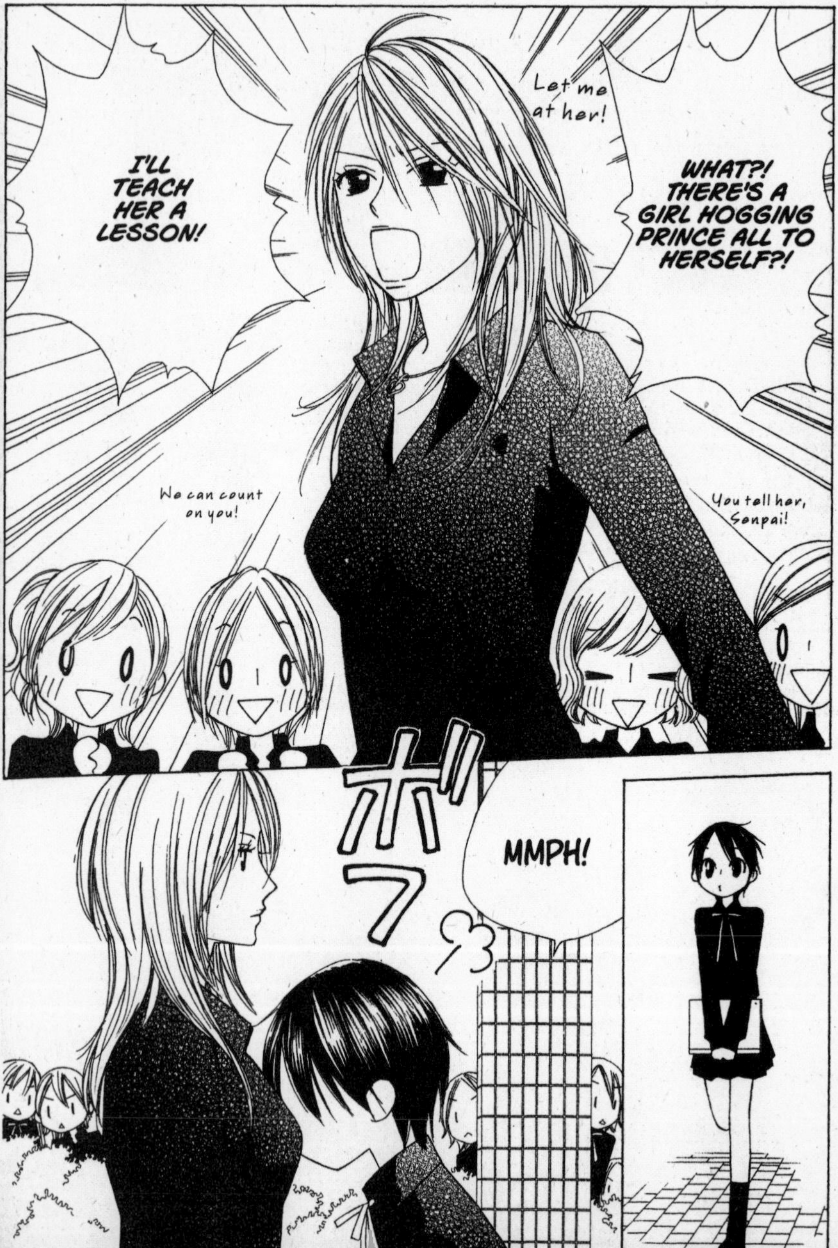

Let me at her!
WHAT?! THERE'S A GIRL HOGGING PRINCE ALL TO HERSELF?!
I'LL TEACH HER A LESSON!
You tell her, Senpai!
We can count on you!
MMPH!
ボフ

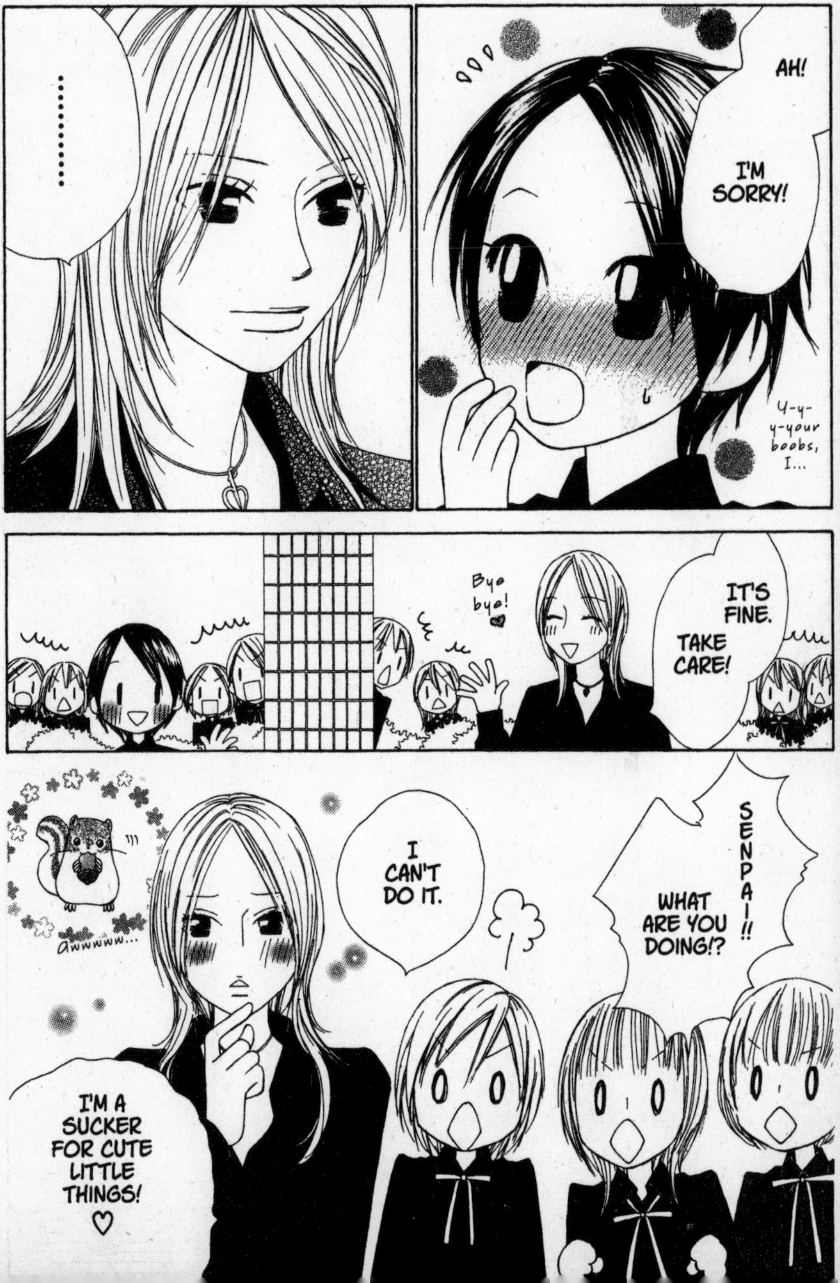
AH!
I'M SORRY!
Y-y-y-your boobs, I...
....
IT'S FINE. TAKE CARE!
Bye bye! ♥
SENPAI!!
WHAT ARE YOU DOING!?
I CAN'T DO IT.
awwwww...
I'M A SUCKER FOR CUTE LITTLE THINGS! ♡

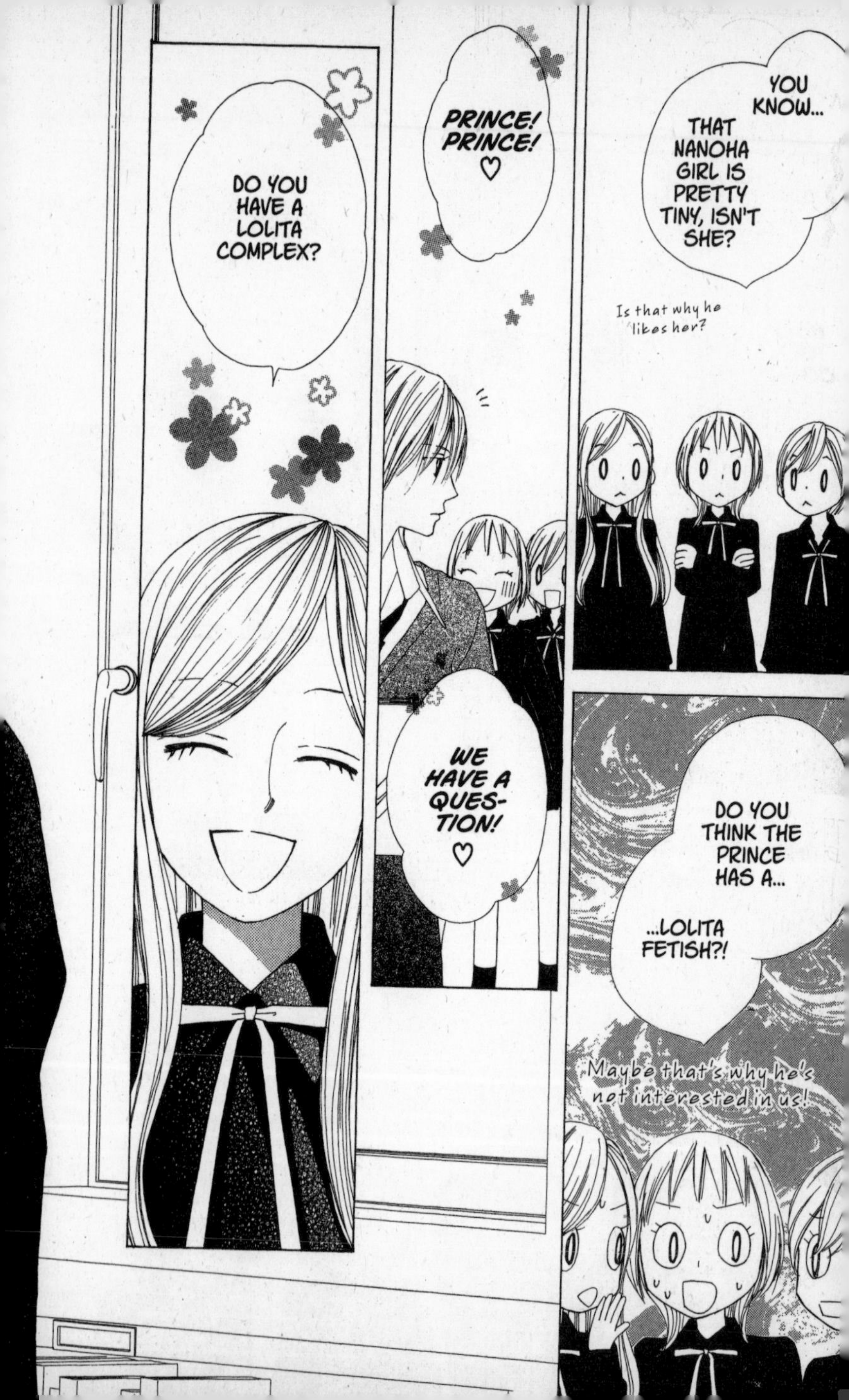
YOU KNOW... THAT NANOHA GIRL IS PRETTY TINY, ISN'T SHE?
Is that why he likes her?
DO YOU THINK THE PRINCE HAS A... ...LOLITA FETISH?!
Maybe that's why he's not interested in us!
PRINCE! PRINCE! ♡
WE HAVE A QUESTION! ♡
DO YOU HAVE A LOLITA COMPLEX?

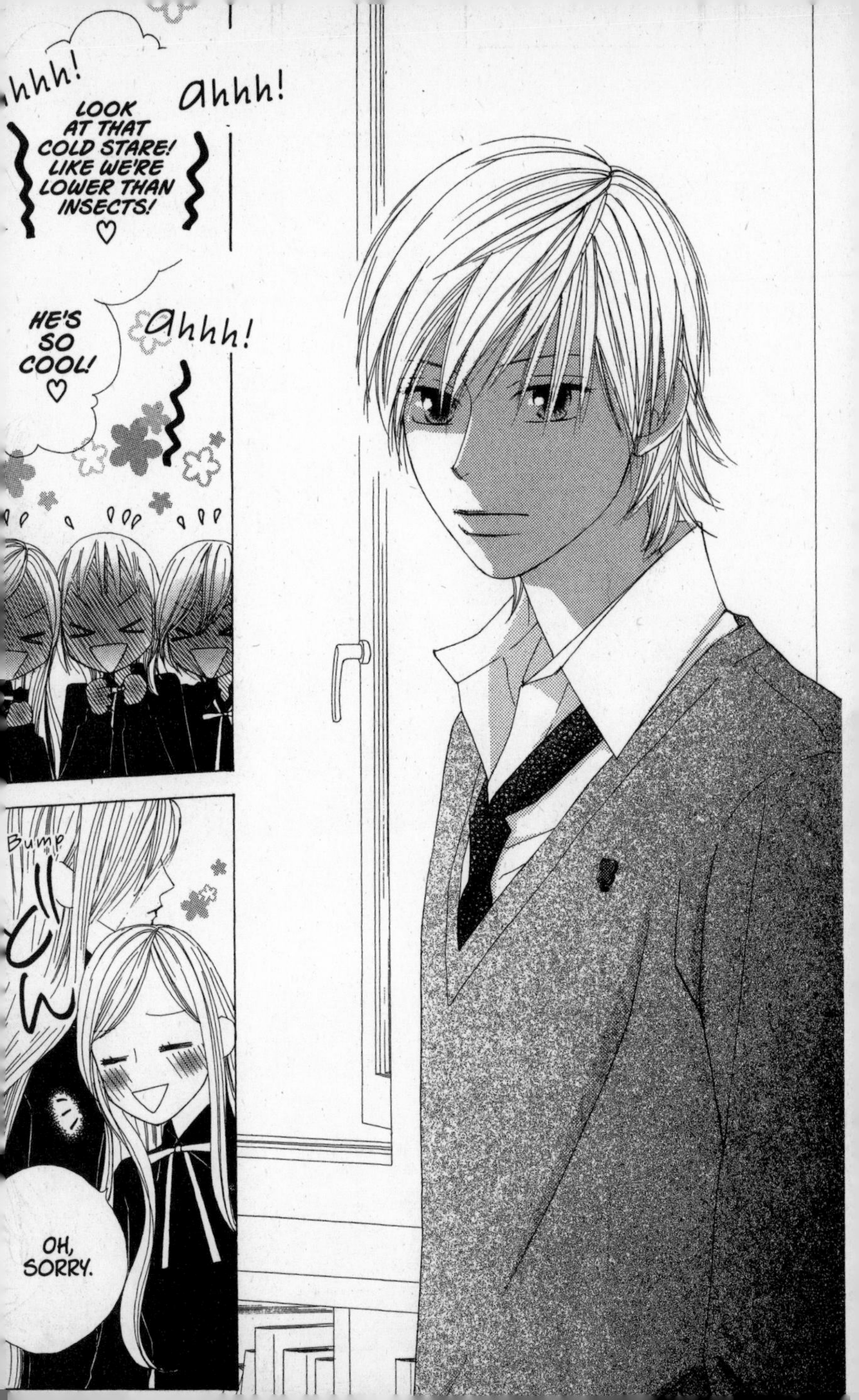
ahhh!
hhh!
LOOK AT THAT COLD STARE! LIKE WE'RE LOWER THAN INSECTS! ♡
ahhh!
HE'S SO COOL! ♡
Bump
OH, SORRY.

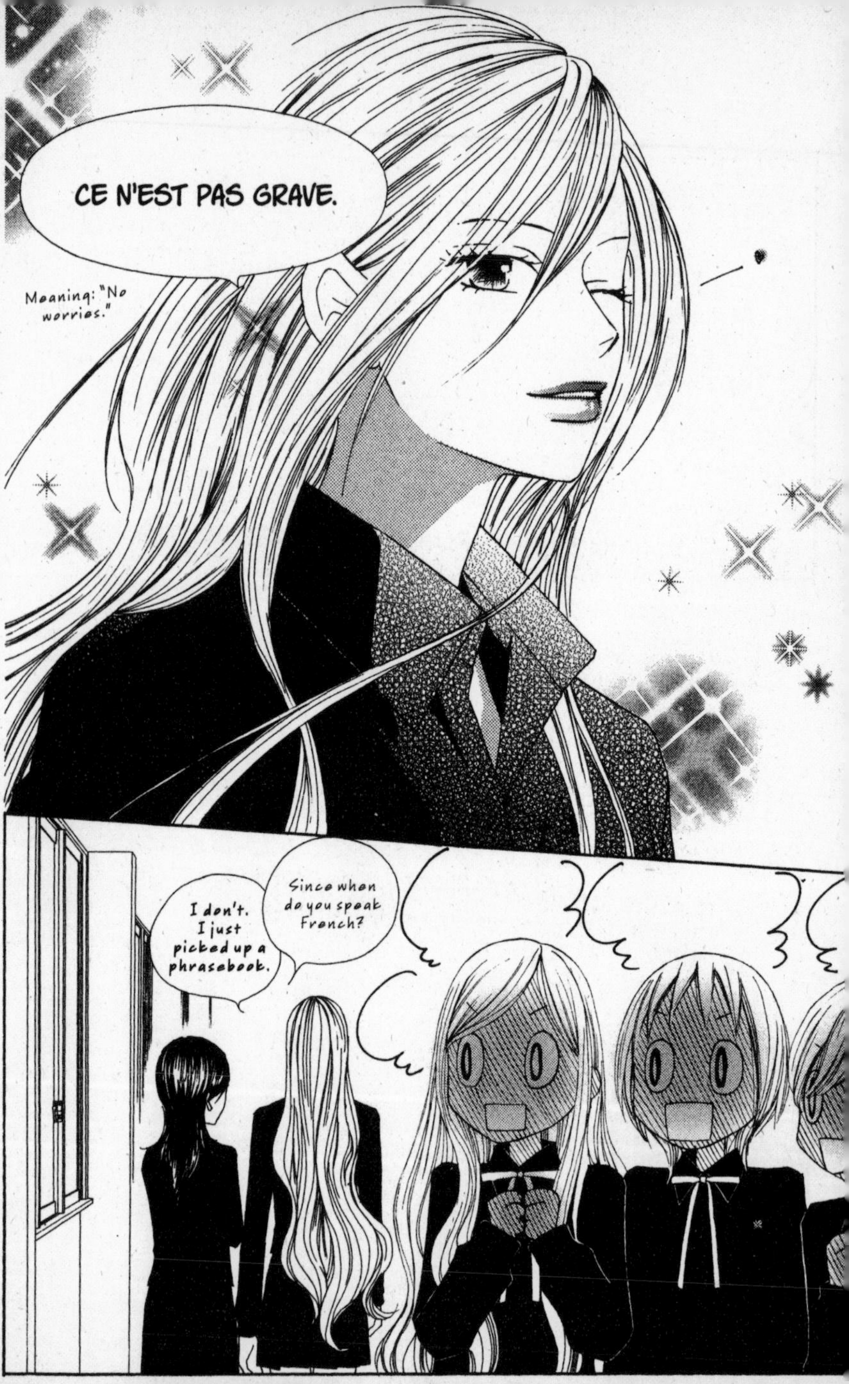
CE N'EST PAS GRAVE.
Meaning: "No worries."
Since when do you speak French?
I don't. I just picked up a phrasebook.

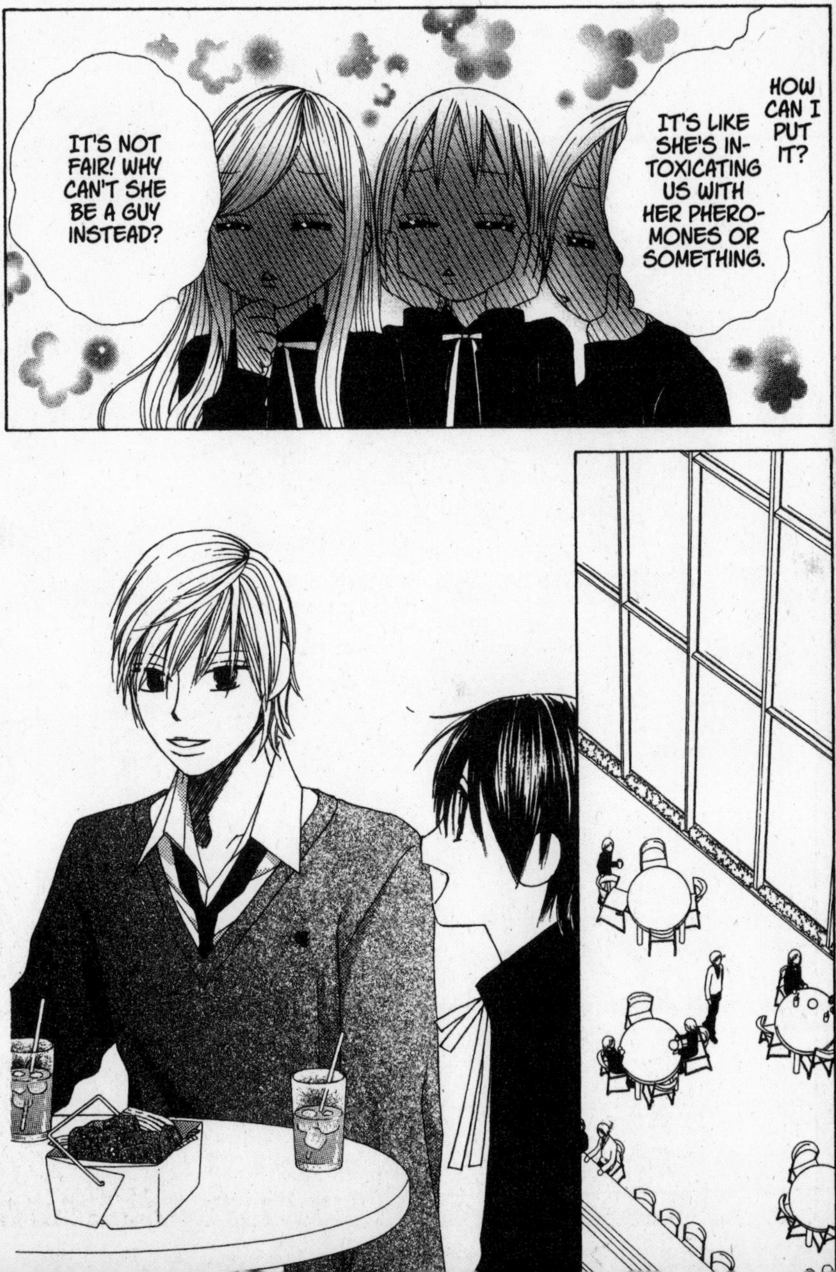
HOW CAN I PUT IT?
IT'S LIKE SHE'S IN-TOXICATING US WITH HER PHERO-MONES OR SOMETHING.
IT'S NOT FAIR! WHY CAN'T SHE BE A GUY INSTEAD?

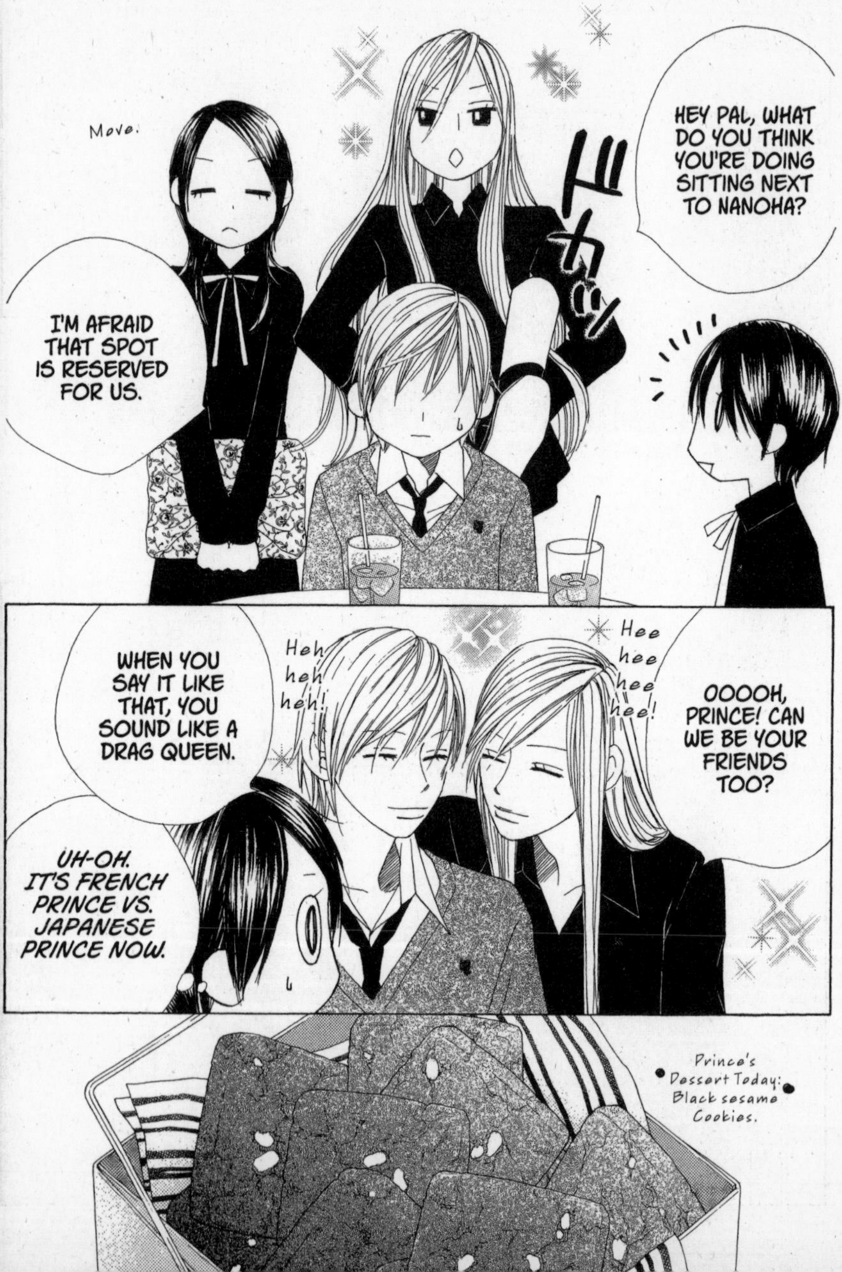
HEY PAL, WHAT DO YOU THINK YOU'RE DOING SITTING NEXT TO NANOHA?
Move.
I'M AFRAID THAT SPOT IS RESERVED FOR US.
OOOOH, PRINCE! CAN WE BE YOUR FRIENDS TOO?
Hee hee hee hee!
Heh heh heh!
WHEN YOU SAY IT LIKE THAT, YOU SOUND LIKE A DRAG QUEEN.
UH-OH. IT'S FRENCH PRINCE VS. JAPANESE PRINCE NOW.
Prince's Dessert Today: Black sesame Cookies.

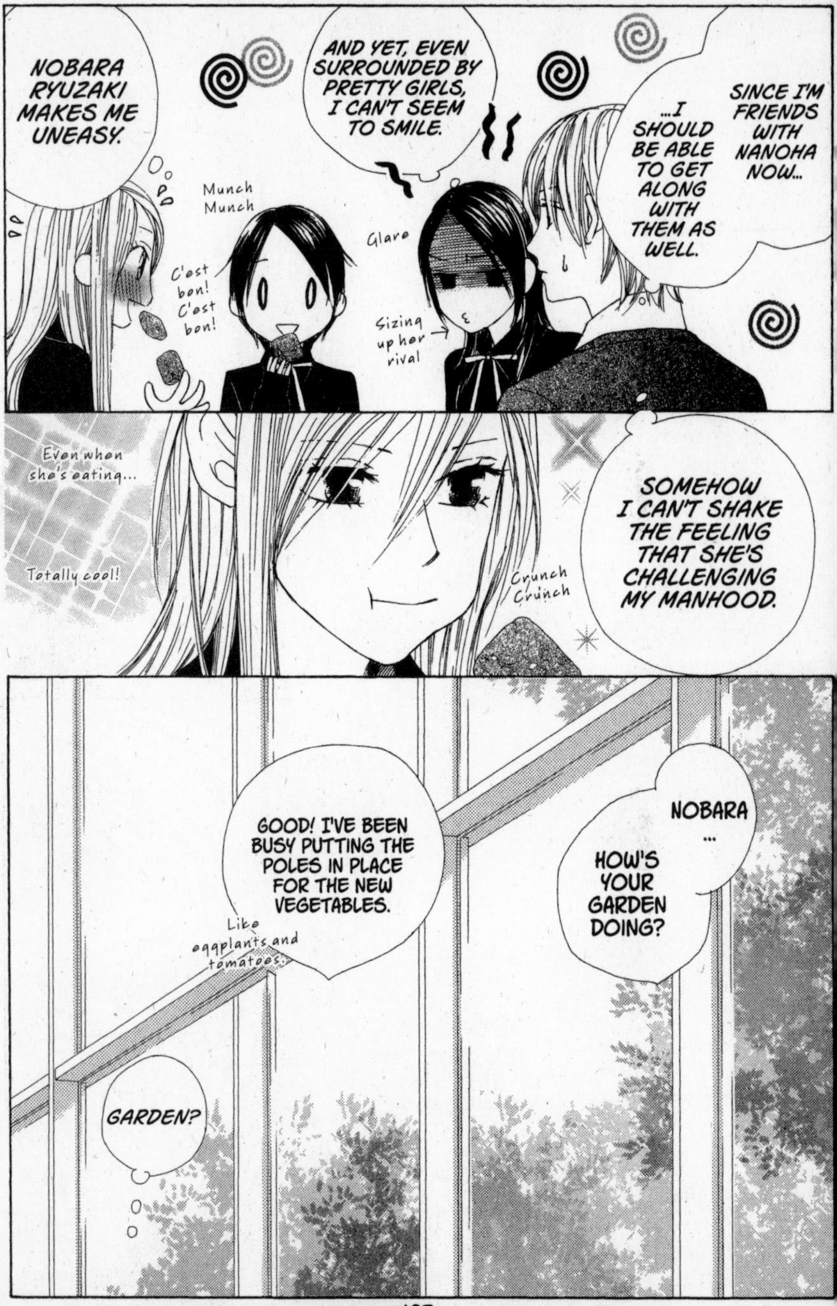
SINCE I'M FRIENDS WITH NANOHA NOW...
...I SHOULD BE ABLE TO GET ALONG WITH THEM AS WELL.
AND YET, EVEN SURROUNDED BY PRETTY GIRLS, I CAN'T SEEM TO SMILE.
Glare
Sizing up her rival
Munch Munch
C'est bon! C'est bon!
NOBARA RYUZAKI MAKES ME UNEASY.
SOMEHOW I CAN'T SHAKE THE FEELING THAT SHE'S CHALLENGING MY MANHOOD.
Crunch Crunch
Even when she's eating...
Totally cool!
NOBARA... HOW'S YOUR GARDEN DOING?
GOOD! I'VE BEEN BUSY PUTTING THE POLES IN PLACE FOR THE NEW VEGETABLES.
Like eggplants and tomatoes.
GARDEN?

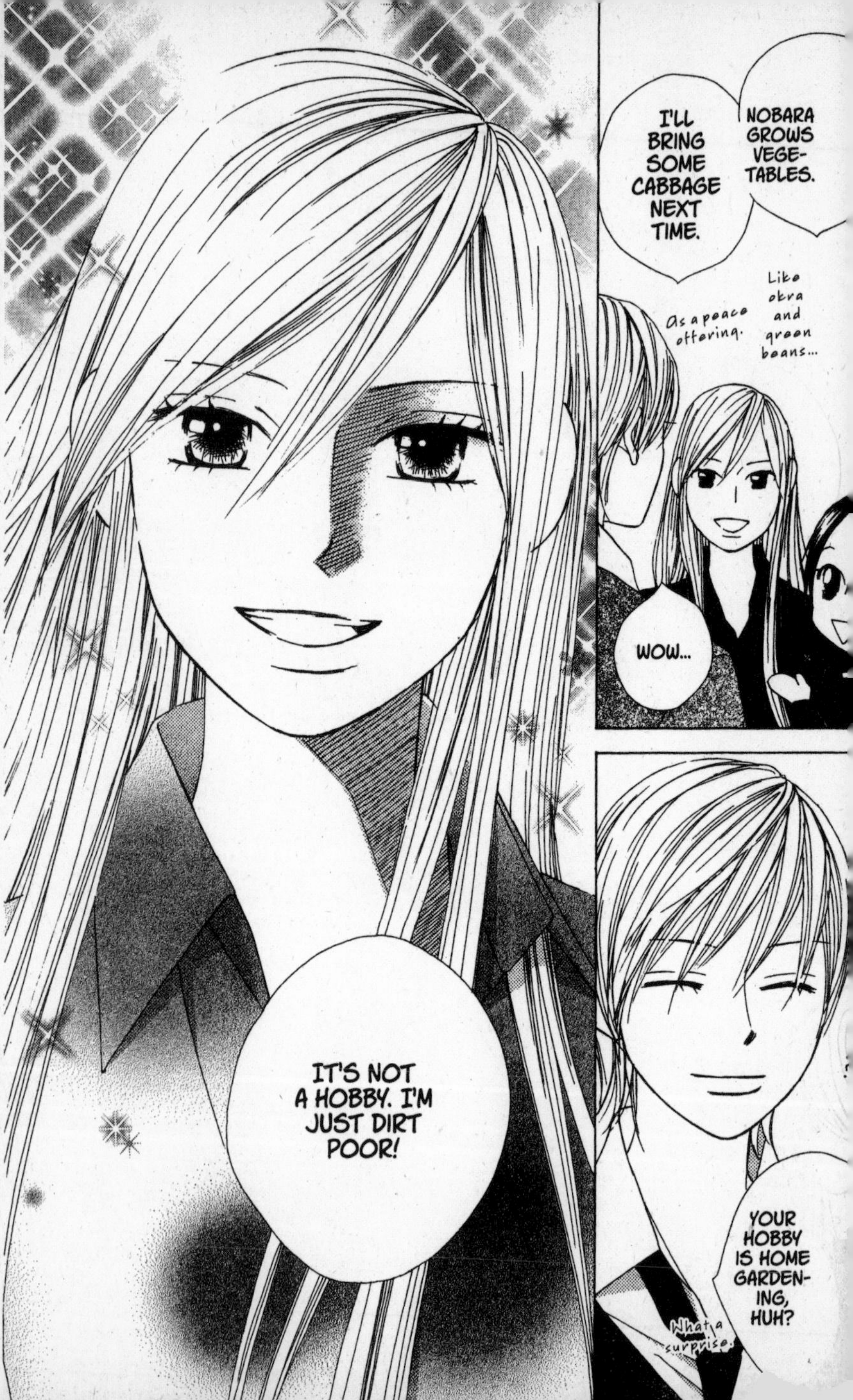
NOBARA GROWS VEGE-TABLES.
I'LL BRING SOME CABBAGE NEXT TIME.
Like okra and green beans...
As a peace offering.
WOW...
YOUR HOBBY IS HOME GARDEN-ING, HUH?
What a surprise.
IT'S NOT A HOBBY. I'M JUST DIRT POOR!

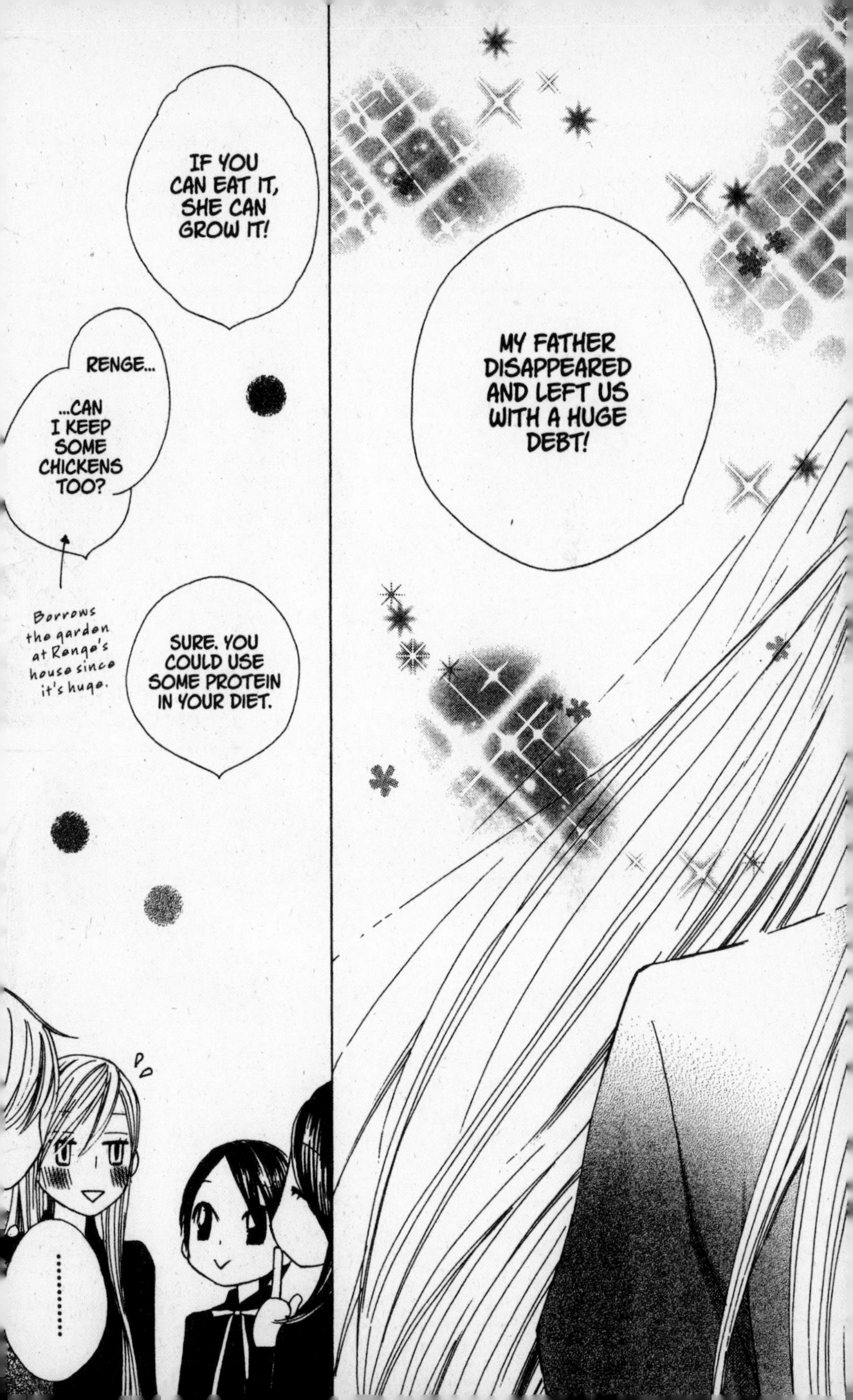
MY FATHER DISAPPEARED AND LEFT US WITH A HUGE DEBT!
IF YOU CAN EAT IT, SHE CAN GROW IT!
RENGE...
...CAN I KEEP SOME CHICKENS TOO?
Borrows the garden at Renge's house since it's huge.
SURE. YOU COULD USE SOME PROTEIN IN YOUR DIET.
....

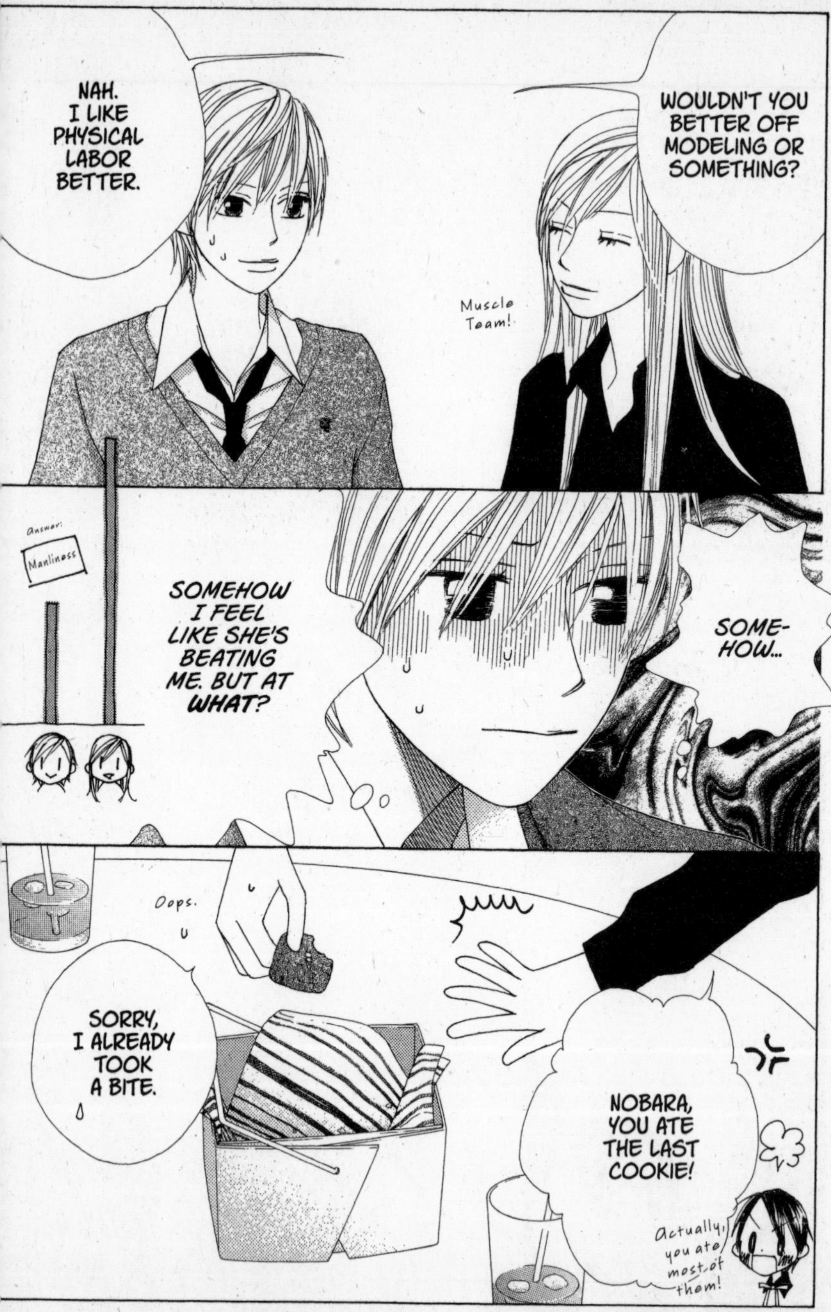
WOULDN'T YOU BETTER OFF MODELING OR SOMETHING?
Muscle Team!
NAH. I LIKE PHYSICAL LABOR BETTER.
SOME-HOW...
SOMEHOW I FEEL LIKE SHE'S BEATING ME. BUT AT WHAT?
Answer:
Manliness
NOBARA, YOU ATE THE LAST COOKIE!
Actually, you ate most of them!
Oops.
SORRY, I ALREADY TOOK A BITE.

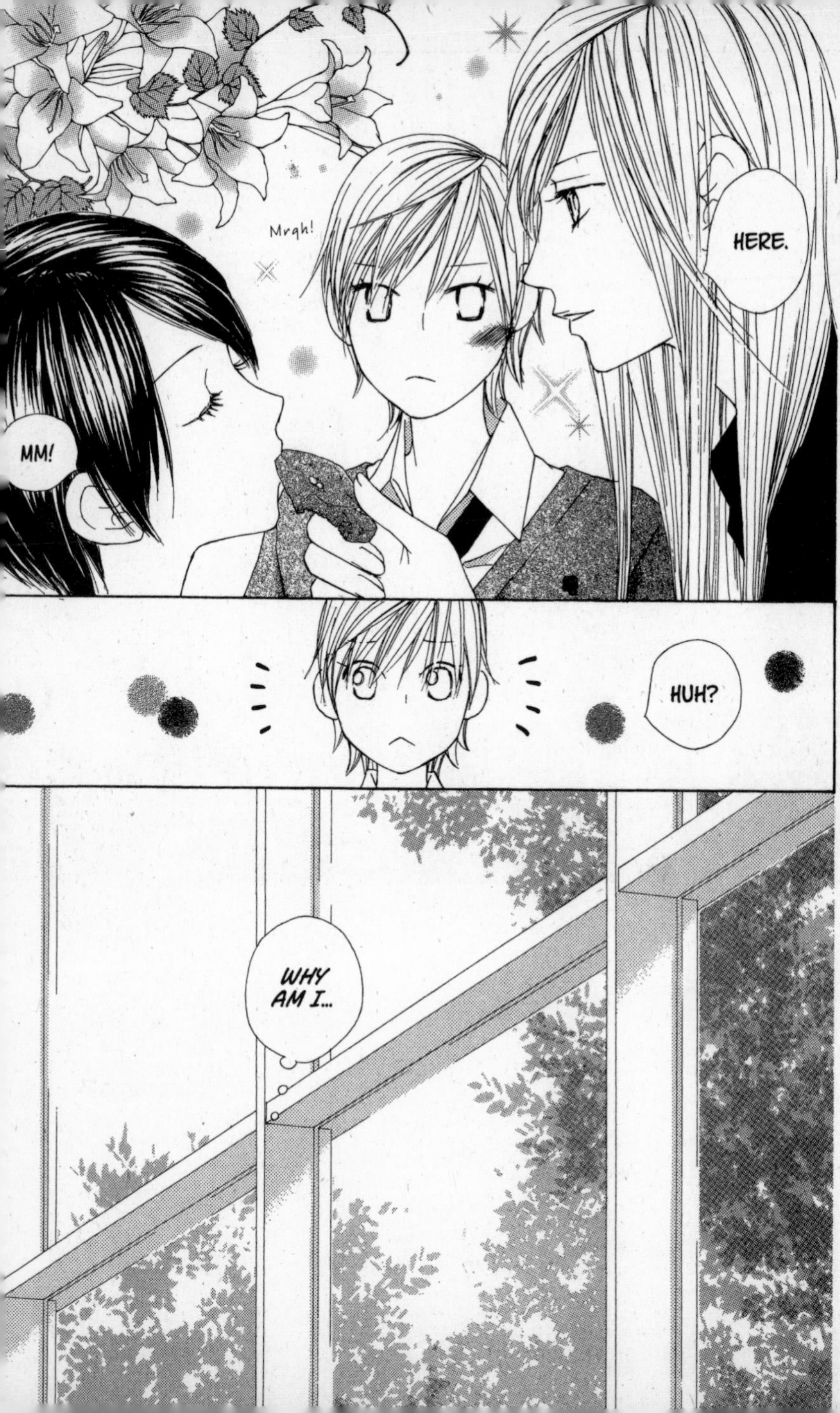
HERE.
Mrgh!
MM!
HUH?
WHY AM I...

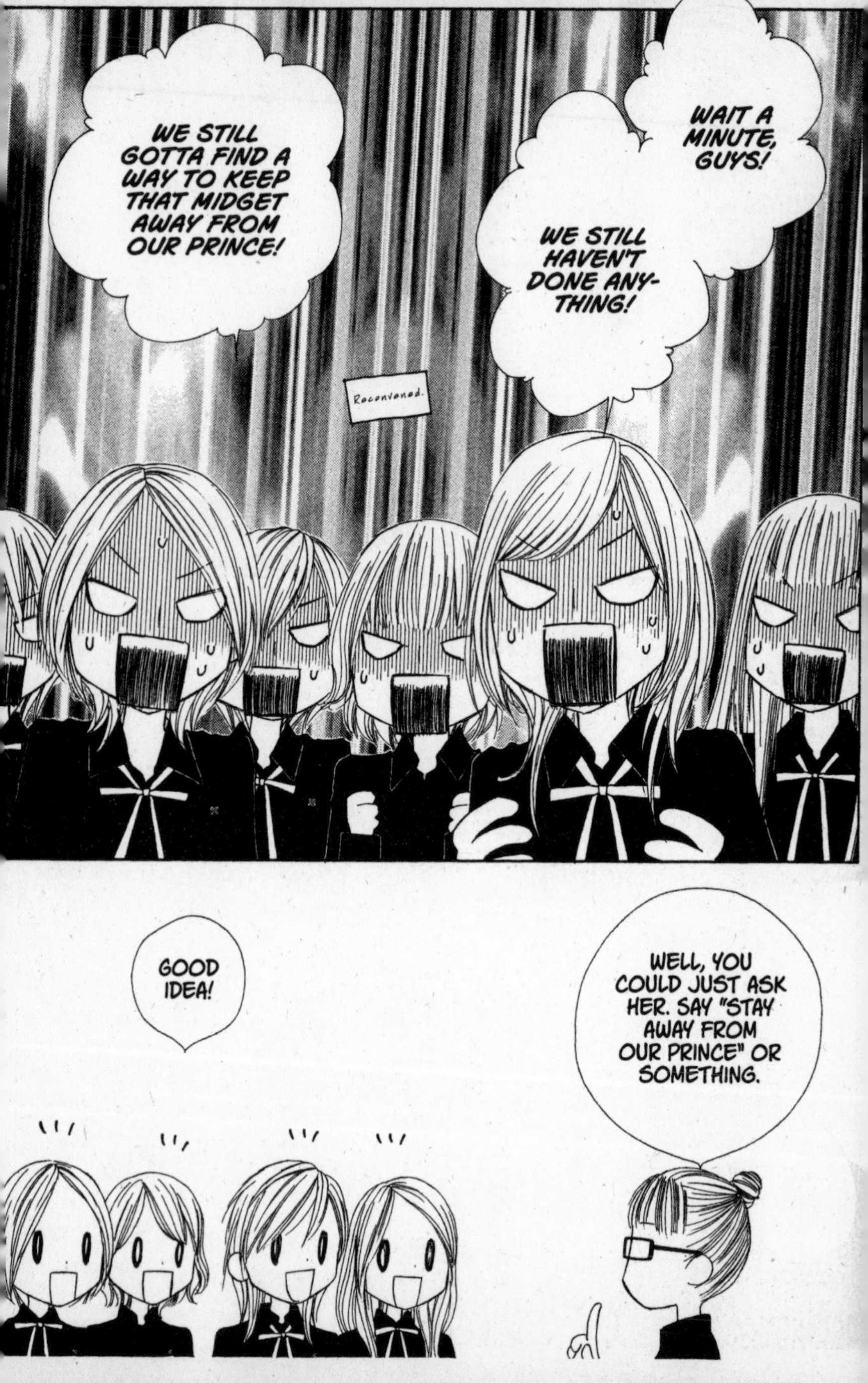
WAIT A MINUTE, GUYS!
WE STILL HAVEN'T DONE ANY-THING!
WE STILL GOTTA FIND A WAY TO KEEP THAT MIDGET AWAY FROM OUR PRINCE!
Reconvened.
WELL, YOU COULD JUST ASK HER. SAY "STAY AWAY FROM OUR PRINCE" OR SOMETHING.
GOOD IDEA!

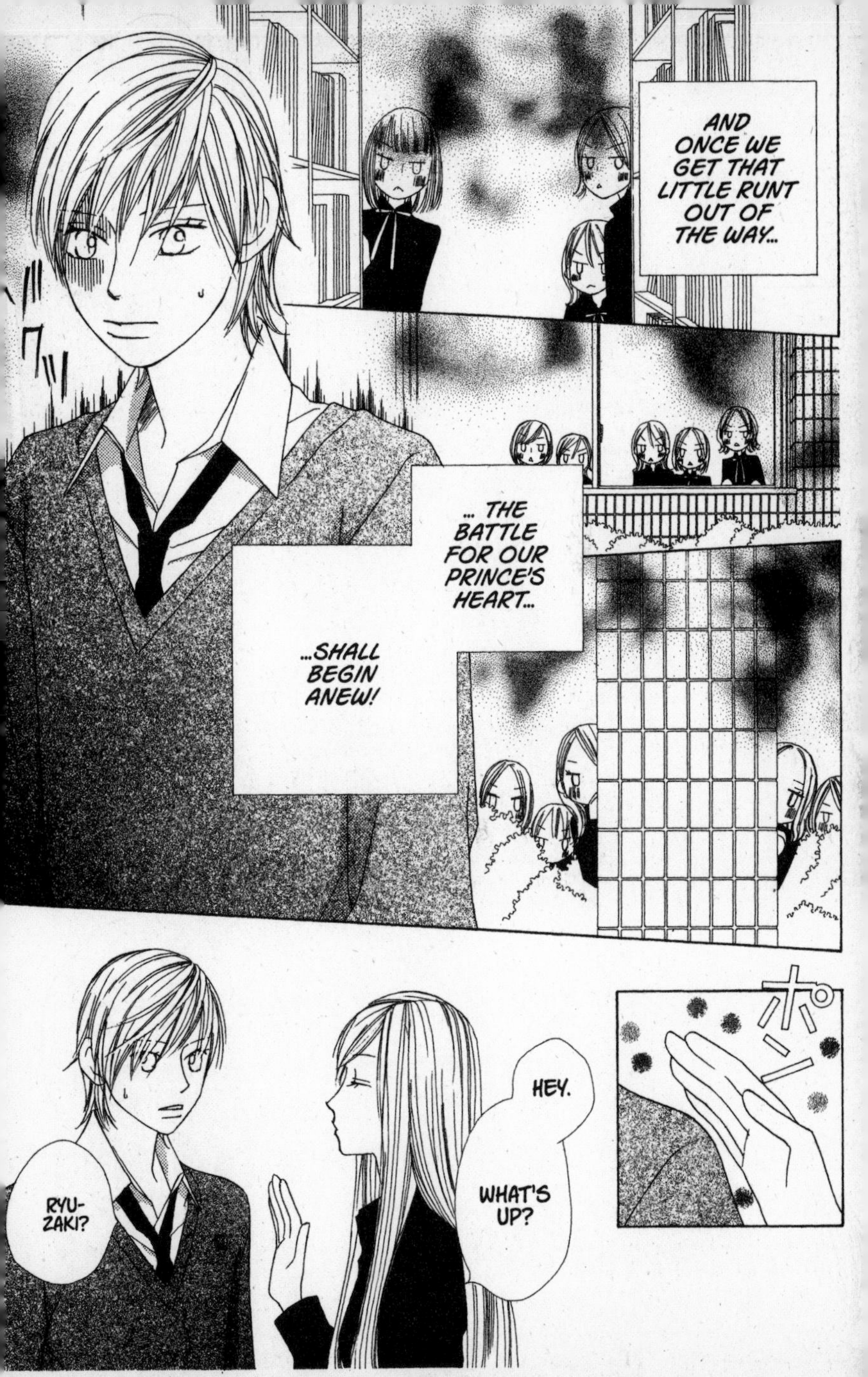
AND ONCE WE GET THAT LITTLE RUNT OUT OF THE WAY...
... THE BATTLE FOR OUR PRINCE'S HEART...
...SHALL BEGIN ANEW!
HEY.
WHAT'S UP?
RYU-ZAKI?

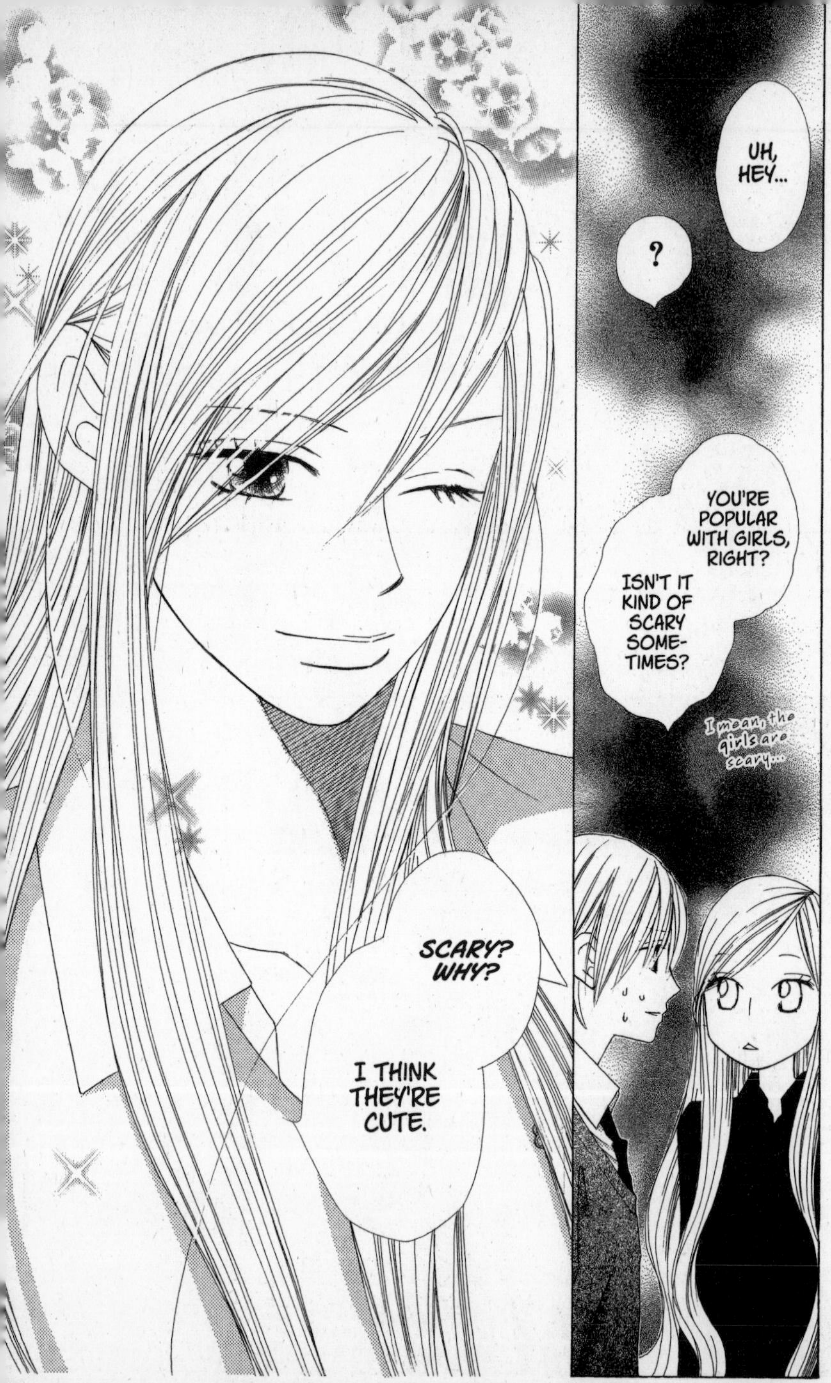
UH, HEY...
?
YOU'RE POPULAR WITH GIRLS, RIGHT?
ISN'T IT KIND OF SCARY SOME-TIMES?
I mean, the girls are scary...
SCARY? WHY?
I THINK THEY'RE CUTE.

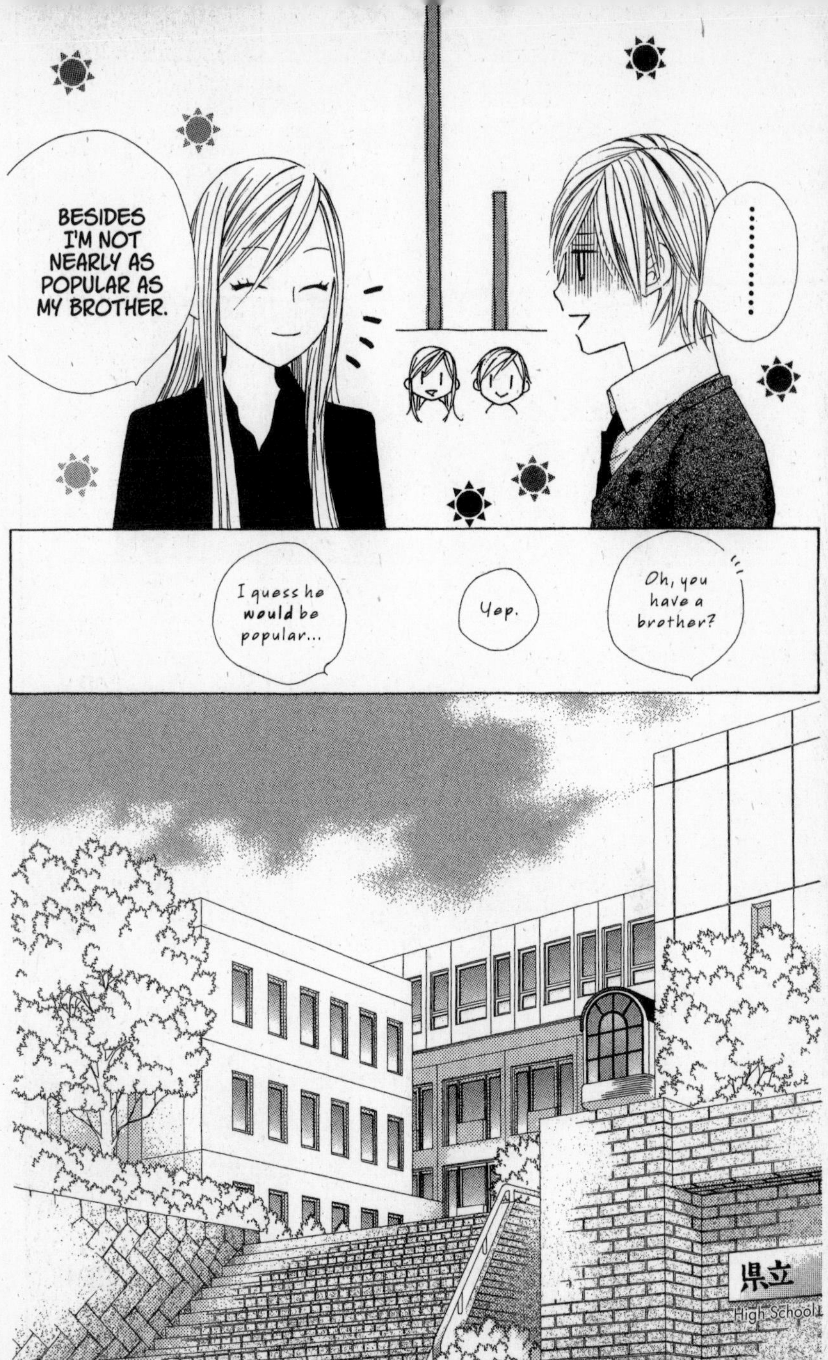
......
BESIDES I'M NOT NEARLY AS POPULAR AS MY BROTHER.
Oh, you have a brother?
Yep.
I guess he would be popular...
県立
High School

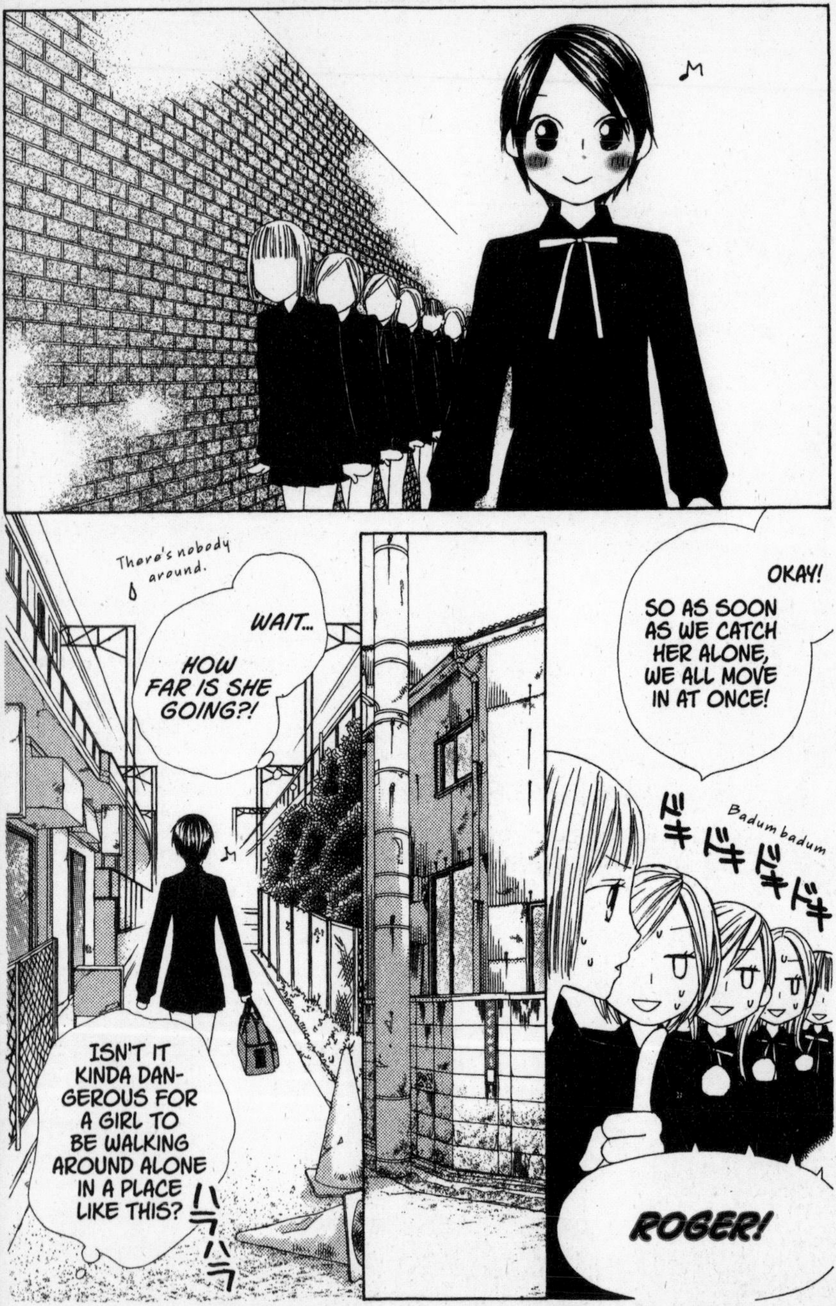
OKAY!
SO AS SOON AS WE CATCH HER ALONE, WE ALL MOVE IN AT ONCE!
ドキドキドキドキ
Badum badum
ROGER!
WAIT... HOW FAR IS SHE GOING?!
There's nobody around.
ISN'T IT KINDA DANGEROUS FOR A GIRL TO BE WALKING AROUND ALONE IN A PLACE LIKE THIS?
ハラハラ

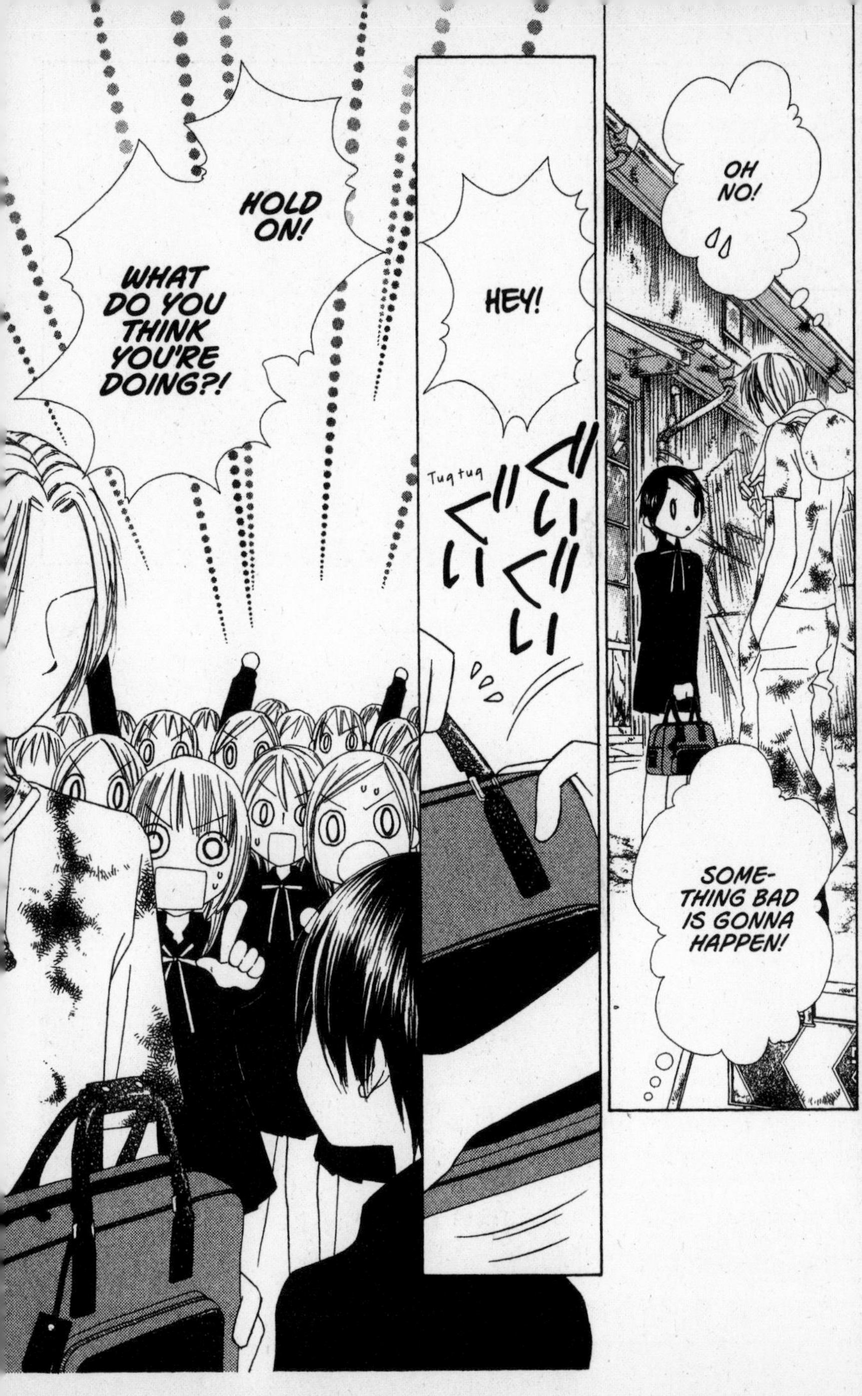
OH NO!
SOME-THING BAD IS GONNA HAPPEN!
HEY!
Tug tug
HOLD ON!
WHAT DO YOU THINK YOU'RE DOING?!

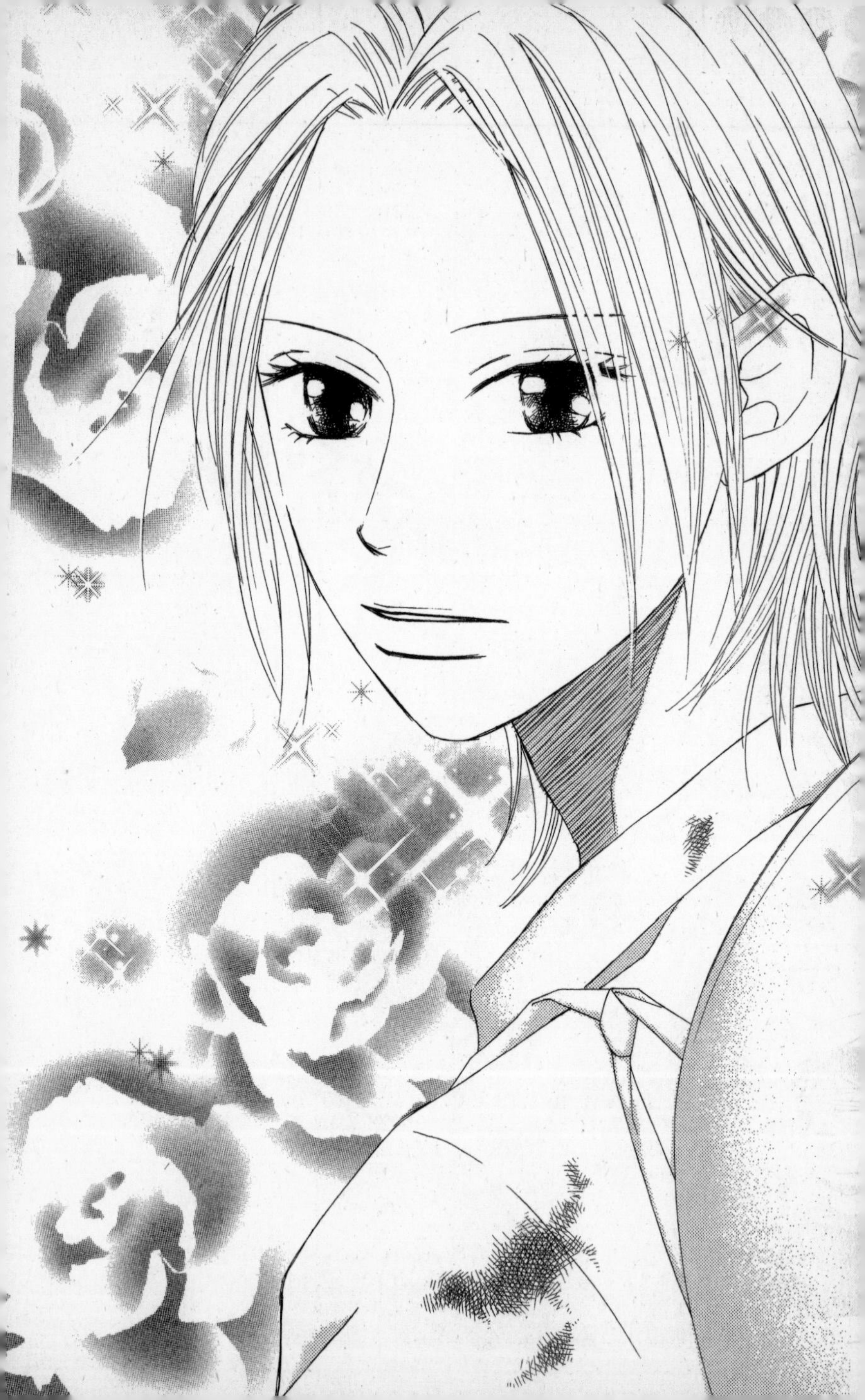

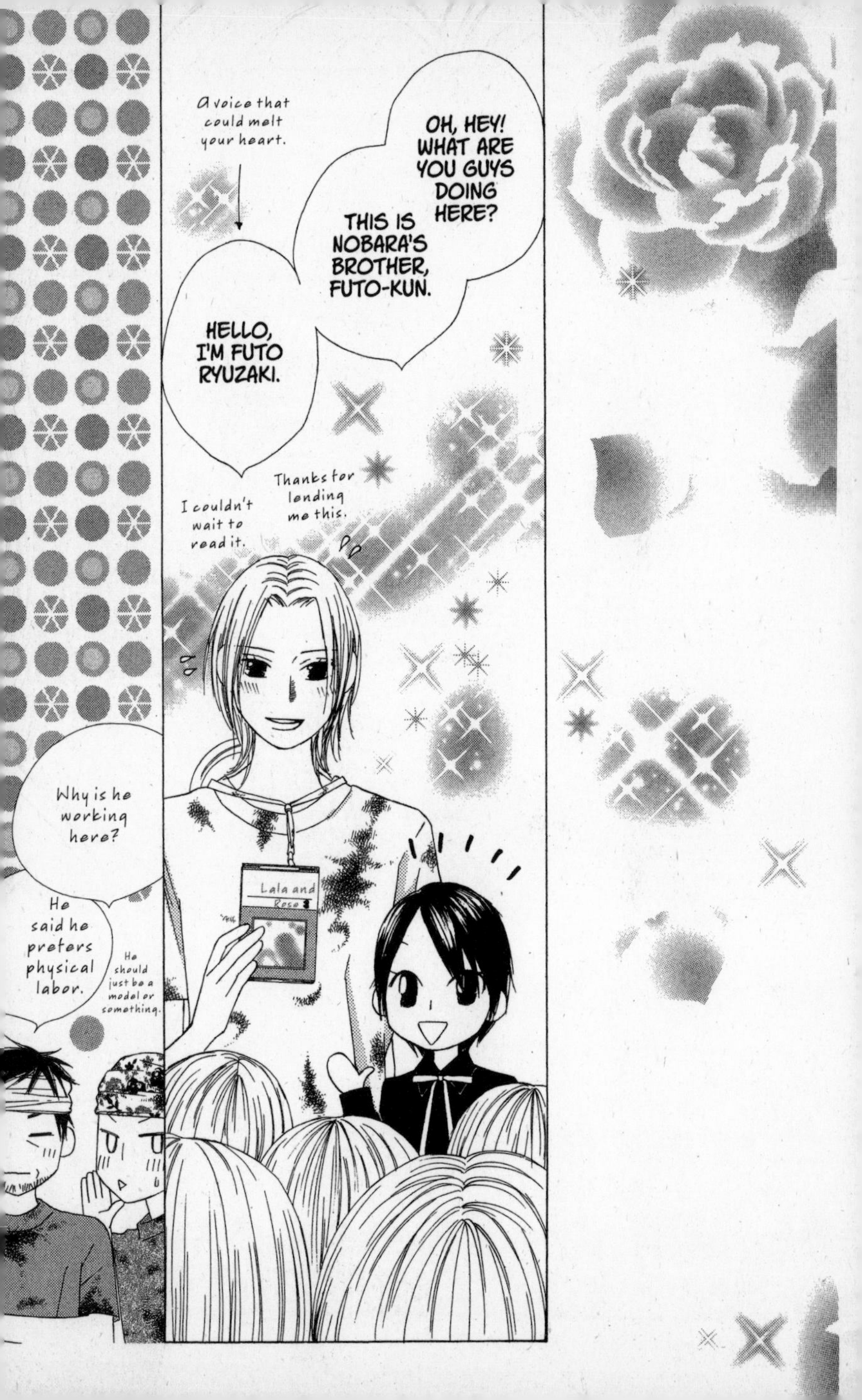
OH, HEY! WHAT ARE YOU GUYS DOING HERE?
THIS IS NOBARA'S BROTHER, FUTO-KUN.
A voice that could melt your heart.
HELLO, I'M FUTO RYUZAKI.
Thanks for lending me this.
I couldn't wait to read it.
Lala and Rose 3
Why is he working here?
He said he prefers physical labor.
He should just be a model or something.

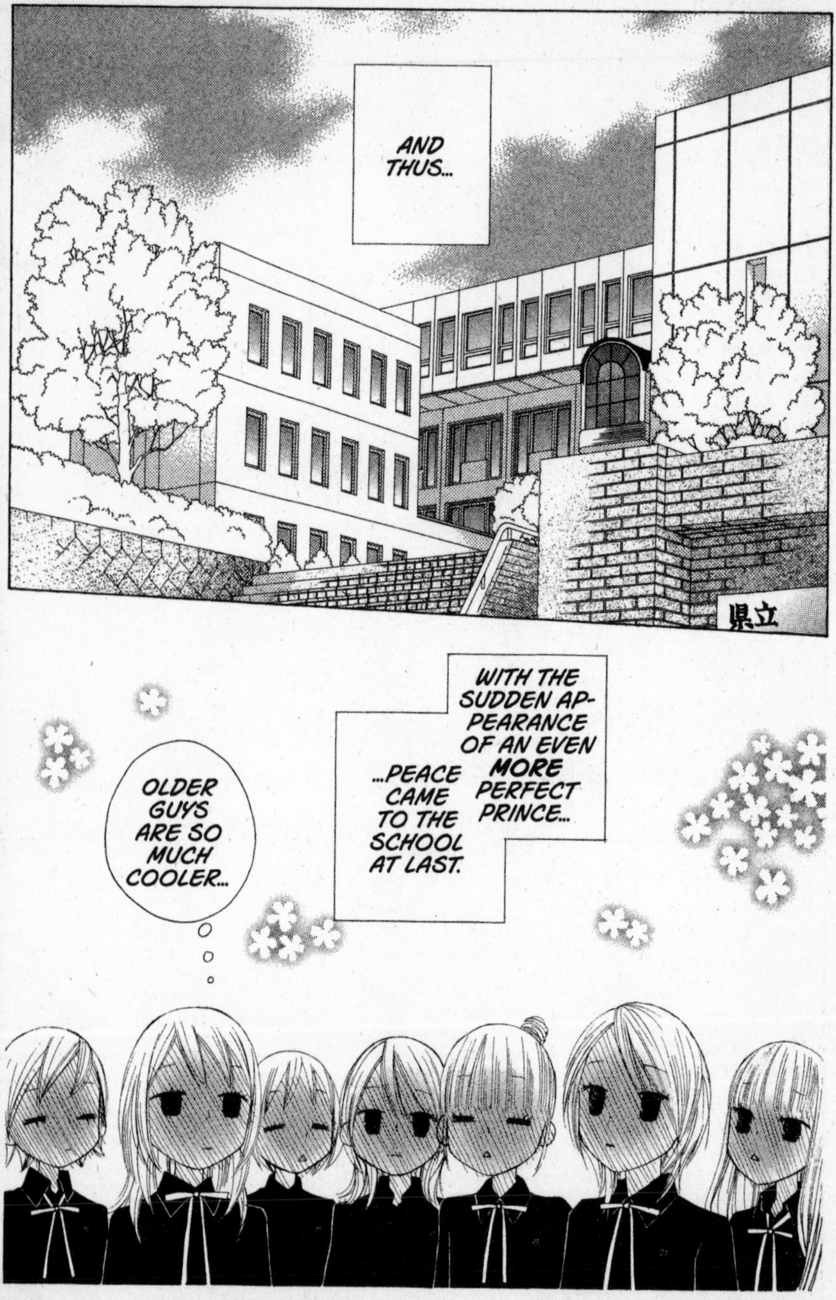
AND THUS...
県立
WITH THE SUDDEN AP-PEARANCE OF AN EVEN MORE PERFECT PRINCE...
...PEACE CAME TO THE SCHOOL AT LAST.
OLDER GUYS ARE SO MUCH COOLER...

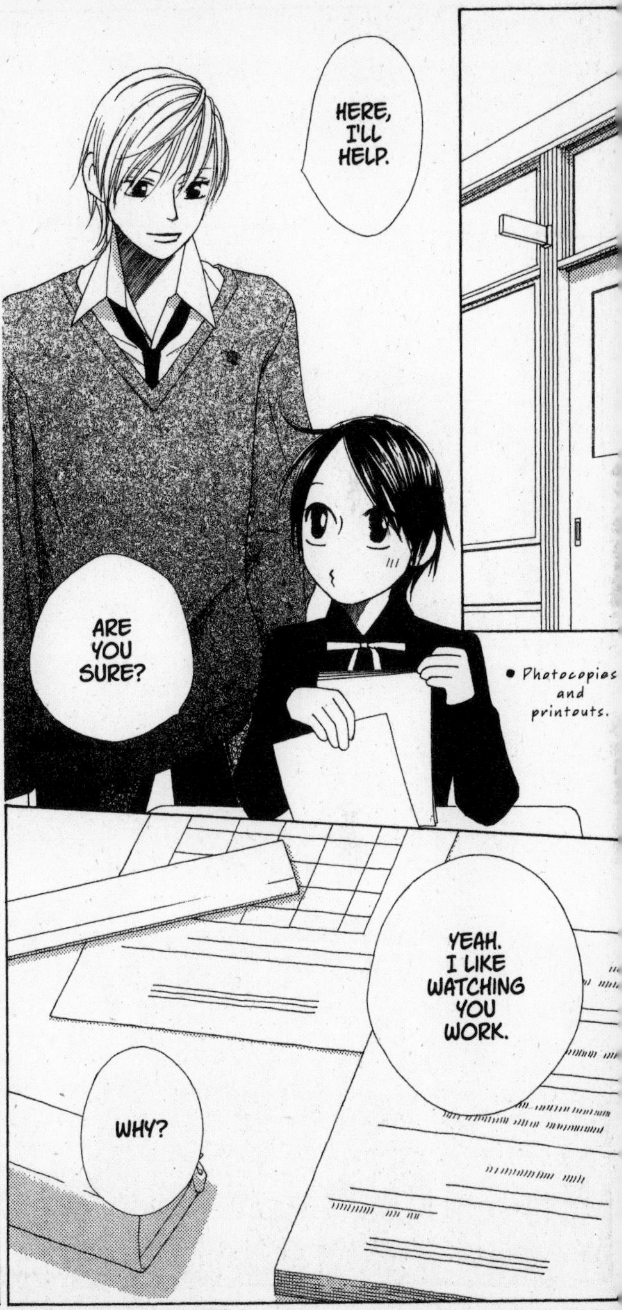
HERE, I'LL HELP.
ARE YOU SURE?
• Photocopies and printouts.
YEAH. I LIKE WATCHING YOU WORK.
WHY?

6

Thank you for reading.

It's been 15 years since my debut but this is only my second series.

Ha ha!

So little experience!

Anyway, this series covers one year in the character's lives, so the next volume is the final one!

I hope you enjoy it all the way through!

See you!

Masami Tsuda

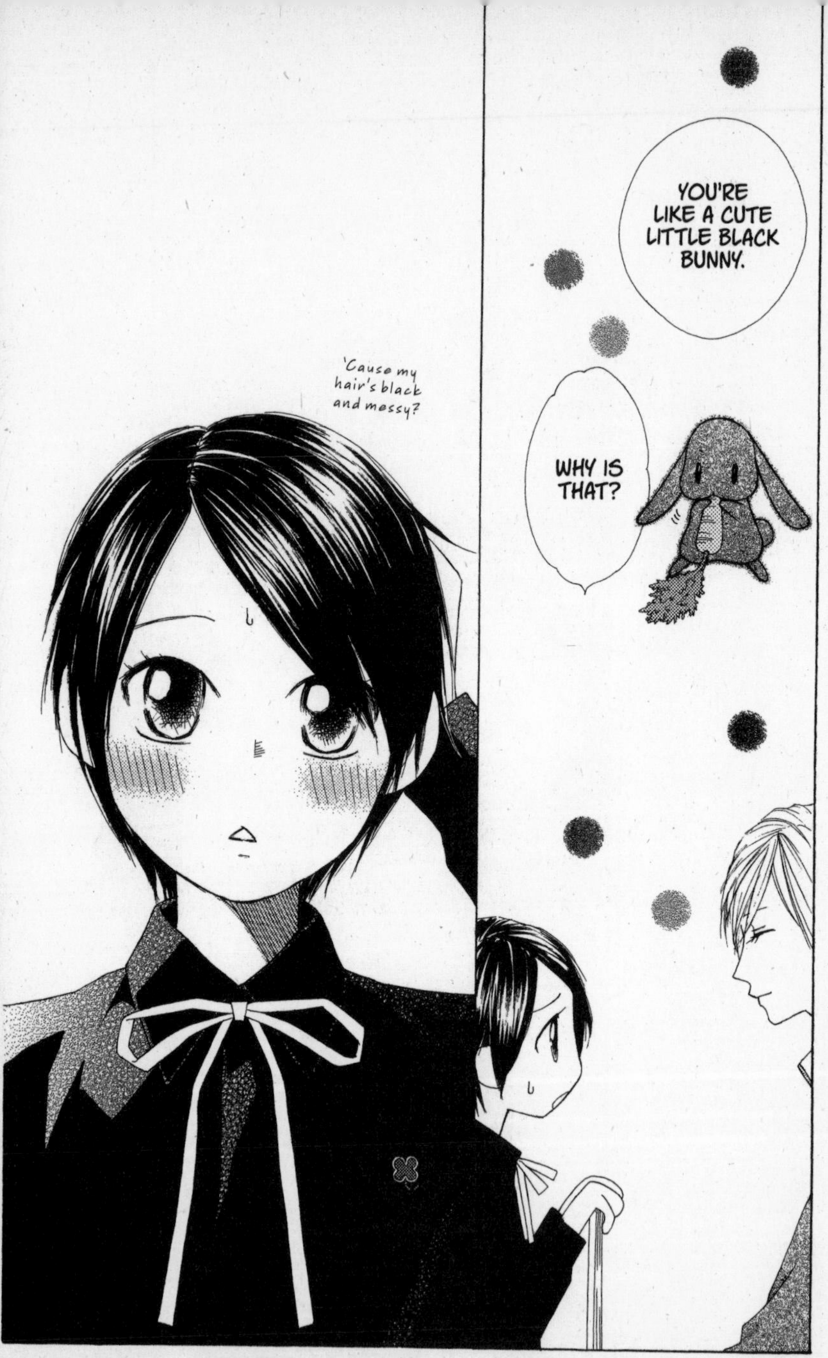
YOU'RE LIKE A CUTE LITTLE BLACK BUNNY.
WHY IS THAT?
'Cause my hair's black and messy?

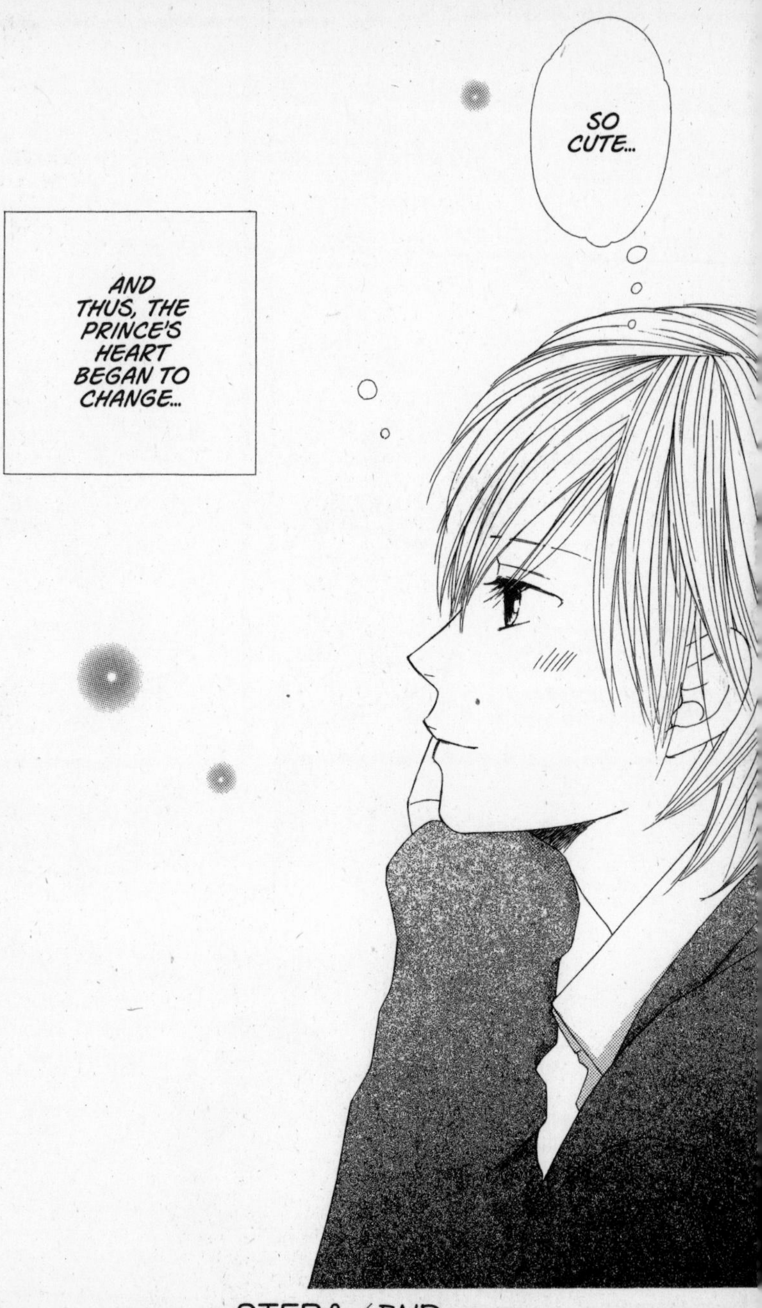
SO CUTE...
AND THUS, THE PRINCE'S HEART BEGAN TO CHANGE...

STEP 6 / END

TSUDA'S-DIARY

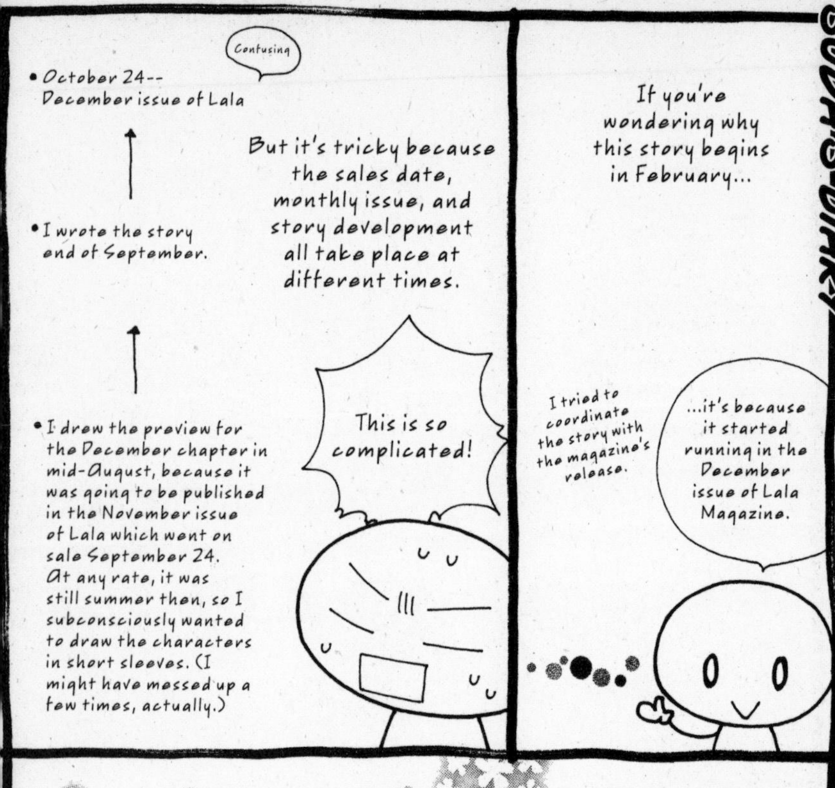
If you're wondering why this story begins in February...
...it's because it started running in the December issue of Lala Magazine.
I tried to coordinate the story with the magazine's release.
Confusing
• October 24-- December issue of Lala
• I wrote the story end of September.
• I drew the preview for the December chapter in mid-August, because it was going to be published in the November issue of Lala which went on sale September 24. At any rate, it was still summer then, so I subconsciously wanted to draw the characters in short sleeves. (I might have messed up a few times, actually.)
But it's tricky because the sales date, monthly issue, and story development all take place at different times.
This is so complicated!
Anyway, after all that I decided to coordinate the story with the monthly issue so that I wouldn't get confused. I played with the character names a bit too.
<Flower Group>
Renge (Lotus)
Nanoha (Rapeseed flower)
Nobara (Wild rose)

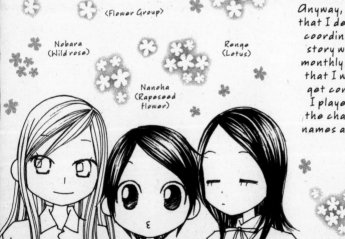

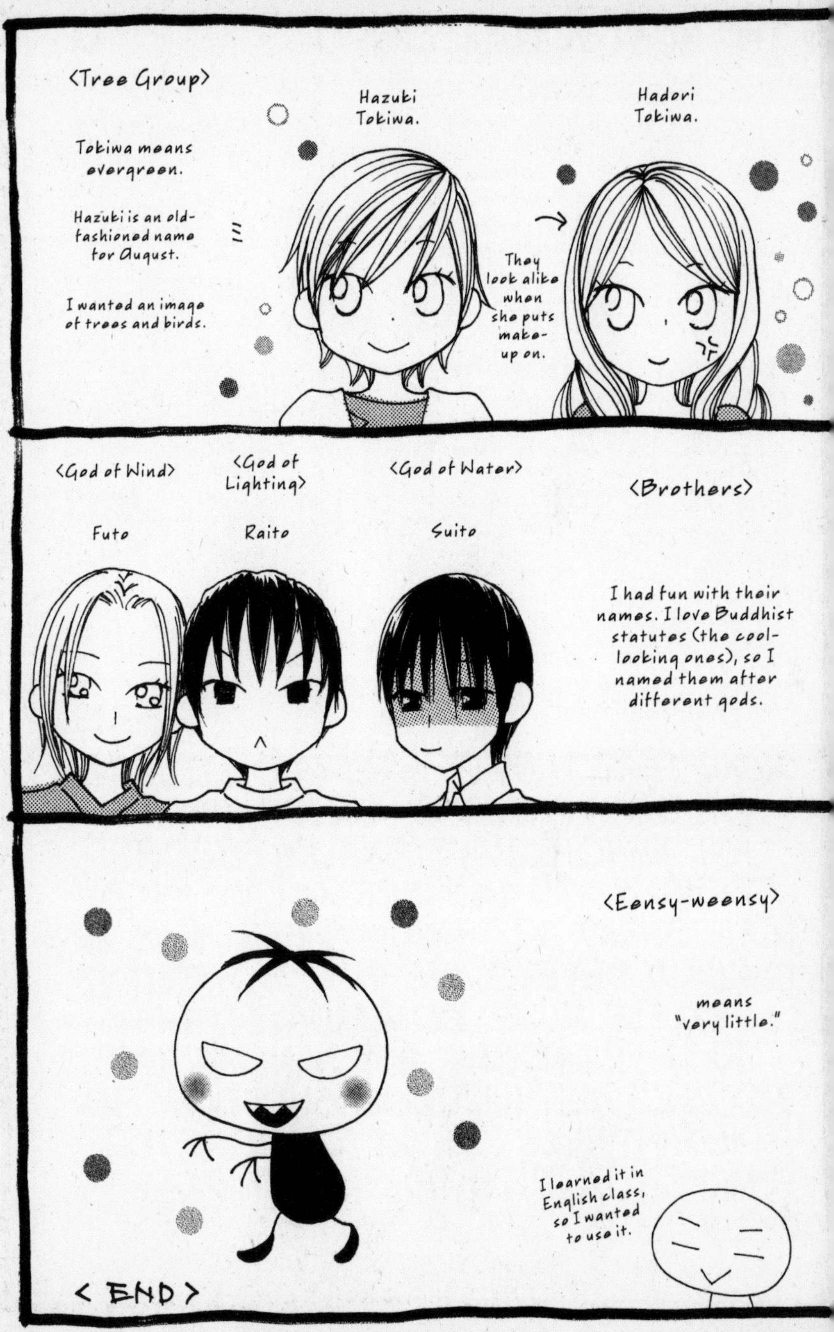

Hadori Tokiwa.
Hazuki Tokiwa.
<Tree Group>
Tokiwa means evergreen.
Hazuki is an old-fashioned name for August.
They look alike when she puts make-up on.
I wanted an image of trees and birds.
<Brothers>
<God of Water>
Suito
<God of Lighting>
Raito
<God of Wind>
Futo
I had fun with their names. I love Buddhist statutes (the cool-looking ones), so I named them after different gods.
<Eensy-weensy>
means "very little."
I learned it in English class, so I wanted to use it.
< END >

eensy weensy
MONSTER

NOW THAT THEY'VE STOPPED GETTING ON EACH OTHER'S NERVES, HAZUKI AND NANOHA HAVE FINALLY BECOME FRIENDS, AND THEIR RELATIONSHIP IS FLOURISHING. BUT HAZUKI'S FEELINGS ARE QUICKLY DEVELOPING INTO SOMETHING A LITTLE MORE COMPLICATED THAN JUST FRIENDSHIP, AND NANOHA HAS NO CLUE WHY HAZUKI IS SUDDENLY SO DISTANT. WILL HER LITTLE MONSTER MAKE A RETURN TO SAVE THE DAY?

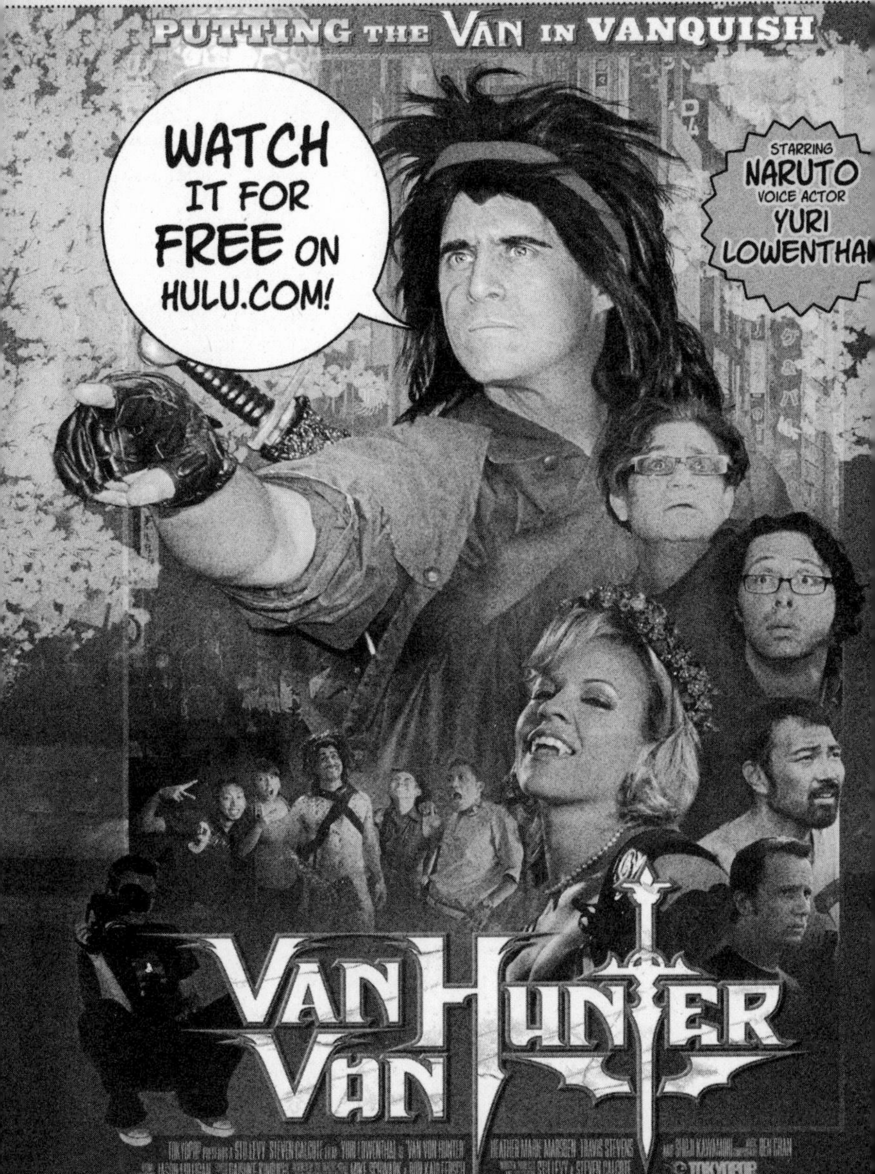
PUTTING THE VAN IN VANQUISH
WATCH IT FOR FREE ON HULU.COM!
STARRING NARUTO VOICE ACTOR YURI LOWENTHAL
VAN VON HUNTER

STOP!

This is the back of the book.
You wouldn't want to spoil a great ending!

This book is printed "manga-style," in the authentic Japanese right-to-left format. Since none of the artwork has been flipped or altered, readers get to experience the story just as the creator intended. You've been asking for it, so TOKYOPOP® delivered: authentic, hot-off-the-press, and far more fun!

1
2
3
4
5
6
7
8
9
10

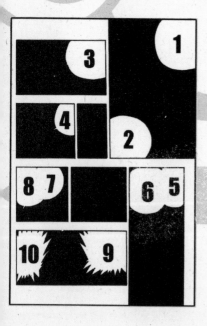

DIRECTIONS

If this is your first time reading manga-style, here's a quick guide to help you understand how it works.

It's easy... just start in the top right panel and follow the numbers. Have fun, and look for more 100% authentic manga from TOKYOPOP®!

THE MANGA REVOLUTION • LEADING THE MANGA REVOLUTION • LEADING

漫画革命

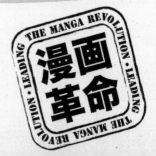